1982

LEARNING AND MEMORY
An introduction

The Dorsey Series in Psychology

Advisory Editors
Wendell E. Jeffrey
University of California, Los Angeles

Salvatore R. Maddi
The University of Chicago

LEARNING AND MEMORY

An introduction

Jack A. Adams

Professor of Psychology
University of Illinois at Urbana-Champaign

1980   Revised Edition

The Dorsey Press   Homewood, Illinois   60430
Irwin-Dorsey Limited   Georgetown, Ontario   L7G 4B3

ISBN 0-256-02314-X
Library of Congress Catalog Card No. 79–55218
Printed in the United States of America

1 2 3 4 5 6 7 8 9 0 MP 7 6 5 4 3 2 1 0

Preface

THE first edition of this book was published in 1976. The emphasis of that edition was on the experimental psychology of learning and memory for college and university students, and the emphasis of this revised edition is the same. The hope is that the book will move the student's appreciation of learning and memory from an intuitive to a scientific one. We all have an intuitive understanding of learning and memory processes, but intuition is not the objective substance of which a science of behavior is built. Psychologists have been doing laboratory experiments for 100 years and experiments on learning and memory for almost that long, and the facts of these experiments are the objective building blocks of psychology as a science. As time goes on and the facts accumulate, we begin to see regularities that are the laws of the science. Beyond the laws are theories which organize the laws into a conceptual structure. Unlike physics, however, psychology is a young science, and our engagement with laws and theories is more often pursuit than capture. Even though our scientists have been inventive and energetic, the identification of variables and the untangling of their relationships for behavior is a difficult enterprise that can proceed slowly, and so the science of behavior is a mixture of solid achievements and unfulfilled quests. This book documents both the achievements and the quests.

A measure of the accomplishments of a science is the extent to which its findings can be applied in solving practical problems. As psychology strives toward scientific maturity and as its variables and laws are identified more and more, it begins to acquire weapons in its scientific arsenal that can be used to ease our way in this world. Behavior modification and behavior therapy are names that are given to applications of learning principles in the home, the school, and the clinic, and they are widely used today for changing behavior that is inappropriate or un-comfortable. Biofeedback is the application of learning principles to the regulation of physiological responses such as blood pressure, heart rate, and muscular tension. Mnemonic devices are aids that improve our remembering, and modern psychology has taken an interest in them and given us new evidence on their validity and uses. All of these applications are evidence of psychology's growing scientific power to help us achieve useful behavioral ends, and they have not been ne-glected in these pages.

Before launching the revised edition of a book it is wise to have observers take a critical look at the strengths and weaknesses of the first edition. James Fritzen, Frank Marzocco, and David Mostofsky served in this observer role. James Fritzen then reviewed the manuscript for this revised edition. Harry Kalish reviewed Chapter 9 on applications of learning. The reviews improved the book. I am grateful for the help that these constructive critics gave me.

January 1980   Jack A. Adams

Contents

one

LEARNING

1

Introduction to learning

WHY BOTHER with the scientific study of learning when we seem to know so much about it already? From the beginning, humans have seen the benefits of learning for the transmission of cultural knowledge and the teaching of useful skills. That schools have existed for thousands of years is evidence of some understanding of the principles of learning and of our application of them, as is less formalized learning in the parent teaching skills to the child. Why bother with the scientific study of learning if societies have been accomplishing all of these complex kinds of learning for so long?

The answer is that folk wisdom cannot be discounted, but neither can it be canonized. Through trial and error people "luck into" many relationships in their world that are useful and which are later elevated to principles when the phenomena come under the scrutiny of scientific investigators. That a primitive physician might rub dirt on a wound and prevent infection is understandable in terms of our modern knowledge about penicillin mold. The difference between the primitive physician and a modern physician lies in the identification of cause and effect and the added sophistication that it brings. The primitive physician probably believed that the dirt had curative powers in its own right or, more remotely, that a god of healing worked through the physician and the dirt to accomplish the cure. But those cures were fortuitous cures because the primitive physician did not really understand the responsible agent in the dirt and why it worked as it did, and so was as likely to use the dirt for a headache. The modern physician knows the specific relationship between the penicillin mold and infection and knows when and when not to apply it. Through systematic observation, usually in laboratory experiments, scientists have determined the specific relationship between penicillin mold and infection, and have ruled out alternative explanations that were plausible in the beginning. Once having established a reliable relationship between penicillin mold and infection, the investigators can pursue related lines of investigation and can devise new strains of mold for even more effective cures. Except by accident, the primitive physician had no way of discovering a different kind of dirt with greater healing power.

The same is true of the common sense knowledge of learning that people have distilled from centuries of everyday experiences. People learn—but it is never clear why the teaching operations that are performed achieve the behavioral results that they do. One teacher might assume that reading while standing is important for a child first learning to read because she has always had her students read while standing and they have always learned to read. But the more fundamental operation in the situation is practice repetitions of the reading material, with standing irrelevant. By knowing through research that practice is a fundamental variable for reading, and standing an indifferent variable, more systematic and effective training can be accomplished and lines of research can be suggested to make even more effective uses of practice.

But suppose prescientific people did not misidentify the variables in a cause and effect relationship as our primitive physician did. They are then in a position to have a measure of control over aspects of their world, but only a small measure. Power is limited without the more comprehensive knowledge that systematic science can bring. Someone may have learned enough mechanics to build a footbridge, but lack the technical power to build the Golden Gate Bridge. Similarly, in the field of learning, we have known for thousands of years that a wide variety of animals can be taught various behavioral acts with food as reward. Granting that the lay person has some understanding of rewards and their power to effect behavior, that knowledge is crude and probably no greater than the primitive person's knowledge of physics when building the footbridge. The science of physics can lead to the Golden Gate Bridge, and so can the pursuit of rewards and their mechanisms by psychologists lead to scientific power in the control of behavior. Today, our knowledge of rewards and how they work is being used routinely in regulating behavior in the home, the classroom, and the clinic. It takes the institutionalized agencies of science, doggedly pursuing knowledge century after century, to eventually give us an impressive power in the control of our world.

The nature of scientific laws

The fundamental goal of a science is the uncovering of scientific laws for its subject matter, and for the psychology of learning as an arm of the science of psychology, the goal is finding the laws that relate the behavior we call learned to the events that determine it. A field becomes worthy of the name "science" to the extent that it has its phenomena described by scientific laws.

What is a scientific law? A *scientific law* is a generalization about characteristics of events that we observe. A scientific law has an event which is predicted, called the *dependent variable,* and one or more events which do the predicting, called *independent variables.* Any reliable relationship between dependent and independent variables can be a scientific law. The law can be qualitative, of a simple "if–then" form, such as: If a response is rewarded, then it will be learned. Or the law can be quantitative: The probability of a response occurring is an exponential function of the number of rewarded trials.

What does a scientific law do for us, apart from giving a careful statement of a relationship in the world? There are two consequences of a scientific law, and they usually go together: *prediction* and *control.* All scientific laws allow prediction. The position of the moon tomorrow can be predicted from the position of the moon today, and a dog will perform the trick of rolling over more reliably after it has been rewarded for it 20 times rather than twice. Most scientific laws allow control, in addition to prediction, because manipulation of the independent variables determines what happens to the dependent variable and so puts us in control of the dependent variable. In this sense of control, the position of the moon cannot be controlled, although the behavior of a dog can be controlled by rewarding it or not. We like to have the sciences arm us with power to control the physical world, although we are less sure about psychology and the control of human behavior. Humans have a strong subjective sense of free will and find it morally repugnant that someone can control them. Yet a moment's reflection should dispel that attitude because our behavior is being manipulated in countless ways all the time. Any parent, for example, is a massive controller of a child's behavior even though the control is cloaked in such euphemisms as love, concern, and parental responsibility.

An important property of scientific laws is that they be as general as possible. If the law of gravity was specific it might predict only the fall of 10-lb. bodies, and it would be a good law within its narrow domain. But the law of gravity which physics has found for us is a general law for all objects of our world. This single expression gives us enormous power in predicting and controlling the trajectories of bodies, and it is a great scientific achievement.

What do specific and general laws look like in psychology? Most of our laws in psychology are rather specific, which is typical of a young science. We find the correlation between reading performance and a test of vocabulary, or the relationship between the rate of learning a list of words and the length of the list; laws such as these are low-order. They can be good laws but their domain of operation is narrow, like predicting the fall of 10-pound objects. In time we will integrate these specific laws into more masterful relationships, but now we have little of them. Integration has been tried, however, and the psychology of learning has been one of the arenas where attempts have been made.

From the turn of the century until about 1950 there was a strong urge to put the specific laws of learning together into a comprehensive principle of learning. It failed, but not for want of effort. Such prominent learning scientists as E. L. Thorndike, C. L. Hull, and E. R. Guthrie each expressed a general law of learning which they believed would explain all animal and human learning. All of these people made admirable attempts, with the loftiest of scientific goals in mind, but they traveled a rocky road, and none of their laws have acceptance today. No one today is attempting a general law on learning; time has given us a feeling of caution that those who went before us lacked. Now, when we consider what we know about the different types of learning for a wide variety of response classes, we are awed by the prospect of a general law that can embrace them all. Indeed, the prospect may be illusory. Psychology may not be able to follow the model of the physical sciences with their general laws.

Is the finding of laws the end of scientific activity in psychology? Certainly it is a major goal, but not the end. Beyond laws is theory, where we specify a few abstract principles that organize the laws and transcend them. Theory will often contain hypothetical, unobservable states. Atoms and electrons are examples from physics, and they have been eminently useful theoretical constructions. In the psychology of learning such unobservables as "habit" and "image" have been used in theoretical attempts.

How we define and study learning

That we have no general law of learning means that we have a number of specific laws. If learning has so many different manifestations, how do we define and study it?

The learning of a response is an inferred state of the organism. Learning results from defined kinds of experience which produce a relatively stable potential for subsequent occurrences of the response. The storage and retrieval of this relatively stable potential is the topic of memory.

The parts of this definition deserve several comments:

1. Learning is an inferred state of the organism. Learning is not observed directly but is inferred from the performance of an organism, and this is a complication because learning is not the only state that affects performance. Learning psychologists distinguish between *learning* and *performance.* A student who knows the material very well (learning) may be lacking in academic motivation and flunk out (performance). Fatigue can obscure learning. High skill cannot be revealed when an athlete is tired. The point is that we cannot always accept observed performance as an undistorted mirror of learning. It is the job of the learning psychologist to understand the determinants of the different states and to know how to manipulate and control them.

2. Learning results from defined kinds of experience. It is self-evident that learning occurs from "defined kinds of experience"; obviously not any kind of experience produces learning. Nevertheless the statement is worth making because it is the job of the learning psychologist to determine those particular kinds of experiences that produce the state called learning. An animal will learn if food reward is delivered after the response. Will it also learn if a rock is delivered? In this book we will encounter various kinds of operations that produce learning.

3. Learning is a relatively stable potential for subsequent occurrences of the response. If today we reward an animal every time it makes a response, there is a good chance that it will make the response tomorrow. A relatively stable potential for responding has developed.

4. The storage and retrieval of the relatively stable potential is the topic of memory. Learning and memory are two sides of the same behavioral coin. Learning is acquisition of a persistent disposition to respond, and memory is its storage over time and its activation when recollection takes place. When a response is learned today and then is made tomorrow, we say that the response has been remembered. The storage of the response potential is in memory. If the response does not occur, we say it is forgotten. But what does "forgetting" mean? Has something happened to the response potential while it was in memory storage? Is it weakened by some process? Or does a response potential exist full strength in memory, but the retrieval mechanism has failed to activate it into a response? These are the kinds of questions that are met when memory is engaged as a research topic.

One would think that learning would be difficult to study because it is rather generally defined as a stable tendency to react, and yet it is meaningfully studied in many experiments each year. Here is how to collect data on learning, and it is not as difficult as it might seem:

1. Define a response that can be reliably observed. This is the dependent variable.

2. Define one or more operations that you can reliably manipulate and believe to be learning operations. These are the independent variables.
3. Create learning opportunities where the response is performed under the conditions defined by the independent variables.
4. Observe changes in the response.
5. Rule out changes in the response as a function of nonlearning states such as motivation and fatigue.
6. If the response shows improvement over the training series and some persistence with time is observed, then learning has occurred.

Following these six steps gives learning data and starts you down the road to law-finding. Consider how we would teach a dog to lift its paw and use the situation to observe learning. First we would objectively define lifting of the paw and reliably distinguish it from any other movements of the foot that might occur. Next, we would choose an independent variable that would induce learning—e.g., a food reward every time the dog lifted its paw. A series of learning trials would then be administered, where the dog is given a piece of food every time it raises its paw, and the occurrence or nonoccurrence of paw-lifting is recorded on each trial. On the first block of ten trials only one instance of paw-lifting behavior may be observed, but nine instances might well be observed on the last ten trials. This change in behavior would be identified as learning, and reasonably so.

Summary

Our concern with science had its beginning in the knowledge and skill that were important for accomplishing the tasks of everyday life. As science became formalized and institutionalized, its concerns became systematic as it sought the laws of natural phenomena. A scientific law is a generalization about observable events, is a relationship between events called independent and dependent variables, and gives the power of prediction and usually the power of control over the dependent variable.

A law of learning is a relationship between measures of behavior that are the dependent variables and determinants of the measures, called independent variables. A law of learning must have nonlearning effects eliminated, and when this is done the law of learning will reflect a relatively stable tendency to react under the conditions specified by the law. Learning operations produce a state that has some persistence over time, and the persistent state is called memory. Thus, learning and memory are closely related.

2

Classical conditioning

THIS CHAPTER is about one of the main kinds of learning, called *classical conditioning*. Often it is called *Pavlovian conditioning* or *respondent conditioning*. Classical conditioning was discovered by the great Russian physiologist Ivan P. Pavlov (1849–1936) at about the turn of the century. Today there is awareness that E. B. Twitmyer of the United States independently discovered classical conditioning about the same time. His discovery was the substance of his doctoral dissertation, completed in 1902, at the University of Pennsylvania. Twitmyer reported his findings at a meeting of the American Psychological Association in 1904, but the audience was indifferent to them. Twitmyer failed to follow his dissertation findings with additional research, and nothing came of them. The findings lay in the library until eventually they were published in the interests of the historical record (Twitmyer, 1974). Pavlov, on the other hand, went after the implications of his observations with the vigor that characterizes a great scientist. His many experiments on classical conditioning provide guidance to investigators even today. Pavlov's major book on conditioning (Pavlov, 1927) is one of the great source books in the experimental psychology of learning.

The background and essentials of classical conditioning

HOW CLASSICAL CONDITIONING WAS DISCOVERED

It may be wrong to say that Pavlov's discovery of conditioning was an act of serendipity, a happy accident like a farmer looking for a cow and discovering a diamond mine, but there was an element of serendipity. Pavlov was influenced strongly by the mid–19th century writings of the Russian physiologist I. M. Sechenov (1829–1905). It was through Sechenov that he became attracted to the concept of the reflex, a biologically endowed response based on the energizing of sensory nerves to a spinal or brain connection, which in turn fires motor nerves that activate the reflex. Under the impact of Darwin's theory of evolution, Pavlov saw reflexes as adaptive mechanisms that contributed to biological survival. With this frame of reference, Pavlov was studying the reaction of the dog's salivary glands to food in the mouth. Salivation is a natural reflex because it facilitates the passage of food in the alimentary canal. Pavlov observed that the salivary glands did not need direct stimulation of food in the mouth but could be activated by the sight or odor of food, the sight of the food dish, or the sound of the footsteps of the attendant who regularly brought the food. The puzzle was one of understanding how with experience stimuli at a distance could activate the reflex. Soon he came to call these acquired reactions *conditioned reflexes*, and he distinguished them from *unconditioned reflexes*, which were biologically endowed and unlearned. (Hereafter, the text will drop the term "reflex" and replace it with "response," in accord with a longstanding practice in psychology.)

DEFINITION OF CONDITIONING

Pavlov's preliminary observations were followed by systematic laboratory studies. As a result of Pavlov's systematic work, the formation of a conditioned response is seen to have five ingredients:

1. The *unconditioned stimulus* (UCS), which has a stable power to elicit a response.
2. The *unconditioned response* (UCR), which is elicited by the UCS.
3. The *conditioned stimulus* (CS), which is a neutral stimulus that has no power to elicit the UCR.
4. The *conditioned response* (CR) which the CS comes to elicit as a learned response. It resembles, but is not the same as, the UCR.
5. The CS and UCS are presented repeatedly, with the CS preceding the UCS and with a defined temporal spacing.

Figure 2–1 shows a commonly used experimental arrangement of the five ingredients that readily leads to conditioning. Pavlov used dogs as subjects and ordinarily studied salivation as the response, which is elicited as a UCR by such UCS as food or weak acid in the mouth. Typical CS stimuli for Pavlov were such stimuli as a bell, a tone, or a buzzer. Figure 2–2 shows one of Pavlov's experimental setups for studying conditioned salivation in the dog. The saliva flows through an inci-

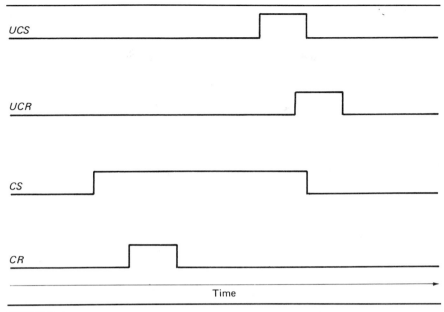

FIGURE 2–1
An example of the four basic events of classical conditioning. The deflection indicates the onset and the offset of the event.

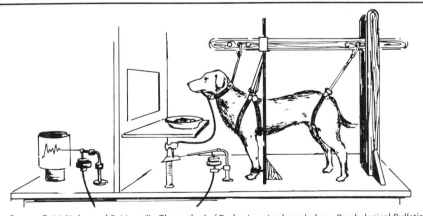

Source: R. M. Yerkes and S. Morgulis, The method of Pavlov in animal psychology. *Psychological Bulletin,* 1909, 6, 257–273.

FIGURE 2–2
An experimental arrangement which Pavlov used to study conditioned salivation in the dog.

sion in the mouth and is collected in a beaker and the amount is recorded. The dog is in a soundproof room to prevent extraneous stimuli from interfering with the conditioning process.

MEASUREMENT OF THE CONDITIONED RESPONSE

By definition, the UCR occurs on every trial in response to the UCS, but the CR develops gradually over the trials when the CS and the UCS are paired. How do we chart the course of learning for the CR?

A measure that has been used throughout the history of classical conditioning is the magnitude of the CR; it is the measure that Pavlov used. The amount of saliva emitted in response to the CS in a specified period of time, such as 30 seconds, documented the strength of the CR for Pavlov. In the beginning the CS elicited no saliva, but with trials the amount steadily increased.

The number of CRs in a block of trials is perhaps the most commonly used measure today. In the first block there are few or no CRs, but the frequency of them steadily increases until, eventually, 100 percent is reached. The CR can be recorded on every trial if its occurrence is remote enough in time from the UCS and its UCR so there is no confusion between them. If this requirement cannot be met then the test trial method is used, where only the CS is presented and the presence or absence of a CR is recorded. The test trial is interspersed occasionally among the regular trials.

GENERALITY OF CONDITIONING

If someone told you that classical conditioning applied only to salivation in Russian dogs, you would dismiss it as trivial. The fact is that classical conditioning is a type of learning with great generality that cannot be dismissed. There is hardly an organism, a type of response, a UCS, or a CS, that has not figured in classical conditioning at one time or another. Planaria, paramecia, rats, cats, dogs, pigs, monkeys, and human children and adults are among the organisms that have been conditioned. Salivation, eyeblink, leg flexion, and finger withdrawal have been some of the responses that have been conditioned. Unconditioned stimuli, and the unconditioned responses that they elicit, have been food or weak acid to elicit salivation, airpuff to elicit the eyeblink, and electric shock to elicit leg flexion or finger withdrawal. The CS can be, presumably, any stimulus that does not elicit the UCR in the situation, and thus is neutral. Examples are lights, tones, horns, buzzer, rotating fans, heat, odors, and clicks. In a kind of classical conditioning called interoceptive conditioning, which has been most extensively studied in Russia (Razran, 1961), distended balloons, jets of air, and liquid irrigation of the animal gut have been used as the CS for the salivation CR.

KINDS OF CONDITIONING

There are four kinds of classical conditioning, and they are defined by the relationship between the CS and the UCS. The four relationships are illustrated in Figure 2–3. If the CS and UCS come on together and go off together, it is *simultaneous conditioning*. For example, a light (CS) and a shock (UCS) to the finger going on and off together is a case of simultaneous conditioning for the finger withdrawal response (CR). When CS onset is before the UCS and persists until UCS onset or later, it is *delayed conditioning*. If the CS is terminated before the onset of the UCS, such that there is a time delay between them, it is *trace conditioning*. Finally, the UCS can precede the CS, which is a case of *backward conditioning*.

Whether or not backward conditioning is a reliable effect is controversial. Razran (1956), on the basis of a review of the studies of backward conditioning in the United States and Russia, concluded that it can occur but that the effect is not as reliable as forward conditioning. Others are not so sure. One explanation for backward conditioning is *pseudoconditioning*, where the UCS, particularly if it was noxious like electric shock, can place the subject in an aroused state. The subsequent occurrence of virtually any stimulus could produce a response resembling the CR. Thus, the CS occurring after the UCS would elicit a response

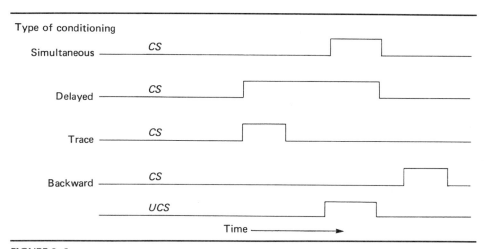

FIGURE 2–3
The four basic kinds of classical conditioning. They differ in the temporal relationship between the CS and the UCS.

that would resemble a CR, and the unwary might interpret the CR as a genuine instance of learning.

HIGHER-ORDER CONDITIONING

The kind of conditioning that we have been discussing, in which a CS is paired with a UCS, is called first-order conditioning to set it off from higher-order conditioning. Consider second-order conditioning. After a CR is firmly associated with the CS, a new stimulus is repeatedly paired with the CS. After a number of pairings, the new stimulus will come to elicit the CR. Third-order conditioning is difficult to establish. Pavlov (1927, pp. 34–35) could not do it with food and weak acid that were the UCS for salivation, but he was able to do it when the UCS was a strong stimulus like electric shock.

ACQUISITION VARIABLES

The variables that have the biggest effect on the acquisition of conditioning are number of trials, schedules of reinforcement, and the CS–UCS interval. The intensity of the CS and the UCS are two other variables that are known to influence conditioning but whose effects are smaller and have been surrounded with controversy (Hall, 1976, chap. 4). Only number of trials, schedules of reinforcement, and the CS–UCS interval will be discussed in this section.

Number of trials Investigators have conditioned many kinds of responses, but in recent years the nictitating membrane of the albino rabbit has enjoyed some popularity. The nictitating membrane is a thin membrane that is present in many animals and is like an inner eyelid. When the eye is stimulated briefly by an airpuff or an electric shock, the nictitating membrane moves horizontally across the surface of the eye to about the midline of the pupil. The choice of the nictitating membrane is not arbitrary because the albino rabbit and its nictitating membrane have advantages over other animals and response systems. The albino rabbit will remain passive for a rather long time, which makes conditioning easy. And the natural, spontaneous response of the nictitating membrane is low, which means that there are few spontaneous responses that can be confused with conditioned responses.

An example of conditioning the nictitating membrane of the rabbit is an experiment by Berger and Thompson (1978). A tone was the CS and an airpuff was the UCS. The UCS occurred 250 milliseconds (250 one thousandths of a second) after CS onset and had a duration of 100 milliseconds, with the UCS and the CS terminating simultaneously. This arrangement defines a case of delayed conditioning (Figure 2–3). An experimental group had the CS and UCS paired on each trial, with a

CS-alone test trial among each block of eight paired trials. A control group had the CS and UCS unpaired and randomized. The results for two days of training are shown in Figure 2–4. As expected, the control group shows no conditioning because of the inappropriate sequencing of the CS and the UCS. By contrast, the sequencing of the CS and the UCS that defines delayed conditioning for the experimental group shows a nice learning curve. The percentage of conditioned responses is a steadily increasing function of number of trials.

Schedules of reinforcement   How necessary for conditioning is it to deliver the UCS on every acquisition trial? The pairing of the CS and the UCS is one of the basic requirements of conditioning, but the UCS may

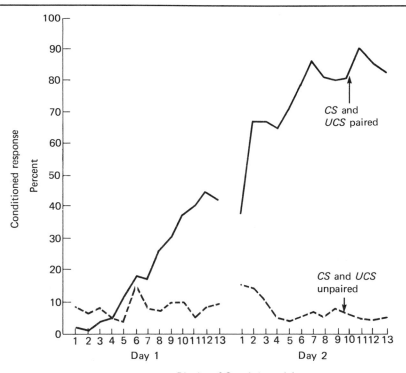

Source: T. W. Berger and R. F. Thompson, Neuronal plasticity in the limbic system during classical conditioning of the rabbit nictitating membrane response. I.   The hippocampus. *Brain Research,* 1978, *145,* 323–346. Reprinted by permission of Elsevier/North-Holland Biomedical Press.

FIGURE 2–4

Classical conditioning of the nictitating membrane of the rabbit. The CS and the UCS were systematically paired in conditioning. A control condition had the same number of CS and UCS events as the group that learned, but the events were unpaired and randomly presented.

not be required on every trial for effective conditioning to occur. How often the UCS is presented and the patterning of trials with the UCS is the topic of *schedules of reinforcement*. The topic did not amount to much until a study by Humphreys (1939) showed that the schedule of reinforcement in acquisition is an important variable for extinction of the response when the UCS is completely withdrawn. We will turn to the topic of extinction, including the Humphreys study, in a moment.

In classical conditioning the frequency of CRs in acquisition is directly related to the percentage of trials on which the UCS is presented. This principle is illustrated in Figure 2–5 by data from a study by Grant and Schipper (1952) on human eyeblink conditioning. The experimental variable was percentage of trials on which the UCS was delivered. Attend only to trial blocks 1–12, which are acquisition data; the last 5 blocks are extinction trials that will be discussed later. The greater the frequency of CS and UCS pairings, the higher the performance level in acquisition.

This study by Grant and Schipper could be faulted by saying that with a constant number of acquisition trials, the higher the percentage of UCS events the greater the number of UCS events, and so it is not surprising that the level of conditioning and percent UCS events are positively related. Hartman and Grant (1960) answered this criticism in

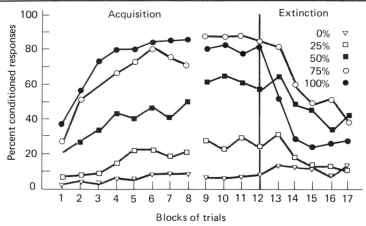

Source: D. A. Grant and L. M. Schipper, The acquisition and extinction of conditioned eyelid responses as a function of the percentage of fixed-ratio random reinforcement. *Journal of Experimental Psychology*, 1952, 43, 313–320. Reprinted by permission of the American Psychological Association.

FIGURE 2–5
Effect of percent of reinforcement (occurrence of the UCS) on occurrence of the conditioned eyeblink response in acquisition and extinction.

a study from the same laboratory. Again using eyeblink conditioning, they held number of UCS events constant for each percentage by allowing number of trials to vary, and their findings were very similar to those of Grant and Schipper in Figure 2–5.

CS–UCS interval   A key variable for classical conditioning is time interval between the CS and the UCS. The interval is called the CS–UCS interval, and it can be positive, designating forward conditioning, or it can be negative, indicating backward conditioning. A study by Smith, Coleman, and Gormezano (1969) included both positive and negative intervals, with the emphasis on positive intervals because of the unreliability of backward conditioning. Their approach was conditioning of the nictitating membrane of the albino rabbit. The CS was a 50-millisecond tone and the UCS was a 50-millisecond shock. The CS–UCS intervals were −50 milliseconds (backward conditioning), 0 milliseconds (overlap of the CS and UCS), and 50, 100, 200, 400, and 800 milliseconds as intervals for forward trace conditioning. Each interval had a different group assigned to it. A control group had the CS and UCS unpaired and randomized. The results are shown in Figure 2–6. There was no evidence of conditioning by the control group, or the −50, 0, and 50-milliseconds groups. The remaining groups, however, showed good conditioning. The 200- and 400-millisecond intervals produced rapid conditioning, achieving the maximum after relatively few trials, but the 100- and 800-millisecond intervals conditioned more slowly. Based on the conditioning of human subjects, the optimum CS–UCS interval was once held to be in the 500-millisecond range (Reynolds, 1945; Spooner and Kellogg, 1947), but for the rabbit and its nictitating membrane the optimum interval is in the 200–400 millisecond range. Noble, Gruender, and Meyer (1959) obtained an optimum interval of two seconds for fish. Now we know that the optimum depends on the species and upon the response that is conditioned.

EXTINCTION

General features   The five ingredients that were listed in the earlier section "Definition of Conditioning" are what is needed to cause the reliable occurrence of the CR. Having done so, we are faced with the next question: How do we eliminate the CR after having established it? This is the topic of *extinction*, and here is its definition for classical conditioning: *Extinction is reduction in the level the CR by withdrawal of the UCS.* Take away the UCS and repeatedly present the CS, and the occurrence of the CR will decline steadily. One of the characteristics of extinction is that response elimination is not permanent. Allow a time interval after the extinction trials and then present the CS again. The CR

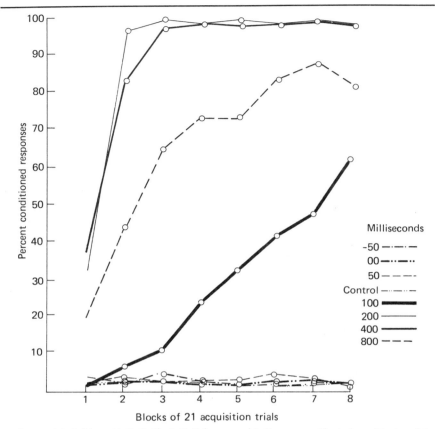

Blocks of 21 acquisition trials

Source: Adapted from M. C. Smith, S. R. Coleman, and I. Gormezano, Classical conditioning of the rabbit's nictitating membrane response at backward, simultaneous, and forward CS–UCS intervals. *Journal of Comparative and Physiological Psychology,* 1969, 69, 226–231. Copyright 1969 by the American Psychological Association. Reprinted by permission.

FIGURE 2–6

Effects of the time interval between the CS and the UCS. The numerical value is the interval in milliseconds between the CS and the UCS. A positive value means that the CS precedes the UCS, the zero value means overlap of the CS and the UCS, and the negative value is backward conditioning where the UCS precedes the CS. The control condition had the CS and the UCS randomly paired.

will reappear, although it may not occur quite as frequently as before. The reappearance of the CR over a time interval after extinction is called *spontaneous recovery.*

Table 2–1 has representative extinction findings from Pavlov's laboratory (Pavlov, 1927, p. 58), and they show how a fully learned response can be diminished in the behavioral repertoire by presentation of the CS

TABLE 2–1
Extinction and spontaneous recovery of a
conditioned salivation response in the dog.

Time	Drops of saliva
1:42 P.M.	8
1:52 P.M.	3
2:02 P.M.	0
(interval of 20 minutes)	
2:22 P.M.	7

Source: I. P. Pavlov, *Conditioned Reflexes.* (An-
rep, trans.). Oxford: Oxford University Press, 1927.
Reprinted by permission of the Oxford University
Press.

alone. As usual, a dog was the subject and salivation was the response. The CS was sight of meat powder presented a short distance away at ten-minute intervals, and in three trials the CR is completely extinguished. A 20-minute rest was given, and spontaneous recovery was then observed where the CR bounced back to nearly its original level. Pavlov found that salivation in the dog had near 100 percent spontaneous recovery, but it is not always the case.

Grant, Hunter, and Patel (1958) had their subjects learn an eyeblink response to a criterion of eight CRs in ten consecutive trials, and they were then extinguished to a criterion of five successive trials without CRs. A second extinction was one, two, four, or eight hours after the first, and the number of CRs obtained in the second extinction was taken as the amount of spontaneous recovery. The results are shown in Figure 2–7, and the recovery curve levels out at about 60 percent.

The number of trials to extinguish a CR decreases with the number of times that the CR has undergone extinction. Porter (1938) found that it took seven trials to extinguish a conditioned eyeblink response the first time, and only two trials the third time. Pavlov (1927, p. 54) reported that with repeated extinction some dogs will extinguish their salivation response in one trial.

Extinction and schedules of reinforcement A potent variable for the rate of extinction, or the speed with which the response drops out of the behavioral repertoire, is *schedules of reinforcement.* This topic has been studied more extensively with reward learning (Chapter 3), but within the context of classical conditioning it means the percentage of trials in which the CS and UCS are paired. The experiment which opened this topic and motivated other investigators to explore it was by Humphreys (1939). Before Humphreys, other investigators casually explored the ef-

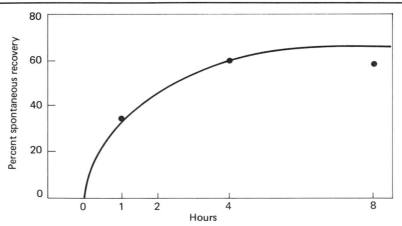

Source: D. A. Grant, H. G. Hunter, and A. S. Patel, Spontaneous recovery of the conditioned eyeblink response. *Journal of General Psychology*, 1958, 59, 135–141. Reprinted by permission of *The Journal Press*.

FIGURE 2–7
Spontaneous recovery as a function of time for the conditioned eyeblink response.

fects of intermittent reinforcement on extinction, but nothing came of the topic until the Humphreys experiment.

Humphreys classically conditioned the human eyeblink response. His experiment had three groups. Group I had 96 acquisition trials with the UCS on every trial. Group II had 96 acquisition trials also but with the UCS assigned randomly to half the trials. Group III had 48 acquisition trials but with the UCS on every one of them, which gave it the same number of UCS occurrences as Group II. The difference between Group II and Group III was whether the UCS occurred on some or all of the acquisition trials. All groups then were given 24 extinction trials, and the results are shown in Figure 2–8. Group II, with intermittent occurrences of the UCS, had a slower rate of extinction than the other two groups which had 100 percent occurrences of the UCS. Figure 2–5 has the eyeblink conditioning data of Grant and Schipper (1952), and it also shows the same effect. The last five blocks of trials are the extinction trials, and the group which had the UCS 100 percent of the time in acquisition had the fastest rate of extinction.

Why did the Humphreys study arouse interest? The reason was the theoretical climate of the day. At that time the psychology of learning was entrenched in the concept of habit. In the case of classical conditioning, the more trials where the CS and the UCS were paired the greater the habit strength and the stronger the CR. One of the measures of habit strength commonly used was resistance to extinction, with the rationale

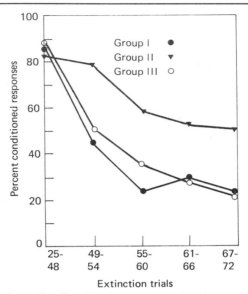

Source: L. G. Humphreys, The effect of random alternation of reinforcement on the acquisition and extinction of conditioned eyeblink reactions. *Journal of Experimental Psychology*, 1939, *25*, 141–158. Reprinted by permission of the American Psychological Association.

FIGURE 2–8
Effect of partial reinforcement on extinction of the conditioned eyeblink response. Group II had 50 percent reinforcement, Groups I and III had 100 percent reinforcement. The first point of a curve is the average of the 24 preceding acquisition trials.

being that responses with high habit strength require more extinction trials to eliminate them than responses with weak habit strength. Humphreys assailed this relationship with his data, which showed that intermittent pairing of the CS and UCS produced greater resistance to extinction than pairings on every trial. The finding created difficulty for the prevailing view of habit strength and extinction because, somehow, fewer pairings produced greater resistance to extinction.

Humphreys put forward the *expectancy hypothesis* to explain his data. The CR in acquisition occurs in anticipation of the UCS, and the nonoccurrence of the CR in extinction is in anticipation of nonoccurrence of the UCS. Consider Group I, which received the UCS on 100 percent of the acquisition trials. The shift from occurrence of the UCS to nonoccurrence of the UCS readily changes the expectancy; so the result is rapid extinction. Now consider Group II that had the UCS on half of the acquisition trials. When the UCS is removed in the extinction trials, the subjects discriminate extinction trials from acquisition trials poorly because the UCS had been omitted on some of the acquisition trials. As a consequence, the expectancy of the UCS is maintained longer in extinction and a greater number of CRs occur than when the UCS occurred 100 percent of the time in acquisition.

Theories of classical conditioning

As one of the thriving research areas of experimental psychology, classical conditioning has produced thousands of experiments and a wealth of data that is an attractive lure for theorists. Pavlov himself was a theorist. Even today, Pavlov's theoretical terminology and concepts are visible in the experimental literature. Pavlov believed that the close or simultaneous pairing of the CS and the UCS produces a state of *excitation*, and the increasing occurrence of the CR with trials is because of an increase in excitatory strength. The co-occurrence, or contiguity of the CS and UCS, is fundamental to the development of excitation. The inverse of excitation, called *inhibition*, is used to account for decrement in the CR. Excitation and inhibition combine algebraically to provide the net potentiality for the CR. When the UCS is withdrawn in extinction and the CS alone is repeatedly presented, inhibition increases and the result is the decrement in the CR that is extinction. Inhibition is unstable. Allow sufficient time between extinction trials, and inhibition will dissipate. The resulting increase in level of the CR is spontaneous recovery.

Modern investigators of classical conditioning often will use excitation and inhibition as terms in their theoretical thinking, but some of them will not necessarily use the terms in the same way as Pavlov. A modern view of excitation and inhibition (Rescorla, 1967, 1969a, 1969b, 1975) is cognitive in its orientation, placing emphasis on the subject's learned capability for extracting information from environmental events and responding on the basis of it. The CS and the UCS can occur in a variety of relationships, and the way that they occur and the relationships that are perceived determine whether nothing, excitation, or inhibition is formed. The principle of contiguity is not strictly held in this formulation. Rather, the approach is more statistical. When the CS and UCS are presented randomly, there is no structure to perceive and nothing to learn. If the CS and the UCS are positively correlated, where the UCS follows the CS on at least some of the trials, then excitation is formed and the CR occurs. The stronger the positive correlation the better the conditioning; so if the UCS follows the CS on every trial the acquisition of the CR should be relatively rapid, which it is. Following this logic, if the CS and the UCS have a negative correlation, where the CS reliably predicts the nonoccurrence of the UCS, the organism will develop inhibition and a reliable tendency for the CR *not* to occur. When excitatory and inhibitory tendencies exist simultaneously, they combine, as they did for Pavlov, algebraically. This *informational view*, as it is called, it prominent in thinking of theorists today. The informational view of classical conditioning is under development and is striving to widen the range of data that it can explain. The development has taken place mostly in fear conditioning, and currently the informational view has the strongest explanatory power there. The informational view will be encountered again in Chapter 6 on punishment and fear.

Summary

In classical conditioning there is the presentation of an event called the unconditioned stimulus (UCS) which reliably elicits an unconditioned response (UCR). A neutral stimulus, called the conditioned stimulus (CS), is presented in accompaniment with the UCS and the UCR, and the result of repeated presentation of these events is that the CS comes to evoke a new learned response called the conditioned response (CR). Everything from primitive organisms to the human have been classically conditioned; it is a fundamental kind of learning.

Reliable acquisition of conditioning occurs when the CS precedes the UCS. Backward conditioning, where the UCS precedes the CS, is unreliable. Important variables for acquisition are the number of trials where the CS and the UCS are paired, the percentage of trials on which the CS and the UCS are paired, and the time interval between the CS and the UCS.

Extinction is reduction in the level of the CR by withdrawal of the UCS. A major variable for the rate of extinction is percentage of acquisition trials on which the UCS is paired with the CS. Pairing the CS and the UCS on all of the acquisition trials produces faster extinction than omitting the UCS on some of them. Extinction is unstable because the extinguished CR tends to recover spontaneously with time after extinction.

References

Berger, T. W., & Thompson, R. F.   Neuronal plasticity in the limbic system during classical conditioning of the rabbit nictitating membrane response. I.   The hippocampus. *Brain Research,* 1978, *145,* 323–346.

Grant, D. A., Hunter, H. G., & Patel, A. S.   Spontaneous recovery of the conditioned eyelid response. *Journal of General Psychology,* 1958, *59,* 135–141.

Grant, D. A., & Schipper, L. M.   The acquisition and extinction of conditioned eyelid responses as a function of the percentage of fixed-ratio random reinforcement. *Journal of Experimental Psychology,* 1952, *43,* 313–320.

Hall, J. F.   *Classical conditioning and instrumental learning: A contemporary approach.* Philadelphia: Lippincott, 1976.

Hartman, T. F., & Grant, D. A.   Effect of intermittent reinforcement on acquisition, extinction, and spontaneous recovery of the conditioned eyelid response. *Journal of Experimental Psychology*, 1960, *60*, 89–96.

Humphreys, L. G.   The effect of random alternation of reinforcement on the acquisition and extinction of conditioned eyelid reactions. *Journal of Experimental Psychology*, 1939, *25*, 141–158.

Noble, M., Gruender, A., & Meyer, D. R.   Conditioning in fish (*Mollienisia Sp.*) as a function of the interval between CS and US. *Journal of Comparative and Physiological Psychology*, 1959, *52*, 236–239.

Pavlov, I. P.   *Conditioned reflexes.* (Anrep translation). Oxford: Oxford University Press, 1927.

Porter, J. M., Jr.   The modification of conditioned eyelid responses by successive series of non-reinforced elicitations. *Journal of General Psychology*, 1938, *19*, 307–323.

Razran, G.   Backward conditioning. *Psychological Bulletin*, 1956, *53*, 55–69.

Razran, G.   The observable unconscious and the inferable conscious in current Soviet psychophysiology: Interoceptive conditioning, semantic conditioning, and the orienting reflex. *Psychological Review*, 1961, *68*, 81–147.

Rescorla, R. A.   Pavlovian conditioning and its proper control procedures. *Psychological Review*, 1967, *74*, 71–80.

Rescorla, R. A.   Conditioned inhibition of fear. In N. J. Mackintosh and W. K. Honig (Eds.), *Fundamental issues in associative learning.* Halifax: Dalhousie University Press, 1969, pp. 65–89. (a)

Rescorla, R. A.   Pavlovian conditioned inhibition. *Psychological Bulletin*, 1969, *72*, 77–94. (b)

Rescorla, R. A.   Pavlovian excitatory and inhibitory conditioning. In W. K. Estes (Ed.), *Handbook of learning and cognitive processes* (Vol. 2). Hillsdale: Erlbaum, 1975, pp. 7–35.

Reynolds, B.   The acquisition of a trace conditioned response as a function of the magnitude of the stimulus trace. *Journal of Experimental Psychology*, 1945, *35*, 15–30.

Smith, M. C., Coleman, S. R., & Gormezano, I.   Classical conditioning of the rabbit's nictitating membrane response at backward, simultaneous, and forward CS–UCS intervals. *Journal of Comparative and Physiological Psychology*, 1969, *69*, 226–231.

Spooner, A., & Kellogg, W. N.   The backward conditioning curve. *American Journal of Psychology*, 1947, *60*, 321–334.

Twitmyer, E. B.   A study of the knee jerk. *Journal of Experimental Psychology*, 1974, *103*, 1047–1066.

3

Instrumental learning and positive reinforcement

THIS CHAPTER is about reinforcement, one of the most powerful determiners of behavior that psychologists know. We have always known
that behavior can be changed by rewarding some responses and not
others, and we have used this knowledge in ways we saw as advantage-
ous. Hard work earns more pay than idleness, the boy who does his
chores receives his weekly allowance, otherwise not, and the college
student hitchhiking home has a long wait rewarded with a ride direct to
the home town and learns that patience has a payoff. By experimentally
studying reinforcement, psychologists have extended our knowledge
about it and have increased the range of situations where it can be
applied. In Chapter 9 we will discuss various uses of positive reinforcement for human betterment, ranging from biofeedback to the regulation
of maladaptive behavior of hospital patients.

Psychologists prefer the term "reinforcement" to "reward," although
some use them interchangeably. The distinction is made between positive reinforcement, punishment, and negative reinforcement. Positive
reinforcement deals with events that are probably pleasant, while punishment and negative reinforcement are concerned with unpleasant
events. *Positive reinforcement* is any event that follows a response and
increases the chances of the response occurring again. *Punishment*, on
the other hand, is any event that follows a response and decreases the
likelihood of the response occurring again. *Negative reinforcement* is any

event whose *removal* increases the chances that a response will occur. Suppose that a child is afraid of a dog. She runs away, removing the dog from her sight. The dog is a negative reinforcer the removal of which increases the chances that the child will run away the next time the dog is encountered. This chapter is about positive reinforcement. Punishment and negative reinforcement, dealing as they do with the consequences of aversive events, have a chapter of their own.

Definitions, distinctions, and procedures

Reinforced learning comes under the classification of *instrumental learning*. The subject is an active agent in instrumental learning because the subject's response is instrumental in producing the reinforcement. Reinforced learning can have a stimulus which becomes the cue for occurrence of the response. An example is saying "Roll over" to your dog, and every time that it obeys you reward it with meat. Soon it will roll over reliably to your command. Or reinforced learning can occur without a specific stimulus. In this latter case you give your dog a piece of meat every time that it rolls over, and here also it will roll over regularly although you will not have it under the control of a command. Skinner (1938) called the instrumentally learned response without a specific stimulus an *operant*, and its instrumental learning is often called *operant learning*. When the response is with an identifiable stimulus, called the *discriminative stimulus*, it is called a *discriminated operant*. The command "Roll over" is the discriminative stimulus for the discriminated operant that you teach your dog.

THE FIVE ESSENTIALS OF REINFORCED LEARNING

Here is what it takes to demonstrate learning through positive reinforcement:

1. A defined response class Behavior is complex, continuous, and multidimensional, and out of it all we must choose the response class that we want to learn and which we will reinforce. The response class chosen does not matter just as long as it can be objectively and reliably observed. The response can be big, like rewarding a speech, or it can be small, like rewarding the lift of a finger. And we can reward a response of any precision. A dog can be rewarded for rolling over in a precise way, such as rolling to the left in 1.5 seconds, or we can ignore the precision of the roll just so long as the dog rolls over.

2. Reinforcement Like response class, the definition of reinforcement is generous providing it meets certain criteria. Most fundamental is that the reinforcer must be an event the occurrence of which increases the level of the defined response. Reinforcement can be a piece of food to the dog when it rolls over, or it can be a pat on the dog's head. Anything is accepted as a reinforcer if it works by increasing the level of the designated response.

3. Motivation A response has to occur before it can be reinforced, and this means an organism motivated enough to behave. Laboratory animals customarily are made hungry or thirsty before they are put in a learning situation for food or water reward.

4. Correlation of reinforcement with occurrence of the response class The response and the reinforcement do not always have to occur together, although often they do. More important is that the relationship between response and reinforcement be reliable and predictable in some sense. The reinforcement can occur after every response, every tenth response, or after responding has been in progress for 30 seconds, but whatever the relationship it must be a predictable one.

5. Reinforcement must follow the response There is little evidence that learning can occur when reinforcement precedes the response.

PERFORMANCE MEASURES AND LABORATORY TASKS

The heart of reinforced learning is that the level of the response is at an indifferent level before reinforcement, and with reinforcement the performance level increases. Psychologists mostly use standard measures and laboratory tasks for the systematic manipulation of reinforcement variables so that the transition from the indifferent state to the learned state can be charted and controlled.

The frequency of response measure Frequency of response is a fundamental measure for instrumental learning. Before learning, the response occurs infrequently, and after the learning process has begun the number of responses increase.

Figure 3–1 shows a simple kind of apparatus where response frequency is the measure. It is a T-maze, and it is a choice discrimination task. The early history of maze learning is filled with various kinds of complex mazes with many turns and blinds, but the complexity of these mazes made the control of relevant variables difficult. By the 1940s psychologists were turning to the T-maze as a simple choice learning situation better suited to their experimental purposes. Rats are usually the experimental subjects in T-mazes, and the task might be learning to turn left on each trial. Every time the animal turns left it is rewarded in the goal box at the end of the run, otherwise not, and soon it is turning left on more and more of the trials until eventually it does it 100 percent of the time.

The most common device to produce the frequency of response measure is the Skinner box, named after B. F. Skinner who invented it, in

28

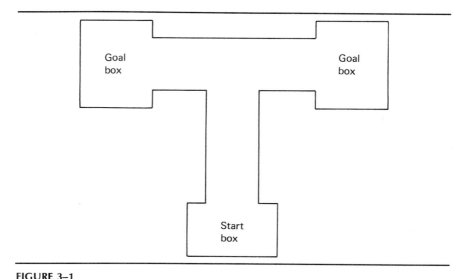

FIGURE 3–1
The T-maze—a device which often has been used in research on animal learning. The animal is rewarded when it chooses the correct goal box.

which an animal subject learns to press a bar or a key for food or water reward. Usually the animal is a rat or a pigeon. Figure 3–2 has a picture of the Skinner box. The Skinner box is often used in the study of operant learning. The response occurs at the discretion of the animal; so the number of responses per unit of time, or the rate of response, is a primary index of learning. The frequency of responses that occurs per unit of time can be plotted, and this is shown in Figure 3–3, but it is also common to cumulate response frequencies over time. The latter produces a cumulative frequency curve (Figure 3–4), and the rate of responding is revealed in the slope of the curve (steep slope-fast responding). Standard recording apparatus to produce a cumulative curve is commercially available for connecting to Skinner boxes. Other apparatus that is attached to Skinner boxes is called programming apparatus, and it is used mainly to control the delivery of reinforcement. The experimenter may want reinforcement of every response, every other response, or the first response that occurs after each 30-second interval. Programming and recording equipment for Skinner boxes has become sophisticated. Some laboratories have fully automated arrays of Skinner boxes.

Latency of response as a measure Latency, or the time between occurrence of a signal and the occurrence of a response, is another measure that is used in instrumental learning. The "straight runway" or

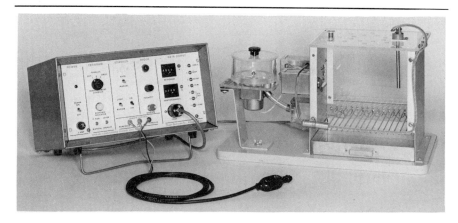

Source: Ralph Gerbrands Company, Inc., Arlington, Mass.

FIGURE 3–2

A bar-press apparatus, often called the *Skinner box,* that is commonly used in research on animal learning. Pressing of the bar produces a reward.

"straight alley," which is shown in Figure 3–5, is an example of a learning apparatus from which a latency measure is obtained. The animal is confined in the start box, and at a signal, often the raising of the door between the start box and the alley, the animal runs to the goal box where it receives reinforcement. The time between the signal and reach-

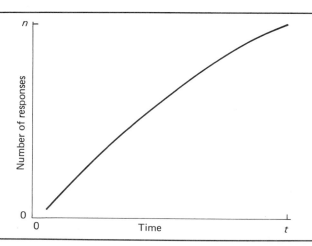

FIGURE 3–3

Learning often produces an increase in the number of responses. The curve of learning can be plotted in terms of the number of responses made per unit of time.

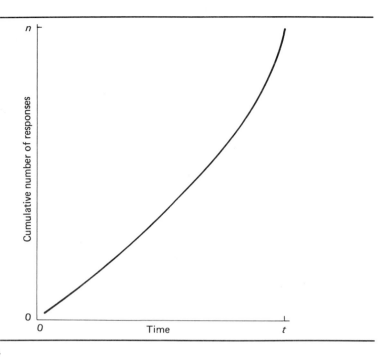

FIGURE 3–4
A cumulative frequency curve, derived from the data shown in Figure 3–3. The number of responses for successive units of time in Figure 3–3 are added to produce the function shown here. The more responses per unit of time the steeper the slope of a cumulative frequency curve.

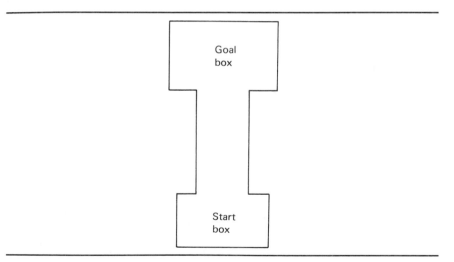

FIGURE 3–5
A device that is commonly used in research on animal learning, called the *straight runway*. The animal is rewarded for running from the start box to the goal box, and the time to make the run is recorded.

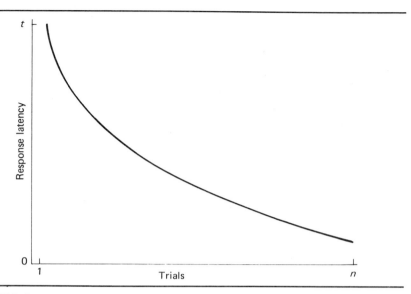

FIGURE 3–6
A learning curve in terms of the time to make the response, or response latency, as it is usually called.

ing the goal box is *response latency*. Slowness of response can be deliverately reinforced and trained, but in many skills an increase in learning and an increase in speed of responding go together. The straight runway is such a situation. Figure 3–6 shows a learning curve with latency as the measure.

Sometimes investigators will plot the reciprocal of latency, which is called speed. A speed curve increases with learning, and this is intuitively appealing to some, although it contains no more information than the latency curve.

Schedules of reinforcement and learning

In Chapter 2 on classical conditioning we saw that the frequency with which the UCS occurred in conditioning trials was a variable for both acquisition and extinction, and no less is true for instrumental learning. In fact, schedules of reinforcement, which is the banner under which this research area flies, has been studied mostly in instrumental learning situations; investigators of classical conditioning have studied it less. This section is about the effects of different schedules on the learning of a response and maintenance of the response after it has been learned.

For a long time psychologists studied continuous reinforcement, where every response of the specified kind was reinforced. Why continuous reinforcement was codified in the procedures of learning is a mystery. Perhaps an unverbalized reason was that the study of learning required the development of a learned response, and continuous reinforcement was a reliable way of doing it. Maybe another reason was that the withdrawal of reinforcement is the defining operations of extinction and the lowering of responsiveness (to be discussed later in this chapter), and so an investigator might have reasoned that intermittent reinforcement with its occasionally unreinforced responses is, in part, the condition of extinction. Why should we risk weakening a response when learning is the study of its strengthening? Whatever the reasons, they were not enough to constrain B. F. Skinner who challenged this orthodoxy in the 1930s. Skinner (1956), in discussing his curiosities as a young scientist, questioned the conventional wisdom of continuous reinforcement and tried reinforcing only some of a rat's responses. Instead of the response becoming intermittent like the reinforcement, it carried on at a steady rate. Since then, Skinner and his followers have been forerunners in research on reinforcement, and have investigated many kinds of programs, or schedules, of delivery for reinforcement. Today continuous reinforcement is considered only a special case, of minor interest in its own right.

The reasons for studying intermittent reinforcement have become compelling since the 1930s. Research has demonstrated that schedules of reinforcement are powerful determiners of behavior. No less important is that behavior in our everyday world is seldom reinforced continuously. The reward of publication comes to a striving young writer only for some articles, and a child in the classroom has only some efforts praised by the teacher. Our understanding of such behavior depends on understanding the effects of intermittent reinforcement.

THE FOUR BASIC SCHEDULES

The two main schedules of reinforcement are the *ratio schedule* and the *interval schedule*. The *fixed schedule* and the *variable schedule* are principal subtypes of the two main ones. A ratio schedule has reinforcement delivered after a fixed number of responses, which means that a fixed number of nonreinforced responses can occur before the reinforcement. Time is an irrelevant variable for a ratio schedule; number of responses is the factor that determines the delivery of reinforcement. An interval schedule requires that a given amount of time goes by before a response is reinforced, with number of responses irrelevant. Whether a schedule is fixed or variable depends upon the constancy of the ratio or the time factor.

First, let us consider each of the four basic schedules and its effect on response acquisition, or the original learning of the response, and on response maintenance.

The fixed-ratio schedule When a specified number of responses must occur before a reinforcement is delivered, and this number is a constant throughout learning, we have a fixed-ratio or *FR* schedule. If the subject is reinforced after every 50th response the schedule is designated *FR* 50. The schedule *FR* 1 is reinforcement after every response, which is continuous reinforcement, and it is a special case of the fixed-ratio schedule. In cases of infrequent reinforcement it is necessary to start the subject on a low ratio and gradually increase it until performance under the high ratio is attained.

Figure 3–7 shows the four basic schedules plotted in terms of cumulative frequency of response, so the steeper the slope of the curve the

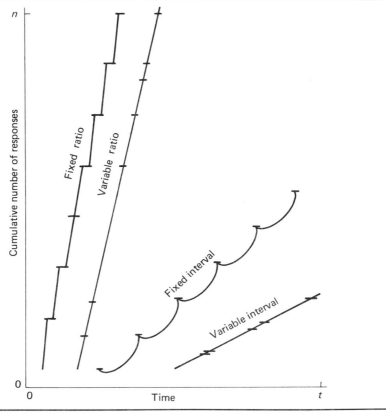

FIGURE 3–7
The four basic schedules of reinforcement.

faster the response. The short horizontal lines on curves represent points of reinforcement. As shown, the ratio schedules can produce a relatively high rate of responding.

Figure 3–8 has data from a study by Boren (1961) which show the rate of bar pressing in rats as a function of size of the fixed-ratio schedule. Boren used schedules that ranged from continuous reinforcement to 20 : 1. Figure 3–8 shows that rate of responding increases rapidly as the ratio increases, and then levels off. The form of the function is more important for our purposes than absolute level of the response rate, which can depend on type of animal and type of task. Pigeons pecking a key for grain reinforcement, for example, have a faster response rate than rats pressing bars.

Apparently high rates of fixed-ratio responding are unpleasant (Azrin, 1961; Appel, 1963; Thompson, 1964). Appel (1963) had two keys for his pigeons. Pecking the left-hand key delivered grain as reinforcement on a fixed-ratio schedule. A peck on the right-hand key terminated the reinforcement on the left-hand key until the bird pecked the right-hand key a second time. Appel had fixed ratios increase from 80 to 240, and the pigeons used the right-hand key increasingly as the size of the ratio increased. The right-hand key was almost invariably used after the reinforcement was received and before the next run of responses began. It

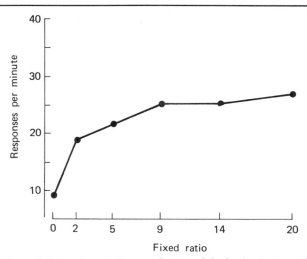

Source: J. J. Boren, Resistance to extinction as a function of the fixed ratio. *Journal of Experimental Psychology*, 1961, *61*, 304–308. Copyright 1961 by the American Psychological Association. Reprinted by permission.

FIGURE 3–8

Average performance level as a function of the size of the fixed-ratio schedule of reinforcement.

would seem that working hard for a reinforcement is unpleasant, and the animal will sometimes vote itself temporary relief once the reinforcement is received.

The world is full of examples of reinforcement under fixed-ratio schedules. A frequently cited example is the piece-rate system in a factory, where the production of *n* units produces a payment. Historically, trade unions have opposed the piece-rate system because it extracts high production levels from workers to the point, it is contended, of being inhumane. Management undoubtedly is less discontented with the high production than are the unions.

The variable-ratio schedule As the name implies, reinforcement comes after a variable number of responses rather than after a fixed number, as in the fixed-ratio schedule. This does not mean that the reinforcement is random but rather that it has a statistical definition and occurs after a specified number of responses *on the average*. Consider a variable-ratio schedule of 50, which is called *VR* 50. Reinforcement may be after 2 responses or 200, but over a long series of responses the subject will be rewarded for every 50 responses on the average. Figure 3–7 shows that the response rate for the variable-ratio schedule can be high.

Brandauer (1958) conducted an experiment that shows how behavior is controlled by the variable-ratio schedule. He used pigeons as his subjects and key-pecking as the response. Response rate as a function of ratios ranging from 1 to 400 is shown in Figure 3–9. The curve in Figure 3–9 has its similarities to the one in Figure 3–8 for fixed-ratio schedules. A limit to response rate is attained at a modest ratio, and it remains about the same thereafter.

The best example of the variable-ratio schedule is gambling with a slot machine. A slot machine will average a certain level of payoff, with the occurrence of payoff unsystematic and variable. You can win 3 plays in a row, or lose 50 in a row. Some psychologists would say that the gambler has a need for gambling which is being satisfied by frequent playing, but learning psychologists are more inclined to say that a high response rate is being sustained by a variable-ratio schedule.

The fixed-interval schedule A fixed-interval schedule is periodic. The first response that occurs after the specified period of time has passed is reinforced. A subject might be reinforced after every two minutes (*FI* 2) or every five minutes (*FI* 5). No matter how few or how many responses are made within the interval, reinforcement is not forthcoming until the time interval has passed.

Figure 3–7 shows the performance function for the fixed-interval schedule, and it is characterized by a moderate rate of responding and a distinct scallop effect. The moderate rate is intuitively understandable because a high response rate has no payoff in reinforcement. Only re-

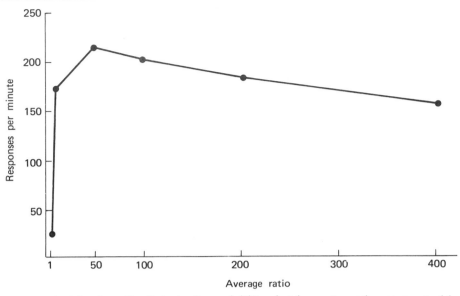

Source: C. M. Brandauer, The effects of uniform probabilities of reinforcement upon the response rate of the pigeon. Unpublished doctoral dissertation, Columbia University, 1958. Adapted from table 2.

FIGURE 3–9
Average performance level as a function of the size of the variable-ratio schedule of reinforcement.

sponses at specified points in time have payoff. Subjects could perform perfectly under a fixed-interval schedule if they were perfect time keepers and had within them physiological clocks that would tick off the exact interval between reinforcements. A subject would need to respond only at the times designated by the inner clock. The curve for the fixed-interval schedule in Figure 3–7 does suggest that some kind of rudimentary timekeeping is going on. After reinforcement, the response rate drops off because the subject knows that some time must pass before reinforcement is available again. As the interval continues the subject seems to develop a feeling that the time of reinforcement is approaching because the response rate picks up and guarantees a reinforcement shortly after it becomes available.

Wilson (1954) investigated the effect of size of the fixed interval on behavior, using rats as his subjects and bar pressing as the task. The intervals ranged from one sixth of a minute to 6 minutes. The results are shown in Figure 3–10. The curve in Figure 3–10 has the opposite trend of the curves shown in Figures 3–8 and 3–9. One reason is that animals learn something about the time requirements of their task. An animal in the one-minute interval need respond only once a minute to be rein-

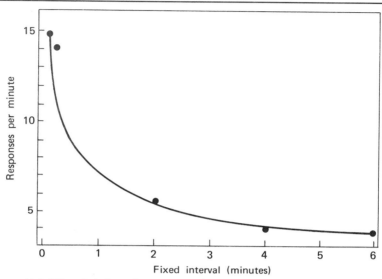

Source: M. P. Wilson, Periodic reinforcement interval and number of periodic reinforcements as parameters of response strength. *Journal of Comparative and Physiological Psychology*, 1954, *47*, 51–56. Copyright 1954 by the American Psychological Association. Reprinted by permission.

FIGURE 3–10
Average performance level as a function of the size of the fixed-interval schedule of reinforcement.

forced, and a six-minute interval needs a response only once every six minutes for reinforcement. Once a degree of time discrimination is learned, animals assigned longer intervals will make fewer responses than animals with shorter intervals.

An example of a fixed-interval schedule is feeding a child at regular times, ignoring pleas for food between meals. No matter how much the child might cry for food, feeding would occur only when he or she cries the first time after feeding time arrives. Crying would increase as the time of feeding approaches, and decrease after feeding, as the scallop effect in Figure 3–7 implies.

The variable-interval schedule A variable-interval schedule is aperiodic. Responses are reinforced after varying time intervals, the length of which averages out to the time value that defines the schedule. The subject might, for example, be rewarded for the first response after Minute 1, Minute 3, Minute 6, Minute 11, etc., with a reinforcement occurring every 5 minutes on the average (*VI* 5). As with the fixed-interval schedule, the number of responses within the interval is irrelevant; only the first response after the interval receives the reinforcement. Figure 3–7 shows that the variable-interval schedule has a low rate, and the performance curve is smooth. As with the fixed-interval schedule the subject gets nothing for high rates of responding; so response rate tends to be low.

Catania and Reynolds (1968) used pigeons and the key-pecking response to investigate the effects of variable-interval schedules that ranged from 12 to 427 seconds, and their results are shown in Figure 3–11. The longer intervals induced a slower rate of responding, as fixed intervals do (Figure 3–10), and probably for the same reason: The animals develop some power to keep time, and with the longer intervals they learn that occasional responding, properly timed, can gain as many reinforcements as frequent responding. Timekeeping should be less

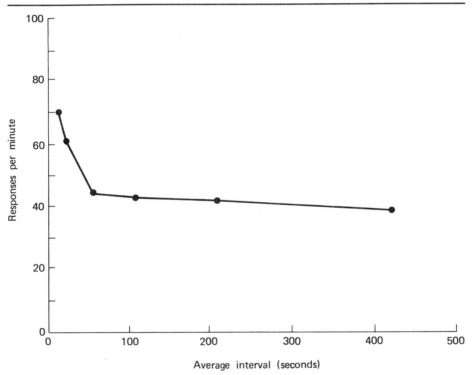

Source: A. C. Catania and G. S. Reynolds, A quantitative analysis of the behavior maintained by interval schedules of reinforcement. *Journal of the Experimental Analysis of Behavior*, 1968, *11*, 327–383. Copyright 1968 by the Society for the Experimental Analysis of Behavior, Inc.

FIGURE 3–11
Average performance level as a function of the size of the variable-interval schedule of reinforcement.

precise with the variable-interval schedule, however, because of its statistical definition where a particular schedule is an average of several intervals and so has uncertainty associated with it. That the decline of the curve in Figure 3–11 is slight relative to the curve for fixed-interval schedules in Figure 3–10 is testimony to less precise timekeeping with variable-interval schedules.

An example of a variable-interval schedule is fishing. On the average you catch a fish every hour, but you could catch two of them in a five-minute period and then have a three-hour wait for the next one.

SUPERSTITIOUS BEHAVIOR

Schedules of reinforcement are various kinds of intermittent reinforcement, and they can explain different kinds of everyday behavior, as we have seen. A major kind of everyday behavior which intermittent reinforcement can explain, and which has not been discussed, is superstitious behavior.

Why does the dice player blow on the dice each time before throwing? Why does the football coach wear a "lucky hat" to the game? According to a learning interpretation these "meaningless" pieces of behavior first occurred in accidental association with reinforcement (winning the roll of the dice, winning the football game), and this increased their probability of occurrence in the future. The superstitious act may not have been rewarded regularly, but reward occurred often enough to insure the act's frequent occurrence. Skinner (1948) was the first to demonstrate the learning of superstitious behavior. He found that pigeons who received a pellet of food irrespective of their behavior came to perform bizarre acts, like turning around two or three times in a ritualistic dance, or repeatedly pecking the upper corner of the cage. These eccentric elements of behavior accidentally came to be paired with reinforcements from time to time, and eventually they occurred with some regularity. The reason for superstitious acts being strange is that they are uncontrolled and accidental at the time of reinforcement, and so they have a bizarre character. We think there is nothing eccentric about kinds of behavior that we deliberately choose for learning. Thus, we choose key-pecking as the response which we reinforce for a pigeon, and we think it a perfectly normal unit of behavior; but when we play no role in the choosing we see the behavior as bizarre. Normal or eccentric, the behavior is covered by the same laws of reinforcement.

COMBINATIONS OF REINFORCEMENT SCHEDULES

Much of the research on schedules of reinforcement has used simple situations like pressing a single bar or a single key. However, investigators of schedules of reinforcement have gone beyond simple situations and have asked how two or more schedules operating in a situation regulate the response sequence. Each stimulus or response element can have its own schedule of reinforcement so that the behavioral sequence is not simply determined. There are many possibilities when we consider the various schedules of reinforcement and the elements that can be arranged. Here are some of the prominent possibilities that have been investigated.

Concurrent schedules Concurrent schedules involve choice among simultaneous response options, with each option associated with a different schedule of reinforcement. A typical experimental arrangement would have two keys for a pigeon with a different schedule of reinforcement on each key. More than two keys can be used. The investigator who uses a concurrent schedule must insure that choice behavior is occurring and that he does not encourage sequential behavior where the peck of one key is immediately followed by the peck of another and reinforcement. In this latter case, it is the pattern of two pecks that is being reinforced rather than the choice between two keys. To insure choice behavior, a time delay is introduced, called the *change-over delay*, where reinforcement for a response is withheld if the other response has occurred within the last second or two.

The impressive characteristic of a concurrent schedule is that the percentage of responses for an option is determined by the percentage of reinforcements available at the option. The pioneering study of this relationship was by Herrnstein (1961). The pigeons of his experiment had two keys, each with a different variable-interval schedule of reinforcement. Various pairs of variable-interval schedules were used for different sessions of the experiment. The change-over delay was 1.5 seconds. Herrnstein's results are shown in Figure 3–12, which has the proportion of responses given to the left-hand key, and Herrnstein calls it the *Matching Law*. There is a virtually perfect relationship between the proportion of reinforcements from both keys that is available on the left-hand key, and the proportion of responses that the left-hand key receives. When a variable-interval schedule on the left-hand key is chosen such that it delivers, for example, 20 percent of the reinforcements that are available from both keys, then the left-hand key will receive about 20 percent of the key pecks. The right-hand key, which delivers 80 percent of the reinforcements, will receive about 80 percent of the pecks. The birds could have pecked either key exclusively, but instead they divided their time in accord with the Matching Law.

Other commonly used combinations Here is a sample of other kinds of schedules that have been studied. They do not involve response choice as the concurrent schedules.

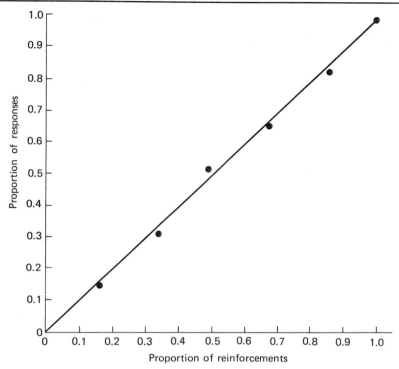

Source: Adapted from R. J. Herrnstein, On the law of effect. *Journal of the Experimental Analysis of Behavior,* 1970, *13,* 243–266. Copyright 1970 by the Society for the Experimental Analysis of Behavior, Inc.

FIGURE 3–12
When a concurrent schedule of reinforcement with two response options has a different schedule of reinforcement associated with each option, an animal will divide its responses in accord with the percentage of reinforcements that each schedule delivers. This is called the Matching Law.

A chained schedule is a sequence of different stimuli, each with its own schedule, with a single reinforcement delivered at the end of the sequence. For example, a key for a pigeon will have four different colors, each with a different schedule of reinforcement, and the requirement of each schedule must be met before reinforcement is obtained.

A tandem schedule has schedules of reinforcement acting in succession, with a single reinforcement programmed by the schedules, and without a different stimulus for each schedule. For example, the color of the key remains unchanged but the pigeon must respond accordingly to, say, four different schedules before reinforcement is obtained.

A multiple schedule has different schedules of reinforcement in succession, each with a different stimulus. When a schedule is completed, a reinforcement is delivered, the stimulus changes, and another schedule goes into effect. For example, a blue key has a variable-interval schedule associated with it and, when reinforcement is received and the key turns red, a fixed-ratio schedule goes into effect.

Extinction

In Chapter 2 we saw that the extinction of a classically conditioned response is by withdrawing the UCS and repeatedly presenting the CS alone. In the case of a response instrumentally learned with positive reinforcement, the definition of extinction is similar: *Extinction is reduction in performance by the withdrawal of reinforcement.*

Figure 3–13 shows extinction data from a rat in a Skinner box, reported by Skinner (1938). Food reinforcement was withdrawn and the part of the cumulative-response curve before the intersecting line is the classic extinction effect, where the animal's responsiveness steadily declines until it stops responding altogether. The intersecting line is a 48-hour rest period where the animal was returned to the home cage and, upon return to the experimental task, another established effect for extinction appears—spontaneous recovery, or the regaining of some responsiveness with time after extinction. At the end of the first session the animal had ceased responding and was extinguished, but on return to the box it temporarily had a rapid rate of responding and then eventually stopped responding again. Ellson (1938) showed that spontaneous recovery of bar-pressing in the rat is a gradually increasing func-

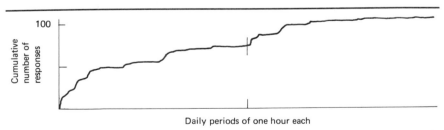

Daily periods of one hour each

Source: B. F. Skinner, *The Behavior of Organisms.* Englewood Cliffs, N.J.: Prentice-Hall, 1965. Adapted by permission of Prentice-Hall, Inc.

FIGURE 3–13
A cumulative response curve which shows extinction, a 48-hour rest at the point of the intersecting line, and spontaneous recovery.

tion of time, rising to a maximum of about 50 percent of the strength that was held before the rest interval.

PROMINENT VARIABLES THAT AFFECT EXTINCTION

In Chapter 2 we saw that in acquisition the number of CS–UCS pairings and schedules of reinforcement are potent influences on extinction of a classically conditioned response. Essentially the same can be said of a response that is instrumentally learned with positive reinforcement.

Number of reinforcements "Resistance to extinction" has been a useful notion for the psychology of learning. Any variable that induces more responses in extinction than another is said to increase resistance to extinction. For a rather long time, number of reinforcements was thought to be related positively to resistance to extinction, and this view was especially held by those who believed that reinforcement affected a response by the strengthening of habit. The greater the number of responses reinforced in learning the greater the habit strength and the greater the resistance to extinction. This position was not arbitrarily held. There have been a number of experiments which show that resistance to extinction increases with number of reinforcements (Williams, 1938; Perin, 1942; Wilson, 1954; Harris and Nygaard, 1961; Dyal and Holland, 1963).

The difficulty with the view that number of reinforcements and resistance to extinction are positively related is that exceptions have appeared in the literature from time to time. These exceptions go under the heading of the *overtraining extinction effect.* The gist of the overtraining extinction effect is that with a large number of reinforcements, often measured in hundreds, resistance to extinction can be reduced (e.g., Sperling, 1965; Senkowski, 1978). The habit-centered viewpoint that asserted the positive relationship between number of reinforcements and resistance to extinction does not accommodate the overtraining extinction effect gracefully. For that matter, no one else has a suitable theory of it either.

Schedules of Reinforcement The discovery that extinction rate was slowed with intermittent reinforcement in acquisition was with classical conditioning, but most of the research since then has been with instrumental learning and positive reinforcement. A study by Weinstock (1954) is a representative experiment. Rats were the subjects, and the apparatus was an L-shaped runway where food was the reinforcement. Running speed was the measure of performance. Four groups of animals were given 75 acquisition trials with either 30, 50, 80, or 100 percent reinforcement. Twenty extinction trials followed. The results for extinction are shown in Figure 3–14. The 100-percent, or continuous-

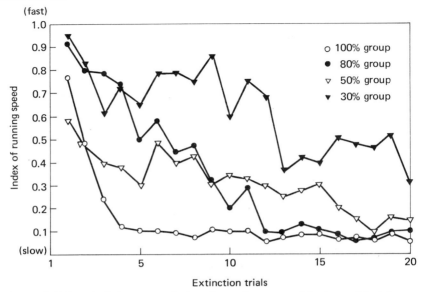

Source: S. Weinstock, Resistance to extinction of a running response following partial reinforcement under widely spaced trials. *Journal of Comparative and Physiological Psychology*, 1954, 47, 318–322. Reprinted by permission of the American Psychological Association.

FIGURE 3–14

Extinction of a running response as a function of percent reinforcement in acquisition. The more frequent the reinforcement in acquisition the more rapid the extinction.

reinforcement, group, had a faster rate of extinction than any of the groups in partial-reinforcement conditions. The 30 percent group had the most resistance to extinction even though it had the least number of reinforcements in acquisition.

Earlier in this chapter we looked at the acquisition of bar pressing in rats as a function of size of the fixed-ratio schedule. The study that we examined was by Boren (1961), and he reported extinction data also. His extinction data, covering fixed ratios from continuous reinforcement to 20 : 1, are shown in Figure 3–15. Similar to the Weinstock findings in Figure 3–14, extinction is fastest with continuous reinforcement. Higher fixed ratios increased the resistance to extinction.

So that you do not think that the partial-reinforcement effect on extinction is limited to pigeons and rats, the favorite laboratory animals of learning psychologists, consider a study by Grossman (1973) who taught honeybees to suck sugar solution from a tube. He reinforced every entry to the tube (continuous reinforcement) or every fifth entry (a fixed ratio

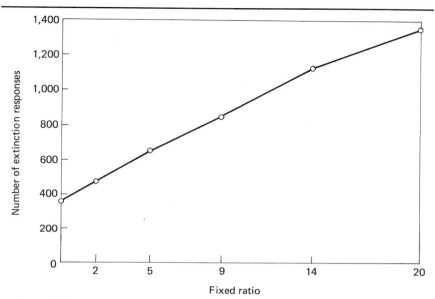

Source: J. J. Boren, Resistance to extinction as a function of the fixed ratio. *Journal of Experimental Psychology,* 1961, *61,* 304–308. Reprinted by permission of the American Psychological Association.

FIGURE 3–15
The number of responses in extinction as a function of several values for the fixed-ratio schedule of reinforcement in acquisition.

of 5 : 1). The bees on the 5 : 1 schedule made twice as many responses in extinction as those that had continuous reinforcement.

THEORIES OF PARTIAL-REINFORCEMENT EFFECTS ON EXTINCTION

The discrimination hypothesis—a reasonable hypothesis that failed Mowrer and Jones (1945) conducted one of the early studies of intermittent reinforcement and extinction, and they offered the *discrimination hypothesis.* Mowrer and Jones used a Skinner box with food reinforcement for their rat subjects, and they hypothesized that pressing the bar and turning to the trough and eating food establishes distinctive patterns of stimulation. In extinction, after 100 percent reinforcement, there is no more eating of food, the patterns of stimulation change, the animal discriminates the change, and soon stops its bar pressing as a result. When reinforcement is intermittent, the stimulus patterns in acquisition are ambiguous because the bar press is sometimes followed by eating responses and sometimes not, and so noneating trials are similar to extinction trials. The animal has trouble distinguishing acquisition trials from extinction as a result, and so its responding persists longer.

Tests of the discrimination hypothesis failed to support it. A consistent finding in the psychological literature is that partial reinforcement increases resistance to extinction even though trials of continuous reinforcement occur between the partial-reinforcement trials and the extinction trials. The trials of continuous reinforcement occurring just before extinction should make the discrimination between reinforced trials and nonreinforced extinction trials easy, thus upsetting the usual effects of partial reinforcement on extinction, but this is not so. Theios (1962), Quartermain and Vaughan (1961), Rashotte and Surridge (1969), and Leung and Jensen (1968) report data which show the standard effects of partial reinforcement on extinction even though considerable amounts of continuous reinforcement intervened.

The sequential hypothesis The findings of Weinstock (1954) in Figure 3–14 show that resistance to extinction increases as the percentage of reinforced trials decreases. Is percent reinforcement the basic determiner of resistance to extinction? Is that all there is to it? There are two other ways of viewing the matter.

The first way is that *number* of nonreinforced trials in acquisition, not percent of reinforcements, is the fundamental determiner of resistance to extinction. As percent of reinforcement decreases, the number of nonreinforced trials increases, and so perhaps number of nonreinforced trials is the most basic variable of all. With total number of trials held constant in acquisition, percent reinforcement and number of nonreinforced trials are reciprocally related, but if total number of acquisition trials is allowed to vary, then the two measures can be dissociated. An experiment by Lawrence and Festinger (1962, Experiment 5) established that number of nonreinforced trials was a potent variable for resistance to extinction. An S-shaped runway was the task, with rats as subjects and food as the reward. Their groups had either 33, 50, 67, or 100 percent reinforcement, with subgroups having different numbers of trials to dissociate percent reinforcement and number of nonreinforced trials. Extinction to a criterion followed, and trials to criterion was the measure. The partial-reinforcement groups had more trials to extinction than the continuous-reinforcement group, which is the standard finding. But, when the trials-to-extinction measure was examined as a joint function of percent reinforcement and number of nonreinforced trials, the nonreinforced trials were found to be the most important determiner of behavior. Trials to extinction increased linearly with number of nonreinforced trials. Uhl and Young (1967) conducted a similar experiment, using bar pressing as the response for rats to learn. Their results were the same—the number of nonreinforced trials, not percent reinforcement, was the strong determiner of resistance to extinction.

The second way is that number of nonreinforced trials *in a sequence* between reinforced trials is the primary variable rather than percent reinforcement or the total number of nonreinforced trials in acquisition. It is true that the total number of nonreinforced trials will increase as percent reinforcement decreases, but it is also true that the length of the run of nonreinforced trials between reinforcements will increase. Which is the more fundamental variable for extinction? Gonzalez and Bitterman (1964) probed this possibility with rats as the experimental subjects, bar pressing as the task, and food as the reinforcement. One group had 100 percent reinforcement in training, 2 had 60 percent, and 2 had 30 percent. The 60 percent groups had either short or long runs of nonreinforced trials between reinforcements, as did the 30 percent groups, where a short run was as many as 5 nonreinforced trials and a long run was as many as 16 nonreinforced trials. After extensive training, extinction to a criterion followed. As expected, the partial-reinforcement groups had greater resistance to extinction than the 100 percent-reinforcement group but, more importantly, the long-run groups had greater resistance to extinction than the short-run groups. Capaldi (1964, 1966, 1967) has used findings such as these as the foundation of his *sequential hypothesis.*

The sequential hypothesis is grounded, primarily, in the memories of nonreinforced trials (Capaldi, 1971). The memory states for reinforced and nonreinforced trials are assumed to be different. The instrumental response becomes conditioned to memory traces of nonreinforced trials in acquisition, and the longer the run of nonreinforced trials in extinction the greater the chances that the instrumental response will occur and prolong the extinction.

The theoretical assertion that longer runs of nonreinforced trials in acquisition will produce greater resistance to extinction has been verified. Gonzalez and Bitterman (1964) found that longer runs of nonreinforced trials produced greater resistance to extinction than shorter runs. Capaldi (1964) found the same thing when he varied the length of the run of nonreinforced trials before a reinforcement in a straight runway with rats, with percent reinforcement constant.

A merit of a worthy scientific hypothesis is that it will generate a number of provable assertions, sometimes counter-intuitive ones. As we have seen, resistance to extinction increases as the percent reinforcement decreases. The sequential hypothesis squares with this well-known finding because the lower percentages of reinforcement will have the longer sequences of nonreinforced runs. However, if a training situation with a higher percent reinforcement was designed to have some longer sequences of nonreinforced trials than a lower percent reinforcement situation, then greater resistance to extinction should be found for the higher percent reinforcement, which reverses the standard finding. This was the good idea of Capaldi and Stanley (1965), and they tested it with rats, a straight runway, food reinforcement, and running speed as the measure. Their results are shown in Figure 3–16 for extinction days, and they deserve to be compared with Weinstock's finding in Figure 3–14. As the sequential hypothesis predicts, the highest percent reinforcement has the greatest resistance to extinction (fastest running time in this case).

The frustration hypothesis Amsel (1958, 1962, 1967) has been the architect of a frustration theory which includes partial-reinforcement effects on extinction. Frustration is determined by such variables as the blocking of an ongoing response, the delay of reinforcement, or the reduction in size of an anticipated reinforcement, but Amsel's focus for partial reinforcement is frustration through the omission of anticipated reinforcement.

Amsel's theory says that positive reinforcement increases the strength of an instrumental response and also produces a learned anticipation of

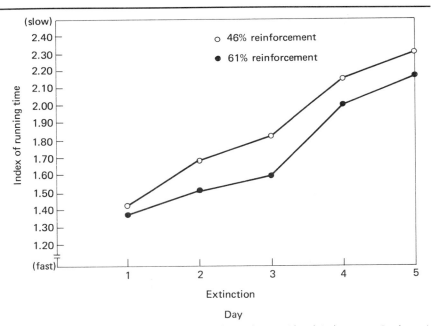

Source: E. J. Capaldi and L. R. Stanley, Percentage of reward versus N-length in the runway. *Psychonomic Science*, 1965, *3*, 263–264. Reprinted by permission of The Psychonomic Society, Inc.

FIGURE 3–16
Evidence for the sequential hypothesis. Shown is a reversal of the standard effect of partial reinforcement on extinction, which was predicted by the hypothesis.

the reinforcement. Nonreinforcement of the response thwarts anticipation of the reinforcement, and frustration results. Frustration is a drive, or motivational state, that becomes conditioned to the stimuli of the situation, and it energizes behavior whenever it is aroused. The frustration is elicited by the stimuli in extinction, the subject responds more energetically, and extinction is prolonged as a consequence. There is no frustration when acquisition is under continuous reinforcement; so resistance to extinction is lower than under partial reinforcement.

A fundamental line of proof for the frustration hypothesis is showing that omitted reinforcements have an energizing effect on behavior. The experiment which made this point was by Amsel and Roussel (1952). They trained rats in preliminary trials to run two straight runways for food reinforcement. After training, the animals were given test trials. Half of the test trials on Runway A were reinforced and half were not. Runway B was reinforced on every trial. Each trial on Runway A was followed immediately by a trial on Runway B. The measure of performance was running time. The results are presented in Figure 3–17.

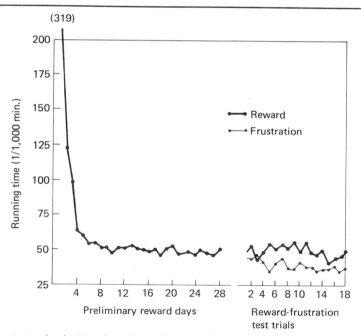

Source: A. Amsel and J. Roussel, Motivational properties of frustration: I. Effect on a running response of the addition of frustration to the motivational complex. *Journal of Experimental Psychology*, 1952, 43, 363–368. Reprinted by permission of the American Psychological Association.

FIGURE 3–17

Evidence that frustration has an energizing effect on behavior. Running time in a straight runway is faster after reward omission than after reward.

Running times on the left-hand side of the figure are for the preliminary trials where all runs were reinforced. Running times on the right-hand side are the times for runs in Runway B which were preceded by runs in Runway A that were reinforced on only half the trials. A run in Runway B following nonreinforcement in Runway A was a frustration test and, according to Amsel's theory, should be faster than after a reinforcement in Runway A. The empirical outcome confirmed the theory. Running times in Runway B were faster on the frustration tests.

Conclusions on theories of partial reinforcement and extinction   The sequential hypothesis can be seen as a competitor of the frustration hypothesis, both seeking to explain the same data. Yet, they need not be. The sequential hypothesis is rooted in learning and memory, and the frustration hypothesis is based on motivation. Learning theorists would mostly agree that learning and memory as well as motivation are both needed to account for performance; so perhaps it is best to see the two hypotheses as complementary.

THE ODOR OF NONREINFORCEMENT: A DIFFICULTY FOR THEORIES OF PARTIAL REINFORCEMENT

Experimental psychologists pride themselves in their control of the experimental environment. Environmental stimuli are so fundamental in the regulation of behavior that an experimenter must give very close attention to their control if his findings are to be interpretable. It is troublesome, therefore, to find a line of evidence that the behavior of the animal itself can alter the environment; environmental stimuli are not under complete control of the experimenter but are partly contributed by the subjects themselves. This evidence is developing into a potential difficulty for the conduct and interpretation of experiments on partial reinforcement.

The evidence is mounting that there are distinctive odors associated with nonreinforcement, and possibly reinforcement, and that these odors are influential stimuli for behavior. These odors are of a class of stimuli called *pheromones* which an animal emits and which arouse a reaction in another animal (Gleason and Reynierse, 1969, Birch, 1974). Because the pattern of reinforcements and nonreinforcements is the essential stuff of partial reinforcement, it is clear that any pheromones associated with them is a variable to be reckoned with. All of the hypotheses on partial reinforcement that have been reviewed count on memory of past stimuli associated with reinforcements and nonreinforcements, not current chemical stimuli resulting from past reinforcements and nonreinforcements, to determine behavior. No hypotheses about such behavior have ever considered odors as an influential variable, nor have any controls for them ever been used. The accumulating evidence is that an animal can be influenced by the odors from its own previous nonreinforced behavior or the nonreinforced behavior of another animal.

An experiment by Wasserman and Jensen (1969) is an example of how odor can effect the running behavior of rats in a straight runway. After preliminary training, their experimental animals were given test runs where the floor of the runway was covered with paper which was either new, had been traversed by an animal on nonreinforced extinction trials, or traversed by an animal on reinforced trials. They found that runs down the alley on papers that had been used by animals during extinction were substantially slower than runs when new or reinforcement paper was used.

Morrison and Ludvigson (1970), using rats in a T-maze, made choice contingent upon discrimination of an odor of reinforcement or nonreinforcement at the choice point. The "odor of reward" was created by allowing a hungry rat to eat at the choice point. The "odor of nonreward" was created by allowing a hungry rat to spend the same amount of time at the choice point without eating. These odors, if they existed, were to be cues for a turn in the maze. If odor can be a discriminative stimulus the animal should be able to choose a particular arm of the maze when the odor is present and receive reinforcement for it. One group received odor of reward as a cue for turning into one arm of the maze and odor of nonreward for turning into the other arm. A second group received odor of reward as a cue for one arm and clean floor paper (intended as a minimum odor condition) as a cue for the other arm. A third group had odor of nonreward and clean paper as cues, and a fourth group had clean paper on all trials. The results were that only the groups which had the odor of nonreward as a cue showed any learning of the discrimination.

The tenor of the research literature is that nonreinforcement has a distinctive odor associated with it and that reinforcement does not. Moreover, there is the clear indication that the odor of nonreinforcement is aversive and animals will avoid it (Mellgren, Fouts, and Martin, 1973; Collerain and Ludvigson, 1977; Collerain, 1978). Collerain and Ludvigson (1977) and Collerain (1978) have conducted a series of experiments which show that rats will learn to escape a compartment where another rat has experienced nonreinforcement for its performance. These investigators discuss the "frustration odor" that is produced by nonreinforcement. If nonreinforcement produces frustration (Amsel's experiments are evidence that it does), and frustration produces odor, then we cannot understand how the reinforced and nonreinforced trials of partial reinforcement sequences influence behavior until the effects of odor are clarified. Pheromones are a puzzle to be solved before theorizing in this field can advance, it would seem.

Summary

This chapter was concerned with positive reinforcement, which is often called reward. Positive reinforcement is defined as any event that follows a response and increases the probability of occurrence of the response. Positive reinforcement is sought by the subject (e.g., food), in contrast to negative reinforcement which is unpleasant and causes learning by virtue of its removal (e.g., electric shock).

Reinforcement is not always delivered after every response but is sometimes delivered intermittently according to a schedule. The two basic schedules of reinforcement are ratio schedules, where reinforcement occurs after a specified number of responses irrespective of time, and interval schedules, where reinforcement is delivered on a time schedule irrespective of number of responses. Each of these two basic schedules are further classified into fixed and variable schedules, depending whether number of responses or time between reinforcements is fixed or is variable with a statistical definition.

The withdrawal of positive reinforcement produces a decrease in the probability of responding, and this effect is called extinction. The most powerful determiner of extinction is schedules of reinforcement. Extinction of a response that has been learned under continuous reinforcement is fast relative to one that has received intermittent reinforcement. The number of reinforcements administered in learning is also an important determiner of extinction.

References

Amsel, A.   The role of frustrative nonreward in noncontinuous reward situations. *Psychological Bulletin*, 1958, *55*, 102–119.

Amsel, A.   Frustrative nonreward in partial reinforcement and discrimination learning: Some recent history and a theoretical extension. *Psychological Review*, 1962, *69*, 306–328.

Amsel, A.   Partial reinforcement effects on vigor and persistence: Advances in frustration theory derived from a variety of within-subjects experiments. In K. W. Spence and J. T. Spence (Eds.), *The psychology of learning and motivation* (Vol. 1). New York: Academic Press, 1967, pp. 1–65.

Amsel, A., & Roussel, J.   Motivational properties of frustration: I. Effect on a running response of the addition of frustration to the motivational complex. *Journal of Experimental Psychology*, 1952, *43*, 363–368.

Appel, J. B.   Aversive aspects of a schedule of positive reinforcement. *Journal of the Experimental Analysis of Behavior*, 1963, *6*, 423–428.

Azrin, N. H.   Time-out from positive reinforcement. *Science*, 1961, *133*, 382–383.

Birch, M. C. (Ed.) *Pheromones*. North-Holland Research Monographs: Frontiers of Biology (Vol. 32). Amsterdam: North-Holland, 1974.

Boren, J. J. Resistance to extinction as a function of the fixed ratio. *Journal of Experimental Psychology*, 1961, *61*, 304–308.

Brandauer, C. M. The effects of uniform probabilities of reinforcement upon the response rate of the pigeon. Unpublished doctoral dissertation, Columbia University, 1958.

Capaldi, E. J. Effect of N-length, number of different N-lengths, and number of reinforcements on resistance to extinction. *Journal of Experimental Psychology*, 1964, *68*, 230–239.

Capaldi, E. J. Partial reinforcement: An hypothesis of sequential effects. *Psychological Review*, 1966, *73*, 459–477.

Capaldi, E. J. A sequential hypothesis of instrumental learning. In K. W. Spence and J. T. Spence (Eds.), *The psychology of learning and motivation* (Vol. 1). New York: Academic Press, 1967, pp. 67–156.

Capaldi, E. J. Memory and learning: A sequential viewpoint. In W. K. Honig and P. H. R. James (Eds.), *Animal memory*. New York: Academic Press, 1971, pp. 111–154.

Capaldi, E. J., & Stanley, L. R. Percentage of reward vs. N-length in the runway. *Psychonomic Science*, 1965, *3*, 263–264.

Catania, A. C., & Reynolds, G. S. A quantitative analysis of the behavior maintained by interval schedules of reinforcement. *Journal of the Experimental Analysis of Behavior*, 1968, *11*, 327–383.

Collerain, I. Frustration odor of rats receiving small numbers of prior rewarded running trials. *Journal of Experimental Psychology: Animal Behavior Processes*, 1978, *4*, 120–130.

Collerain, I., & Ludvigson, W. Hurdle-jump responding in the rat as a function of conspecific odor of reward and nonreward. *Animal Behavior & Learning*, 1977, *5*, 177–183.

Dyal, J. A., & Holland, T. A. Resistance to extinction as a function of number of reinforcements. *American Journal of Psychology*, 1963, *76*, 332–333.

Ellson, D. G. Quantitative studies of the interaction of simple habits: I. Recovery from the specific and generalized effects of extinction. *Journal of Experimental Psychology*, 1938, *23*, 339–358.

Gleason, K. K., & Reynierse, J. H. The behavioral significance of pheromones in vertebrates. *Psychological Bulletin*, 1969, *71*, 58–73.

Gonzalez, R. C., & Bitterman, M. E. Resistance to extinction in the rat as a function of percentage and distribution of reinforcement. *Journal of Comparative and Physiological Psychology*, 1964, *58*, 258–263.

Grossman, K. E. Continuous, fixed-ratio, and fixed-interval reinforcement in honeybees. *Journal of the Experimental Analysis of Behavior*, 1973, *20*, 105–109.

Harris, P., & Nygaard, J. E. Resistance to extinction and number of reinforcements. *Psychological Reports*, 1961, *8*, 233–234.

Herrnstein, R. J. Relative and absolute strength of response as a function of frequency of reinforcement. *Journal of the Experimental Analysis of Behavior,* 1961, *4,* 267–272.

Herrnstein, R. J. On the law of effect. *Journal of the Experimental Analysis of Behavior,* 1970, *13,* 243–266.

Lawrence, D. H., & Festinger, L. *Deterrents and reinforcement.* Stanford: Stanford University Press, 1962.

Leung, C. M., & Jensen, G. D. Shifts in percentage of reinforcement viewed as changes in incentive. *Journal of Experimental Psychology,* 1968, *76,* 291–296.

Mellgren, R. L., Fouts, R. S., & Martin, J. W. Approach and escape to conspecific odors of reward and nonreward in rats. *Animal Learning and Behavior,* 1973, *1,* 129–132.

Morrison, R. R., & Ludvigson, H. W. Discrimination by rats of conspecific odors of reward and nonreward. *Science,* 1970, *167,* 904–905.

Mowrer, O. H., & Jones, H. Habit strength as a function of the pattern of reinforcement. *Journal of Experimental Psychology,* 1945, *35,* 293–311.

Perin, C. T. Behavior potentiality as a joint function of the amount of training and the degree of hunger at the time of extinction. *Journal of Experimental Psychology,* 1942, *30,* 93–113.

Quartermain, D., & Vaughan, G. M. Effect of interpolating continuous reinforcement between partial training and extinction. *Psychological Reports,* 1961, *8,* 235–237.

Rashotte, M. E., & Surridge, C. T. Partial reinforcement and partial delay of reinforcement effects with 72-hour intertrial intervals and interpolated continuous reinforcement. *Quarterly Journal of Experimental Psychology,* 1969, *21,* 156–161.

Senkowski, P. C. Variables affecting the overtraining extinction effect in discrete-trial lever pressing. *Journal of Experimental Psychology: Animal Behavior Processes,* 1978, *4,* 131–143.

Skinner, B. F. *The behavior of organisms.* New York: Appleton-Century, 1938.

Skinner, B. F. Superstition in the pigeon. *Journal of Experimental Psychology,* 1948, *38,* 168–172.

Skinner, B. F. A case history in scientific method. *American Psychologist,* 1956, *11,* 221–233.

Sperling, S. E. Reversal learning and resistance to extinction: A review of the rat literature. *Psychological Bulletin,* 1965, *63,* 281–297.

Theios, J. The partial reinforcement effect sustained through blocks of continuous reinforcement. *Journal of Experimental Psychology,* 1962, *64,* 1–6.

Thompson, D. M. Escape from S^D associated with fixed-ratio reinforcement. *Journal of the Experimental Analysis of Behavior,* 1964, *7,* 1–8.

Uhl, C. N. & Young, A. G. Resistance to extinction as a function of incentive, percentage of reinforcement, and number of nonreinforced trials. *Journal of Experimental Psychology,* 1967, *73,* 556–564.

Wasserman, E. A., & Jensen, D. D. Olfactory stimuli and the "pseudo-extinction" effect. *Science*, 1969, *166*, 1307–1309.

Weinstock, S. Resistance to extinction of a running response following partial reinforcement under widely spaced trials. *Journal of Comparative and Physiological Psychology*, 1954, *47*, 318–322.

Williams, S. B. Resistance to extinction as a function of the number of reinforcements. *Journal of Experimental Psychology*, 1938, *23*, 506–522.

Wilson, M. P. Periodic reinforcement interval and number of periodic reinforcements as parameters of response strength. *Journal of Comparative and Physiological Psychology*, 1954, *47*, 51–56.

4

Mechanisms and theories of positive reinforcement

THE LAST CHAPTER held that there are a wide variety of events that can serve as positive reinforcers in instrumental learning, and no attempt was made to specify what they are or how they might work. A nonanalytical position like this is called *empirical reinforcement*, which asserts the reality of reinforcement but has no explanation for it. Psychologists interested in theory are discontented with the empirical reinforcement view and they hope that someday a masterful theorist will come along and link all reinforcers together with a single theory. This day has not arrived. In the meantime, this chapter discusses the various kinds of reinforcers and the prominent theoretical attempts to explain why they work as they do.

Secondary reinforcement

Learning psychologists make the distinction between primary reinforcement and secondary reinforcement. *Primary reinforcement* does not depend on the learning history of the organism; it is closely identified with reinforcers that aid biological survival. Responses that are learned for food reward or water reward are examples. *Secondary reinforcement*, however, depends upon a history of learning; experience determines whether or not a stimulus will be a reinforcer.

There is an intuitive reasonableness about a hungry organism learning a response for food reinforcement, and the intuition is not without its scientific justification. A response that is learned through primary reinforcement becomes a reliable way of obtaining something that contributes to biological survival. It is not surprising that the processes of evolution have given us learning through primary reinforcement, and if that was all there is to reinforced learning we would have a tidy biological explanation. A difficulty arises in the fact that most of the positive reinforcers that influence the learning of human behavior do not have much to do with biological needs. An adult works for paper (money), and a child studies hard in school in exchange for words of praise from the teacher. How can these seemingly neutral stimuli serve as reinforcement?

The psychologist's answer is that a neutral stimulus gains reinforcing power by association with the response being learned, the primary reinforcement, or both. Neutral stimuli that have gone through this associative process will develop the power to maintain behavior and reward new learning, just as primary reinforcers do, and they are called *secondary reinforcers* or *conditioned reinforcers*. If this generalization is true, it means that any neutral stimulus can be a reinforcer with the proper associative history, and so we come to have an explanation of why we will learn for money or a smile. With the different learning history that each of us has, it is not surprising that what is reinforcing for one does nothing for another. The problem with secondary reinforcement is that it has had an indecisive theoretical history, and we lack a convincing explanation of why so many different neutral stimuli reinforce so many so well.

The emphasis throughout this chapter will be with positive secondary reinforcement, based on primary reinforcement such as food and water for the appetitional drives of hunger and thirst. The association of neutral stimuli with aversive events will be covered in Chapter 6 on punishment and fear.

BACKGROUND: EARLY STUDIES THAT DEFINED THE TOPIC

The first demonstration of secondary reinforcement was by Frolov in Pavlov's laboratory (Pavlov, 1927, pp. 33–34), using classical conditioning procedures (see Chapter 2). Using the Frolov experiment as a point of departure, Williams (1929) conceived the idea of using a neutral stimulus that had been paired with primary reinforcement as reinforcement for the learning of a new response in an instrumental learning situation. Rats were Williams's subjects, and she first imbued a white goal box with secondary reinforcing power by regularly rewarding the response to it in a simple discrimination situation. These animals were then shifted to a complex, multiple maze with a neutral goal box and were allowed to wander around, one trial a day, for eight days. On Day 9 the white goal box from the discrimination training was introduced as the goal box for the multiple maze, and at this point the animals had a substantial drop in errors relative to control groups that had had no prior secondary reinforcement training. The white goal box, however, gradually began to lose its secondary reinforcing powers because errors began to increase as test trials continued in the multiple maze. Williams asked if the white goal box had taken on the rewarding power of food, and she concluded that it had.

Skinner (1938, pp. 82–83) obtained the same kind of results with rats in the bar-press Skinner-box situation. A click of the food magazine was first associated with eating out of the food tray, and then click of the food magazine (now empty) was used to reinforce bar pressing. Definite learning of bar pressing occurred but the rate of bar pressing decreased after a while as the click began to lose its secondary reinforcing powers, which is the same phenomenon observed by Williams. Perhaps the most widely cited of the early studies on secondary reinforcement were by Wolfe (1936) and Cowles (1937). Chimpanzees were taught to insert poker chips in a vending machine for raisins and peanuts. Cowles taught his animals to learn a new choice response, in which poker chips with their newly acquired secondary reinforcing power served as the reward.

The early studies that we have reviewed so far have all used a secondary reinforcer for the learning of a new response, but another line of evidence emerged in an experiment by Bugelski (1938). He used rats as subjects, and bar press in the Skinner box as the response. With the bar absent, the animals were first trained to eat food pellets delivered from a food magazine that had a distinctive click. The bar was then introduced, and the animal had to learn to press it to receive the food from the magazine with the click. The test for secondary reinforcement came in the extinction trials that followed, in which food no longer followed the bar press. Half of the animals had the click accompanying the bar-press and half did not. The animals who received the click in extinction gave 30 percent more responses than those who did not have it.

SOME ISSUES ABOUT SECONDARY REINFORCEMENT

The foregoing section discussed the viewpoint that a neutral stimulus can develop the power of reward and can be used for the learning of new responses. Investigators continued to generate research in support of this reinforcement interpretation, but they were not without their debates about the mechanisms of secondary reinforcement as time went on.

The discriminative stimulus hypothesis   A notable debate centered on the conditions of pairing the neutral stimulus and the response being learned with primary reinforcement. Is it necessary to have a response learned with primary reinforcement for the neutral stimulus to become a secondary reinforcer? Or is the response merely the device for producing the primary reinforcement, the pairing of which with the neutral stimulus is the defining condition for secondary reinforcement? Skinner (1938, p. 82) believed that the association of the neutral stimulus and primary reinforcement was sufficient. Hull (1943, pp. 97–98) accepted this but went even further and said it was necessary that a response be made to the neutral stimulus and that it be strengthened with primary reinforcement. Keller and Schoenfeld (1950) took the same position when they said it was necessary for the neutral stimulus to control the response by having the response learned to it. Such stimuli are called discriminative stimuli, and this view of secondary reinforcement has been called the *discriminative stimulus hypothesis.*

The discriminative stimulus hypothesis was put to test in an experiment by Schoenfeld, Antonitis, and Bersh (1950). Two groups of rats were trained in bar pressing. One group had a light turned on for one second after the bar press had delivered the food and the food was being eaten, which is a pairing of the stimulus and the reinforcer. The other group was not administered the light. The tests were extinction trials, in which food was withdrawn and both groups received the one-second light for each bar press. If only pairing with primary reinforcement is required for secondary reinforcement, the group that received the light in training should enjoy secondary reinforcement benefits in extinction and emit more responses than the other group. The extinction performances of the two groups did not differ, as it turned out, and it can be concluded that more than the pairing of the neutral stimulus and the primary reinforcer was involved, which is what the discriminative stimulus hypothesis implies. Using an entirely different technique, Stein (1958) came up with evidence that contradicted this experiment by Schoenfeld and his colleagues. Stein's study was based on the knowledge that direct electrical stimulation of the brain can have positive reinforcing effects. His approach, which was ingenious, was to repeatedly pair a tone as a neutral stimulus with electrical brain stimulation of the rat. The animal made no response to get the positive reinforcer; so if the tone worked as a secondary reinforcer in the learning of a new response it might be taken as evidence against the discriminative stimulus hypothesis. In the tests that followed the pairings, the tone was available as a secondary reinforcer for bar pressing, and the result was a significantly higher rate of responses than for control conditions.

The short life of secondary reinforcers   Another debate concerned the temporariness of secondary reinforcing effects in laboratory experiments. From the first experiment by Frolov it was noticed that the secondary reinforcing stimulus loses its power after a few trials, in an extinction-like fashion, and from time to time it must be re-paired with the response and its primary reinforcer for a restoration of potency. The short life of secondary reinforcers has been observed repeatedly by investigators, and they find it troublesome in explaining the durability of reinforcers such as money in the everyday world. Secondary reinforcement as conceived and studied in the laboratory could be on the wrong track for explaining reinforcers such as money, but conversely it could be on the right track with only more understanding and elaboration needed. Maybe the secret of durable secondary reinforcement lies in grasping the role of intermittent reinforcement. Consider money once again. The pairing of money with primary reinforcers is not a continuous reinforcement schedule because often money is received for an act without an accompanying primary reinforcement; the act, the money and primary reinforcement are paired only occasionally. Saltzman (1949), in a well-known experiment on the learning of a new response with secondary reinforcement, first taught his rats to run down a straight runway to a distinctive goal box for food, and then used the goal box as the reward to learn the choice response in a T-maze. Klein (1959) used the same procedure as Saltzman except that he used several schedules of intermittent primary reinforcement in the straight runway, and he found that the rate of learning the T-maze increased as the percentage of primary reinforcements in the runway decreased from 100 to 20 percent. But the most notable work on intermittency and secondary reinforcement was by Zimmerman (1957, 1959).

Zimmerman (1959) used rats as his experimental subjects and sought to imbue a buzzer with secondary reinforcing powers in a straight runway situation. The animal was placed in the start box, the buzzer was sounded, and then the door of the start box was raised and the animal ran down the runway for a food reward, sometimes, at the other end. The food reward was on a variable-ratio schedule. The buzzer, however, occurred on every training trial. The test was the learning of a new response in the same runway apparatus. The start box now had a bar present, and the rat had to press the bar one or more times, depending on the schedule, to sound the buzzer and open the door for an opportunity to run to an empty goal box. The buzzer–door event first occurred for every bar press, then was changed to a variable-ratio schedule, and finally to a fixed-ratio schedule. The animals were run on the test until they stopped bar-pressing. The interesting thing about this experiment is its contrast with earlier experiments that found secondary reinforcement effects so temporary. Zimmerman's animals pressed the bar for thousands of responses over 10–14 days. Wike and Platt (1962) also obtained impressively high levels of responding with a task and procedures about the same as Zimmerman's. Apparently durable secondary reinforcement is related to intermittent rewarding, and if so, we move much closer to understanding the high effectiveness of secondary rewards in everyday life.

A standard scientific tactic is to look at an investigator's data and ask if they are a result of entirely different variables than the investigator believed. Looking at this tactic in action provides good insight into how scientists think and work, and the reaction to Zimmerman's experiment is a good example of it. There were others who looked at Zimmerman's findings and concluded that they were a consequence of frustration as an aversive state of affairs. As with fear, an organism will learn responses which give freedom from frustration. Experiments by Daly (1969) and Daly and McCroskery (1973) have shown that rats will learn bar pressing and hurdle-jumping to escape the frustration produced by denying them anticipated rewards. In the Zimmerman experiment the animal is confined in the start box in the periods between buzzer–door events, and it is reasonable to suggest that the bar pressing was sustained by escape from the frustration of confinement.

Consider the experiment by McNamara and Paige (1962) on escape as the reward, not the secondary reinforcing stimulus, as in the Zimmerman experiment. Their experiment was procedurally very similar to Zimmerman's. In training, the rat was placed in a start box and when the experimenter sounded the cue (a buzzer or a light), the animal was allowed to go to the goal-box for food. Fifty percent reinforcement was used in training, with one half of the animals receiving buzzer on reinforced trials and light on nonreinforced trials (or vice versa). On the test sessions the rats were divided into two groups, in which a bar press as the new response being learned now allowed escape to an empty goal-box. One group had the reinforced cue come on with the bar press, and the other the nonreinforced cue, with both being on a continuous reinforcement schedule. The results were consistent with Zimmerman's, in which hundreds of bar presses occurred on the test sessions. But of most interest was that the latency of the bar-press response became *faster* with trials. *Learning* was taking place, rather than the waning of secondary reinforcing powers for a stimulus that is customarily found on test trials in which a new response is learned. And, bar pressing occurred just as efficiently for the nonreinforced cue as the reinforced cue. If secondary reinforcement had been the determiner of the behavior the reinforced cue should have produced the most bar-presses.

A similar experiment with a similar outcome was by Wike, Platt, and Knowles (1962). Rats were used, and they followed Zimmerman's procedures closely. An experimental group and four control groups were used. The experimental group was treated the same as Zimmerman's animals. Training to impart secondary reinforcing powers to a new stimulus (buzzer) preceded the test in which a bar press, allowing escape from the box and sounding the buzzer for every five presses of the bar, was the new response to be learned. The control groups had no secondary reinforcement training, only the test with the bar pressing. The four control groups were:

Control Group I: Receive the buzzer and escape from the box for every fifth press of the bar.
Control Group II: Escape from the box on every press of the bar but no buzzer.
Control Group III: Receive a buzzer for every fifth press of the bar but no escape permitted.
Control Group IV: Pressing of the bar produced no buzzer and no escape.

If the buzzer is a secondary reinforcing stimulus, as Zimmerman said, then the experimental group should do better than all of the control groups which had no secondary reinforcement training. But if escape is the fundamental variable operating, the experiment group and Control Groups I and II should be the same and perform at a higher level than Control Groups III and IV which were denied escape. The latter was the case, and the investigators concluded that escape from frustration, not secondary reinforcement, was the key factor operating in Zimmerman's data. Apparently confinement in the box is frustrating, which is easy to believe for an animal that explores as much as the rat.

In an experimental counterattack, Zimmerman (1963) produced evidence that some genuine secondary reinforcement effects beyond frustration might exist in the kind of situations that have entered this controversy. In this study with rats, Zimmerman paired a light–tone combination with drinking on an intermittent reinforcement schedule, and then used the light–tone combination on an intermittent reinforcement schedule as a secondary reinforcer to train a bar-press response. No escape was permitted from the box. The result was success in training bar pressing in the absence of escape, with a considerable number of bar-press responses emitted over five test sessions. But the number of bar presses was considerably less than Zimmerman (1959) had obtained before, suggesting that escape from the box in the earlier study was a contributing factor, as Zimmerman's critics had implied and documented. Nevertheless, the message of Zimmerman's 1963 experiment is that frustration and escape from it is not the whole story. Zimmerman is supported by a similar experiment (Fox and King, 1961), which compared continuous and intermittent reinforcement in both training and test, and without the possibility of escape. The highest level of performance for the new response acquired with secondary reinforcement occurred when both training and test were under intermittent reinforcement schedules.

SECONDARY REINFORCEMENT AS THE INFORMATION VALUE OF A STIMULUS

Another way of looking at secondary reinforcement is that a stimulus with secondary reinforcing powers has a reliable capability for informing about the occurrence of primary reinforcement. A stimulus is effective as a secondary reinforcer to the extent that it reliably predicts primary reinforcement. Egger and Miller (1962, 1963) have done interesting work on this idea, and their 1962 experiment illustrates the approach. Two stimuli were presented to rats in association with food, in which Stimulus 1 was a light and Stimulus 2 was a tone (or vice versa). For Group A, Stimulus 1 came on 2 seconds before the delivery of a food pellet, and Stimulus 2 came on 1.5 seconds before the pellet. Both stimuli terminated together when the pellet was delivered. Group B had the same stimulus sequence preceding food delivery as Group A, but, in addition, received aperiodic presentations of Stimulus 1 alone without food. A bar-press response that had been previously learned was then extinguished, and the secondary reinforcing strengths of Stimulus 1 and Stimulus 2 were tested in relearning after extinction. Bar-pressing now delivered either Stimulus 1 or Stimulus 2 on a fixed-ratio schedule. The information hypothesis makes two main predictions. First, Stimulus 1 should produce more responses for Group A than Group B because it was associated with food 100 percent of the time for Group A and only part of the time for Group B. Second, Stimulus 2 should produce more responses for Group B than Group A. Stimulus 2 had 100-percent association with food for both groups, but it is totally redundant with Stimulus 1 in the case of Group A and predicted nothing new whereas it was not fully redundant with Stimulus 1 in the case of Group B and was the best predictor of food. The results supported these expectations. Group A had more responses to Stimulus 1 than Group B, and Group B had more responses to Stimulus 2 than Group A. Egger and Miller see their data as consistent with the discriminative stimulus hypothesis, which requires a response to be made to the stimulus, but one can legitimately wonder if the response is necessary at all. Could the secondary reinforcement mechanism be one of getting the organism to comprehend the relationship between stimulus and food and come to "know" that the stimulus "means" food? An interpretation like this is a cognitive one, which implies a power of the organism to relate events in its environment and later use these acquired relationships to guide responding; there is no requirement of a response to be associated with a stimulus. If a rat has been running down a straight alley for food in a white goal-box, and later learns to choose the arm of a T-maze that has the white goal-box, is it because it knows that the white box predicts food? Continuing this reasoning, it can be assumed that a stimulus loses its secondary reinforcement power in a new learning situation because it becomes a promise unfilled. The stimulus no longer predicts primary reinforcement, and responding declines as a result. As we shall see in our discussion of cognitive theory later on in this chapter, the occurrence of the response as a requirement for learning is an item of controversy.

Theories of reinforcement

DRIVE REDUCTION THEORY

Clark L. Hull (1884–1952) was a prominent learning theorist whose ideas about the mechanisms of the learning process were rooted in the theory of biological evolution. The drive-reduction theory of reinforcement, which was a prominent part of Hull's theorizing, holds that biological survival requires sufficient conditions of food, water, air, temperature, intactness of body tissue, etc., and when there is a deviation from an optimum a state of primary need exists. The organism then responds to regain its physiological balance and achieves what is called homeostasis, and the response sequence which reduces the need and optimizes survival is the one that is reinforced and learned. Thus, the hungry animal learns responses that lead to food, and the thirsty animal learns responses that take it to water. Hull said that the organism had a hierarchy of responses available to it in any instrumental learning situation, with one leading to reinforcement and the others not. Initially, responses that fail to produce reinforcement can dominate in the response hierarchy and cause the animal to make inappropriate responses (errors). These inappropriate responses are not reinforced, however, and they extinguish, while the reward-producing response gets stronger and stronger with each reinforcement and eventually dominates the response hierarchy and occurs all the time.

Hull had a highly formalized theory of behavior, much of it stated mathematically (Hull, 1943, 1952). Hull's 1943 book *Principles of Behavior* is an important book in the psychology of learning, and in it Hull defines an increment of habit strength for a response whenever the response produces an event which reduces a need (a reinforcement). For learning to occur, there must be a drive or motivational state that impels the organism to action, and an increment of habit strength for a response accrues each time the drive is reduced and the organism's need state is moved closer to homeostasis.

The drive-reduction theory of reinforcement makes a measure of bio-logical sense, and there is still some credibility for it in the domain of punishment and fear (see Chapter 6), but it has fallen from favor as an explanation for positive reinforcement. There are several reasons for the theory's decline.

One reason is that the time between a primary reinforcement and the reduction of a biological need can often be relatively long as positive reinforcers such as food and water are gradually absorbed into the tis-sues. The result is a long delay of reinforcement—too long for effective learning. The argument has been made that a biological need state is accompanied by internal stimuli, which Hull called drive stimuli, and it is the reduction in their intensity that produces the learning, not the reduction of need. Effects on performance have been found before any nutritive value possibly could be extracted from food (Kohn, 1951), suggesting a usefulness of the distinction between drive and its stimuli, and biological need. A related line of research is concerned with the effect of saccharin as reinforcement in animal learning. Saccharin is a sweet-tasting substance of no nutritive value which is often used as a sugar substitute in diets. Saccharin passes through the body chemically unchanged. Sheffield and Roby (1950) used a T-maze with saccharin solution in the goal box of one of the arms of the maze and water in the other. Hungry, but not thirsty, rats came to choose the saccharin side almost 100 percent of the time. The performance of these animals was almost as good as for rats who received food reinforcement. Whatever the mechanism of saccharin reinforcement, it seems unlikely that it is biological need reduction. A final argument against drive reduction is secondary reinforcement, in which events have the power of reinforce-ment but obviously have no power for reducing biological need. A child will learn the multiplication tables solely for the rewarding praise of the teacher. What biological drives are reduced by praise?

CONTIGUITY THEORY

The theoretical issue raised by contiguity theory is this: Is more than occurrence of a response to a stimulus necessary for learning? The drive-reduction theory of reinforcement says, "Yes, the physiological effect of the reward is necessary," and continguity theory says, "No, only the response is necessary." Edwin R. Guthrie (1886–1959) was the champion of contiguity theory, and his principle of learning is: *A com-bination of stimuli which has accompanied a movement will on its recurrence tend to be followed by that movement* (Guthrie, 1952, p. 23). On the sur-face this principle would seem a denial of the power of reinforcement, but that would be folly because the efficacy of reinforcement is as solidly established as any of our laws in psychology, and Guthrie was not given to folly. Rather, Guthrie said that the function of a reward was to remove the animal from the stimuli acting just before reward. Reward prevents the animal from making other, competing responses to the stimuli, and so when the stimuli occur again the response occurs again. Guthrie studied the escape of animals from a puzzle-box by latch manipulation which was followed by the receipt of a reward on the outside. The obtaining of the food when the animal steps outside the box keeps it from making other responses to the stimuli of the box's interior. On the next trial the animal tends to repeat the latch-manipulating escape response because no other responses have been learned to the surrounding stimuli. One would think that learning would occur in one trial, and indeed it is a theoretical possibility with Guthrie's theory, but stimuli ordinarily will change from trial to trial. Sources of the change might be attentional mechanisms or shifts in internal bodily stimuli which are just as much a part of the stimulus complex as environmental stimuli. The result is that only some of the stimuli associated with the response on the last trial will occur on the next trial, and so the response has less than a perfect chance of occurring. Over a number of trials most of the stimulus elements eventually become connected to the response, and it is then that the response is learned.

What do psychologists think about Guthrie's theory? Unlike Hull's theory, Guthrie's theory was simple in its structure and difficult to test. His almost anecdotal style suggests a lack of rigor, but it is also possible that his relaxed style obscures solid principles of learning. For example, Estes (1950) attempted a mathematical theory of learning that was fundamentally based on Guthrie's thinking, and with some success. All in all, it seems fair to say that today Guthrie's theoretical thinking is not seriously influencing present-day thought about mechanisms of reinforcement. No one has proved it wrong, but not enough psychologists are convinced of its correctness either.

COGNITIVE THEORY

If contiguity theory asks: "Is only a response to a stimulus necessary for learning?" then it might be said that cognitive theory asks if even the response is necessary. A cognitive point of view in learning had some status in the 1930s and 1940s under the stewardship of Edward C. Tolman (1886–1959), and the focus of it was animal learning because that is where Tolman's interests were (Tolman, 1932, 1948, 1958). The cognitive point of view reached a low ebb in the 1950s and then reappeared in the 1960s as an emphasis in human learning and memory, as later chapters of this book will testify. The cognitive atmosphere created by human learning and memory has had its influence on animal psychologists because the 1970s has seen an interest in cognitive theory among them.

The occurrence of a response to a stimulus is not a requirement for learning in Tolman's system. Rather, the organism learns stimulus–stimulus relationships of what leads to what, what goes with what. For example, the stimulus–stimulus relationships for a rat in a maze, which was Tolman's favorite research situation, could be between successive parts of the maze, or between a part of the maze, such as choice point, and the reinforcement at the goal. In human-like fashion, an organism will entertain hypotheses about stimuli and what they mean for goal attainment, and an important part of the learning is the testing of hypotheses and coming up with stimulus sequences that reliably signify the goal. As the learning proceeds the organism develops expectations about stimulus sequences that lead to the goal, and it is reinforcement at the goal that confirms these expectations.

For Tolman, it is perceptual experience that is the heart of learning. The organism extracts information from the environment. Correlations between events are made. Put a rat in an empty T-maze without reward and it will learn that the stimuli of the start box are followed by those of the choice point and both maze arms radiating from the choice point have end compartments. The rat should benefit from this knowledge if later asked to learn the maze with reward. Hull and Guthrie had no implications like these.

The latter example was not chosen frivolously because it is the essentials of a famous experiment by Blodgett (1929) on latent learning. Hungry rats were subjects, and the task was learning a complex maze that had several blind alleys as response possibilities between the start box and the goal box. Three groups of animals were used. One trial a day was administered for seven or nine days. Group I, which was a control group, was given conventional reinforced training, in which reward was found in the goal box after each run. Experimental Group III had the same procedures as the control group except that reward was not introduced until Day 3. Experimental Group II was treated the same as Experimental Group III except that the reward did not begin until Day 7. The results are shown in Figure 4–1. If the animals of the experimental groups had learned nothing on their unrewarded trials, we would expect their learning to begin at the point of the first rewarded trial and be gradual. But such was not the case. Learning rate was precipitous once the reward was introduced, and the performance curves quickly moved to the level of the control group that was rewarded throughout. The Tolmanian explanation of these data is that the animals benefitted from perceptual learning of the maze in the prereward trials. The food reward was in demand for the hungry animals, and when it was introduced they put their knowledge to work and readily solved the maze. The Blodgett findings have been challenged numerous times and in various ways, and the majority of the studies sustain Blodgett and a cognitive

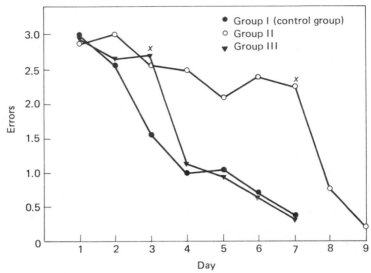

Source: H. C. Blodgett, The effect of the introduction of reward upon the maze performance of rats. *University of California Publications in Psychology*, 1929, *4*, 113–134. Reprinted by permission of the University of California Press.

FIGURE 4–1
Unreinforced exploration of the maze by Groups II and III produced benefits for the rat in subsequent reward learning. The x is the point at which the reward was first introduced. These data have been used to argue against the necessity of reward for learning.

interpretation (MacCorquodale and Meehl, 1954, pp. 199–213). Theories that place a necessity on reward strain to explain how wandering around a maze without reward can produce learning.

McNamara, Long, and Wike (1956) conducted closely related experiments. In their first experiment they used a T-maze and two groups of rats. The control group learned the maze in a standard fashion, with reward after each trial. Training continued until the animals chose the correct side of the maze 95 percent of the time. The experimental group had identical experiences *except* each rat was dragged through the maze in a little basket; each rat was given the same experiences of right and wrong choices as a matched rat in the control group. Both groups were then given the same 16 extinction trials as a test, in which they both ran the maze under standard running conditions. The results were no difference between groups on the test, which is supporting for cognitive theory. A theory that requires a reinforced response for instrumental learning would expect no learning at all by the experimental group. The critical responses in a maze are running movements and, most importantly, choice behavior at the choice point. The animals in the experimental group were required to do neither, yet they learned. Cognitive theory would say that being dragged through the maze in a basket provides an opportunity for perceptual learning about the route to food. In their second experiment, McNamara and his colleagues dramatically reduced extra-maze cues by painting the experimental room black, surrounding the maze with black cloth, and reducing the illumination. Otherwise procedures were about the same as the first experiment. One might expect, theoretically, that the experimental group which must rely on perceptual learning would have some trouble because the visual environment was so degraded. The control group, however, would be expected to fare better. They have the same poor visual environment as the experimental group but they have information from the internal, kinesthetic cues from movement, and the experimental group in the basket is denied it entirely. As expected from a cognitive learning position, the control group learned and the experimental group did not.

Menzel (1978) has a good example of perceptual learning. Chimpanzees were used as subjects. One experimenter carrying a chimpanzee would accompany a second experimenter who hid a piece of fruit in each of 18 randomly selected places in a field. The animal was then returned to the cage and within two minutes released into the field along with control animals who had not seen the food being hidden. In a number of tests of this kind, the chimps given the perceptual experience found 12–13 pieces of fruit per trial on the average. Usually they would go unerringly to where the fruit was hidden. In contrast the control animals found less than one piece, on the average, and then only by searching near the animal who had received the perceptual learning or by begging from it.

Another line of experiments that can be interpreted in terms of perceptual learning is *auto-shaping*. Consider a standard discriminated operant task for a pigeon, which delivered grain reinforcement for pecking a backlighted key every time that the light came on for a few seconds. This is the standard stimulus–response learning situation, in which a response to a stimulus is reinforced; the occurrence of the reinforcer is dependent on the occurrence of the stimulus and the response. There are other possible arrangements of the stimulus, the response, and the reinforcer, however. Consider superstitious behavior, which was discussed in the last chapter. The learning of superstitious behavior is based on the random occurrence of the reinforcement, independent of the stimulus and the response. Now consider one further case in which reinforcement is dependent on the stimulus but not the response. This is the auto-shaping case. Repeatedly, the stimulus occurs and the reinforcement follows it, regardless of the response that the subject is making. Will there be learning from the perceptual experience of repeatedly watching the pairing of the stimulus and the reinforcement? According to Tolman's theory, the pigeon should learn something from watching the light and the reinforcement being paired together, and its eventual performance in keypecking for grain reinforcement when the light comes on should benefit.

This latter experiment is the one which Brown and Jenkins (1968) did as the pioneer experiment on auto-shaping. A pigeon was put in the Skinner box and was exposed to pairings of the key light and grain reinforcement. One group had 160 forward pairings of the light and the reinforcement, in which the light preceded the reinforcement as it would if the key was pecked when the light came on. Another group had 160 reverse pairings. The key was available for pecking at all times. The question was how the experience of watching the light-reinforcer pairings would affect the eventual key-pecking when and if it eventually occurred. If learning to key peck when the light came on was a matter of accidental lucking into the key and pecking it at the right time, then the two groups should perform about the same. As a matter of fact, the group with forward pairing was far superior. All birds with forward pairing learned to peck the key, with an average of 45 trials for the first peck. Only 17 percent of the group with reverse pairing pecked the key even once in the 160 trials.

The Brown and Jenkins study, as convincing as it is, used a relatively free situation which can slightly cloud a clear interpretation. As the effect of watching the stimulus-reinforcer begins to take hold for the group with forward pairings, the birds will begin to take a peck at the key now and then, which means that the reinforcement of a stimulus-response sequence intrudes on the perceptual learning phase. Experimentally, it would be neater if the occurrence of a response and its reinforcement could be separated cleanly from the perceptual learning phase. This is the good experiment of Williams and Williams (1969), which had the same essential auto-shaping procedures that Brown and Jenkins used except that a peck of the key *prevented* reinforcement; there was no way that a stimulus-response sequence could be followed by reinforcement. Nevertheless, the pigeons pecked the key many times, even though it cost them reinforcements. Another approach that has been used is to put a window barrier between the key and the food, and the pigeon, so that the pigeon can watch the stimulus-reinforcer sequence in the perceptual learning phase but cannot make the key-peck response. Parisi and Matthews (1975) used this method. When the window barrier was removed after the perceptual learning phase and the key was made available, the birds pecked the key at a good rate and at a higher level than control groups.

The strong tradition in animal learning has been the strengthening of a response through the reinforcement that follows it, but in recent times we have seen the growth of a modern version of Tolman's theory that relies on perceptual learning. In Chapter 2 we saw that a similar cognitive point of view is prevalent as theory in classical conditioning. It will be fascinating to see if research in the immediate years to come tilts animal learning decisively toward cognitive theory, or whether its advance will be halted by rival theories. Tolman's theory of another day is the germ of useful cognitive theory, but the basic ideas of it need a great deal of refinement to be acceptable by modern standards of theory. The cues and their characteristics that an animal will attend to, and the manner in which the perceptual experience of the cues is translated into the particular action that the animal takes must be defined. Guthrie (1952, p. 143) criticized Tolman on this latter point by saying that "In his concern with what goes on in the rat's mind, Tolman has neglected to predict what the rat will do. So far as the theory is concerned the rat is left buried in thought; if it gets to the food box at the end that is its concern, not the concern of the theory."

PREPOTENT RESPONSE THEORY

The prepotent response theory of reinforcement belongs to David Premack. As are all learning theorists, he is fascinated with the classic issue of why some events are reinforcers and others are not. The theory is refreshing because it bypasses standard positions such as the strengthening of stimulus-response associations and drive reduction. Premack states a theory of reinforcement entirely in terms of responses and their probabilities.

It is always good strategy for a theorist to outline the position that he is reacting against, and Premack (1965, pp. 129–133) discusses the three basic assumptions about reinforcement which all learning psychologists accept:

1.   A reinforcer is a stimulus which if delivered in a certain relation to the response will produce a change in frequency of that response. Some stimuli have the property of reinforcers and some do not.

2.   Reinforcers are trans-situational. A stimulus that is effective as a reinforcer with one response will be effective with many responses, ideally all responses. There is no reason to believe that food will not be a reinforcer for any response of any hungry organism. Psychologists would pay scant attention to a reinforcer that alters the probability of only one response class for one organism.

3.   There are two classes of responses that are associated with reinforcement of animal behavior, but the concern is changing the probability of occurrence for only one of them. We are always concerned with operations that change the probability of response classes such as bar pressing or maze-running, but never eating or drinking.

Premack points out that none of these constitute a theory of reinforcement but rather are the implicit empirical premises that guide all theorists and workers in the field of learning. The first two assumptions unquestionably have empirical foundation, but the knowledge is without much formal structure. No one has ever catalogued what is known about what events are reinforcers. Nor has any one bothered to document the trans-situationality of reinforcers, in which the range of their effectiveness across response classes and organisms is specified. The third assumption has not been tested at all, perhaps because it is the most low key of the three, and it is this third assumption that Premack turns into a theory of reinforcement.

His theory is one of response relations, which is stated in one generalization: *Of any two responses the more probable response will reinforce the less probable one—the prepotent response is the reinforcer.* There are four implications of this generalization that deserve emphasis:

1. Anatomically different responses can be compared directly. For example, ways can be devised to determine the probabilities of barpressing and eating, compare them, and determine which one will reinforce the other.

2. The only thing that matters is the probability of the response, not the variables that determine the probability of response. That response probability might be altered by increasing the time of food deprivation is irrelevant in and of itself—only the probability level matters. This is called the "indifference principle."

3. Reinforcement is a relative property. The most probable response of a set will reinforce all of the other responses, the next most probable response will reinforce all responses of lesser probability but not the response of greater probability, and so on down the scale until the least probable response reinforces no response of the set.

4. The reinforcement relation is reversible. By manipulating the probabilities of Responses A and B, we can cause A to reinforce B and vice versa.

Evidence for Premack's theory is all around us. A food-eating response will reinforce bar pressing in an animal because its probability of occurrence is higher than bar pressing. A boy will learn the multiplication tables (a low probability response) for the opportunity to play baseball (a high probability response). It is problematical, however, whether the boy's listening to Handel's *Organ Concerto in F Major* would be an effective reinforcer for learning the multiplication tables because it is a low probability response also.

A marvelous thing about theory worthy of the name is that it will imply the unexpected while, at the same time, accounting for the known and expected. All theories of reinforcement including Premack's would say that eating reinforces an instrumental motor response, but only Premack's theory predicts the unexpected—that an instrumental motor response like running or bar pressing can reinforce the eating response and increase its probability of occurrence.

Every good drive-reduction theorist knows that first-grade children will play a pinball machine for candy reward, but would they predict that children will eat candy for the opportunity to play a pinball machine? Premack (1959) used this situation to demonstrate such a reversal of reinforcement relations. Premack's theory requires that the probabilities of the two responses first be determined in a free situation, and in a first session he had both candy and the pinball machine freely available. The number of pinball machine responses and pieces of candy eaten by each child were recorded. Some children played the pinball machine more than they ate candy, and they were called the "manipulators." Others had a preference for candy and they were called "eaters." With respect to the theory, pinball playing should be reinforcing for manipulators because it is their most probable response, and candy eating should be reinforcing for eaters for the same reason. In a second session Premack introduced contingency relationships: The pinball machine could not be played unless the candy was eaten, which has the candy eating reinforced by pinball playing; or the candy could not be eaten unless the pinball machine was played, which has pinball playing reinforced by candy eating. Half of the manipulators were in each of these conditions, as were half of the eaters. The theoretical prediction was that pinball playing should reinforce the eating response and increase its frequency for manipulators but not for eaters. Correspondingly, eating should reinforce pinball playing for eaters but not for manipulators. The data which Premack obtained nicely conformed to this theoretical prediction. In another experiment, Premack (1962) found that the opportunity for a rat to run in an activity wheel was reinforcing for the drinking response and increased the probability of its occurrence, which is also a case of reinforcement reversal. The converse is, of course, easily obtained, and is a routine finding. Similarly, Sawisch and Denny (1973) trained pigeons to peck a key and then made the availability of key-pecking dependent upon the eating of free grain. The eating of free grain steadily increased.

A critical test of prepotent response theory lies in verification of the indifference principle. The indifference principle contends that the reinforcing power of a response depends solely on its probability, and it makes no difference how response probability was determined. Premack (1963) tested the reinforcing power of drinking sweet-tasting sucrose liquid and running in an activity wheel for the bar-press response. Rats were the subjects. The independent probability of sucrose drinking was assessed in several free response sessions, and the probability was manipulated by using either 16-, 32-, or 64-percent sucrose in the solution. Free response sessions of wheel running were also held, in which the independent probability of running was manipulated by light- or heavy-force requirements for wheel turning. The various levels of sucrose gave different probabilities for drinking, as did the force requirements for turning the wheel. The results are shown in Figure 4–2, and they meet theoretical expectations. The higher the independent probability of the reinforcer response the greater the power for reinforcing the bar-press response, and it does not matter if reinforcer probability was determined by amount of sucrose or force requirements in wheel turning.

Premack (1959, 1965) recognizes the several problems that exist for his theory, one of which is exemplified by this last experiment, positive though the evidence be. The theory turns on the relations between response probabilities, which means that responses must be counted in a free-response situation to determine their probability of occurrence. But how is a response defined? Is one occurrence of an eating response the

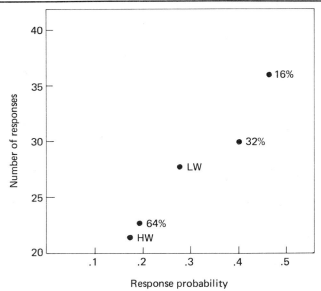

Source: D. Premack, Prediction of the comparative reinforcement values of running and drinking. *Science*, 1963, *139*, 1062–1063. Reprinted by permission of the American Association for the Advancement of Science.

FIGURE 4–2

Evidence for Premack's indifference principle. Shown is the effect of drinking sucrose solution or running in an activity wheel as reinforcement for bar-pressing by the rat. The probability of drinking the sucrose solution or running in the activity wheel is given on the horizontal axis, and it was manipulated by the percent of sucrose concentration (16-, 32-, and 64-percent) and the force requirement to turn the wheel (light, LW; heavy, HW).

entire sequence of seizing, biting, chewing, and swallowing the food, or is each element of the sequence an element to be counted? The definition of "response" is an old problem for experimental psychology, and the issue resurfaces again from time to time. What it means for prepotent reinforcement theory is yet to be determined.

Another difficulty is accounting for learning when no apparent response is associated with the reinforcement. Miller and Kessen (1952) found that rats could learn a T-maze when milk was injected directly into the stomach for the correct choice and saline solution injected for the incorrect choice. Learning was not as fast as when milk reinforcement was taken directly in the mouth in the normal fashion, but learning nevertheless occurred. Premack cannot apply his theory to this situation because of the absence of an observable response when milk is injected into the stomach as the reinforcing event.

In spite of the problems we must score Premack's theory high in inventiveness. Being able to reverse reinforcement relations is a particularly important finding that cannot be generated by competing theories, and our theories of tomorrow must come to grips with it.

Sensory reinforcement

The topic of sensory reinforcement is set off in this separate final section because it does not fit any of the established mechanisms and theories of reinforcement very well. Sensory reinforcement is a young subject matter, being a scant 30 years old, and it will be a while before it fits a larger theoretical scheme.

In one sense sensory reinforcement is poorly named because any reinforcement is a sensory event that follows the response being learned. Notwithstanding, the label is appropriate because it refers to learning that occurs for the reinforcement of stimulus change; so it is sensation in a very fundamental sense that induces learning. When we speak of food reinforcers, for example, we are speaking of a particular class of stimuli that are especially effective for learning when the organism is hungry, but sensory reinforcement is different because it does not specify a class of stimuli that will function as reinforcers, only that there be a sufficient change in stimuli, whatever they are.

The origins of sensory reinforcement lie in exploratory and curiosity behavior. Why does a rat walk around, touch objects, look about, engage in play with other rats, and on and on endlessly? Why does a human being walk around, touch objects, look about, engage in play with other humans, and on and on endlessly? We say these organisms have curiosity and are exploratory, but this is only a description of behavior, not a scientific explanation. Various explanations are possible within established frames of references, although most certainly speculative. One might say that there is an instinct for exploration, that fearful situations are being avoided, that there is a motivation to explore, or that responses to stimuli such as these have been positively reinforced in the past and encountering the stimuli again evokes the responses again. All of these are possibilities, but somehow their use to explain the endless catalog of exploratory and curiosity behavior seems contrived. This topic did not find conceptual direction until the 1950s, when opportunity to explore and encounter (or create) stimulus change was found to be reinforcing for the learning of new responses, just as food might be reinforcing for a hungry animal. The experiments of Harlow, Butler, and Montgomery were pioneering.

Harlow (1950) had a six-unit mechanical puzzle, which is shown in Figure 4–3. At the start of a trial the device was as pictured, and the task was to remove five restraining devices and free the hinge at the bottom. This is child's play for a human, but Harlow's interesting innovation was that he gave it to monkeys to solve without primary reinforcement. Figure 4–4 shows the learning curve, and there is regular learning for no more reinforcement than the stimulation inherent in manipulation of the puzzle. Harlow explained the findings in terms of an externally elicited drive rather than an internal drive such as hunger. The stimuli of the puzzle created the motivation to solve it. It was, as Harlow put it, a "manipulation drive."

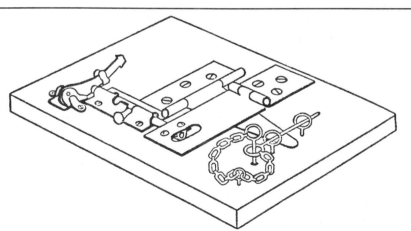

Source: H. F. Harlow, Learning and satiation of response in intrinsically motivated complex puzzle performance by monkeys. *Journal of Comparative and Physiological Psychology*, 1950, 43, 289–294. Reprinted by permission of the American Psychological Association.

FIGURE 4–3
Monkeys will learn to solve this mechanical puzzle without primary reinforcement.

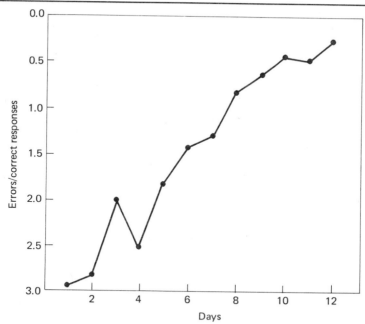

Source: H. F. Harlow, Learning and satiation of response in intrinsically motivated complex puzzle performance by monkeys. *Journal of Comparative and Physiological Psychology,* 1950, *43,* 289–294. Reprinted by permission of the American Psychological Association.

FIGURE 4–4
The learning curve of monkeys for solving the puzzle shown in Figure 4–3. The performance measure is a ratio of errors to correct responses which approaches zero as a limit as number of correct solutions increase and number of errors decrease.

Butler (1953) also used monkeys, and for the experiment he had them in a completely enclosed cage except for two small doors which, when opened, allowed the animal to see the busy laboratory outside. Each door had an identifying colored card, and one of them was designated the correct one; if it was pressed it would come open and give the animal an opportunity to visually explore the laboratory. With no primary reinforcement and only the opportunity for visual exploration as the reward, Butler's monkeys readily learned to press the required door. Butler spoke of a drive for visual exploration; an animal is motivated to seek change in visual stimulation.

Montgomery (1954) and Montgomery and Segall (1955) found that rats would learn to run a Y-maze and a T-maze simply for the opportunity to explore a more complex maze with a number of turns and passageways. The learning was explained by an increase in an "exploratory drive" aroused by the complex maze that was the reward.

About this same time evidence began to appear in psychology literature that rats would learn to press the bar in the Skinner box for only the reinforcement of a light coming on (Kish, 1955; Marx, Henderson, and Roberts, 1955), once again highlighting the significance of stimulus change for learning.

Harlow, Butler, and Montgomery all had notions about stimulus-centered drives determining the behavior. Whether it was manual manipulation, visual exploration, or locomotor exploration, it was a matter of changing patterns of external stimuli, and their effects were assigned the theoretical role of motivation. In one way this was a commendable move because it brought the stimulus effects which these investigators inferred under the heading of motivation, but in another way it was disconcerting to those whose theoretical thinking about motivation was centered on internal homeostatic drives such as hunger and thirst. For these theorists drive was an energizer of behavior that heightened activity level as the animal responded to achieve its reward. How, then, could a drive induced by stimulus change *after* the occurrence of the response affect behavior (Brown, 1953)? If the motivation comes after the response, what impelled the animal to action in the first place? Brown (1953, p. 54) correctly saw that the stimulus-centered theorists were offering a drive increase theory of reinforcement in opposition to drive reduction theory of reinforcement.

About this same time there was a relevant thrust from brain physiology. In the late 1940s physiologists began a program of research on the ascending reticular activating system of the brain (Moruzzi and Magoun, 1949), which is sometimes called the brain-stem reticular formation or, simply, the reticular formation. Heretofore the emphasis of physiologists had been on the cue function of stimuli being processed by the brain, in which the sensory impulse would travel from the receptor to a projection area of the cortex and in which we might become aware of it, discriminate it from other stimuli, learn a response to it, etc. Research on the reticular formation, however, revealed that stimuli follow a second, circuitous route through the reticular formation, which discharges broadly over the cerebral cortex. This function of the reticular formation came to be known as the arousal function because when it was present in an intact animal, the animal was generally alert and responsive; and when the action of the reticular formation was surgically denied, the animal was drowsy and indifferent. Psychologists of a physiological persuasion were quick to see that arousal had implications for motivation if not actually being the physiological basis of motivation. Because of the influence of Hull's theory mostly, psychologists conceived of drive as having a general capability for activating any response that might occur, and the general bombardment of the cortex by the reticular formation was nicely parallel to the general energizing effect of drives. Hebb (1955, p. 249) wrote that stimuli had a cue function and an arousal function, and that the arousal function is synonymous with a general drive state.

The theory of stimulus-centered drive by Harlow, Butler, and Montgomery dovetailed with the arousal view of drive—the reticular formation is activated by stimuli, the reticular formation is the basis of drive, and so stimuli are motivating. When an animal is curious and exploring, it is being motivated by the changing stimulus situation. But why does an organism learn for the reinforcement of stimulus change? Needed was the additional assumption that an increase in motivation can be reinforcing—not only does stimulus change produce an increment of motivation, but the occurrence of the increment is reinforcing for the response that produced it. This assumption is straightforward enough, but its acceptance was questioned by drive-reduction theorists. If hungry and thirsty animals learn by decreasing their hunger and thirst drives, how can drive *increase* produce learning? You cannot have it both ways. Or can you?

The inverted-U hypothesis was the arousal theorists answer to the drive-reduction theorists' criticism; the hypothesis shows how a theory can explain the reinforcing effects of both drive decrease and drive increase (Hebb, 1955; Malmo, 1959; Fiske and Maddi, 1961). To accommodate drive-increase and drive-decrease views of reinforcement within the same arousal theory, one must assume that the degree of arousal is important. When the organism is below the optimum point of arousal an increase in drive is rewarding, and when one is above the optimum point the drive level is aversive and a decrease in drive is rewarding. Butler's monkeys were in a dimly lit cage and low in arousal level. When the door opened their arousal level was increased by the stimulation of the visual scene, and the increase was rewarding. A hungry animal, on the other hand, has excessive arousal that is unpleasant for it and the reduction in internal stimulation that eating provides is rewarding. Berlyne (1967, p. 51) reasons in this fashion, but Fowler (1967, p. 159) properly points out that such reasoning is difficult to work out empirically because we cannot specify optimal levels of stimulation for different classes of stimuli and situations, kinds of organisms, and types of responses. Without knowing the optimal point we do not know where we are on the U-function, and we cannot predict whether a change in stimulation will be an increase or a decrease in arousal and be reinforcing or not. Arousal theory has been useful as an attempt to integrate externally-based drives and internally-based drives, and as a link with contemporary findings in brain physiology, but it is not yet a fully functioning theory of reinforcement.

But is it possible that drive-reduction theory might explain it all, without the complexities of a U-shaped function and both drive increase and drive decrease as the conditions of reinforcement? Yes, is the answer. Myers and Miller (1954), as drive-reduction theorists, proposed such a theory. They assumed that inadequate external stimulation creates a need for stimulation, just as food or water deprivation creates hunger and thirst. When an organism is deprived of sufficient stimulation it develops a *boredom drive*, as it has been called. In accord with drive-reduction theory, the boredom drive is reduced by stimulus change and the change is reinforcing for the response that produced it. With this viewpoint, a theoretical economy is achieved because all drives are related to learning in the same way. There is no need for assuming that drive decrease produces learning in some cases and drive increase in others.

The first major clue that too much exposure to a stimulus can produce a need for stimulus change lay in the research on spontaneous alternation in the choices of rats in a T-maze (Dember and Fowler, 1958; Glanzer, 1958). If the animal turns right on a trial in a T-maze and then is immediately returned to the starting point, the likelihood is high that it will turn left on the next trial. Glanzer (1958) wrote in terms of "stimulus satiation," in which continuing exposure to a stimulus decreases the responding to it and presumably causes the organism to alleviate the satiation with stimulus change. At work was the same fundamental phenomenon that caused Myers and Miller (1954) to suggest a boredom drive that can be reduced by stimulus change. The rat's right-turning on the present trial causes boredom (satiation) with the stimuli in that area of the maze, and it is alleviated on the next trial by turning left and finding new stimuli.

The idea of a boredom drive says that the longer you are exposed to stimuli, the higher the drive level and the greater the need to reduce it by stimulus change. Earlier in this section we examined an experiment by Butler (1953) in which monkeys learned to open a door of an enclosed cage for the reward of visually exploring the laboratory outside. In a later experiment, Butler (1957) used essentially the same procedure but with zero, two, four, or eight hours of visual deprivation in the enclosed cage before the door could be opened momentarily for a brief look. The measure of performance was the number of times after the deprivation period that the door was opened for visual exploration, and Butler found that the frequency of door-opening responses increased as visual deprivation increased from zero to eight hours. As predicted, the greater the boredom drive the greater the need for stimulus change.

In a closely related experiment Fox (1962) kept monkeys in a light-tight box, much the same as Butler, for visual deprivation periods of zero, one, two, three, four, and eight hours after which the pressing of a bar would flash a light for 0.5 seconds and illuminate the inside of the box. The results are shown in Figure 4–5, expressed in terms of number

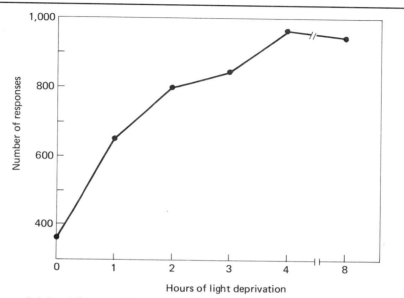

Source: S. S. Fox, Self-maintained sensory input and sensory deprivation in monkeys: A behavioral and neuropharmacological study. *Journal of Comparative and Physiological Psychology,* 1962, *55,* 438–444. Reprinted by permission of the American Psychological Association.

FIGURE 4–5

Using light as the reinforcement, number of bar presses made by monkeys as a function of hours in total darkness.

of bar-presses. The amount of visual stimulation which the animals generate for themselves is almost directly proportional to the amount of visual deprivation, which corresponds to Butler's findings.

Sensory reinforcement has been provocative for the topic of positive reinforcement. Its beginnings in exploratory and curiosity behavior led us to an appreciation of a new class of reinforcers that seems best described as stimulus change or variety. How to bring these new reinforcers in theoretical line with more conventional reinforcers is a challenge, and the concept of boredom drive and its reduction as reinforcement is an interesting approach.

Summary

The purpose of this chapter was to discuss why positive reinforcers work as they do to produce learning. A distinction was made between primary and secondary reinforcement. Primary reinforcers do not depend on the learning history of the organism. Hungry or thirsty animals learning a response with food or water as reinforcement is an example. Secondary reinforcers, however, are based on learning history. A neutral stimulus gains the power of secondary reinforcement through association with the response being learned with primary reinforcement, the primary reinforcer itself, or both. Secondary reinforcement is often used to explain why a seemingly neutral stimulus like a word of praise can be reinforcing.

Drive-reduction theory, contiguity theory, cognitive theory, and prepotent-response theory are prominent attempts to explain the action of positive reinforcers. Drive-reduction theory says that an event will be a reinforcer if it reduces a biological need. Contiguity theory contends that the response need only occur in the presence of a stimulus for learning to occur and for the stimulus to evoke the response reliably. Reinforcement is important only insofar as it insures the stimulus-response association being learned and discourages the occurrence of unwanted responses. Cognitive theory has learning based on the subject's perception of relationships among events in the situation, with neither the reduction of drive nor stimulus-response contiguity required. Prepotent-response theory says that one response will reinforce another; a more probable response such as eating will reinforce a less probable response like bar-pressing. None of these theories is without problems, and none has a wholehearted endorsement.

A type of reinforcement that stands apart from other kinds of reinforcement is sensory reinforcement. Sensory reinforcement occurs when stimulus change is the event which produces learning, as when an animal learns to run a maze for the opportunity to explore. One explanation of how sensory reinforcement produces learning is drive reduction. It is assumed that exposure to stimuli induces boredom, boredom is a drive, and stimulus change reduces boredom.

References

Berlyne, D. E. Arousal and reinforcement. In D. Levine (Ed.), *Nebraska symposium on motivation*. Lincoln: University of Nebraska Press, 1967, pp. 1–110.

Blodgett, H. C. The effect of the introduction of reward upon the maze performance of rats. *University of California Publications in Psychology*, 1929, 4, 113–134.

Brown, J. S. Comments on Professor Harlow's paper. In *Current theory and research in motivation: A symposium*. Lincoln: University of Nebraska Press, 1953, pp. 49–55.

Brown, P. L., & Jenkins, H. M. Auto-shaping of the pigeon's key peck. *Journal of the Experimental Analysis of Behavior*, 1968, 11, 1–8.

Bugelski, B. R.   Extinction with and without subgoal reinforcement. *Journal of Comparative Psychology*, 1938, *26*, 121–134.

Butler, R. A.   Discrimination learning by Rhesus monkeys to visual-exploration motivation. *Journal of Comparative and Physiological Psychology*, 1953, *46*, 95–98.

Butler, R. A.   The effect of deprivation of visual incentives on visual exploration motivation in monkeys. *Journal of Comparative and Physiological Psychology*, 1957, *50*, 177–179.

Cowles, J. T.   Food-tokens as incentives for learning by chimpanzees. *Comparative Psychology Monographs*, 1937, *14*, No. 5.

Daly, H. B.   Is responding necessary for nonreward following reward to be frustrating? *Journal of Experimental Psychology*, 1969, *80*, 186–187.

Daly, H. B., & McCroskery, J. H.   Acquisition of a bar-press response to escape frustrative nonreward and reduced reward. *Journal of Experimental Psychology*, 1973, *98*, 109–112.

Dember, W. N., & Fowler, H.   Spontaneous alternation behavior. *Psychological Bulletin*, 1958, *55*, 412–428.

Egger, M. D., & Miller, N. E.   Secondary reinforcement in rats as a function of information value and reliability of the stimulus. *Journal of Experimental Psychology*, 1962, *64*, 97–104.

Egger, M. D., & Miller, N. E.   When is reward reinforcing? An experimental study of the information hypothesis. *Journal of Comparative and Physiological Psychology*, 1963, *56*, 132–137.

Estes, W. K.   Toward a statistical theory of learning. *Psychological Review*, 1950, *57*, 94–107.

Fiske, D. W., & Maddi, S. R. (Eds.)   *Functions of varied experience.* Homewood: Dorsey, 1961.

Fowler, H.   Satiation and curiosity. In K. W. Spence & J. T. Spence (Eds.), *The psychology of learning and motivation* (Vol. 1). New York: Academic Press, 1967, pp. 157–227.

Fox, R. E., & King, R. A.   The effects of reinforcement scheduling on the strength of a secondary reinforcer. *Journal of Comparative and Physiological Psychology*, 1961, *54*, 266–269.

Fox, S. S.   Self-maintained sensory input and sensory deprivation in monkeys: A behavioral and neuropharmacological study. *Journal of Comparative and Physiological Psychology*, 1962, *55*, 438–444.

Glanzer, M.   Curiosity, exploratory drive, and stimulus satiation. *Psychological Bulletin*, 1958, *55*, 302–315.

Guthrie, E. R.   *The psychology of learning* (Rev. Ed.). New York: Harper, 1952.

Harlow, H. F.   Learning and satiation of response in intrinsically motivated complex puzzle performance by monkeys. *Journal of Comparative and Physiological Psychology*, 1950, *43*, 289–294.

Hebb, D. O.   Drives and C.N.S. (conceptual nervous system). *Psychological Review*, 1955, *62*, 243–255.

Hull, C. L. *Principles of behavior.* New York: Appleton-Century, 1943.

Hull, C. L. *A behavior system.* New Haven: Yale University Press, 1952.

Keller, F. S., & Schoenfeld, W. N. *Principles of psychology.* New York: Appleton-Century-Crofts, 1950.

Kish, G. B. Learning when the onset of illumination is used as reinforcing stimulus. *Journal of Comparative and Physiological Psychology,* 1955, *48,* 261–264.

Klein, R. M. Intermittent primary reinforcement as a parameter of secondary reinforcement. *Journal of Experimental Psychology,* 1959, *58,* 423–427.

Kohn, M. Satiation of hunger from food injected directly into the stomach versus food ingested by mouth. *Journal of Comparative and Physiological Psychology,* 1951, *44,* 412–422.

MacCorquodale, K., & Meehl, P. E. Edward C. Tolman. In W. K. Estes, S. Koch, K. MacCorquodale, P. E. Meehl, C. G. Mueller, Jr., W., N. Schoenfeld, & W. S. Verplanck (Eds.), *Modern learning theory.* New York: Appleton-Century-Crofts, 1954, pp. 177–266.

Malmo, R. B. Activation: A neuropsychological dimension. *Psychological Review,* 1959, *66,* 367–386.

Marx, M. H., Henderson, R. L., & Roberts, C. L. Positive reinforcement on the bar-pressing response by a light stimulus following dark operant pretests with no aftereffect. *Journal of Comparative and Physiological Psychology,* 1955, *48,* 73–75.

McNamara, H. J., Long, J. B., & Wike, E. L. Learning without response under two conditions of external cues. *Journal of Comparative and Physiological Psychology,* 1956, *49,* 477–480.

McNamara, H. J., & Paige, A. B. An elaboration of Zimmerman's procedure for demonstrating durable secondary reinforcement. *Psychological Reports,* 1962, *11,* 801–803.

Menzel, E. W. Cognitive mapping in chimpanzees. In S. H. Hulse, H. Fowler, & W. K. Honig (Eds.), *Cognitive processes in animal behavior.* Hillsdale: Erlbaum, 1978, pp. 375–422.

Miller, N. E., & Kessen, M. L. Reward effects of food via stomach fistula compared with those of food via mouth. *Journal of Comparative and Physiological Psychology,* 1952, *45,* 555–564.

Montgomery, K. C. The role of the exploratory drive in learning. *Journal of Comparative and Physiological Psychology,* 1954, *47,* 60–64.

Montgomery, K. C., & Segall, M. Discrimination based on the exploratory drive. *Journal of Comparative and Physiological Psychology,* 1955, *48,* 225–228.

Moruzzi, G., & Magoun, H. W. Brainstem reticular formation and activation of the EEG. *Electroencephalography and Clinical Neurophysiology,* 1949, *1,* 455–473.

Myers, A. K., & Miller, N. E. Failure to find a learned drive based on hunger: Evidence for learning motivated by "exploration." *Journal of Comparative and Physiological Psychology,* 1954, *47,* 428–436.

Parisi, T., & Matthews, T. J. . Pavlovian determinants of the auto-shaped key-peck response. *Bulletin of the Psychonomic Society,* 1975, *6,* 527–529.

Pavlov, I. P. *Conditioned reflexes.* Oxford: Oxford University Press, 1927.

Premack, D. Toward empirical behavioral laws: I. Positive reinforcement. *Psychological Review,* 1959, *66,* 219–233.

Premack, D. Reversibility of the reinforcement relation. *Science,* 1962, *136,* 255–257.

Premack, D. Prediction of the comparative reinforcement values of running and drinking. *Science,* 1963, *139,* 1062–1063.

Premack, D. Reinforcement theory. In M. Jones (Ed.), *Nebraska Symposium on Motivation.* Lincoln: University of Nebraska Press, 1965, pp. 123–180.

Saltzman, I. J. Maze learning in the absence of primary reinforcement: A study of secondary reinforcement. *Journal of Comparative and Physiological Psychology,* 1949, *42,* 161–173.

Sawisch, L. P., & Denny, M. R. Reversing the reinforcement contingencies of eating and keypecking behaviors. *Animal Learning & Behavior,* 1973, *1,* 189–192.

Schoenfeld, W. N., Antonitis, J. J., & Bersh, P. J. A preliminary study of training conditions necessary for secondary reinforcement. *Journal of Experimental Psychology,* 1950, *40,* 40–45.

Sheffield, F. D., & Roby, T. B. Reward value of a nonnutritive sweet taste. *Journal of Comparative and Physiological Psychology,* 1950, *43,* 471–481.

Skinner, B. F. *The behavior of organisms.* New York: Appleton–Century, 1938.

Stein, L. Secondary reinforcement established with subcortical stimulation. *Science,* 1958, *127,* 466–467.

Tolman, E. C. *Purposive behavior in animals and men.* New York: Century, 1932.

Tolman, E. C. Cognitive maps in rats and men. *Psychological Review,* 1948, *55,* 189–208.

Tolman, E. C. *Behavior and psychological man.* Berkeley: University of California Press, 1958.

Wike, E. L., & Platt, J. R. Reinforcement schedules and bar pressing. Some extensions of Zimmerman's work. *Psychological Record,* 1962, *12,* 273–278.

Wike, E. L., Platt, J. R., & Knowles, J. M. The reward value of getting out of a starting box: Further extensions of Zimmerman's work. *Psychological Record,* 1962, *12,* 397–400.

Williams, D. R., & Williams, H. Auto-maintenance in the pigeon: Sustained pecking despite contingent nonreinforcement. *Journal of the Experimental Analysis of Behavior,* 1969, *12,* 511–520.

Williams, K. A. The reward value of a conditioned stimulus. *University of California Publications in Psychology,* 1929, *4,* 31–55.

Wolfe, J. B. Effectiveness of token-rewards for chimpanzees. *Comparative Psychology Monographs,* 1936, *12,* No. 5.

Zimmerman, D. W. Durable secondary reinforcement: Method and theory. *Psychological Review,* 1957, *64,* 373–383.

Zimmerman, D. W. Sustained performance in rats based on secondary reinforcement. *Journal of Comparative and Physiological Psychology*, 1959, *52*, 353–358.

Zimmerman, D. W. Influence of three stimulus conditions upon the strength of a secondary reinforcement effect. *Psychological Reports*, 1963, *13*, 135–138.

5

Discrimination learning and generalization

WHETHER ALL behavior is under the control of a stimulus or not, it is fair to say that a large share of it is. This chapter is about discrimination learning and stimulus generalization, or simply generalization. Discrimination and generalization are two related aspects of stimulus control. Discrimination learning is responding to one or more stimuli and not others, such as advancing when the light is green and stopping when the light is red. Generalization is the failure of discrimination and therefore is the converse of it. The same response to the red and green light is generalization from one light to another and a failure to discriminate between them. Generalization will be discussed later in the chapter. First, discrimination learning.

Discrimination learning

The best way to understand the essentials of discrimination learning is by example. Figure 5–1 shows the Wisconsin General Test Apparatus, a well-known apparatus for studying discrimination learning in monkeys. In Figure 5–1 the experimenter is presenting a two-choice discrimination problem to the monkey. The experimenter begins a trial with the forward opaque screen lowered so that the animal cannot see the problem being set up. Two stimuli are placed over food wells, with

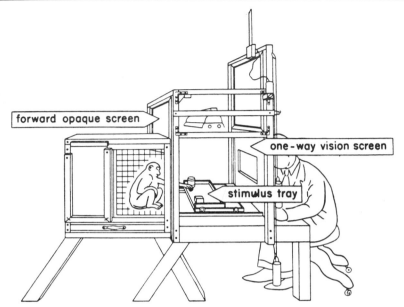

Source: H. F. Harlow, The formation of learning sets. *Psychological Review,* 1949, *56,* 51–65.

FIGURE 5–1
The Wisconsin General Test Apparatus for the study of discrimination learning. See the text for explanation.

food under the stimulus the choice of which is designated as correct. With the stimuli in place, the experimenter lowers the one-way vision screen so that the monkey cannot see him, and then raises the forward opaque screen and allows the monkey to choose one of the stimuli. If the correct stimulus, called S+, is selected, the monkey gets the food in the well beneath it. If the incorrect stimulus, called S−, is chosen, no reward is received. After stimulus selection on a trial, the forward opaque screen is lowered and the monkey is once again isolated while the experimenter sets up the next problem.

In this illustration the animal discriminates the two stimuli and learns to respond differentially by selecting one stimulus and not the other. The problem could be one of form discrimination, with one stimulus a triangle, the other a square, and the triangle rewarded. The experimenter will randomize the left and right positions of the stimuli, and an animal which has learned the discrimination will choose the triangle no matter where it is. Form discrimination is a common kind of laboratory problem, but other kinds of problems have been devised also. A brightness discrimination, in which, for example, an animal would learn to discriminate a black and a white square, is a common type of problem. The learning of a position discrimination has been studied also. Consider again the triangle and the square as stimuli, but with the animal rewarded for responding to the left-hand position. An animal that has learned a position discrimination will chose the left-hand stimulus no matter what it is. In the case of form and brightness discriminations, we say that position is irrelevant. With position discrimination, we say that form and brightness are irrelevant.

The performance curves for two-choice problems start at 50 percent correct because at the start the animal does not know which choice is correct and so is responding by chance. As rewards accrue for the correct response and learning progresses, percent correct increases and moves steadily toward 100 percent. A more complex problem with three choices would start at 33 percent, a four-choice problem at 25 percent, and so on.

This will do for definitions and preliminary observations. Let us turn now to the issue of the effective stimulus, which has occupied so many workers in the field of discrimination learning. An organism is continually bombarded by a complex array of stimuli from both within and without its body. What principles govern selection of the stimulus, or configuration of stimuli, that come to control a response? What is the effective stimulus? Animal discrimination learning has been one of psychology's proving grounds for this topic. The research has had two main themes. One is the *relations issue*. The other is the *attentional issue*, although the research has not been labeled in this way until recent times when attention surfaced as a research interest for psychologists, as it has done regularly throughout psychology's history.

THE RELATIONS ISSUE

An issue that was prominent in discrimination learning for a long time was whether an animal responded to the absolute value of each stimulus or to the relations among the stimuli. Does an animal in a brightness discrimination problem in which it must choose between a white card and a black card respond to the absolute brightness level of each card, or does it respond to white being brighter *in relation* to black? All organisms respond to the absolute values of stimuli because sometimes it is the only basis for response. When there is more than one stimulus present, however, does the brain's perceptual systems compare them and perceive the relation between them as the basis of response? The latter implies a more complex organizing power of perceptual systems.

A convincing study on relations was that made by Lawrence and DeRivera (1954). They used simultaneous discrimination, in which the stimuli are presented together and the animal can apprehend them both and relate them if it can. Rats were the subjects. The apparatus was the Lashley Jumping Stand, in which the animal began a trial on a pedestal in front of two stimulus cards in the windows of a panel. The animal indicated its choice by jumping at a card. If the correct choice was made, the card gave way and the animal received a reward. If the wrong choice was made, the animal struck a card that was locked in the window and fell into a net below. In the initial training, identical cards were over both windows on each trial. The bottom halves of the cards had the same brightness, but the brightness of the top halves was varied across trials. If the top half was lighter than the bottom half, then the animal was required to jump right for a reward. If the top half was darker than the bottom half, then the requirement was to jump left. In terms of theory, the animals could make their choice by responding to the absolute brightness of the top half, or by responding to the relations of top lighter than bottom or top darker than bottom.

Test trials followed the training, and Lawrence and DeRivera arranged them to distinguish the two theoretical points of view. Suppose the two cards in the windows were both light colored, with the top halves the same brightness but the top halves darker than the bottom halves. With both cards now light colored, the animal should jump to the right if it has been responding to the absolute value of brightness. But if the animal has learned stimulus relations, it should jump left because the top half is darker than the bottom half. Various tests of this sort were made, and the result was that 80 percent of them favored relational theory. On the basis of this study and those that followed its lead, it is fair to say that responses can be controlled by absolute values of stimuli, but that relational learning can occur also.

THE ATTENTIONAL ISSUE

Attention is the topic concerned with the selection of stimuli that govern responding. Attention is no problem in many experiments in psychology because the experimenter makes the relevant stimuli for response eminent and unmistakable. But when the stimuli, or dimensions of stimuli, are not deliberately conspicuous and the subject has choice among them, then the choice becomes a behavioral matter of scientific interest to psychology.

Continuity versus noncontinuity The continuity–noncontinuity issue in animal discrimination learning could just as well be called the attentional–nonattentional issue. Stated in attentional terms, the issue is this: Can the animal pay attention to more than one task dimension at a time, or is its capacity to process information limited to one dimension? Does an animal in a multidimensional discrimination learning situation simultaneously and gradually learn something about all task dimensions and their relevance for reinforcement over trials, or does it first pay attention to one task dimension, then another, until it determines the one that leads to problem solution? The former point of view is the *continuity position,* relying as it does on gradual learning about the relevance of all task dimensions. The latter point of view, turning as it does on attention to first one dimension and then another, is the *noncontinuity position.* The controversy was set in motion by Krechevsky (1932), who took a noncontinuity stance and assumed that an animal tested "hypotheses" about the relevance of task dimensions for problem solution, first one and then another. Consider how the noncontinuity position would see the learning of a form discrimination problem with a triangle and a square as relevant stimuli. In the beginning an animal does not know what is being rewarded in the situation; so it might hypothesize that position is the relevant dimension. Because the triangle and the square are randomized with respect to position, the animal will receive some rewards for position responding, but the rewards will be inconsistent and so in time the animal will abandon the position hypothesis for another. If the next hypothesis is that form is relevant, then the hypothesis will be endorsed and the problem will be solved because the animal will discover that S+ is rewarded all of the time and S− is never rewarded. The animal sees the task as a problem-solving situation and proceeds by a process of hypothesis testing and elimination, much as a human would do.

Discrimination learning curves usually will have a *presolution period,* in which the performance stays at the chance level for a while. In a two-choice problem, the curve will stay at 50 percent for a number of trials and then move gradually upward to 100 percent as the animal comes to respond increasingly to S+. The continuity theorists used the presolution period in form discrimination as the point to concentrate their attack on noncontinuity theorists. If, they argued, the animal is learning about only one task dimension at a time, then a reversal of S+ and S− during the presolution period should make no difference because the animal obviously does not have a hypothesis about form. This experimental approach is called *presolution reversal,* and a number of experiments used it. Modern analysts of animal learning (e.g., Sutherland and Mackintosh, 1971; Mackintosh, 1974) agree that these experiments favor the continuity point of view with three lines of evidence: First, reversing S+ and S− during the presolution period retards the speed of problem solution; something about S+ and S− had been learned. Secondly, it was found that animals with position biases in learning a form discrimination could be informative for theory. Some animals will respond either to the left side or the right side in a two-choice situation for some time. Position, however, is irrelevant for the form discrimination; so eventually they give it up and begin responding to the relevant dimension of form. When they do, the response is almost immediately to S+ and seldom to S−. Here again the animals learned something about the pertinence of S+ while also attending to the position dimension. Thirdly, some of the experiments recorded speed of responding to S+ and S− in the presolution period. The speed was faster to S+ than S−, indicating that animals were learning something about S+ while attending to position. Contrary to the noncontinuity point of view, animals can learn about more than one task dimension at a time.

Blocking and overshadowing   Experiments on attention in animal learning have centered on studies of *blocking* and *overshadowing*. These experiments do not deal with discrimination learning, but they are the modern descendants of the continuity-noncontinuity issue that had its origin and resolution in discrimination learning, and so it seems appropriate to discuss them here.

Blocking and overshadowing are distinguished in Table 5–1. In both cases the concern is the effect that the presence of one stimulus has on the effect of another for the control of behavior. The evidence is that one stimulus will impair the effectiveness of another. Put another way, when an animal is attending to one stimulus he will pay less attention to another, which means that blocking and overshadowing have the same theme as the continuity versus noncontinuity issue. There is a difference, however, and it is in a more explicit treatment of attention in the explanation of blocking and overshadowing. The continuity position said that an animal can attend to more than one task dimension at a time, but how attention might be distributed over the dimensions was not an issue. The modern point of view, which is shaped by research on blocking and overshadowing, is that animals can process more than one task dimension at a time, but one dimension will receive more atten-

TABLE 5–1
Blocking and overshadowing defined by experimental design. X and Y are stimulus dimensions. In a blocking experiment, prior training on one of the dimensions, X, will impair learning about another dimension, Y, in the compound XY. In an overshadowing experiment, the presence of X in the compound XY will impair learning about the other dimension, Y.

	Group	Pretraining	Training	Test
Blocking	Control		XY	Y
	Experimental	X	XY	Y
Overshadowing	Control		Y	Y
	Experimental		XY	Y

tion than another. The inverse hypothesis is held by some (Mackintosh, 1974, pp. 583–588), which says that as one task dimension gains power to control behavior the others lose it. Another theory says that attention is paid to task dimensions that inform about reinforcement; redundant, uninformative dimensions are ignored.

An example of this kind of research is work by Kamin (1969) which stimulated the modern interest in animal attentional mechanisms. He used the *conditioned emotional response technique* (which will be discussed in Chapter 6). This technique is a combination of instrumental learning and classical conditioning. The animal is first taught an instrumental response such as bar pressing for food or water reward, and then is given the pairing of a CS and punishment, usually electric shock. The animal becomes afraid of the CS, and the measure of fear is the extent to which the instrumental response is suppressed by the CS when it occurs. Kamin used the blocking paradigm, shown in Table 5–1, for the training of fear. The CS was a compound stimulus that had a light and a sound as elements. Pretraining with one of the CS elements and electric shock almost eliminated the ability of the other element to control the instrumental response. Pretraining had concentrated attention on one CS element at the expense of the other.

Pavlov (1927, chapts. 8 and 16) demonstrated the principle of overshadowing in his experiments on classical conditioning. He conditioned a dog to salivate, using heat and touch as a compound stimulus. When the CS elements were tested separately the touch produced a full salivary response but heat elicited nothing. Bechterev, another Russian who made important contributions to conditioning about the same time as Pavlov, also did experiments on overshadowing. He reported that newborn infants show the overshadowing effect just as animals do (Bechterev, 1933, p. 338).

LEARNING SET

The substantial effort that psychologists have given to the study of discrimination learning has mostly been dedicated to the learning of a single problem, such as learning to choose one form over another. The animal is presented a stimulus pair repeatedly with reward for the correct choice until the correct stimulus is correctly chosen 100 percent of the time and the discrimination is learned. Usually at this point the experiment is finished. Psychologists have not limited their investigations entirely to the single-problem approach, however. Another line of research, that has received a respectable amount of attention, goes under the name of *learning set*. Instead of asking how a single problem is learned, research on learning set asks how an entire class of problems are learned. Define a class of problems, such as two-choice form discrimination, with the stimulus pair being anything whatsoever and with either member of the pair arbitrarily assigned the reward. Learning set is the ability to solve any of such problems efficiently.

An animal who has acquired a learning set does not learn each problem of the class anew. Rather, he comes to have what a casual observer might call an "intelligent strategy." After having acquired a learning set, the animal on a new problem will choose either of the stimuli at random on Trial 1, just as with a single-problem learning. Where learning set and single-problem learning differ is on Trial 2. With single-problem learning, Trial 2 is not much different than Trial 1 because learning is gradual, but with a learning set the success on Trial 2 will be 100 percent and will remain so as long as that particular stimulus pair remains. It is as if the animal fully understands what is S+ and S− no matter what his choice on Trial 1. If he chooses S+ on Trial 1, he knows

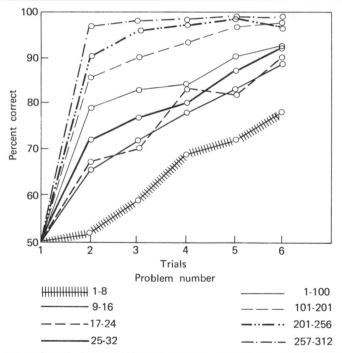

Source: H. F. Harlow, The formation of learning sets. *Psychological Review*, 1949, 56, 51–65.

FIGURE 5–2

The acquisition of a learning set. Six trials were given on each of 312 two-choice form discrimination learning problems. Shown are the learning curves for successive blocks of problems. Learning is slow for the early problems but fast and efficient for the later problems.

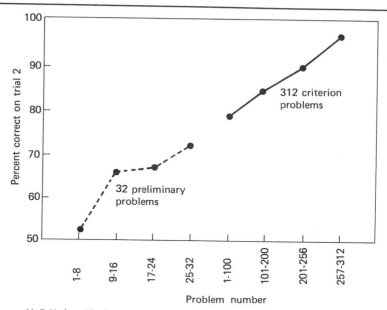

Source: H. F. Harlow, The formation of learning sets. *Psychological Review*, 1949, 56, 51–65.

FIGURE 5–3

Trial 1 of a two-choice discrimination problem is necessarily at the chance level of 50 percent correct, but efficiency on Trial 2 depends upon the degree to which the learning set is developed. Performance on Trial 2 is about at chance level early in the learning, but late in learning, after a large number of problems, performance is virtually 100 percent correct.

which member of the stimulus pair is rewarded and chooses it on every trial thereafter. If he chooses S− on Trial 1, he knows that the other member of the pair is the rewarded one, and so S+ is chosen on every trial thereafter. This is called the win-stay–lose-shift strategy (Levine, 1959, 1965). Research on learning set shows how this skill for a class of problems is acquired.

The prime mover of research on learning set was Harlow (1949), who used monkeys as his subjects and the Wisconsin General Test Apparatus (Figure 5–1). One of the problem types that he chose for study was two-choice form discrimination in which one of two different stimuli is rewarded and one is not. He made up hundreds of problems, using odds and ends of all sorts. A small number of trials, usually no more than six, was given on each problem, and this was repeated for hundreds of problems. Figure 5–2 shows a plot of the results for 312 problems. The important thing to notice is how learning proceeds as a function of number of problems. In the beginning, when the number of problems is small, the learning over the six trials is gradual; no particular efficiency in problem solution is indicated. But notice the final set of problems, in which Problem Block 257–312 is administered. Learning is chance on Trial 1, as it must be, but Trial 2 is virtually 100 percent correct and remains there for the rest of the six trials. The efficiency on Trial 2 is shown more explicitly in Figure 5–3. As Figure 5–3 indicates, compentence on Trial 2 is a steadily increasing function of number of problems. With a learning set the animals can solve any problem of the class with no more than one error, and the way to do it is experience with a large number of problems of the class.

Another type of problem which Harlow studied was the discrimination reversal problem. The animal is run on a two-choice problem for a block of trials and then the reward value of the stimuli is reversed for the next block of trials, and so on. This would seem to be very confusing because S+ and S− regularly change signs, but over a large number of reversals the monkeys acquire the same kind of efficiency that was obtained with the form discrimination problem. Trial 2 efficiency becomes almost perfect after a large number of problems.

Generalization

Generalization, being a lack of tight stimulus control, means that a range of stimuli will elicit a response that has been learned. Your dog will approach you whether your whistle is loud or soft even though all of its training was with a loud whistle. Some have seen stimulus generalization as biologically adaptive, and Pavlov, the great Russian physiologist, was among them (Pavlov, 1927, p. 113). Our behavior would be hopelessly ineffective if we responded only to stimulus values that were present in learning. A jungle animal would not survive very long if its defensive reactions were not sensitive to some variation of cues that signified a threat. Laboratory psychologists, however, have not cared much about generalization as an adaptive mechanism, reasonable though the idea seems. As with all scientists, they are most interested in the variables that determine the phenomenon, and the functional relations among the variables that are the laws.

The laboratory method for the study of stimulus generalization requires that a stimulus, called the training stimulus, elicits a response. Either classical conditioning or instrumental learning procedures can be used. After training, tests without reinforcement are made to see how well values of the stimulus not used in training elicit the response. The extent to which test stimuli elicit the response is generalization. The elicitation of responses without reinforcement is the condition of extinction; so care must be taken to minimize the confounding of extinction and generalization. A solution to the problem is to use intermittent reinforcement in training which, as we saw in Chapters 2 and 3, induces slow extinction and so minimizes the impact of extinction on responses in the generalization tests. Intermittent reinforcement was used in a classic study by Guttman and Kalish (1956). Their experiment came to define the methods that are used in most modern studies of stimulus generalization, and their data illustrate generalization very nicely.

Pigeons in a Skinner box learned by a variable interval schedule to peck a key whose color as the training stimulus was either a wave length of 530, 550, 580, or 600 millimicrons. (To the human eye, but not necessarily the pigeon eye, these wave lengths represent, approximately, green, yellow-green, yellow-orange, and orange.) At the generalization test the same color or a different one was presented, and the pecking rate determined. Figure 5–4 has the findings, and curves such as these are called *generalization gradients*. Notice that the best performance on the test is for the training stimulus, that responses occur for a range of stimuli around the training stimulus, and that performance falls off rapidly when the color of the stimulus is changed.

THEORIES OF GENERALIZATION

Pavlov (1927) was a physiologist; so it is not surprising that his explanation of generalization was physiological. He believed that generalization from the training stimulus to similar stimuli was due to a spreading wave of excitation across the cortex. Pavlov's theory can be dismissed with the observation that there was no physiological evidence for cortical waves then or now. Later, psychologists (e.g., Hull, 1943), with more behavioral than physiological interests, wrote about the spread of habit strength, just as Pavlov wrote about the spread of cortical excitation. The important thing to notice about both of these theoretical positions is that generalization is seen as an innate propensity of the brain. Generalization will occur naturally via cortical waves or habit structures once a training stimulus comes to elicit a response reliably.

Theoretically, not much came of generalization until the publication of a paper by Lashley and Wade (1946) which raised issues that are the target of argument and experiment until this day. They said that the view of innate generalization was wrong. Generalization, they said occurs because of failure to discriminate the training stimulus from the test stimulus. Indeed, "The 'dimensions' of a stimulus series are determined by comparison of two or more stimuli and do not exist for the organism until established by differential training." (Lashley and Wade, 1946, p. 74). Or "'Stimulus generalization' is generalization only in the sense of failure to note distinguishing characteristics of the stimulus or

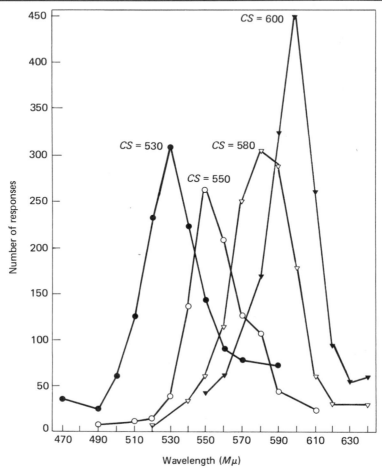

Source: N. Guttman, and H. I. Kalish, Discriminability and stimulus generalization. *Journal of Experimental Psychology*, 1956, *51*, 79–88. Reprinted by permission of the American Psychological Association.

FIGURE 5–4
Generalization gradients for four training stimuli.

to associate them with the conditioned reaction." (Lashley and Wade, 1946, p. 81). Whatever argument there has been about details, the Lashley and Wade theory appeared clear enough in its essentials:

1. Generalization, as an innate property of the brain, is wrong.
2. Generalization is the result of acquired discrimination. Training procedures, of course, must be used to associate a response with the

training stimulus, but that is not the point. The point is that discriminative training with respect to training and test stimuli is required. There is no generalization gradient without discrimination learning. One learns about the dimensions of stimuli by training to discriminate differences between them.

There is a strong and weak interpretation that can be given to the position of Lashley and Wade. The *strong interpretation* says that *all* generalization is a function of discrimination experience with no contribution from innate sources. There should be no generalization along a stimulus dimension if one were raised in an environment in which discriminations along the dimension were denied. The *weak interpretation* says that there *may* be contributions to generalization from innate sources, but nevertheless training in discriminating the values of a stimulus dimension will affect generalization.

The conclusion of research studies on the strong interpretation is negative. Experiments (Rudolph, Honig, and Gerry, 1969; Mountjoy and Malott, 1968; Tracy, 1970; Riley and Leuin, 1971; Terrace, 1975) reared the quail, ducklings, or chickens that were their subjects in monochromatic light, such as an orange light. The monochromatic light gave no opportunity to make discriminations with respect to a color. Then, for a response on which they had been trained, they were given generalization tests for several colors. All experiments reported significant generalization gradients; so a contention that all generalization is a function of discrimination experience is wrong.

A conclusion that generalization is not entirely a function of discrimination experience does not mean that discrimination training will not affect generalization. This is the weak interpretation of the Lashley and Wade position, and it turns out to be true. The most well-known evidence for it was presented in a study by Jenkins and Harrison (1960). Jenkins and Harrison compared the effects of discriminative and nondiscriminative training on the generalization gradient. A tone was the stimulus, pigeons were the subjects, and key-pecking was the instrumental response. In nondiscriminative training, a 1000 Hz tone sounded continuously whether a bird was responding and being reinforced or not. In discriminative training, reinforcements were received only when the tone was sounding, and they could not be had when the tone was off. The test for generalization evaluated response level in which the stimuli were no tone, 300, 450, 670, 1,500, 2,250, 3,500, and 1000 Hz (the training stimulus). The results for nondiscriminative training are shown in Figure 5-5, and the tone acquired no stimulus control over the response—the gradient is flat. But discriminative training was different, as Figure 5-6 shows. The tone had strong control over the response. Newman and Baron (1965) obtained the same results as Jen-

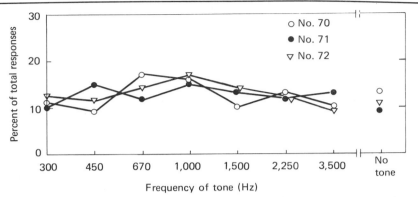

Source: H. M. Jenkins and R. H. Harrison, Effect of discrimination training on auditory generalization. *Journal of Experimental Psychology*, 1960, 59, 246–253. Reprinted by permission of the American Psychological Association.

FIGURE 5–5
The generalization gradients of three pigeons who had nondiscriminative training.

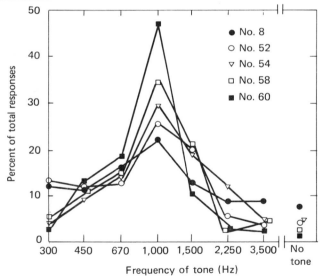

Source: H. M. Jenkins, and R. H. Harrison, Effect of discrimination training on auditory generalization. *Journal of Experimental Psychology*, 1960, 59, 246–253. Reprinted by permission of the American Psychological Association.

FIGURE 5–6
The generalization gradients of five pigeons who had discriminative training.

kins and Harrison in an experiment that used very similar procedures. Their training stimulus was a vertical line on the key which the pigeon pecked, and the generalization tests were with angular changes of the line. Findings such as this are gratifying for scientists because they speak to the generality of results, and they dispel any reservations that the Jenkins and Harrison findings are somehow uniquely associated with tones.

In a later study Jenkins and Harrison (1962) further demonstrated the power of discrimination training for shaping generalization gradients. Two pigeons from the 1960 experiment were used so that their data could be used for comparison. Again key-pecking was the response, and again tones were used as the discriminative stimuli. This time, however, S+ was a 1,000 Hz tone and S– a 950 Hz tone. The results are shown in Figure 5–7. The gradient with the dashed line is from the 1960 experiment where tone and no-tone were S+ and S–, respectively. The gradients of the 1962 experiment are shown by the solid line, and the discriminative training for closely spaced tones has the effect of sharply steepening the gradients. Here again there is evidence of the importance of discrimination training for generalization.

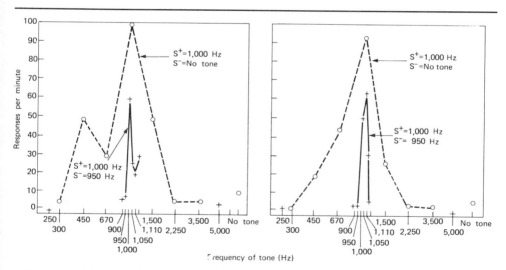

Source: Adapted from H. M. Jenkins and R. H. Harrison, Generalization gradients of inhibition following auditory discrimination learning. *Journal of the Experimental Analysis of Behavior,* 1962, 5, 435–441. Copyright 1962 by the Society for the Experimental Analysis of Behavior, Inc.

FIGURE 5–7

Effects of discrimination training on the generalization gradient. The wider gradients are from Jenkins and Harrison (1960) and are based on a tone–no-tone discrimination training, in which the tone was 1,000 Hertz. The very narrow gradients are based on discrimination training with two tones, one 950 and one 1,000 Hertz.

Why does discrimination training affect the generalization gradient? In the discussion of discrimination learning earlier in this chapter, we saw that an important set of issues and experiments was based on attention, or the variables and mechanisms that determine the selection of stimuli that govern responding. If discrimination learning is an important determinant of the generalization gradient, then we should expect attention to be a factor for generalization also. Consider the Jenkins and Harrison (1960) experiment again. One could easily contend that the gradients are steep in Figure 5–6 because discrimination training correlated the tone with reinforcement, forcing the pigeon to pay attention to it. The tone was significant for the bird and it made a difference when the tone was changed in the generalization tests. We can infer that the Guttman and Kalish experiment (Figure 5–4) was a case of discriminative training. Maximum exposure to the lighted key occurred when a bird was pecking it and getting reinforcement, and minimum exposure occurred when a bird was not pecking it and not being reinforced.

The reason that the gradients are flat in Figure 5–5 is that the nondiscriminative training did not force attention to the tone; so when the tone was varied in the generalization tests, it had no effect because the pigeon had been paying no attention to it in the first place. If this explanation is true, then we have said more about attention than about generalization. An explanation is still lacking as to why stimulus variation on the generalization tests produce the orderly gradients that they do. Pavlov may have been correct in saying that generalization is fundamentally a property of the perceptual systems of the brain, although certainly he was wrong about cortical waves. We are closer than we once were to an explanation of generalization, but we are still lacking a fundamental theory.

OTHER VARIABLES FOR GENERALIZATION

Schedules of reinforcement Guttman and Kalish (1956), in their classic study on generalization, used a variable interval schedule of reinforcement to minimize the effects of extinction in nonreinforced generalization tests. The success of their approach has prompted the exploration of reinforcement schedules on generalization, and an example is an experiment by Hearst, Koresko, and Poppen (1964) in which generalization as a function of different variable interval schedules was investigated. Pigeons were the subjects and key-pecking was the response. The training stimulus was a vertical line on the key, and the generalization tests were different angular orientations of the line. A variable interval schedule specifies the average time at which a response produces a reinforcement, and in this experiment the schedules were 30 seconds, 1, 2, 3, and 4 minutes. The results are shown in Figure 5–8. More frequent reinforcement produced the steeper gradient.

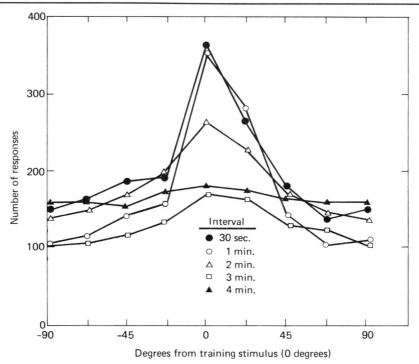

Degrees from training stimulus (0 degrees)

Source: Adapted from E. Hearst, M. B. Koresko, and R. Poppen, Stimulus generalization and the response-reinforcement contingency. *Journal of the Experimental Analysis of Behavior,* 1964, *7,* 369–380. Copyright 1964 by the Society for the Experimental Analysis of Behavior, Inc.

FIGURE 5–8
The schedule of reinforcement is a variable for the generalization gradient. Shown are gradients for five variable interval schedules. The schedules with the most frequent reinforcement produce the steepest gradients. The training stimulus was a vertical line (0 degrees). The test stimuli had various degrees of tilt.

Amount of training   Using the same procedures as in the 1964 experiment by Hearst and his associates discussed above, Hearst and Koresko (1968) did two experiments on amount of training and its effect on the generalization gradient. Training on a 1-minute variable interval schedule was given for 2, 4, 7, or 14 days. The results are presented in Figure 5–9. The more the training the steeper the gradient.

INHIBITORY GENERALIZATION GRADIENTS

Without saying so, we have been discussing the *excitatory generalization gradient,* in which a training stimulus, S+, is reinforced so that it elicits a response reliably. The generalization gradient is produced by

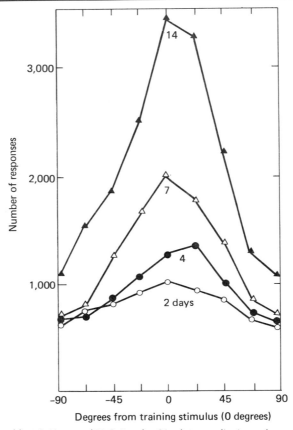

Source: Adapted from E. Hearst and M. B. Koresko, Stimulus generalization and amount of prior training on variable-interval reinforcement. *Journal of Comparative and Physiological Psychology*, 1968, 66, 133–138. Copyright 1968 by the American Psychological Association. Reprinted by permission.

FIGURE 5–9
Effects of amount of training on the generalization gradient. Daily sessions of 2–14 days were administered.

variation in S+ along one of its dimensions. In a discrimination situation, however, we have another stimulus called S− which is not reinforced and for which the subject is trained not to respond. The S− has a generalization gradient also, and it is called the *inhibitory generalization gradient*; there is a spread of the tendency *not* to respond around S− which is greatest at S− and less as S− is varied along one of its dimensions.

Honig et al. (1963) did an experiment on the inhibitory gradient, using pigeons as subjects and key-pecking as the response. A line on the key was S+ for one group and S− for another. For each group a blank key was the other stimulus. As in other experiments that used a line on the key as the essential stimulus, changes in the angular orientation of the line were the generalization tests. The nice thing about this experiment is that it produces, for comparative purposes, an excitatory gradient and an inhibitory gradient under common conditions.

The findings of the Honig et al. study are shown in Figure 5–10. The convex excitatory gradient is as we have encountered before, but the concave inhibitory gradient is new to our discussion. The lowest point is at S−, and the level of responding gradually increases as the line is changed systematically in the generalization tests; it is opposite in

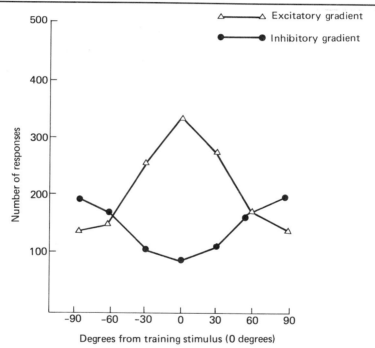

Source: Adapted from W. K. Honig, C. A. Boneau, K. R. Burstein, and H. S. Pennypacker, Positive and negative generalization gradients obtained after equivalent training conditions. *Journal of Comparative and Physiological Psychology,* 1963, *56,* 111–116. Copyright 1963 by the American Psychological Association. Reprinted by permission.

FIGURE 5–10

Variation around the positive stimulus that has been reinforced in training produces an excitatory generalization gradient. This is the convex curve, and it is the spread of responding across a stimulus dimension. Variation around a stimulus that has not been reinforced produces the concave curve, called an inhibitory generalization gradient. The inhibitory generalization gradient is a spread of a tendency not to respond.

trend to the excitatory gradient. There is a gradient of not responding, just as there is a gradient of responding.

Summary

Discrimination and generalization are about the stimulus control of behavior. Discrimination is the responding to one stimulus and not others. Generalization is the failure of discrimination. There is generalization when we make the same response to stimuli and fail to discriminate between them.

The relations issue was a prominent one in the field of discrimination learning for a long time. The question was whether an animal responded to the absolute value of a stimulus or to the relations among stimuli. In a brightness discrimination problem the animal may choose between a white stimulus and a black stimulus on the basis of the absolute brightness level, or it may respond to white being bright in relation to black. The consensus of the research that has been done is that response to the absolute value of stimuli can occur but that relational responding occurs also.

Other prominent issues in discrimination learning have been concerned with attention. Attention is a topic concerned with the selection of stimuli that govern responding. Attention is no issue when the experimenter makes the stimulus unitary and unmistakable, but when the stimulus is multidimensional and the subject has choice among the dimensions, then attention enters as an issue for psychology. The continuity-noncontinuity controversy asked if an animal could pay attention to more than one stimulus dimension at a time during discrimination learning. The answer that research gave to this question was yes. More recent attentional concerns have been with blocking and overshadowing, or whether paying attention to one stimulus degrades attention to another. The evidence is that one stimulus can impair the effectiveness of another.

Most of the effort in discrimination learning has been given to the learning of a single problem, such as learning to choose one form over another. Research on learning set, however, asks how an entire class of problems is learned. Give a small number of trials on each of a large number of discrimination problems of the same kind and the subject will become highly proficient in solving that type of problem.

The laboratory method for the study of generalization is to train the subject to respond to a stimulus and then test with similar stimuli to see if the response occurs to them also. If it does, generalization is demonstrated. A controversy has been whether generalization is innate or learned, and the answer appears to be both. Animals raised in controlled environment where they are denied experience with certain kinds of stimuli nevertheless will show generalization with respect to them. Learning to discriminate between the training and test stimuli also affects generalization, demonstrating an influence of learning. In addition to discrimination training, schedules of reinforcement and amount of training are important variables for amount of generalization. Generalization can be excitatory, in which the spread of responding is with respect to the training stimulus that has been reinforced, or it can be inhibitory, in which there is a spread of nonresponding with respect to the stimulus that has not been reinforced.

References

Bechterev, V. M.   General principles of human reflexology. (Emma and Wm. Murphy translation), London: Jarrolds, 1933.

Guttman, N., & Kalish, H. I.   Discriminability and stimulus generalization. *Journal of Experimental Psychology*, 1956, *51*, 79–88.

Harlow, H. F.   The formation of learning sets. *Psychological Review*, 1949, *56*, 51–65.

Hearst, E., Koresko, M. B., & Poppen, R.   Stimulus generalization and the response-reinforcement contingency. *Journal of the Experimental Analysis of Behavior*, 1964, *7*, 369–380.

Hearst, E., & Koresko, M. B.   Stimulus generalization and amount of prior training on variable-interval reinforcement. *Journal of Comparative and Physiological Psychology*, 1968, *66*, 133–138.

Honig, W. K., Boneau, C. A., Burstein, K. R., & Pennypacker, H. S.   Positive and negative generalization gradients obtained after equivalent training conditions. *Journal of Comparative and Physiological Psychology*, 1963, *56*, 111–116.

Hull, C. L.   *Principles of behavior*. New York: Appleton-Century, 1943.

Jenkins, H. M., & Harrison, R. H.   Effect of discrimination training on auditory generalization. *Journal of Experimental Psychology*, 1960, *59*, 246–253.

Jenkins, H. M., & Harrison, R. H.   Generalization gradients of inhibition following auditory discrimination learning. *Journal of the Experimental Analysis of Behavior*, 1962, *5*, 435–441.

Kamin, L. J.   Predictability, surprise, attention, and conditioning. In B. A. Campbell and R. M. Church (Eds.), *Punishment and aversive behavior*. New York: Appleton-Century-Crofts, 1969, pp. 279–296.

Krechevsky, I.   Hypotheses in rats. *Psychological Review*, 1932, *39*, 516–532.

Lashley, K. S., & Wade, M.   The Pavlovian theory of generalization. *Psychological Review*, 1946, *53*, 72–87.

Lawrence, D. H., & DeRivera, J.   Evidence for relational transposition. *Journal of Comparative and Physiological Psychology*, 1954, *47*, 465–471.

Levine, M.   A model of hypothesis behavior in discrimination learning set. *Psychological Review*, 1959, *66*, 353–366.

Levine, M.   Hypothesis behavior. In A. M. Schrier, H. F. Harlow, & F. Stollnitz (Eds.), *Behavior of nonhuman primates: Modern research trends* (Vol. 1). New York: Academic Press, 1965, pp. 97–127.

Mackintosh, N. J. *The psychology of animal learning.* New York: Academic Press, 1974.

Mountjoy, P. T., & Malott, M. K. Wavelength generalization curves for chickens reared in restricted portions of the spectrum. *Psychological Record,* 1968, *18,* 575–583.

Newman, F. L., & Baron, M. R. Stimulus generalization along the dimension of angularity. *Journal of Comparative and Physiological Psychology,* 1965, *60,* 59–63.

Pavlov, I. P. *Conditioned reflexes.* (G. V. Anrep trans.). Oxford: Oxford University Press, 1927.

Riley, D. A., & Leuin, T. C. Stimulus-generalization gradients in chickens reared in monochromatic light and tested with a single wavelength value. *Journal of Comparative and Physiological Psychology,* 1971, *75,* 399–402.

Rudolph, R. I., Honig, W. K., & Gerry, J. E. Effects of monochromatic rearing on the acquisition of stimulus control. *Journal of Comparative and Physiological Psychology,* 1969, *67,* 50–57.

Sutherland, N. S., and Mackintosh, N. J. *Mechanisms of animal discrimination learning.* New York: Academic Press, 1971.

Terrace, H. S. Evidence for the innate basis of the hue dimension in the duckling. *Journal of the Experimental Analysis of Behavior,* 1975, *24,* 79–87.

Tracy, W. K. Wavelength generalization and preference in monochromatically reared ducklings. *Journal of the Experimental Analysis of Behavior,* 1970, *13,* 163–178.

6

Punishment and fear

THERE ARE stimuli which innately frighten us. Without learning, a baby is startled by a loud noise, and it will recoil if its hand touches a flame. But a catalog of unlearned reactions to noxious stimuli is of less interest to the learning psychologist than how we become afraid of situations that are ordinarily neutral. Why does a dog cringe and whine when it hears the approaching footsteps of the person who regularly beats it? The rhythmic sound that is approaching footsteps has no innate capability to frighten the animal. Why does the child run away from a home where the tyrannical parent regularly abuses him or her? Newborn babies are not genetically endowed with a fear of parents, so the child's fear must have been acquired through experience. It is these learned reactions to punishment that fascinate learning psychologists.

In a pioneering experiment, Watson and Rayner (1920) conditioned a baby (little Albert, as he is affectionately remembered in psychology) to be afraid of stimuli that were previously neutral to him. A classical conditioning procedure was used, with a loud sound as a UCS to arouse fear reliably. The loud sound was a steel bar which was struck behind the child's head. A live white rat was used as the CS. At the outset Albert was unafraid of the rat, but when the loud sound and the rat were paired repeatedly, Albert developed a strong fear of the rat. The investigators then went on to demonstrate generalization by showing that the fear reactions would occur when Albert was shown a rabbit, a dog, or even a sealskin coat. The importance of this study is that fear can be a learned state and subject to the same laws of learning as any response.

Fear has its origins in punishment; so it is appropriate to discuss reactions to punishment before discussing how fear is learned in a punishing situation.

Punishment

A punishing situation has three levels of analysis. Consider the case of a mother who punishes a child for stealing pennies from her purse. At one level of analysis the punishment stops the stealing. At another level the child develops a fear reaction to the mother, and at still another level the child runs away from home to avoid the feared mother. Only the first level will be discussed in this section, in which the concern is with punishment and how it reduces the probability of a response. The other levels of analysis will be discussed in later parts of this chapter in which fear and avoidance learning are discussed.

There are two conditions that establish a punishment situation:

1. There is a response that has been rewarded, has strength, and is ongoing. The purpose of punishment is to reduce the occurrence of this response.
2. The ongoing response is delivered a punishing stimulus.

The issue is the reduction in performance produced by the punishing stimulus, and the amount of reduction that is achieved is importantly a function of the strength of the ongoing response and the intensity and duration of the punishment. In experimental work the punishing stimulus almost always is electric shock, and understandably because shock can be painful and because its intensity and duration can be exactly controlled. Psychologists have been slow in studying other kinds of punishing events and their characteristics.

STRENGTH OF THE ONGOING RESPONSE AND PUNISHMENT

A primary variable for the effectiveness of punishment is the strength of the ongoing response that is punished. The more times the unwanted response has been rewarded, the more persistent it will be and the more punishment it will take to eliminate it. The child who has been successfully stealing pennies from mother's purse for a year may not be deterred by one spanking.

The experimental illustration of this principle is a study by Kaufman and Miller (1949). They used five groups of rats and trained them to run down a straight runway for food reinforcement. Different strengths of

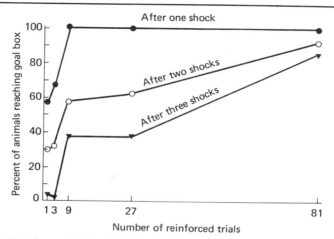

Source: L. E. Kaufman and N. E. Miller, Effect of number of reinforcements on strength of approach in an approach-avoidance conflict. *Journal of Comparative and Physiological Psychology,* 1949, *42,* 65–74. Reprinted by permission of the American Psychological Association.

FIGURE 6–1
Data which demonstrate that a punishment situation can be described as approach-avoidance behavior. An approach response in rats is trained with food reinforcement and is deterred when punishing electric shock is delivered.

the running response were defined by the number of reinforcement given to each group, which were 1, 3, 9, 27, and 81 reinforcements. After this training the animal had punishment trials in which a brief shock was delivered when the rat took the food. Figure 6–1 has the findings, plotted in terms of percent of animals who reached the goal box as a function of number of reinforcements in training and three punishing shocks. The punishment is effective in eliminating the running behavior, and it is least effective for the largest number of reinforcements.

INTENSITY OF PUNISHMENT

Because of our direct experience with many psychological variables and in observing their effects on ourselves and others, we sometimes have good intuition on how a variable might effect behavior. The intensity of punishment is one of these variables. We all have been punished and have delivered punishment, and it would be our intuitive feeling that strong punishment eliminates unwanted behavior more quickly than weak punishment. Laboratory research supports this intuition, with the bonus of more detail than common sense provides. Karsh (1962) did a study with rats in which intensity of punishment was the

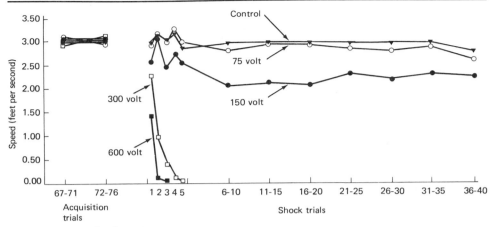

Source: E. B. Karsh, Effects of number of rewarded trials and intensity of punishment on running speed. *Journal of Comparative and Physiological Psychology*, 1962, 55, 44–51. Reprinted by permission of the American Psychological Association.

FIGURE 6–2
Effects of intensity of punishment on running speed.

experimental variable. She used a straight runway as her research apparatus. Speed of running was the measure of performance. After 75 food-rewarded trials she gave 40 punishment trials during which the animal was shocked when it touched the food cup. Five groups of animals were used, with each group receiving a different intensity of shock on the 40 punishment trials: 0, 75, 150, 300, and 600 volts. The results are shown in Figure 6–2. The final trials of acquisition show the final preshock performance, and the punishment that followed was effective in lessening performance, with larger consequences for the greater amounts of punishment. With the highest amounts of shock the animals very quickly stopped running altogether, as shown by zero speed in Figure 6–2.

DURATION OF PUNISHMENT

The effects of the duration of punishment are illustrated for us in a study by Church, Raymond, and Beauchamp (1967). Rats and a Skinner box were used, and the rats were first trained to press the lever for food reward, and this went on for five daily sessions. The next ten sessions were punishment sessions, in which some of the responses continued to be rewarded with food but some were also punished with shock. There were six groups of animals, with each group receiving a different duration of shock (intensity of shock held constant): 0.00 (control condition), 0.15, 0.30, 0.50, 1.00 and 3.00 seconds. The results are presented in

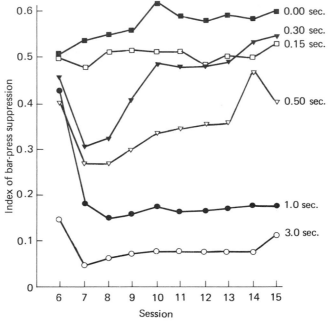

Source: R. M. Church, G. A. Raymond, and R. D. Beauchamp, Response suppression as a function of intensity and duration of punishment. *Journal of Comparative and Physiological Psychology,* 1967, 63, 39–44. Reprinted by permission of the American Psychological Association.

FIGURE 6–3
Effect of duration of punishment on bar-pressing behavior in the rat. The rat's behavior is represented in terms of suppression of the bar-pressing that had been trained with food. Higher values of the index mean less suppression.

Figure 6–3 in terms of a measure of suppression of the bar-pressing response. There is a clear relationship: The longer the punishment the more effective it is in eliminating a response.

Avoidance learning

Reduction in an ongoing response is the most straightforward consequence of punishment, but it is only one aspect. Another facet, which theorists have found more challenging, is behaving in such a way as to do something about the punishing situation. Psychologists do not believe that punishing stimuli weaken a response and work in an opposite fashion to the strengthening effects of reward. Instead, subjects actively do something to lessen the discomfort, and it is this learning of new responses that psychologists have found so interesting. Basically, this learning occurs in two kinds of situations, depending whether the subject can avoid the punishment or not. In *escape learning* it cannot avoid the punishment. The subject always receives the punishment on a trial but it can escape it by making a response, and it is the learning of this response which psychologists study. An example would be a rat placed in a box with an electrified floor. At the start of each trial the shock is delivered and the rat will learn that it can escape it by jumping from the box. But no matter how efficiently it performs its escape response, it will always receive the shock at the beginning of each trial. In the second kind of punishment-induced learning, called *avoidance learning*, the subject can learn to avoid punishment all together. Continuing with the rat-in-the-box example, an avoidance learning situation might sound a tone for ten seconds before the shock is delivered on a trial, and the avoidance response which the rat learns is to jump out of the box in the ten seconds before the shock comes on when the tone sounds. Avoidance learning has the anticipatory fear of punishment, and it is a kind of learning which has fascinated learning psychologists and which will primarily occupy our interests in the remainder of this chapter. The theoretical concern with punishment and fear began in the 1930s, and it has been accelerating ever since.

Consider a puzzle such as this, with classical conditioning as the frame of reference. According to the laws of classical conditioning (Chapter 2), the pairing of the CS and the UCS is a fundamental circumstance of learning, with the learning increasing with number of CS–UCS pairings. Brogden, Lipman, and Culler (1938) ran an experiment with guinea pigs which used an activity cage that rotated on a shaft as the animal ran in place with the cage moving beneath its feet. The CS was a tone, the UCS was electric shock, and the UCR was movement; the animal had to learn to move when it heard the tone. One group of animals had the standard classical conditioning arrangement, in which the CS and UCS were always paired together and the shock was unavoidable. A second group was treated the same except that its animals could avoid the shock by making a movement in the CS–UCS interval. Figure 6–4 shows the results plotted in terms of anticipatory movements to the CS. The bottom curve is the group which received the standard classical conditioning procedure, and they had a modest amount of learning. But notice the top curve for the second group which could avoid the shock. They had far fewer pairings of the CS and the UCS than the other group because they came to avoid the shock regularly, and yet they learned so much faster. Why this apparent failure of the laws of classical conditioning? How could a few CS–UCS pairings produce better learning than many?

TWO-FACTOR THEORY

In one of the most important papers in the psychology of learning, Mowrer (1947) said that the data by Brogden, Lipman and Culler are understandable if we see punishment and avoidance as needing *both* classical conditioning and instrumental learning to explain them, *and* if we bring fear into the analysis. He said that fear was an internal state that was learned, that fear was an uncomfortable motivating state, and that the fear would motivate the subject to learn forms of behavior that would remove it. Mowrer said that the fear was an emotion learned by the principles of classical conditioning and that the avoidance behavior that followed was learned instrumentally. The reward for the instrumental learning was reduction in fear, and any response that eliminated fear was thereby rewarded and learned. This is the theory of reward learning called *drive reduction theory* (Chapter 4). Hunger and thirst are examples of unlearned primary drives because their satisfaction is necessary for biological survival. Fear, however, is a *secondary drive* because it is learned.

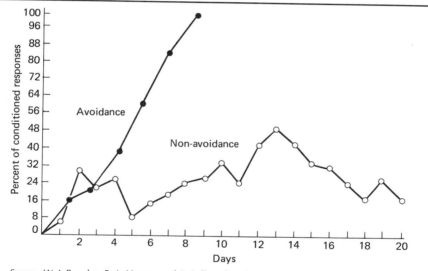

Source: W. J. Brogden, E. A. Lipman, and E. Culler, The role of incentive in conditioning and extinction. *American Journal of Psychology*, 1938, *51*, 109–117. Reprinted by permission of the University of Illinois Press.

FIGURE 6–4

With electric shock as the UCS in classical conditioning, anticipatory avoidance of the shock speeds the rate of conditioning.

Stage 1: Classical conditioning of the fear response

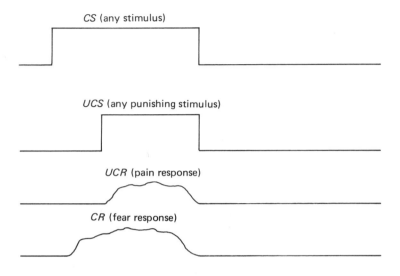

CS (any stimulus)

UCS (any punishing stimulus)

UCR (pain response)

CR (fear response)

Stage 2: Instrumental learning of an avoidance response

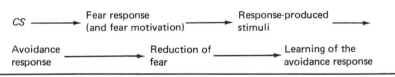

CS ⟶ Fear response (and fear motivation) ⟶ Response-produced stimuli ⟶

Avoidance response ⟶ Reduction of fear ⟶ Learning of the avoidance response

FIGURE 6–5
The stages of Mowrer's two-factor theory. Fear is learned in Stage 1 by classical conditioning, and avoidance behavior is instrumentally learned in Stage 2 when it produces fear reduction.

Mowrer's theory of emotional learning is called *two-factor theory* because it uses both classical conditioning and instrumental learning as explanatory tools. In more detail, the theory makes these assumptions:

1. Pain is an innate response of the autonomic nervous system.
2. Pain can be conditioned to any stimulus. The aspect of the pain response that is conditioned to a stimulus is called fear. The learning of fear is by classical conditioning.
3. Fear is motivating.
4. Fear has cue (stimulus) properties which are called response-produced stimuli.

5. Response-produced stimuli can become the cue for any response through learning.
6. The reduction of the fear motivation is a basis for instrumental learning.

Figure 6–5 shows how these assumptions produce the learning of fear and an avoidance response based on its reduction. A good theory has scope, and two-factor theory has it because it says that fear can become conditioned to any stimulus and that any avoidance response will be learned that reduces fear. Human experience supports this assertion. Can you think of a stimulus to which someone, somewhere, is not afraid? Can you think of a response that is not made by someone, somewhere, in avoidance of fearful stimuli?

A demonstration of two-factor theory, in which fear was classically conditioned and an arbitrary avoidance response was learned to remove a fearful stimulus, was carried out by Brown and Jacobs (1949). They used rats and an apparatus with two compartments separated by a guillotine door which created a wall. With the door lifted, there was a low barrier between the two compartments. The door was down for the classical conditioning of the fear, and an animal was administered 22 training trials in which a light-tone combination (CS) was paired with shock (UCS). Test trials followed, in which the door was lifted to reveal the barrier. The CS was turned on and when the animal jumped the

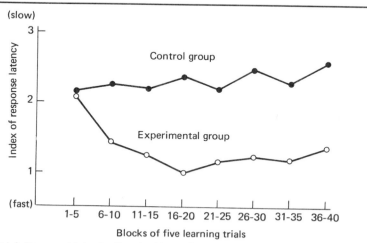

Source: J. S. Brown, and A. Jacobs, The role of fear in the motivation and acquisition of responses. *Journal of Experimental Psychology*, 1949, 39, 747–759. Reprinted by permission of the American Psychological Association.

FIGURE 6–6
Learning of an avoidance response to escape a stimulus which arouses fear.

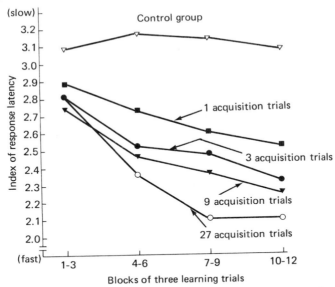

Source: H. I. Kalish, Strength of fear as a function of the number of acquisition and extinction trials. *Journal of Experimental Psychology,* 1954, 47, 1–9. Reprinted by permission of the American Psychological Association.

FIGURE 6–7

The learning of a response to avoid a stimulus which arouses fear. The curve parameter is number of times the stimulus was paired with electric shock which, according to two-factor theory, determines the degree of fear.

barrier the CS was turned off. Theoretically, fear has been conditioned to the CS, and the animal can avoid the fear-arousing CS by jumping the barrier. There were two groups of animals: an experimental group that received the treatment just described and a control group that was treated the same except that it was never shocked. The results given in Figure 6–6 are presented in terms of the time to make the barrier-crossing response. The control animals wandered about in random exploration as animals do, and often crossed the barrier, so that a latency measure was obtained for them also. But notice the curve for the experimental group. It is a standard learning curve; the animals respond with increasing speed to escape the fear-producing CS. Brown and Jacobs, in their test of two-factor theory, interpret the findings in support of it.

Kalish (1954) investigated the learning of an avoidance response as a function of the number of CS–UCS pairings which, according to two-factor theory, determines the amount of fear. Different groups of rats were given either 0 (control group), 1, 3, 9 or 27 paired presentations of a

light-buzzer CS and shock as the UCS in a box, and then were transferred to a hurdle-jumping task such as Brown and Jacobs used, where
the CS would turn on and then turn off when the animal crossed the
barrier. The measure of performance was latency of jumping the hurdle,
just as in the Brown and Jacobs experiment. Kalish's results are shown
in Figure 6–7. The greater the number of CS–UCS pairings and fear, the
more readily the avoidance response was learned.

Both the Brown and Jacobs experiment, and the Kalish experiment,
had the classical conditioning of fear precede the instrumental learning
of the avoidance response, which has a tidiness about it because it
separates the learning of fear and avoidance as two-factor theory does.
Commonly, however, research workers in this field will use a task in
which fear and avoidance are learned together. One such device is the
two-way shuttle box, shown in Figure 6–8 (Solomon and Wynne, 1953),
and it is similar to the hurdle-jumping task. The floor is electrified, and
there is a barrier between two compartments. When a guillotine gate is
lifted, there remains a hurdle in the center of the box. Any distinctive
stimulus can be a CS, and its onset is followed by shock. The avoidance
response to be learned is jumping over the hurdle and into the other
compartment during the CS–UCS interval before the shock comes on.
The guillotine gate is then closed until the next trial, at which time the

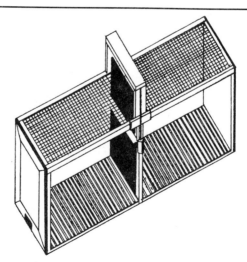

Source: R. L. Solomon, and L. C. Wynne, Traumatic avoidance learning: Acquisition in normal dogs.
Psychological Monographs, 1953, 67, Whole No. 354. Reprinted by permission of the American Psychological Association.

FIGURE 6–8
A two-way shuttle box for dogs commonly used in research on avoidance behavior.

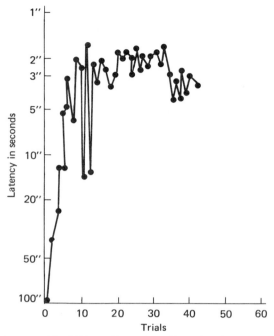

Source: R. L. Solomon, and L. C. Wynne, Traumatic avoidance learning: Acquisition in normal dogs. *Psychological Monographs,* 1953, 67, Whole No. 354. Reprinted by permission of the American Psychological Association.

FIGURE 6–9

Representative shuttle box data from one dog. Punishing shock was received when a response took longer than ten seconds. A response in less than ten seconds avoided the shock.

animal is required to jump back to the first compartment. The interest in the shuttle box is the study of avoidance learning, but, strictly, it is an escape-avoidance task. In the beginning trials, before it learns to avoid, the animal is shocked each time before the hurdle is jumped, and so at this point it is an escape situation. In the later trials the animal anticipates the shock by jumping over the hurdle when the CS comes on, and so it is now an avoidance task.

Representative shuttle box data from one dog are shown in Figure 6–9 (Solomon and Wynne, 1953). The CS was a dimming of lights above the box, and the CS–UCS interval was ten seconds which required that the dog jump over the hurdle within ten seconds or be shocked. It can be seen that the initial responses were longer than ten seconds, which means that the animal was shocked. In these initial trials there was pairing of the CS and UCS for the classical conditioning of fear, but after that the animal learned to avoid shock because responses occurred in less than ten seconds. The learning of the avoidance response was somewhat gradual because there are two responses after the avoidance learning began which had latencies longer than ten seconds and the dog was shocked. Thereafter, the fearful animal always responded in two to three seconds after onset of the CS and was never shocked again.

Extinction of an avoidance response

GENERAL CHARACTERISTICS

The extinction of an avoidance response requires withdrawal of the punishing UCS, but there is more to extinction than the withdrawal of punishment. According to two-factor theory there is the emotional state of fear that is supporting the avoidance response. To extinguish the avoidance response we must extinguish fear also.

There are many people who never conquer their fear of water and systematically avoid swimming all of their lives. The punishment that originally induced the fear of water is long gone, but the avoidance behavior continues unabated. Such things are common knowledge to us, and so experimental evidence on the resistance of avoidance responses to extinction will come as no surprise. Figure 6–10 shows data for the extinction of a hurdle-jumping response. The study is by Solomon, Kamin, and Wynne (1953). They used dogs as subjects and the shuttle box shown in Figure 6–8 as their research apparatus. As in the Solomon and Wynne (1953) study, the CS was a dimming of lights, shock was the UCS, and the CS–UCS interval was ten seconds. After 10 consecutive acquisition trials in which shock was administered if the animal did not leap the barrier within ten seconds, 200 extinction trials were given in which shock was always omitted. Notice that over the 200 trials the avoidance response is very efficient, occurring as it does between one and two seconds after the onset of the CS, and there is no sign of a decrease in response proficiency that ordinarily characterizes behavior in experimental extinction. Two hundred extinction trials without decrement is a long series, certainly longer persistence than one would expect for learning by positive reinforcement. Some investigators have reported many hundreds of extinction trials without a decline in avoidance behavior.

Obviously more must be done to extinguish the avoidance response than withdraw the punishing UCS. The UCS must be withdrawn, of

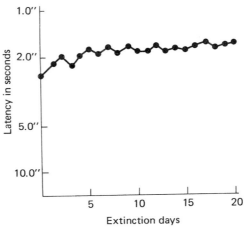

Source: R. L. Solomon, L. J. Kamin, and L. C. Wynne, Traumatic avoidance learning: The outcomes of several extinction procedures with dogs. *Journal of Abnormal and Social Psychology,* 1953, *48,* 291–302. Reprinted by permission of the American Psychological Association.

FIGURE 6–10
Attempt to extinguish the avoidance response in the two-way shuttle box by withdrawing the UCS. Two hundred extinction trials were administered.

course, but this operation guarantees only that no new fear learning will occur—it does not guarantee the repeated unreinforced elicitation of the fear state and thus its weakening by extinction. That the avoidance response can continue so long in extinction without decline shows that fear is not weakening, and this could be embarrassing for two-factor theory because the occurrence of the avoidance response should bring an unreinforced elicitation of the fear response and its extinction. But maybe two-factor theory is correct in principle but vague on details. Maybe the occurrence of an avoidance response does not bring a full-blown occurrence of the fear response and, thus, a full-fledged extinction trial for it. Maybe the avoidance response is fired by a very slight arousal of fear so that the full occurrence of the avoidance response does not necessarily mean a full occurrence of the fear response. The result is that the fear response never has full, unreinforced elicitations and so it undergoes little extinction. Solomon and Wynne (1954) conceived this idea and called it the *principle of anxiety conservation.* The person afraid of water does not need a massive fright reaction to avoid swimming, but merely avoids swimming and protests disinterest in it with only the slightest feelings of fear and unpleasantness. The individual is not only avoiding a punishing experience but fear as well. How, then, is fear extinguished?

WAYS OF EXTINGUISHING FEAR

Flooding If the principle of anxiety conservation is true, then the proper extinction procedure is to prevent the avoidance response and repeatedly present the fearful CS in the absence of the UCS so that the fear response is repeatedly elicited in full strength and extinguished. A number of experiments have been done using this procedure, which goes under the names of *flooding, blocking,* or *response prevention.* A representative one is by Schiff, Smith and Prochaska (1972). Schiff and his associates used a straight runway with an electrified floor, and the animal (the rat) started a trial in a start box with the door to the runway alley closed. At the start of the trial the CS was sounded (it was "white noise," which sounds like the rush of a waterfall) and the door was opened. If the animal made it to the goal box within ten seconds the CS was turned off and shock was escaped; otherwise the animal was shocked. After an animal reached a criterion of learning, it was administered the flooding treatment, in which it was shut in the start box with the CS sounding and the animal blocked from making the avoidance response. The experimental variable was amount of flooding time. The extinction of the avoidance response followed, which was the same as the initial training phase except that shock was never administered, and it was continued to a criterion of not responding. The results are shown in Figure 6–11, in which trials to extinction are plotted as a function of blocking time. The more the subject was held in the presence of the fearful CS the less likely it was to make the avoidance response. And Shipley (1974) has shown that the important thing in flooding is the total exposure time to the CS; it does not matter how the total time is broken up.

The elimination of fear is one explanation of extinction of the avoidance response under the two-factor theory. Alternatively it has been suggested that the subject under restraint in the flooding situation learns another response, perhaps one of immobility, as fear is reduced when the CS is terminated, and on the extinction trials this newly learned response to the CS interferes with the execution of the avoidance response and reduces its frequency of occurrence. Fear is unaffected; only a conflicting response has been learned which acts in opposition to the avoidance response and lowers its performance level, making it seem as if the fear supporting the avoidance response has been reduced. This is called the interference, or counterconditioning, hypothesis.

Black (1958) had an inventive test of the counterconditioning hypothesis. He used dogs which were held in a harness, and they were required to learn a head-turning response to a tone CS as an avoidance response to shock. He then placed an experimental group of animals

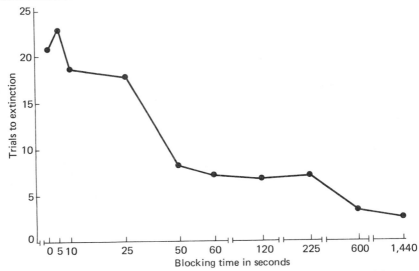

Source: R. Schiff, N. Smith, and J. Prochaska, Extinction of avoidance in rats as a function of duration and number of blocked trials. *Journal of Comparative and Physiological Psychology,* 1972, *81,* 356–359. Reprinted by permission of the American Psychological Association.

FIGURE 6–11
The extinction of an avoidance response by blocking the avoidance response and forcing the subject to endure the fearful stimulus.

under curare and gave extinction by repeated presentation of the tone. In a final session, with the effects of curare worn off, the experimental animals were given a standard extinction series of the head-turning response, and comparison was with control animals that did not have the extinction treatment under curare but were otherwise treated the same. The idea of the experiment was that the animals under curare could not conceivably learn a competing motor response because their muscles could not function, so any effect of the extinction procedures in the curare session must be on the extinction of fear. The results in the final session supported the view that the extinction of an avoidance response is dependent on the extinction of fear, not the learning of a competing response. The experimental animals required about one sixth as many trials as the control animals to reach a criterion of extinction.

CS termination We saw in Chapter 3 that the discrimination hypothesis has been held as an explanation of the partial reinforcement effect in extinction. The omission of reinforcements some of the time in acquisition, and all of the time in extinction, creates a perceived similarity between acquisition and extinction that increases the persistence of a response being extinguished. The subject has a hard time knowing when acquisition ends and extinction begins; so he responds in extinction as he did in acquisition. The same hypothesis has been used to explain the persistence of an avoidance response in extinction. The subject with a well-learned avoidance response has not experienced the UCS for a while; so from the subject's point of view there is no difference when the UCS is withdrawn in extinction. The avoidance response is prolonged as a result. An implication of the discrimination hypothesis is that the avoidance response would extinguish more readily if the acquisition and extinction trials were made discriminably different. The standard procedure is for the CS to terminate with the avoidance response, both in acquisition and extinction, but if the CS in extinction was delayed beyond occurrence of the avoidance response, then acquisition and extinction would be distinguishable and extinction should proceed more rapidly. Katzev (1967) did an experiment on delay of CS termination in extinction. He used rats and a shuttle box (similar to the one shown in Figure 6–8). The CS was a buzzer-light combination, and the UCS was electric shock. All animals were given 200 training trials, in which the shock was avoided if the barrier-crossing avoidance response was made within five seconds after CS onset and in which the CS was terminated promptly when the response occurred. In extinction, where the shock was withdrawn, the animals were divided into two groups. Group 1 had the CS terminate when the avoidance response occurred, or terminate after five seconds if no avoidance response occurred. Group 2 had the same procedure for failure to avoid, but it had the CS continue for 20 seconds after a successful avoidance response. The results are shown in Figure 6–12. The standard extinction procedure gave high persistence of the avoidance response for Group 1, but Group 2 extinguished very rapidly.

A problem with the Katzev experiment is that it confounds the CS termination variable with amount of exposure to the CS. Group 2, which had the CS continue after the avoidance response, had more exposure to the CS than Group 1. Flooding experiments show that exposure to the CS is a fundamental variable for the extinction of fear, and so the more rapid extinction found for Group 2 could be a flooding effect and have nothing to do with the point of CS termination. Katzev and Berman (1974) answered this criticism with an experiment that jointly studied CS termination and CS exposure, and they concluded that the time of CS termination was a genuine variable for the extinction of avoidance behavior. The CS exposure time turned out to be a variable also, however, which is expected from the flooding experiments.

Katzev entertained the discrimination hypothesis, but other possible explanations lie within two-factor theory. If the CS arouses fear, and if

126

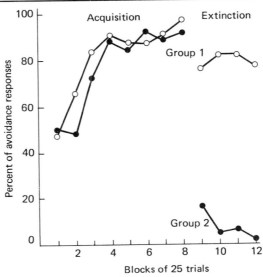

Source: R. Katzev, Extinguishing avoidance responses as a function of delayed warning-signal termination. *Journal of Experimental Psychology*, 1967, *75*, 339–344. Reprinted by permission of the American Psychological Association.

FIGURE 6–12
Delay of CS termination after the avoidance response hastens the extinction process.

CS offset at the time of the avoidance response reduces fear and reinforces the response, then delay of CS offset is delay of reinforcement and it reasonably can be expected to lower the level of the avoidance response. In the same vein, if CS offset produces reinforcing effects, its delay until after the avoidance response could reward whatever response happens to be ongoing, such as exploring or crouching or relaxing. These could be considered interfering responses that reduce the occurrence of avoidance response.

The cognitive point of view

STATUS OF TWO-FACTOR THEORY

Two-factor theory has explanatory value, but in recent years doubts have arisen about it (Rescorla and Solomon, 1967; Seligman and Johnston, 1973). Psychophysiological measures have been a source of data. The heart beats faster when you are afraid because it receives impulses from the autonomic nervous system which is the main physiological residence of fear, according to two-factor theory; so an experimental test of two-factor theory would be to record heart rate in an avoidance learning situation. Heart rate, as an index of fear, should increase when the CS occurs and subside when the CS is withdrawn, and heart rate should correlate with the extinction of the avoidance response, which is based on fear.

Black (1959) has the most well-known experiment on heart rate and fear. He used the same apparatus and head-turning response as in his earlier study (Black, 1958), which was discussed earlier. Heart rate during acquisition acted about as expected under two-factor theory, although the interpretation is not unequivocal. On an acquisition trial there was a sharp increase in heart rate when the CS came on, and then it subsided in a few seconds after the CS terminated, just as would be expected if the CS was arousing fear and heart rate was an index of it. But body movement increases heart rate also; so was the heart rate increase due to fear or the motor act of head turning? Black had to conclude that muscular activity confounded whatever effects fear had on heart rate. Despite this confounding, the heart rate function had *some* correspondence in acquisition to theoretical expectations, but even that was not found for extinction. If heart rate is an index of fear that is sustaining the avoidance response, it should be high at the start of extinction and return to normal when the avoidance response is extinguished. Black found that heart rate returned to normal in one sixth the trials it took the avoidance response to extinguish. This is small comfort for two-factor theory.

Thus, there are problems with some of the details of two-factor theory as it was originally formulated. What remains of the theory today is the central thesis that the laws of fear conditioning are the same as the laws of classical conditioning, that this conditioning has important effects on avoidance learning, and that fear is probably motivational (Rescorla and Solomon, 1967; Maier, Seligman, Solomon, 1969). This is a weaker statement than the original two-factor theory because it does not state how fear and an avoidance response are related. It is far from an inconsequential statement, however. To know that the laws of fear learning are the same as the laws of classical conditioning, and to know that avoidance behavior is importantly determined by them, is an important scientific generalization.

The two-factor theory of fear and avoidance learning is in the stimulus/response, drive/reduction tradition of learning (Chapter 4). Fear is a learned response, and the avoidance response which is instrumental in reducing the aversive motivation accompanying the fear response is learned also. Because of problems that are developing for two-factor theory there is interest in cognitive interpretations of fear and avoidance behavior, of which the informational view is the most prominent.

INFORMATION AND THE CLASSICAL CONDITIONING OF FEAR

We saw in Chapter 2 that a theory of classical conditioning since Pavlov has been contiguity, in which an essential condition of learning is the pairing of the CS and the UCS, and that lately there has been interest in the informational view, in which the perceived correlation of events is the basis of learning. Given the CS, what are the chances of the UCS occurring? What is the probability of a UCS in the absence of a CS?

Rescorla has been an advocate of the informational view, and in one of his experiments (Rescorla, 1968) he used the *conditioned emotional response* technique, which is a method of measuring fear, to test his idea. Rescorla's use of this technique took the standard form of teaching a rat to press a bar for food. Once this act had been acquired the animal underwent classical conditioning of fear, in which a tone CS was paired with shock UCS. Later the animal was returned to bar pressing for food, and occasionally the tone was sounded. The tone had acquired the power to elicit fear, and the amount of fear was measured by suppression of the bar-pressing behavior (sometimes this approach is properly called *conditioned suppression*). The experimental variable was the probability that the UCS would occur in the presence or absence of the CS. Conditioned suppression occurred only when the CS had some correlation with the UCS. When the correlation was absent, and the UCS was just as likely to occur in the absence as in the presence of the CS, suppression was absent. Contiguity does not seem to be the basis of learning because the CS and the UCS occurred together on occasion when the correlation was absent. When there was information in the events and some prediction was possible the conditioning of fear occurred.

INFORMATION AND THE INSTRUMENTAL LEARNING OF AVOIDANCE

If the fear state is learned by classical conditioning and the processing of information in the CS and UCS events, why cannot the avoidance response be learned in the same way by processing the information in response and outcome events? Seligman, Maier, and Solomon (1971) have spoken for this point of view and it runs in parallel with Rescorla's view of classical conditioning. The subject can learn the regularities between his responding and outcome, it is hypothesized. If the response regularly leads to avoidance of a punishing stimulus the subject can learn it, and if the punishment and the behavior are uncorrelated the subject can learn this state of affairs also. In this latter case he will be punished regardless of his behavior, and he will learn that there is nothing he can do about punishment. Later on, when the circumstances have been changed and the subject is given the opportunity to make an avoidance response, he may be indifferent to the opportunity because the uncorrelated behavior and punishment in his past ill suits him for adaptive responding. This line of thinking supports the rapidly expanding research on *helplessness*. The gist of helplessness is that the experience of unavoidable and unpredictable punishment creates a reluctance to avoid punishment when it becomes predictable and possible.

Helplessness   Mowrer and Viek (1948) reported an experiment in which hungry rats were shocked after eating. The rats were more likely to eat food when the electric shock could be turned off with a jump in the air than when it could not. The rats in the two situations were equated for amount of shock received, and so according to two-factor theory the same amount of fear should have developed. Yet, unpredictable shock produced a greater suppression of eating behavior than predictable shock. This provocative finding lay dormant until Overmier and Seligman (1967) reopened the topic.

Overmier and Seligman used two apparatus units in their experiment. One unit was a cloth hammock in which their dog subjects were slung for receiving unsignaled, inescapable shocks. The other unit was a two-way shuttle box for the learning of avoidance behavior. The procedure was to give experimental animals strong, unsignaled, unpredictable shocks in the hammock, followed 24 hours later by avoidance training in the shuttle box, in which the CS was the dimming of illumination and the CS–UCS interval was ten seconds. The control animals received no treatment prior to avoidance training. The avoidance behavior of the control and the experimental animals differed in striking ways. The experimental animals were much slower than the controls in their avoidance response and about half of them never escaped shock at all. And, the experimental dogs were qualitatively different from the control dogs in the shuttle box. In the initial trials they acted like the naive control dogs—whimpering, howling, and urinating as they were shocked, but there was a strong tendency to give up and accept the shock. Sometimes an experimental dog would cross the barrier and escape the shock, but learning was not affected very much because on the next trial the dog was likely to sit passively and accept the shock. In appearance it was helpless and depressed, and it was experimentally made that way.

Tests of a cognitive view of helplessness   Before one launches on a test of theory it is desirable to eliminate nontheoretical explanations of the phenomenon. One such explanation of helplessness is motor interference. The subject acquires motor responses in the inescapable punishment situation that are incompatible with the avoidance response, and so it appears helpless because its dominant response is a nonavoidance one. Motor interference in this case might be seen as superstitious responding, in which the response that is fortuitously occurring at the time of inescapable shock offset is reinforced. As reasonable as interference might seem as a hypothesis, it slipped from stature when Overmier and Seligman (1967) showed that helpless behavior occurred even when the unsignaled, inescapable shocks were administered to curarized dogs. Curare prevents any motor response whatsoever, and so it becomes difficult to hold a hypothesis which says that helplessness is based on competing motor activity.

Seligman and Maier (1967) made a test of the cognitive view by assuming that prior experience in controlling shock should allow the subject to perceive the effectiveness of its own behavior and should offset the effects of unsignaled, inescapable shock on avoidance behavior. Dogs were their subjects. An escape group was first trained to turn off a shock by turning the head and pressing a panel. The escape group was then given the same unsignaled, inescapable shocks and avoidance training in the same harness and shuttle box apparatus that was used by Overmier and Seligman (1967). A yoked control group received the same treatment as the escape group except that panel pressing was ineffective in controlling the shock. A normal control group received only avoidance training in the shuttle box. The results supported the cognitive theory of helplessness. The escape group which had prior training in shock control performed about the same as the normal control group—both had good success in learning the shuttle box avoidance task. The yoked control group, by contrast, showed typical helplessness behavior by failing to avoid shock on a majority of their trials. As long as experience taught a relationship between behavior and punishment there was adaptive behavior in the avoidance situation. But, when experience left the perception that punishing events are uncontrollable, maladaptive helplessness occurred.

The alleviation of helplessness The control of behavior is a scientific goal of psychology, and so we are as interested in undoing helplessness as in creating it. Seligman and Maier (1967) showed that prior acquaintance with shock-behavior contingencies prevented helplessness from occurring, and this idea can be used to alleviate helplessness after it is formed. Seligman, Maier, and Geer (1968) used the same apparatus and about the same procedures as Overmier and Seligman (1967), discussed above. Their treatment for modifying helplessness had two phases, and their approach, which has its roots in cognitive view, was to expose the dog to the punishment/response contingency after it had acquired helplessness so that it could perceive a relationship between behavior and punishment. The first phase was to lower the barrier of the shuttle box and call to the dog while it was being shocked, trying to induce its escape. One dog responded to this treatment, but the remainder of the dogs were subjected to a second phase in which they were placed on a leash and dragged from shock to the safe area of the shuttle box. The forcible procedure worked. The helplessness syndrome was broken up in all cases. Avoidance tests in a shuttle box followed, and all animals learned to avoid.

Helplessness and human depression The similarities between human depression and learned helplessness may be more than accidental, and Miller and Seligman (1973) and Seligman (1975) believe that the principles of helplessness explain depression. The natural world contains such events as wars, accidents, and economic catastrophes that occur independently of our behavior, and these can be forms of unpredictable punishment that contribute to human depression. Depression and helplessness have much in common—passivity, inability to cope, and paralysis of the will. We saw in laboratory work that this kind of behavior in dogs can be alleviated by showing them relationships between their behavior and events in the world. Like the laboratory dog, the human can become helpless when a behavior repeatedly fails to cope with situational demands. And, like the dog, the human can be adaptive again when taught effective coping behavior. Caution must be used in drawing correspondence between helplessness in the dog and depression in the human. In their most recent theoretical formulation, Seligman and his associates (Abramson, Seligman, and Teasdale, 1978) have tailored their thinking more to the human circumstance while retaining the insights that research on animals has provided.

Signaled versus unsignaled punishment A basic part of the procedure to create helplessness is unsignaled punishment. Repeatedly inflict a subject unpredictably with punishment that cannot be escaped and the maladaptive behavior that is helplessness often will be found. Singling out the dimension of unsignaled punishment and looking at it alone, we find that there are other behavioral effects of it. One of these is gastrointestinal lesions, of which ulcers and erosions are the types (Weiss, 1977). Ulcers are long-lasting and, in the worst cases, can penetrate the wall of the stomach or duodenum. Erosions, which are often called stress ulcers, develop rapidly and are not as severe because they may heal in a few days and they almost never perforate. It is erosions which are experimentally produced in animals, and unsignaled punishment is a way to do it.

Weiss (1970) used rats in his experiment to compare the effects of signaled and unsignaled punishment. A rat was restrained in a cylinder and had inescapable shock administered through the tail. The experiment had three groups of rats. One was a control group that received no shock. Another was a predictable shock group, for which a tone signal always began ten seconds before each shock. There was no relationship between tone and shock for a third group. After the experiment the animals were sacrificed and the lesions in their stomachs were counted and measured. The third group with the unpredictable punishment had the largest number of lesions and their lesions were the largest in size.

The helplessness experiments and the Weiss experiment on stress ulcers show that unsignaled punishment contributes to bodily damage and to an inability to cope behaviorally. If other evidence is needed to show that unsignaled punishment is unpleasant and unwanted, there are experiments which show that subjects will choose signaled over unsignaled punishment. Even though both alternatives are inescapable and punish equally, the signaled punishment is preferred. Badia and Culbertson (1972, Experiment II) used rats as subjects and bar pressing as the response to show the preference of signaled over unsignaled punishment. Punishment was inescapable. The rat would begin a session with unsignaled shock, but the press of the bar would turn on a light and indicate a three-minute period where a tone would always precede a shock by five seconds. At the end of three minutes the light would go out and the schedule would return to unsignaled shock until the bar was pressed again. The animals spend 80–95 percent of their time in the signaled condition. In another experiment, Badia and his colleagues (Badia, Culbertson, and Harsh, 1973) found that rats preferred signaled shock that was 4–9 times longer in duration and 2–3 times more intense than unsignaled shock.

Psychologists are not agreed on why signaled punishment is preferred to unsignaled punishment. The most favored hypothesis is the *safety signal hypothesis* (Seligman and Binik, 1977), which holds that when punishment is signaled the subject knows when and when not to be afraid, and when punishment is unsignaled the subject is in a state of fear all of the time because he never knows when he will be hit by the punishment. Another hypothesis, of earlier vintage, is the *preparatory response hypothesis* (Perkins et al., 1966) which asserts that when punishment is signaled regularly the subject learns a preparatory response that lessens the impact of the punishment. Tensing your muscles and bracing yourself when you know a blow is coming is an example.

Summary

A punishing, aversive stimulus and the fear that results from it have strong effects on behavior. A punishing stimulus has the effect of reducing the probability of response occurrence, and its effectiveness is positively related to stimulus intensity and duration.

A consequence of punishment is fear and avoidance of the fearful situation, and Mowrer's two-factor theory has been a prominent attempt to explain them. Two-factor theory assumes that fear is a learned emotional state acquired by classical conditioning (one factor), and that avoidance behavior is instrumentally learned by fear reduction as the avoidance response takes the subject from the fearful situation (the second factor). Extinction of an avoidance response is accomplished by prevention of the avoidance response and the repeated presentation of the stimulus which controls the fear. The unreinforced elicitation of fear brings its extinction and a decrease in the avoidance response based on it.

Another explanation of fear and avoidance learning is the information hypothesis, which is a cognitively oriented theory. The information hypothesis assumes that the subject learns the correlation between stimulus events presented to it and its response and the resulting outcome. Avoidance will be learned when there is a regular relationship between the avoidance response and elimination of the punishing, fearful stimuli, but when a correlation is absent and punishment is unpredictable and unavoidable, the subject will perceive that there is nothing it can do to eliminate the punishment and so it does not avoid. The failure to avoid an aversive situation and the willingness to endure it is called helpless behavior. Unpredictable punishment shows its unpleasantness in other ways. Animals will choose predictable over unpredictable punishment when given a choice. Predictable punishment, even when it is longer in duration and more intense than unpredictable punishment, will be preferred. Moreover, unpredictable punishment produces stress ulcers.

References

Abramson, L. Y., Seligman, M. E. P., & Teasdale, J. D. Learned helplessness in humans: Critique and reformulation. *Journal of Abnormal Psychology,* 1978, *87,* 49–74.

Badia, P., & Culbertson, S. The relative aversiveness of signalled vs. unsignalled escapable and inescapable shock. *Journal of the Experimental Analysis of Behavior,* 1972, *17,* 463–471.

Badia, P., Culbertson, S., & Harsh, J. Choice of longer or stronger signalled shock over shorter or weaker unsignalled shock. *Journal of the Experimental Analysis of Behavior,* 1973, *19,* 25–32.

Black, A. H. The extinction of avoidance responses under curare. *Journal of Comparative and Physiological Psychology,* 1958, *51,* 519–524.

Black, A. H. Heart rate changes during avoidance learning in dogs. *Canadian Journal of Psychology,* 1959, *13,* 229–242.

Brogden, W. J., Lipman, E. A., & Culler, E. The role of incentive in conditioning and extinction. *American Journal of Psychology,* 1938, *51,* 109–117.

Brown, J. S., & Jacobs, A. The role of fear in the motivation and acquisition of responses. *Journal of Experimental Psychology,* 1949, *39,* 747–759.

Church, R. M., Raymond, G. A., & Beauchamp, R. D. Response suppression as a function of intensity and duration of punishment. *Journal of Comparative and Physiological Psychology*, 1967, *63*, 39–44.

Kalish, H. I. Strength of fear as a function of the number of acquisition and extinction trials. *Journal of Experimental Psychology*, 1954, *47*, 1–9.

Karsh, E. B. Effects of number of rewarded trials and intensity of punishment on running speed. *Journal of Comparative and Physiological Psychology*, 1962, *55*, 44–51.

Katzev, R. Extinguishing avoidance responses as a function of delayed warning-signal termination. *Journal of Experimental Psychology*, 1967, *75*, 339–344.

Katzev, R. D., & Berman, J. S. Effect of exposure to conditioned stimulus and control of its termination in the extinction of avoidance behavior. *Journal of Comparative and Physiological Psychology*, 1974, *87*, 347–353.

Kaufman, E. L., & Miller, N. E. Effect of number of reinforcements on strength of approach in an approach-avoidance conflict. *Journal of Comparative and Physiological Psychology*, 1949, *42*, 65–74.

Maier, S. F., Seligman, M. E. P., & Solomon, R. L. Pavlovian fear conditioning and learned helplessness: Effects on escape and avoidance behavior of (*a*) the CS–US contingency and (*b*) the independence of the US and voluntary responding. In B. A. Campbell and R. M. Church (Eds.), *Punishment and aversive behavior*. New York: Appleton-Century-Crofts, 1969, pp. 299–342.

Miller, W. R., & Seligman, M. E. P. Depression and the perception of reinforcement. *Journal of Abnormal Psychology*, 1973, *82*, 62–73.

Mowrer, O. H. On the dual nature of learning: A reinterpretation of "conditioning" and "problem-solving." *Harvard Educational Review*, 1947, *17*, 102–148.

Mowrer, O. H., & Viek, P. An experimental analogue of fear from a sense of helplessness. *Journal of Abnormal and Social Psychology*, 1948, *83*, 193–200.

Overmier, J. B., & Seligman, M. E. P. Effects of inescapable shock upon subsequent escape and avoidance responding. *Journal of Comparative and Physiological Psychology*, 1967, *63*, 28–33.

Perkins, C. C., Jr., Symann, R. G., Levis, C. J., & Spencer, H. R., Jr. Factors affecting preference for signal-shock over shock-signal. *Journal of Experimental Psychology*, 1966, *72*, 190–196.

Rescorla, R. A. Probability of shock in the presence and absence of CS in fear conditioning. *Journal of Comparative and Physiological Psychology*, 1968, *66*, 1–5.

Rescorla, R. A., & Solomon, R. L. Two-process learning theory: Relationships between Pavlovian conditioning and instrumental learning. *Psychological Review*, 1967, *74*, 151–182.

Schiff, R., Smith, N., & Prochaska, J. Extinction of avoidance in rats as a function of duration and number of blocked trials. *Journal of Comparative and Physiological Psychology*, 1972, *81*, 356–359.

Seligman, M. E. P. *Helplessness.* San Francisco: Freeman, 1975.

Seligman, M. E. P., & Binik, Y. M. The safety signal hypothesis. In H. Davis & H.M.B. Hurwitz (Eds.), *Operant-pavlovian interactions.* Hillsdale: Erlbaum, 1977, pp. 165–180.

Seligman, M. E. P., & Johnston, J. C. A cognitive theory of avoidance learning. In F. J. McGuigan and D. B. Lumsden (Eds.), *Contemporary approaches to conditioning and learning.* New York: Wiley, 1973, pp. 69–110.

Seligman, M. E. P., & Maier, S. F. Failure to escape traumatic shock. *Journal of Experimental Psychology,* 1967, *74,* 1–9.

Seligman, M. E. P., Maier, S. F., & Geer, J. H. Alleviation of learned helplessness in the dog. *Journal of Abnormal Psychology,* 1968, *73,* 256–262.

Seligman, M. E. P., Maier, S. F., & Solomon, R. L. Unpredictable and uncontrollable aversive events. In F. R. Brush (Ed.), *Aversive conditioning and learning.* New York: Academic Press, 1971, pp. 347–400.

Shipley, R. H. Extinction of conditioned fear in rats as a function of several parameters of CS exposure. *Journal of Comparative and Physiological Psychology,* 1974, *87,* 699–707.

Solomon, R. L., Kamin, L. J., & Wynne, L. C. Traumatic avoidance learning: The outcomes of several extinction procedures with dogs. *Journal of Abnormal and Social Psychology,* 1953, *48,* 291–302.

Solomon, R. L. & Wynne, L. C. Traumatic avoidance learning: Acquisition in normal dogs. *Psychological Monographs,* 1953, *67,* No. 354.

Solomon, R. L., & Wynne, L. C. Traumatic avoidance learning: The principles of anxiety conservation and partial irreversibility. *Psychological Review,* 1954, *61,* 353–385.

Watson, J. B., & Rayner, R. Conditioned emotional reactions. *Journal of Experimental Psychology,* 1920, *3,* 1–14.

Weiss, J. M. Somatic effects of predictable and unpredictable shock. *Psychosomatic Medicine,* 1970, *32,* 397–408.

Weiss, J. M. Psychological and behavioral influences on gastrointestinal lesions in animal models. In J. D. Maser & M. E. P. Seligman (Eds.), *Psychopathology: Experimental models.* San Francisco: Freeman, 1977, pp. 232–269.

7

Biological constraints on learning

The traditional view of learning

The previous chapters implicitly represent a scientific model of learning that can be called the *traditional view*. The traditional view is fashioned after the Newtonian model in physics in the sense that it seeks general laws that cover a full range of the phenomena from smallest to largest. Laws of motion and gravitational forces apply to a falling pea and a falling star, and similarly learning psychologists have sought principles that embrace learning phenomena from amoeba to humans. Guthrie, Hull, Skinner, Thorndike, and Tolman were systematizers for the psychology of learning, and none of them for a moment doubted the eventual realization of general laws of learning.

Seligman (1970, p. 407) said that the traditional view was guided by the *assumption of equivalence of associability*, which holds that any response of any animal can be associated with any stimulus, and the laws of acquisition, extinction, delay of reinforcement, etc., can be worked out with any arbitrary animal, response, or stimulus. Studying a simple animal was perfectly acceptable because it had learning processes in common with all animals and, being simple, was amenable to good scientific control. The rat and the pigeon have been studied extensively by psychologists because it was believed that general laws of behavior can be found for all animals, and that something can be learned about them by studying the rat and pigeon. Of course such complex animals as humans would have more complex functions than simple animals but this obvious fact altered nothing. It is possible for complex relations to be derived from combinations of simple laws, and so the complexities of behavior deterred no one. Animal psychologists and human psychologists stood shoulder to shoulder in a grand search for the general laws of learning. It was "a period of heroic optimism" (Hinde, 1973, p. 1).

Underlying the traditional view and its faith in general laws was the assumption of an orderly biological universe, progressing from simple animals to complex ones. Aristotle proposed a classification of animals that was of graded complexity, and a scale of animals on a dimension of complexity has been called the *scala naturae* or the *phylogenetic scale*. At the bottom of the scale were simple animals such as sponges, in the middle of the scale were such animals of intermediate complexity as fish, reptiles, and birds, and at the top were humans. The *scala naturae* had its origins in a concern with organization of the biological world, but, as Hodos and Campbell (1969) point out, it also had theological ramifications in which God was perfect, angels somewhat less perfect, humans more imperfect, and so on down the scale to such formless blobs as the sponge. Too, the *scala naturae* was seemingly compatible with Charles Darwin's biological theory of evolution, in which animals were seen on a continuum, evolving from simple to complex. This conception of evolution was consistent with the traditional view of learning because the belief in general laws was complemented by a belief in general biological processes.

Another thrust of the traditional view of learning, usually unverbalized, was that instinct, or the genetic determinants of behavior, mattered little. Instinct as a topic has had an uneven history in psychology, with its lowest point being a facile process in which every aspect of behavioral activity was explained by an instinct that determined it. There was an instinct for eating, playing, smiling, fighting, and so on, and instinct psychology fell into low repute because behavior was being explained by naming it. Behaviorism, or stimulus-response psychology as it is so often called, was given its first strong statement by John B. Watson (Watson, 1913), and as it became a powerful influence on the American psychological scene there was an elevation of learning to the top of psychology's scientific hierarchy and a downgrading of instinct. Behaviorism was a scientific philosophy of environmentalism, in which behavior was controlled by environmental circumstances and learning was the mechanism of adjustment to the environment. In the long-running nature-nurture controversy, nurture won for behaviorism. If pressed, a staunch behaviorist might have admitted that genetics was a determinant of certain features of behavior, such as the primary drives of hunger and thirst, and the senses, but learning was master and pursuit of the general laws of learning was a prime goal of experimental psychology. The result was thousands of experiments on rats and pigeons in standardized laboratory apparatuses such as Skinner boxes, with the confidence that general laws of learning would someday emerge. The observing of rats and pigeons, or any other animal, for that matter, outside the laboratory where they normally live was virtually unheard of. This was not a misspent emphasis because many important behavioral regularities were uncovered, as we saw in preceding chapters.

Learning and instinct

Somewhat parallel with American behaviorism was a scientific study called *ethology*, which was centered in Europe (e.g., Tinbergen, 1951; Eibl-Eibesfeldt, 1975). Ethologists are one kind of zoologist, and their scientific interest is the unconstrained behavior of animals in their natural settings. Each scientist observes phenomena that will yield regularities that are important to him or her, and for the ethologist it is behavior in the natural, free setting, just as it is the restricted, controlled laboratory setting for the behaviorist. Instinct rather than learning is the focus of ethology. Ethologists give much of their attention to *fixed action patterns*, which are relatively stereotyped, complex behavioral sequences that are triggered by *sign stimuli* and are independent of experience. Fixed action patterns have strong genetic determinants, are the same within a species, and are usually different between species. Ranging far beyond the rat and the pigeon, ethologists have observed a generous portion of the animal kingdom and have seen a rich array of fixed action patterns that exist at the time of the animal's birth, or come to exist with maturation, and all without learning. Without denying learning, the ethologists found a central place for the genetic determinants of behavior that are shaped by forces defined by Darwin's theory of biological evolution.

Evolution theory says that organisms are modified by change in the genetic composition of the species and natural selection. Genetic combinations emerge by mating, rarely by mutation, which is a fundamental alteration of gene structure. Gene variability gives variability in the characteristics of a species, and natural selection operates on this variability to produce characteristics that help in the struggle for existence. Life is hard, and members of a species compete in a brutish struggle for food, water, survival against enemies, etc. Members of the species who have the most favorable characteristics emerge victorious in the competition and are naturally selected to breed new generations who also will tend to have good survival characteristics, and so on. It is "survival of the fittest," as the classic phrase has it, and the important thing to remember is that behavior is every bit as important for survival as anatomical characteristics. It is important for evolution to have produced a long neck for the giraffe so that it can reach the high leaves of trees on the African plains where it lives, but it is also important for the evolutionary processes to give it the behavior to flee the leopards that lurk in wait for it. A newborn giraffe must have an instant, unlearned capability to flee if it is to survive. Certainly giraffes would be doomed if the fleeing behavior was dependent upon a gradual learning process.

Concern with instinct in modern American psychology came late. In 1950 the American comparative psychologist, Frank A. Beach, published a prophetic article (Beach, 1950) that suggested a usefulness of the ethological approach, but it aroused only minor attention at the time because the learning-centered view was so strong in experimental psychology. It was not until some years later when Breland and Breland (1961) published an article entitled "The Misbehavior of Organisms" that American psychologists began to have cautious second thoughts about the traditional view that had dominated for so long. The Brelands were putting their psychological skills to work in training animals for zoos, television commercials, and commercial exhibits. The nature of their work required them to train a variety of animals, and they found that the "general laws" of learning from laboratory work with the rat and pigeon were not as general as they had surmised.

One of their projects was the teaching of raccoons to pick up coins and deposit them in a small box. The raccoon has "hands" like a primate, and it seemed a simple matter to reinforce it with food for putting coins in the container. Teaching it to pick up one coin and deposit it in the box was easy enough, but trouble came when the problem was changed to picking up and depositing two coins. The raccoon would not let go of the coins. Instead, its time was spent in rubbing the coins together and dipping them into the container. This seemingly eccentric behavior produced no reinforcement, and it would seem that nonreinforcement would extinguish the behavior, but not so. The rubbing behavior became worse and worse until the project had to be abandoned. In a similar project the Brelands set to train a pig to drop large wooden coins in a "piggy bank." The coins were placed several feet from the bank and the pig was required to carry them to the bank and deposit them. A partial reinforcement schedule of one reinforcement for four or five coins deposited was used, and the pig readily learned the act. But as the training regime progressed the pig's behavior degenerated. The coin would be picked up well enough, but on the way to the bank the pig would drop the coin, root it, toss it up in the air, root it along, and so on. This problem behavior might have been dismissed as the unknown peculiarities of a particular pig, but it was found in other pigs as well.

The Brelands came to the conclusion that the behavior of these animals represented a failure of learning theory—the animals simply did not do what they were trained to do. The particular behaviors to which these animals drifted were examples of instinctive food-getting behavior which no training could overcome. The raccoon exhibited its well-known "washing behavior," and the rooting behavior of pigs is known to the most casual visitor of a farm. The Brelands did not throw out the learning principles that they were trying to use, for that would have been hasty, but they did conclude that the rejection of instinct has weakened the psychologists power to predict and control behavior.

Evidence for biological constraints on learning

There is a wealth of data to consider once one begins to face the issue of unlearned, instinctive behavior (e.g., Bolles, 1970, 1971, 1973; Eibl-Eibesfeldt, 1975; Hinde, 1969; Hinde and Stevenson-Hinde, 1973; Hodos and Campbell, 1969; Seligman, 1970; Scott, 1967), and the theoretical thrust of these data is to urge a reappraisal of the traditional view about general laws of learning. The traditional view has established opinions about stimuli, responses and the reinforcers that associate them, and all of this becomes attenuated when instinct enter the picture.

Stimulus specificity It is the traditional view that all stimuli bombarding the senses have equal potentiality for response until learning operations give some stimuli control over behavior and deny it to others. This view has truth in it, but it is also true that evolution has tuned some receptors for a highly selective reaction to stimuli. Some aspects of the impinging stimulus energy fire an adaptive response and others do not. Hinde (1969, p. 43) cites von Uexküll's observation about the mated female tick who climbs to the top of a bush so that mammals can rush beneath her. She can hang there for a month ignoring all stimuli until she smells butyric acid, a product of mammalian skin glands and the sign of a blood meal. Out of the rich variety of stimuli that impinge on her senses, she has her neural circuitry tuned by evolution to respond only when food is signaled. "Like a gourmet who picks the raisins out of the cake," von Uexküll said.

Evolutionary forces also shape selective reactions through learning by making it easier to learn some responses to stimuli than others. It is critical for movement in the visual field to connote danger and for the animal to be able to learn various avoidance responses. On the other hand, there is little adaptive value in stomach upset becoming associated with visual movement because movement can hardly ever be the cause of the upset; but it is important for flavors to become associated with illness so that avoidance can be learned, and this is especially important for such animals as the rat, which has poor vision and would have trouble discerning whatever distinctive visual features that poisons sometimes have. If evolution is a factor in behavior, then natural selection should cause some responses to be associated more readily with certain classes of stimuli than others as a way of optimizing survival. Garcia and Koelling (1966) did an experiment that demonstrated just this phenomenon, and discounted the traditional view that any response can be learned to any stimulus.

Garcia and Koelling trained one group of rats to drink "bright, noisy water," which was accomplished by a drinkometer that detected the contact of a rat's tongue with the water outlet. Whenever the rat licked the spout, the circuitry of the drinkometer produced a flash of light and click of an electrical relay. Another group was given flavored water containing saccharin. Each group was then divided in half, with one half having electric shock (externally produced pain) following drinking and the other half made ill by the administration of X rays (internally produced pain). They were subsequently tested with either bright, noisy water or the saccharin water, and the results are shown in Figure 7–1. Notice that the X-ray punishment inhibited drinking only when the stimulus was saccharin water, not bright, noisy water. The converse was

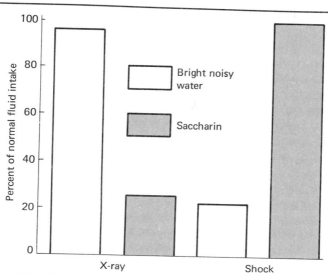

Source: S. Revusky, and J. Garcia. Learned associations over long delays. In G. H. Bower (Ed.), *The psychology of learning and motivation* (Vol. 4). New York: Academic Press, 1970, pp. 1–84. Reprinted by permission of Academic Press, Inc.

FIGURE 7–1

Evidence that the consequences of responding determine the stimuli that come to control the response.

true for shock punishment; only the bright, noisy water inhibited drinking. As Garcia and Koelling (1966, p. 124) said: "The cues, which the animal selects from the welter of stimuli in the learning situation, appear to be related to the consequences of the subsequent reinforcer." Electric shock is an external punishment which can be associated with external stimuli and internal discomfort can be associated with taste cues, but not vice versa.

The Garcia and Koelling experiment might suggest that illness cannot be associated with visual stimuli, but it seems more likely that this is a special feature which evolution has given the rat in deference to its poor vision, highly developed senses of taste and smell, and nocturnal feeding habits. Animals with superior visual equipment that rely on vision in seeking food and drink can learn to avoid ingesting substances that are distinctive in appearance only. Wilcoxon, Dragoin, and Kral (1971) compared rats and bobwhite quail, a bird with a high quality visual system. Both learned to avoid flavored water when it had been followed by illness induced by a drug, but only the quail learned to avoid distinctively colored water that had been associated with illness.

Taste aversion and the problem of punishment delay   One of the longstanding beliefs of psychologists who advocate general laws of behavior is that delivery of positive reinforcement or punishment immediately after the occurrence of a response is most effective, and that effectiveness is decreased with delay of only a few seconds. The limits of delay, in which no effect occurs at all, were probably not established to everyone's satisfaction, but it appeared to be no more than seconds for positive reinforcement (Kimble, 1961) and a minute or two for punishment (Cairns and Perkins, 1972). But suppose that delay of punishment measured in hours was found to be effective in suppressing a response? One would have to suppose that something special was going on, perhaps special enough to threaten one's belief in the general principle about delay of positive reinforcement and punishment that has prevailed for so long. Such is what happened in the field of taste aversion. The previous section described an experiment by Garcia and Koelling (1966) in which animals made sick with X rays inhibited their drinking of saccharin-flavored water. They had an aversion to the taste of it because the saccharin became associated with the sickness as punishment. In a taste aversion experiment with delay, hours can intervene between the response and the sickness.

Taste aversion experiments by Revusky (1968) show how response suppression can occur even after delays measured in hours between response and sickness. The drinking of sucrose solution (sugar water) by rats was the response to be influenced by sickness induced by X-ray radiation. The radiation was administered to various groups of animals 3.5–32 hours after drinking the sucrose. An aversion to the drinking of sucrose solution was found for delays up to 4–8 hours when comparisons with control animals were made. Another experiment has reported taste aversion with delay as long as 13.5 hours (Andrews and Bravemen, 1975).

Psychologists have long thought that they had a general law about delay of positive reinforcement and punishment, but now they were faced with a big exception. Today, in a more biological atmosphere, it is argued that the effectiveness of very long delays in taste aversion experiments cannot be understood without considering the survival advantages of being able to learn over long delays. The animal that learns to avoid eating things that make it sick, whether the delay is short or long, will live longer. Evolutionary processes have shaped a process that contributes to survival of the animal.

A search is in progress for stimulus dimensions that may bridge the long delay with their distinctive, persistent characteristics (Nachman, Rauschenberger, and Ashe, 1977). The reason the search is important is that it asks whether the old law about the importance of short delay of positive reinforcement and punishment should be abandoned in favor of a principle derived from biological and survival considerations. For example, if sucrose solution has an aftertaste that lasts for hours, then aspects of sucrose are present at the time of the sickness, and so the delay is zero, not hours. If this is so, then the biologically based argument is weakened and the old principle stands. Nachman (1970) found that rats could develop a significant aversion to tap water with delays of as much as four hours between drinking and sickness. It seems unlikely that water could have an aftertaste that persists for four hours.

Avoidance behavior   Additional evidence that any response cannot be learned in any situation is avoidance behavior in rats. As we saw in Chapter 6, the rat has been a principal vehicle for the study of punishment and fear, and we have learned a great deal from it. But Chapter 6, like the chapters that preceded it, carried the implication that any response can be learned in any situation, and this implication must now be qualified: There are avoidance situations which rats learn poorly if at all. The occasional failure of avoidance behavior in rats has appeared in the research literature from time to time as a puzzling item. In 1956, Solomon and Brush observed:

> We somehow assume that it is *natural* for organisms to "anticipate" noxious events in an "adaptive" fashion. But it is only after we set up certain special types of environmental event sequences that the avoidance phenomenon emerges. Failure of subjects to learn to avoid are *not* rare, but they are less apt to be reported in scientific papers than are the successes.

And the conditions surrounding failures to learn to avoid are as instructive to the investigator, in many cases, as are the optimum conditions for producing avoidance phenomenon. [1]

Only with the recent interest in biological constraints on learning has this phenomenon come into focus.

Meyer, Cho, and Wesemann (1960) puzzled about the failure of rats to avoid shock by pressing a bar. Their experimental situation was a standard one. A light was the CS and shock was the UCS, and if the animal pressed the bar between light onset and shock onset the light was turned out and the punishing shock was avoided. They had instances of rats being unable to learn this simple avoidance task in several thousands of trials, and it was difficult to understand because they knew that rats could learn avoidance in a running wheel in less than 100 trials (Mote, 1940). And in Chapter 6 we saw the avoidance learning of other locomotor acts. Their puzzlement took the form of two questions. If light produces fear and pressing the bar eliminates the light and the fear, how can avoidance learning fail? Why is the particular form of the response important, with avoidance failing for bar pressing and succeeding with a running response?

Using about the same bar-pressing task as Meyer and his associates, D'Amato and Schiff (1964) also were frustrated in teaching rats to avoid. They ran three experiments. In Experiment I they administered 1,080 avoidance training trials and only two out of eight rats conditioned to any appreciable extent. In Experiment II, after 7,330 trials, only four out of eight attained a reasonable level of performance. In Experiment III, after 1,082 trials, one of eight animals learned to avoid.

Bolles (1969) attacked the question of response form and its relevance for avoidance learning. He found that rats would readily learn a running response to avoid but not one of rearing up and standing on the hind legs. Bolles (1970, 1971, 1973) has been an active analyst of biological constraints on learning, and he interpreted his findings as evidence of *species-specific behavior*, which is another name for instinctive behavior. An animal will learn an avoidance response if the response is consistent with natural defensive reactions that are part of the animal's innate endowment. Running is such a response for a rat. It runs when it is afraid and does not lurch forward and press bars or rear up and stand on its hind legs.

Boice (1970) found avoidance learning of frogs and toads in a shuttle-box task (electric shock as the UCS, opening of a guillotine door as the CS) to be directly proportional to their natively endowed activity level in the natural setting. The leopard frog and the spadefoot

---

[1] M. R. Jones (Ed.), *Nebraska symposium on motivation.* Lincoln: University of Nebraska Press, 1956, pp. 215–216. Reprinted by permission of the University of Nebraska Press.

toad are decidedly passive, the green frog is moderately active, and the Woodhouse toad is very active. The leopard frog and the spadefoot toad showed no avoidance responding, the green frog showed only a little, and the Woodhouse toad showed substantial avoidance learning. The toad can be extremely efficient in avoidance learning if a response is chosen that is particularly relevant to survival in its natural environment. Using the Southern toad's eating response for study and bumblebees as food, Brower and Brower (1962) found that it took only one or two experiences for the toad to learn that bumblebees are noxious. Contrast this swift avoidance learning to Boice's spadefoot toads who could not learn to avoid in the shuttle box task. Findings such as these would be considered mysterious if the animal's behavior in the natural environment was not included in the explanation.

In an open environment rats are known to show *positive thigmotaxis*, or the tendency to remain in contact with objects, like remaining close to a wall while running from one point to another. Grossen and Kelley (1972) hypothesized that this thigmotactic tendency was a species-specific defensive reaction because such predators as birds would have a harder time attacking a rat that was hugging a wall. To test the hypothesis, they asked if rats would become more thigmotactic under defensive motivation. Their apparatus was a large box with an electrifiable grid floor, and the thigmotactic behavior was defined as amount of time spent in contact with the box wall. A 30-minute no-shock session was followed by a 30-minute session of periodic shocks, with the wall-hugging behavior measured throughout. The rats exhibited thigmotactic behavior 67 percent of the time in the no-shock session and 91 percent of the time in the shock session. In a second experiment they asked if rats would learn an avoidance response faster if it capitalized on the thigmotactic tendency. The same apparatus was used as before, and the avoidance response was jumping on a small platform. The platform was placed either in the center of the box or along the wall, and they reasoned that the avoidance response would be learned more readily when the platform was along the wall because it would be consistent with a rat's defensive behavior. One group of rats had the platform along the wall, another had it in the center, and a third had platforms in both positions and had a choice between them. The rat was placed in the box and given ten seconds to make the avoidance response before being shocked. The group with the platform at the wall avoided on 77 percent of the trials, while the group with the platform in the center avoided only 57 percent of the time. The group given choice chose the platform along the wall 92 percent of the time. A third experiment essentially repeated the second one except that the animals were reinforced with food for jumping onto the platform. In this case there were no differences between the three groups, indicating that the behavior shown in the first two experiments was particularly associated with defensive reactions. Here again we have data that are much clearer when we take into account the species-specific behavior of the animal.

How learning influences instincts The previous section said that instinctive behavior patterns influence the learning of a response. Instinctive behavior is defined as response sequences that are genetically endowed and independent of experience. The point of this section is that instinctive response sequences can rely on learning for their refinement.

Hailman (1969) describes the eating behavior of the chick of the common laughing gull, which breeds on the eastern shore of North America. The sequence begins with the parent lowering its head and pointing its beak downward in front of the chick. As a form of begging behavior, or so it appears, the chick pecks at the bill, grasps the parent's bill in its own, and strokes it downward. With repetitions of this sequence, the parent regurgitates partly digested food and the chick eats it. Hailman studied the accuracy with which the chick pecks the bill of the parent. If the instinctive sequence is fully formed at birth, independent of experience, then the chick should be as accurate at birth as it ever will be. In tests, however, Hailman found that only one third of the pecks of newly hatched chicks struck the parent's bill, but after two days the percentage rose to 75 percent. Experience is a factor in refining instinctual behavior.

A young squirrel, inexperienced at nut cracking, will gnaw randomly at a nut until it breaks at some place. Eibl-Eibesfeldt (1975) points out that the experienced squirrel goes about the task differently, and efficiently. It cuts a broad furrow down the side of the nut from top to bottom, and maybe on the other side of the nut also. The lower teeth are then inserted into the crack and the nut breaks into halves. Here again, experience is a factor in behavior that is basically instinctual.

Imprinting

Imprinting is a fascinating case of learning because it occurs only in a narrow time span for the newly born animal. *Imprinting* is the learning of an identification and following response—a kind of social attachment by exposure to a stimulus, and it is learning that can occur at only one period in an animal's lifetime. Imprinting did not escape the attention of Sir Thomas More who reported it in his book *Utopia* published in 1518 (see Kevan, 1976). Over 100 years ago, in 1873, D. A. Spalding (Spalding, reprinted, 1954) gave an account of imprinting that anticipated modern research:

Chickens as soon as they are able to walk will follow any moving object. And, when guided by sight alone, they seem to have no more disposition to follow a hen than to follow a duck, or a human being. Unreflecting onlookers, when they saw chickens a day old running after me, and older ones following me miles and answering to my whistle, imagined that I must have some occult power over the creatures, whereas I simply allowed them to follow me from the first.

The more contemporary research of Hess (1959) puts imprinting on a firm experimental footing and illustrates it nicely.

Hess used wild mallard ducks as his experimental subjects. The eggs were hatched in an incubator and the newly born ducks were kept in a small box until the imprinting experience, which was conducted with the apparatus shown in Figure 7–2. Following time intervals ranging from 1 to 32 hours after birth, the young mallard was put in the imprinting apparatus with a decoy model of a male duck which moved along a circular runway and gave out with duck-like sounds. This procedure

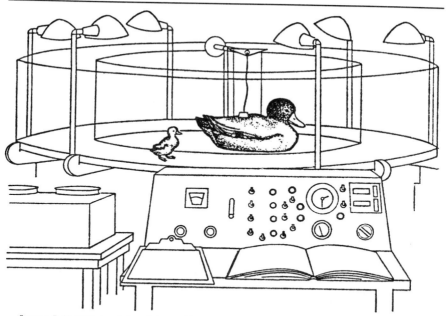

Source: E. H. Hess, Imprinting. *Science*, 1959, *130*, 133–141. Reprinted by permission of the American Association for the Advancement of Science.

FIGURE 7–2

Apparatus used for the imprinting of ducklings. A duckling was given systematic exposure to the decoy as it moved around the runway.

148

went on for about an hour, after which the duckling was returned to the incubator and subsequently tested. The test was four discrimination tests, in which the duckling had to chose between the male mallard model and a female model which differed from the male in its coloration. The male model gave the same duck-like sound as before and the female model emitted a recording of the actual call of a mallard female calling her young. The duckling was released between the two models who were four feet apart and the interest was in the one it chose. The four tests were: both models stationary and silent; both models stationary and calling; the male stationary and the female calling; and the male stationary and silent and the female moving and calling. The percentage of times which the duckling chose the male model on all four tests is shown in Figure 7–3 as a function of the time between birth and the imprinting experience. Notice how critical that time is as a variable for learning. Imprinting in the duckling is only possible in a narrow span of hours after birth.

It is not necessary that the imprinted object resemble the species of the young subject. Hinde, Thorpe, and Vince (1956) imprinted coots and moorhens to follow a box or a man, just as if it were the mother, although not all stimuli imprint with equal effectiveness (Bateson, 1973, p. 102). Hess (1959, p. 140) was the imprinting stimulus for a jungle fowl cock and succeeded in alienating its affections. Even after five years it was attracted to humans and had nothing to do with the female of its species. A lay person looks affectionately at an animal mother and its baby following along and speaks of infant love of the mother, but maybe there is nothing more involved than the mother being present during the critical imprinting period. Infant devotion or not, the baby

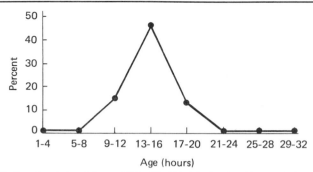

Source: E. H. Hess, Imprinting. *Science*, 1959, *130*, 133–141. Reprinted by permission of the American Association for the Advancement of Science.

FIGURE 7–3

In a choice discrimination test, percent of time that ducklings chose the imprinted decoy as a function of time between birth and the imprinting experience.

that is imprinted by its mother and stays close to it greatly enhances its chances of survival.

As with any behavioral phenomenon, there are a number of variables involved in imprinting, and the underlying processes are not understood very well (Sluckin, 1965; Bateson, 1973). Nor do all species imprint with equal efficiency. Hess (1959, p. 140) reports that some species visually imprint poorly if at all. For example, Hess was unable to visually imprint the wood duck with the same success as the mallard. Klopfer (1959), however, cautions that the behavior of the species in its natural environment must be considered if we are to determine the conditions of imprinting. The mallard lives in open nests, and natural selection would tune it for responsiveness to visual stimuli. The wood duck, on the other hand, lives in holes in trees, and imprinting to auditory stimuli would be most adaptive for it. Presumably Hess would have had more luck with the wood duck if an auditory pattern such as a duck call had been used as the imprinting stimulus.

Chapter 4 examined the various theories of positive reinforcement, and why some events reinforce a response and others do not. The investigators of imprinting have turned up another line of evidence that reinforcement theorists should weigh because the investigators have found that a stimulus presented to a young animal in the critical period can subsequently be used as a reinforcer in an instrumental learning situation. Hoffman et al. (1966) pioneered this line of research. Ducklings were the subjects, and the imprinting stimulus was a white plastic milk bottle moving along a track. There were six imprinting sessions in the first two days after hatching, which the investigators estimated was the critical imprinting period for them. The remaining ducklings had the same amount of imprinting, but were not exposed during the critical imprinting period. The response to be learned was key-pecking. One test was made in the imprinting sessions and one during the key-pecking sessions. The test during the imprinting sessions determined if the ducklings would follow the milk bottle as it moved by them, as an imprinted duckling would follow its mother. The other test asked if a duckling that was shown the moving milk bottle for 12 seconds as reinforcement after it pecked the key would learn key-pecking. The results were that only the ducklings imprinted in the critical early period followed the milk bottle and learned key-pecking. Those ducklings with late imprinting did neither.

Broad implications for laws of learning

The implications of this chapter are that the traditional view of learning which seeks general laws of learning that sweep across animals, responses, and stimuli must be revised. The adaptive pressures of the environment cause genetic differences between behaviors within a specie and between species, as Darwin's theory of evolution said, and these innate differences undermine transcendent laws of learning. Darwin's theory has been with us for over 100 years, and the scientific study of learning for a bit more than half of that. How could the psychology of learning have missed the implications of Darwin's exquisite scientific achievement? Where did the psychology of learning go wrong? There are three main influences that obscured learning's scientific vision, and although they have been mentioned earlier in this chapter they bear mentioning again for the sake of summary and elaboration.

First was the powerful influence of behaviorism on the American scene. Its environmentalism gave experimental psychology in the United States a powerful interest in learning. The concern with environmentalism and learning was so strong that it led to cursory dismissal of innate influences on learning. The pursuit of environmentalism has not been an empty scientific effort because environmental variables are obviously of enormous significance and we have learned a great deal about them under behaviorism's flag.

Second, the psychology of learning was enamored with models from the physical sciences which have wide, general laws; we saw a science of behavior that eventually would have the same form as physics and chemistry. That we should envy success and seek it for ourselves is understandable, but perhaps our efforts were too imitative. There is no necessity for lawfulness to have the same form in different sciences, and perhaps we should have been more sensitive to the special direction that behavioral laws might take. Physics and chemistry have nothing like evolution that would restrict the generality of their laws.

Third has been the false belief in the phylogenetic scale. Whatever touch the psychology of learning has had with evolution theory has been here, and it has been wrong. Hodos and Campbell (1969) see the problem as one of mistaking the phylogenetic scale with the *phylogenetic tree*. The phylogenetic scale is our ordering of organisms according to their complexity as we see it, much as Aristotle did. Thus, we rank the rat, the monkey, and the human in order of increasing complexity, and then we impose evolution theory on the order as a unifying explanation. Furthermore, we study the rat and the monkey and assume the findings have relevance for the human because they are ordered in a hierarchy bonded by evolution theory. What is wrong with this thinking is that it is the biological world as we see it, not necessarily as it is. The phylogenetic tree is the empirical estimate of the biological world as it is, based on the data of paleontology and comparative morphology. The phylogenetic scale has an order and continuity that we give to it; the phylogenetic tree has discontinuities and independent lines of evolutionary development that nature gives to it. Figure 7–4 is a phylogenetic

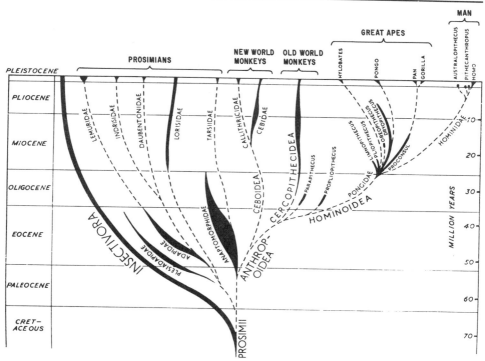

Source: J. Z. Young, *The life of vertebrates.* 2d ed. Oxford: Clarendon Press, 1962. Reprinted by permission of the Clarendon Press.

FIGURE 7–4

Phylogenetic tree showing the probable time of origin and relationships of primates.

tree of primate lines. Monkeys have their linkages to humans in the far past, but the most striking thing about them is their independent lines of development; so anyone who studies monkeys as a route to understanding the human is playing a risky game. Biological adaptation to the demands of their environment has given monkeys physical and behavioral characteristics that is neither inferior not superior to other species but is simply adaptation to the environment. Monkeys may or may not have characteristics similar to man. As Scott (1967, p. 72) said:

> Subhuman primates are not small human beings with fur coats and (sometimes) long tails. Rather they are a group which has diversified in many ways, so that they are different from each other as are bears, dogs, and raccoons in the order Carnivora. The fact that an animal is a primate therefore does not automatically mean that its behavior has special relevance to human behavior.[2]

[2] *Annual Review of Psychology*, 1967, Vol. 18, p. 72. Reprinted by permission of Annual Reviews, Inc.

152

Henry Beston (1928), in his book *The Outermost House*, said it in the special way that gifted writers have:

> Remote from universal nature, and living by complicated artifice, man in civilization surveys the creature through the glass of his knowledge and sees thereby a feather magnified and the whole image in distortion. We patronize them for their incompleteness, for their tragic fate of having taken form so far below ourselves. And therein we err, and greatly err. For the animal shall not be measured by man. In a world older and more complete than ours they move finished and complete, gifted with extensions of the senses we have lost or never attained, living by voices we shall never hear. They are not brethren, they are not underlings; they are other nations, caught with ourselves in the net of life and time, fellow prisoners of the splendour and travail of the earth.[3]

What is the future of law and theory in the psychology of learning? The neglect of evolution and the innate determinants of behavior is a significant omission, and it must be remedied. Lockard (1971, p. 172) believes that the answer lies in adoption of evolution theory as the "one great theoretical principle that unites all of behavior." Lockard is correct in implying that we must embrace evolution more warmly than before, but he oversteps when he dismisses learning almost entirely (p. 174) and says that it is not the key to animal behavior because most behavior is not acquired. There is truth in this statement, particularly if one has a biologist's view of the animal kingdom, which is mostly insects. Lockard says that most behavior is instinctive. But what this viewpoint ignores is that evolution gave many, many animals, including some insects (Eibl-Eibesfeldt, 1975, chap. 13; Hinde, 1973, p. 9), the power of plasticity, or *learning*. If evolution is master as Lockard says, then evolutionary processes must have recognized the environment as an inconstant, uncertain place, and the animals that can readily cope with its new events and relationships through learning have a marvelous adaptive mechanism. Indeed, learning is the supreme adaptive mechanism, and we should see it as evolution's finest achievement. Learning is not something to be replaced by biology and evolution but to be reconciled with it.

Accommodation must be made to evolutionary influences on behavior, and one possible direction is to accept evolutionary determinants of the myriad units of behavior for over a million species on earth and proceed to study and record them. These behavioral elements could have independent genetic determinants, and so there would be a nearly infinite number of behavior elements to investigate, without hope for or attempts at integration. Libraries of disconnected facts and descriptions

---

[3] H. Beston, *The outermost house.* New York: Holt, Rinehart & Winston, 1928, p. 25. Reprinted by permission of Holt, Rinehart and Winston, Inc.

would be produced. Psychology would have some lawfulness and predictive power under these circumstances but of a low order.

A more reasonable approach is to believe that any science worthy of the name must have laws and theory of some generality and, while the great dreamed-of generalizations of yesteryear may not be achievable, laws of some limited generality probably are. Many animals have common environmental problems and have comparable drives to satisfy, and it is likely that laws can be found for these communalities. Principles of positive reinforcement that mainly have been worked out on rats and pigeons are now regularly applied to human behavior under the heading "behavior modification" (Chapter 9). Principles of fear learning and extinction, from rats, pigeons, and dogs, have some success at the human level and are used for the treatment of fear under the name of "behavior therapy." Such generalizations across species give us hope for laws of some scope.

Biological constraints on learning are just that—constraints. They are not the destroyers of laws of learning but the framework within which learning operates. Within these constraints laws of learning of some generality can be found. The early faith that any animal can learn any response to any stimulus is in doubt. A more viable faith may be that many animals can learn many responses to many stimuli, and we can find the laws that relate them. Biology can be a source for explanation when we apply a law and, say, find that one species learns slowly and another rapidly even though the same law is at work. And, biology will help us understand why a law breaks down and has the limits that it does.

Summary

The traditional view of the laws of learning has physics as the model, in which laws of very wide scope are possible. Psychology has assumed that a law of learning will specify the conditions under which any organism can learn any response to any stimulus. The present evidence is that biological factors restrict the scope of behavioral laws. Instinctive response patterns can interfere with an arbitrary response that has been selected for learning. For example, evolution has endowed the rat with positive thigmotaxis, which is the tendency to remain close to objects and avoid open spaces, and it is a factor when the behavior being learned involves movement in open spaces and with respect to objects. Another example of biological constraints is imprinting, in which certain responses can be learned only at a specific time in an organism's life.

Today we have doubts about general laws of learning. Some generality is undoubtedly possible, but biological constraints will define limitations on the stimuli that can come to control responses through learning, on the responses that can be learned, and on the organisms that can learn them.

References

Andrews, E. A., & Braveman, N. S. The combined effects of dosage level and interstimulus interval on the formation of one-trial poison-based aversions in rats. *Animal Learning & Behavior,* 1975, *3,* 287–289.

Bateson, P. P. G. Internal influences on early learning in birds. In R. A. Hinde and J. Stevenson-Hinde (Eds.), *Constraints on learning.* New York: Academic Press, 1973, pp. 101–116.

Beach, F. A. The snark was a boojum. *American Psychologist,* 1950, *5,* 115–124.

Beston, H. *The outermost house.* New York: Holt, Rinehart & Winston, 1928.

Boice, R. Avoidance learning in active and passive frogs and toads. *Journal of Comparative and Physiological Psychology,* 1970, *70,* 154–156.

Bolles, R. C. Avoidance and escape learning: Simultaneous acquisition of different responses. *Journal of Comparative and Physiological Psychology,* 1969, *68,* 355–358.

Bolles, R. C. Species-specific defense reactions and avoidance learning. *Psychological Review,* 1970, *77,* 32–48.

Bolles, R. C. Species-specific defense reactions. In F. R. Brush (Ed.), *Aversive conditioning and learning.* New York: Academic Press, 1971, pp. 183–233.

Bolles, R. C. The comparative psychology of learning: The selective association principle and some problems with "general" laws of learning. In G. Bermant (Ed.), *Perspectives on animal behavior.* Glenview: Scott, Foresman, 1973, pp. 280–306.

Breland, K., & Breland, M. The misbehavior of organisms. *American Psychologist,* 1961, *16,* 681–684.

Brower, L. P., & Brower, J. V. Z. Investigations into mimicry. *Natural History,* April 1962, 8–19.

Cairns, G. F., Jr., & Perkins, C. C., Jr. Delay of punishment and choice behavior in the rat. *Journal of Comparative and Physiological Psychology,* 1972, *79,* 438–442.

D'Amato, M. R., & Schiff, D. Long-term discriminated avoidance performance in the rat. *Journal of Comparative and Physiological Psychology,* 1964, *57,* 123–126.

Eibl-Eibesfeldt, I. *Ethology: The biology of behavior.* Second Edition. New York: Holt, Rinehart & Winston, 1975. (E. Klinghammer translation).

Garcia, J., & Koelling, R. A. Relation of cue to consequence in avoidance learning. *Psychonomic Science,* 1966, *4,* 123–124.

Grossen, N. E., & Kelley, M. J. Species-specific behavior and acquisition of avoidance behavior in rats. *Journal of Comparative and Physiological Psychology,* 1972, *81,* 307–310.

Hailman, J. P. How an instinct is learned. *Scientific American,* 1969, *221,* December, 98–106.

Hess, E. H. Imprinting. *Science,* 1959, *130,* 133–141.

Hinde, R. A. *Animal behaviour.* New York: McGraw–Hill, 1969.

Hinde, R. A. Constraints on learning—An introduction to the problems. In R. A. Hinde & J. Stevenson–Hinde (Eds.), *Constraints on learning.* New York: Academic Press, 1973, pp. 1–19.

Hinde, R. A., & Stevenson-Hinde, J. (Eds.). *Constraints on learning.* New York: Academic Press, 1973.

Hinde, R. A., Thorpe, W. H., & Vince, M. A. The following response of young coots and moorhens. *Behaviour,* 1956, *9,* 214–242.

Hodos, W., & Campbell, C. B. G. Scala naturae: Why there is no theory in comparative psychology. *Psychological Review,* 1969, *76,* 337–350.

Hoffman, H. S., Searle, J. L., Toffey, S., & Kozma, F., Jr. Behavioral control by an imprinted stimulus. *Journal of the Experimental Analysis of Behavior,* 1966, *9,* 177–189.

Kevan, P. G. Sir Thomas More on imprinting: Observations from the sixteenth century. *Animal Behaviour,* 1976, *24,* 16–17.

Kimble, G. A. *Hilgard and Marquis' conditioning and learning.* Second Edition. New York: Appleton-Century-Crofts, 1961.

Klopfer, P. H. Imprinting. *Science,* 1959, *130,* 730.

Lockard, R. B. Reflections on the fall of comparative psychology: Is there a message for us all? *American Psychologist,* 1971, *26,* 168–179.

Meyer, D. R., Cho, C., & Wesemann, A. F. On problems of conditioning discriminated lever-press avoidance responses. *Psychological Review,* 1960, *67,* 224–228.

Mote, F. A. Correlations between conditioning and maze learning in the white rat. *Journal of Comparative Psychology,* 1940, *30,* 197–219.

Nachman, M. Learned taste and temperature aversions due to lithium chloride sickness after temporal delays. *Journal of Comparative and Physiological Psychology,* 1970, *73,* 22–30.

Nachman, M., Rauschenberger, J., & Ashe, J. H. Stimulus characteristics in food aversion learning. In N. W. Milgram, L. Krames, and T. M. Alloway (Eds.), *Food aversion learning.* New York: Plenum, 1977, pp. 105–131.

Revusky, S. H. Aversion to sucrose produced by contingent X-irradiation: Temporal and dosage parameters. *Journal of Comparative and Physiological Psychology,* 1968, *65,* 17–22.

Revusky, S., & Garcia, J. Learned associations over long delays. In G. H. Bower (Ed.), *The psychology of learning and motivation* (Vol. 4). New York: Academic Press, 1970, pp. 1–84.

Scott, J. P. Comparative psychology and ethology. *Annual Review of Psychology,* 1967, *18,* 65–86.

Seligman, M. E. P. On the generality of the laws of learning. *Psychological Review,* 1970, *77,* 406–418.

Sluckin, W. *Imprinting and early experience.* Chicago: Aldine, 1965.

Solomon, R. L., & Brush, E. S. Experimentally derived conceptions of anxiety and aversion. In M. R. Jones (Ed.), *Nebraska symposium on motivation.* Lincoln: University of Nebraska Press, 1956, pp. 213–305.

Spalding, D. A.   Instinct. *MacMillan's Magazine,* 1873. Reprinted in *British Journal of Animal Behavior,* 1954, 2, 2–11.

Tinbergen, N.   *The study of instinct.* Oxford: Clarendon Press, 1951.

Watson, J. B.   Psychology as the behaviorist views it. *Psychological Review,* 1913, 20, 158–177.

Wilcoxon, H. C., Dragoin, W. B., & Kral, P. A.   Illness-induced aversions in the rat and quail: Relative salience of visual and gustatory cues. *Science,* 1971, 171, 826–828.

Young, J. Z.   *The life of vertebrates* (2nd ed.). Oxford: Clarendon Press, 1962.

8

Animal and human verbal learning

THE CHAPTERS on positive reinforcement, classical conditioning, and punishment and fear were intended to express laws of learning for all kinds of responses, including verbal responses. Why, then, a chapter on verbal learning? There are three reasons. First, there is the enormous importance of language; how we learn, remember, and use it in thought has always been an important part of philosophy and psychology. Part II of this book is about memory, and it will underscore a preoccupation with verbal materials. Second, there are verbal learning ideas and methods that do not fit the ideas and methods often associated with animal learning, as explained in earlier chapters. Third, there is a lively interest today in animal language learning, particularly with chimpanzees. If animal language learning were merely teaching animals another response class such as bar pressing, then there would be no exceptional interest in it. It would appear, however, that animals can learn important dimensions of spoken language, and this discovery has changed our thinking about the intellectual capabilities of animals, the nature of similarities and differences between the human and animals, and the meaning of language communication. Because earlier chapters have mostly been devoted to animal behavior, there is transitional ease in beginning this chapter with animal language learning.

157

Animal language learning

Those who are unfamiliar with recent psychological literature, and even some who are familiar with it, will tell you that humans can talk and animals cannot. Common experience is one origin of this opinion because a dog does not engage us in conversation. Beyond common experience, the point of view is entrenched in Western civilization and has been held by great thinkers of ancient and modern times (Linden, 1976).

Plato, who lived about 400 B.C. in Greece, and his pupil Aristotle, saw the human as a creature of rationality and reason and the animal as a brute, perhaps a clever one sometimes, but a brute nevertheless who lived by the biological design that nature had given it. René Descartes, a 17th-century philosopher, echoed this classical view by asserting that humans alone have the power of reason, that animals were unthinking machines, and that language was part of the difference between the human and animals. Thus, as the ancients before Copernicus had seen the earth as the center of the universe with all revolving around it, so the human was preeminent in the biological world.

Charles Darwin and his theory of evolution took the human out of the center of the biological universe. His theory held that humans and animals have common lines of development and thus opened the possibility that humans and animals have more similarities than had been previously believed. This new scientific position eventually gave birth to comparative psychology that saw the behavior of the entire animal world as its domain, and it is not surprising that a challenge of the human's unique capability for language should come from it. Can a chimpanzee, it was asked, learn the essentials of our language? The human and the chimp have a biological connection somewhere in remote history. Even though different survival pressures have molded distinctive characteristics for each, it is also possible that common survival pressures could force a common need for communication and similar mechanisms for accomplishing it.

Speech is oral and language is symbolic, and so speech and language are not the same. Language is a code and, being a code, can be expressed in any number of mediums. Language expressed as speech develops in the human child through social contact with adults who are routinely using the language. The early attempts to cultivate language in the chimpanzee used this very human approach by raising the chimp as a child in a psychologist's home. Although these chimps learned many things and equalled or excelled human children in a number of ways, speech was not one of them (Kellogg, 1968). In the most notable attempt by the Hayses (Hayes and Nissen, 1971), the chimp learned to speak only seven words. The chimp has good sensory and intellectual capabilities with an intellect probably similar to that of the child when the child is learning its language (Hayes and Nissen, 1971); so why not speech and language? Limber (1977) lists four reasons:

1. *Vocal tract differences.* The chimp has a vocal apparatus (Lieberman, 1968; Lieberman, Klatt, and Wilson, 1969) that appears to prevent it from producing the full range of human speech sounds.
2. *Central nervous system differences.* Even if there were not vocal tract differences between the chimpanzee and the human, there may be differences in brain function that prevent the chimpanzee from having language and speech.
3. *Cognitive differences.* If language is the mapping of symbols on thought, then maybe the chimpanzee does poorly because it has little to say. Perhaps so, but chimpanzees are not incompetent. They have good capabilities for solving problems, and in learning, memory, the senses, and perception (Hayes and Nissen, 1971).
4. *Genetic predisposition for language.* Natural selection has designated the human and not the chimpanzee for language. We have a potential for language and the chimpanzee does not.

The breakthrough in our thinking about language learning in chimps came with the decision to abandon speech. To prove that the chimpanzee can learn the essentials of the English language does not require that it be turned into a junior version of a talking human. Speech is not the only way that language can be expressed. The deaf human does very well with his hands, and the chimpanzee has excellent motor capabilities also. This is the direction taken by the Gardners (Gardner and Gardner, 1971) with their chimp Washoe. They taught her American Sign Language, the language used by the deaf of North America. The deaf may sometimes finger-spell letters, but usually they produce signs that are manual symbols of words.

The other major investigators of language learning in the chimpanzee have abandoned speech also, but they do not use sign language. Premack (1971, 1976) taught his chimp Sarah with pieces of arbitrarily shaped plastic that were the words of the vocabulary. The pieces of plastic were backed with metal which adhered to a magnetized slate, and a sentence could be formed by assembling two or more of the pieces. Rumbaugh (Rumbaugh, 1977) has used symbols also, but with computer control of them for the training of his chimp Lana. The computer records all responses and dispenses reinforcement as prescribed.

These projects take years to complete because, like the human child, the chimpanzee learns language slowly. The details of all these projects cannot be covered here. Instead, only the Gardners' Washoe project will be examined in detail. The reason for focussing on Washoe is that the American Sign Language has special advantages for the study of language learning in the chimp. The advantages are mainly two: first, American Sign Language is a recognized language that linguists have formally analyzed. Working in an understood, acknowledged language is important when an issue can be one of deciding whether the chimp is actually using language or not. Second, American Sign Language is in the English language, and so the performance of the chimpanzee can be compared with the performance of our children. A good comparison is with young children who are learning the language just like the chimpanzee.

The American Sign Language was the only form of communication used with Washoe. Several teaching methods were used in learning the signs: reinforcement, imitation, and guidance, in which the experimenter demonstrated the sign by manipulating and shaping the hands and fingers of the chimpanzee into the proper positions. Because the chimpanzee moves a great deal so that sign-like behavior is going on all the time, and because even when they are learned the signs lack the refinement that a human can give it, there is the problem of knowing when a sign is learned. The Gardners established the strict criteria of having a new sign seen by three different observers and for it to occur on 15 consecutive days. By these criteria, Washoe learned 85 signs in three years and 132 signs in a little over four years. Many terms in a language are concepts, in which one word refers to many things. Many of Washoe's signs fulfilled the definition of a concept. Her sign for *more* was first used to ask for more tickling, but subsequently it was used for requesting more food, more drink, and more brushing. The sign *open* was first used for three particular doors, but then it came to be used for all doors, as well as for all containers and for the turning on of water faucets. Longer combinations of signs, sentences, began to emerge, such as *please tickle more*. In the first three years 245 different combinations of three or more signs were recorded.

Does Washoe use the English language and communicate with it as humans do? Attempts to teach language to chimpanzees has forced analysts to turn attention to a definition of language independent of speech so that the question of whether the chimpanzees have language or not can be faced. Linguists are not agreed on a definition of language, but there would not be much disagreement on the following:

1. Language is a set of signs that is used in communication.
2. There are a number of different signs that are the vocabulary.
3. The signs can be used symbolically, remote in time and space from events themselves.
4. Conceptual signs which apply to more than one object or situation are in the vocabulary.
5. An utterance is appropriate to a situation.
6. The signs can be combined into patterns (sentences) that have meaning beyond the signs. Novel sentences are possible, which

gives language "openness," as it has been called. The sentences are governed by rules, or syntax.

By these criteria, Washoe seems to approximate a language user, but there have been doubters (Bronowski and Bellugi, 1970; Lenneberg, 1971; Limber, 1977). Mostly the doubts are about the chimpanzee's ability to form sentences that are creative and novel; the chimpanzee is still seen by some as the brute that the ancients thought him to be. The chimpanzee may be clever and she may be capable of learning many things, but language as the human uses it is not among them.

The Gardners adopted a stance that sidesteps the difficulties of defining language and asking whether Washoe speaks it or not. They carefully recorded the language behavior of Washoe in such a way that it can be compared with the speech of children, and they made the comparison (Gardner and Gardner, 1975a) by using the findings of Brown (1968). Brown had obtained language data on three preschool children who were in the early stages of learning how to speak. The data compared were answers to *Wh* questions, which are questions that begin with such words as who, what, and where. Example questions and replies by Washoe were "Who you?" "Me Washoe." "What color?" "Bird white." Washoe used 91 different signs in reply to 500 questions. The Gardners concluded that if Washoe had been a preschool child "her replies to the *Wh* questions of this sample would place her at a relatively advanced level of linguistic competence." (Gardner and Gardner, 1975a, p. 255).

It is difficult to say how far the Gardners can take Washoe in language learning. Washoe had a rather late start. The training did not begin until she was one year old, and it took six months to teach her two signs, *come gimme* and *more*. An earlier start might have produced a much greater language proficiency. In response to this possibility, the Gardners (Gardner and Gardner, 1975b) acquired two newly born chimpanzees and began exposing them to American Sign Language 1–2 days after birth. At the age of six months one of the chimpanzees knew 15 signs and the other knew 13 signs. How much these new chimps can learn remains to be seen.

Human verbal learning

ASSOCIATIONISM

A good share of psychology's concern with learning has been the study of associations, such as the association of stimulus and response. Verbal learning is part of that tradition except that the associations are between verbal units.

The concern with verbal associations is a much older concern than reward learning. The far-ranging minds of Plato and Aristotle discussed the association of thoughts and images as part of people's mental apparatus and as a theory of thought. They wrote how events are related in memory and arouse one another in recollection. Aristotle said that mental associations are governed by *similarity* (bronze reminds us of gold), *contrast* or opposites (black reminds us of white), and *contiguity* in space or time (a book reminds us of school). These principles of Aristotle were gradually formed into laws of the association of ideas, which became the foundation of British Associationism, an important philosophical and psychological movement of the 17th–19th century. Thomas Hobbes (1588–1679) was the founder of British Associationism, and with it we associate such prominent names in philosophy as George Berkeley, Thomas Brown, David Hartley, David Hume, John Locke (he gave us the expression "association of ideas"), and James Mill. For them there were four basic laws of the association of ideas: similarity, contrast, temporal contiguity, and spatial contiguity (the debt to Aristotle is obvious). From these four laws they sought to describe the properties of mind as a kind of derivative, building block process. Thus, not all thought processes are simple A-to-B kinds of associations; obviously longer associative chains occur.

The British Associationist school of psychology probably would not have come to much if they had done nothing but proclaim and elaborate their four laws of association. What they did, however, was couple the laws with John Locke's empirical theory of knowledge, and this had vast ramifications that are still debated. All knowledge comes from experience, according to this theory. The mind is a blank tablet at the outset, and all knowledge is acquired through the senses. As events and their associations are experienced, the mind acquires them and gradually comes to build up the structure that is the mature mind. The mind only receives and records; it contributes no relations of its own. It is evident now why this empirical theory of knowledge that relies on the laws of association to populate the mind with ideas and percepts, and relations among ideas and percepts, is so important for the experimental psychology of learning and memory. The organization of events in the mind is determined by the organization of events in experience; so by controlling the organization of events in the world we can control the organization of events in the mind and come to understand them.

Hermann Ebbinghaus (1850–1909) is notable in the history of associationism, learning, and memory because he introduced the experimental study of associations. Before Ebbinghaus, in the tradition handed down from Aristotle and the British Associationists, the interest was a descriptive, nonexperimental one for the existing associative processes in the mind. Ebbinghaus changed all of this and secured his position in the history of psychology. He published a thin book in 1885 (Ebbinghaus, translated edition, 1964) about his research, and each generation of students rediscovers this volume and comes to know on whose shoulders it stands.

Ebbinghaus saw the study of words as too complex for determining the essentials of association because words come with many built-in associations (later investigators saw this as a challenge to be met rather than a barrier). To meet this difficult challenge as he saw it, he invented the nonsense syllable, or, to be exact, a pool of 2,300 of them consisting of all consonant-vowel-consonant combinations. Ebbinghaus presumed that this minimal verbal unit was free of complicating associations and the investigation of its learning would reveal the conditions under which the mind forms associations. His procedure was to make up a list of syllables and read through it at a uniform, rapid rate (Ebbinghaus was his own patient subject). Occasionally Ebbinghaus would stop and test himself without looking at the items, and he would continue in this fashion until he could recite the items in their correct order without error. This was *serial learning*. Theoretically, it is important to see that Ebbinghaus was proceeding according to the tenets of association theory, in which the *contiguity* of items in experience placed the items in memory, and the *frequency* of that experience, or practice trials, determined the strength of the relations between items. And, for the thousands of verbal learning studies that followed, it is worth noting that Ebbinghaus began the tradition of the list, in which number of items correct or number of errors made on a list were typical of measures of performance.

Ebbinghaus' method of serial learning was gradually changed. Ebbinghaus had the items spread out in front of him, and with the items arrayed in front of him there was the possibility that the time devoted to each was uncontrolled, even though Ebbinghaus was a disciplined subject. Stimulated by the work of Ebbinghaus, G. E. Müller and F. Schumann in 1887 undertook work on serial verbal learning, and to control presentation time exactly they arranged the items on a drum and presented them one at a time at a fixed rate through a slit in a screen (Angell, 1894). This was the invention of the memory drum, and a picture of a modern memory drum is shown in Figure 8–1. More than a device for serial learning, a modern memory drum is a device for presenting verbal items at a constant rate, whatever the method.

TWO TRADITIONAL METHODS OF VERBAL LEARNING

Serial anticipation learning The *method of serial anticipation* came into use with the memory drum. The task in serial anticipation learning is to look at the item that is showing and use it as a cue to respond with

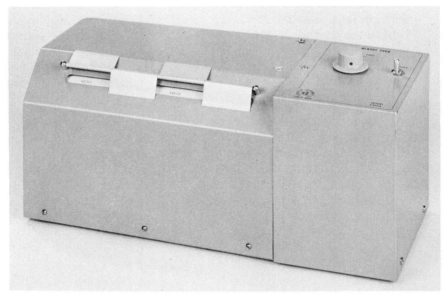

FIGURE 8–1
The memory drum is a device for controlled presentation of a verbal list. The knob at the top controls the rate at which the items are presented at the opening in the front. The tape behind the cover can have up to four different orders of the list typed on it, and the flaps on the front control which order of a list the subject sees on a trial.

the next item of the list before it appears. When the next item appears, the subject uses it to verify the response just given, tries to anticipate the next item before it comes into view, and so on through the list. Once through the list is a trial, and practice repetitions continue until a criterion of performance has been met. Thus, practice might continue until the subject meets the criterion of two consecutive errorless trials, and each subject's score would be the number of trials to achieve the criterion. Or, a fixed number of practice trials could be administered, and the score on each trial would be the number of responses correctly anticipated or number of errors.

After Ebbinghaus the study of verbal associations accelerated, and by the 1920s and the 1930s the psychological literature was generously dotted with studies of serial verbal learning. Starting in the 1940s, however, the method of paired associate learning began to replace serial learning; and although serial learning continued well into the 1960s, it went into decline. By the late 1960s, the method that had given birth to verbal learning was defunct. One reason was a strong interest in memory that brought new methods and techniques, but another reason was a weakness in the method of serial anticipation learning itself. The stimuli and response roles of items were confounded, which made analysis difficult for those of behavioristic persuasion who sought to determine the separate effects of eliciting stimuli and the responses made to them (Young, 1968).

Paired-associate learning   *Paired-associate learning*, which was mentioned in passing above, came into favor because it lacked the confounding of stimulus and response that plagued serial anticipation learning. Being able to study the association of verbal responses to verbal stimuli was commendable in the pre-1960s because animal learning and conditioning studies also were seen in terms of responses being associated with stimuli. Presumably, all of these approaches were reflecting the same laws of learning in different ways, and this was seen as a sound scientific strategy because it was establishing wide generality of the laws.

Each item of the list to be learned in paired-associate learning is a pair of verbal units (words, nonsense syllables, etc.), with the left-hand unit the stimulus term and the right-hand unit the response term. The subject must learn to respond with the response term in the time that the stimulus term is exposed. The three basic methods of paired-associate learning are the study-test method, the anticipation method, and the correction method (Battig, 1965). Paired-associate learning was first used by Mary Calkins, and she used the *study-test method* (Calkins, 1894).

The learning of the verbal pair and the testing of the learning are separated in study trials and test trials in the *study-test method*. On a study trial both terms of each pair are presented together for a fixed period of time, and the subject studies each pair and tries to learn it. Each study trial is followed by a test trial, in which the stimulus term of each pair is presented for a fixed interval and the subject attempts to give the response term paired with it. Thus:

Stimulus term	*Response term*
Study trial	
DOG	STORE
CAR	HOUSE
BICYCLE	GIRL
LADY	TREE
Test trial	
DOG	—
LADY	—
BICYCLE	—
CAR	—

The sequence is study-test, study-test, etc., with a different order of the pairs on each trial, until a criterion of learning is met. Trials to achieve the criterion can be the measure of performance when learning is carried to a criterion. Or a fixed number of trials can be given, in which the number correct on each test trial, or number of errors, is the performance measure.

The *anticipation method* alternates study and test within the trial:

Stimulus term	Response term
DOG	—
DOG	STORE
CAR	—
CAR	HOUSE
BICYCLE	—
BICYCLE	GIRL
LADY	—
LADY	TREE

The stimulus term is displayed for a fixed interval and in that time the subject is tested and must give (that is, anticipate) the response term that is paired with the stimulus term. When the time is up the complete pair is presented for a fixed interval and the subject uses it to check the correctness of each response given, as well as for further learning of the pair. As with the study-test method, practice can be continued until a criterion is met or until a specified number of trials has passed.

A problem with the study-test method and the anticipation method for some purposes is that the number of correct responses for each pair is unequal. If the subject learns to a criterion, the easy items are given correctly first, and the subject continues to give them correctly as the more difficult items are being learned. The result is overlearning of the easy items. The *correction method* remedies this problem by removing a pair from the list when it has met a criterion of learning. Here is an example of two trials of our short example list being learned by the correction method:

Stimulus term	Response term
Trial 1–Study	
DOG	STORE
CAR	HOUSE
BICYCLE	GIRL
LADY	TREE
Trial 1–Test	
LADY	TREE
CAR	HOUSE
BICYCLE	WIFE
DOG	—

Only the responses to CAR and LADY on Trial 1–Test are correct; so they are omitted on the next trial:

Stimulus term	*Response term*
Trial 2–Study	
DOG	STORE
BICYCLE	GIRL
Trial 2–Test	
BICYCLE	FEMALE
DOG	—

And so on, until one correct response is given each item.

Any device that presents material at a standard rate can be used for any of the three methods. A memory drum or a slide projector is common for the study-test and the anticipation methods. The memory drum and the slide projector cannot be used very efficiently for the correction method because the pairs must be manually restructured on each trial. Placing the items on cards allows the items to be easily reorganized on each trial, although the presentation time lacks the precision of the memory drum and the slide projector. A signal light for timing the presentation interval, or a tone through a headset, can easily be rigged for the experimenter, however.

The study of serial learning and paired-associate learning was sometimes seen as the investigation of rote learning, or unmediated learning. The associative bond was commonly seen as habit and was conceived in the same conceptual terms as the habit of the rat for bar pressing. A somewhat more elaborate and realistic conception of the verbal learning process depended on processes akin to longer associative chains which the British Associationists described. Verbal units can have verbal associations, and these associations can be a variable for the verbal learning process. Investigators have scaled verbal items for the number of associations which they elicit, and these scaled values have been used as an experimental variable. C. E. Noble (1952) has been prominent among those who have scaled verbal items in this fashion, and this scaling has come to be called the *meaningfulness* of an item as distinct from the meaning of an item.

Noble's scaling method was to present a subject with an item and allow 60 seconds for the subject to write down as many other words as the stimulus word brought to mind. Noble used two-syllable items, ranging from meaningless artificial words such as NEGLAN, which had few or no associations for most subjects, to meaningful, common words that had many associations for all subjects. Cieutat, Stockwell, and Noble (1958) used these scaled items to investigate the effects of number of associations on paired-associate learning. They had lists of paired associates in which the stimulus terms were either high (*H*) or low (*L*) in meaningfulness, as were response terms. There were four groups for these four conditions: *H-H*, *L-H*, *H-L*, and *L-L*, in which the first letter designates the meaningfulness of the stimulus term and the second letter the meaningfulness of the response term for the pairs that a group used. Learning was by the anticipation method, and 12 practice trials were given. The results are shown in Figure 8–2, and it can be seen that meaningfulness is a strong variable for verbal learning. High meaningfulness of the stimulus term produced more rapid learning than low meaningfulness, whether the meaningfulness of the response term was low or high; the greater the number of associations for the stimulus term the easier a response term can be hooked to it. Meaningfulness of the response terms also made a difference, with high meaningfulness producing a faster rate of learning than low meaningfulness. Pronunciation ease could be a factor for response term effects. The low meaningfulness

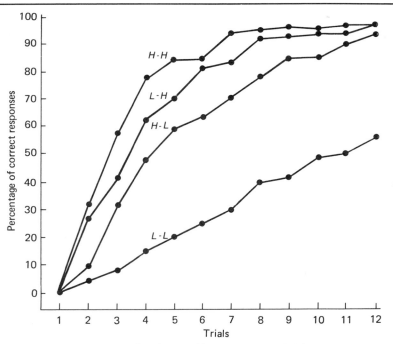

Source: V. J. Cieutat, F. E. Stockwell, and C. E. Noble, The interaction of ability and amount of practice with stimulus and response meaningfulness (*m, m'*) in paired-associate learning. *Journal of Experimental Psychology*, 1958, *56*, 193–202. Reprinted by permission of the American Psychological Association.

FIGURE 8–2

Effects of high (*H*) and low (*L*) meaningfulness of the stimulus and response terms on paired-associate learning.

response terms were artificial words which the subject had never encountered before. The subject first must learn the new elements of the strange word and how to pronounce it before learning to give it as an associate of the stimulus term. A slower learning rate is the result.

The cognitive view of associative learning

SOME HISTORY AND BACKGROUND

In the scientific drama that is the psychology of learning, associationists, or behaviorists as the latter-day ones are often labeled, and cognitive psychologists are antagonists. In Chapter 4 we saw that E. C. Tolman was the chief advocate of cognitive psychology in the realm of positive reinforcement and animal learning, and an influence on him was Gestalt psychology. Gestalt psychology, which had its origins in Germany in 1912, was an intellectual reaction to elementarism in psychology; it emphasized the properties of the whole and the relations among the elements rather than the elements themselves. Gestalt psychology was most interested in perception, but its theoretical ideas about perception had a spinoff for learning. In perception it reacted to *structuralism* as a movement in the psychology of the late 19th and early 20th centuries. Structuralism analyzed complex visual forms and sounds into the elementary parts that comprised the whole pattern. For example, the gestaltists said that it was meaningless to analyze a tune into its notes, ignoring the relations among the notes. The relations are fundamental, and as evidence they cite the ability to sing a tune in the wrong key—the elements are wrong but the pattern is correct. A key point of disagreement between gestaltists and associationists is this matter of relations. Gestalt psychology says that the mind directly apprehends relations (Köhler, 1947; Asch, 1968), along with the parts, whereas associationists hold that both the relations and the parts are learned. This associationist position is consistent with John Locke's philosophy that the mind is a blank tablet at the start and that all mental content is acquired in experience.

The issue of relations clearly divides the associationists and the gestaltists in their interpretation of the verbal learning process. The associationists, who work out of the Ebbinghaus tradition, turn heavily on the principles of contiguity and frequency in the acquiring of a stable relation between verbal units. Experience the pair LAKE–SUGAR enough times and they will come to be associated; and when LAKE is presented as a stimulus SUGAR will occur as a response. Wolfgang Köhler, as a leading theorist for Gestalt psychology, saw it differently (Köhler, 1947, p. 265). He said that LAKE–SUGAR can evoke pictures, or images, in the mind, and it is these images that give the words of the pair an organization into a whole. Moreover, organization of the elements *is* the learning. Contiguity in experience, and frequency of experience, are fundamental for verbal learning but only insofar as they affect the organizational process. Not all verbal learning uses imagery; patterns might be wholly verbal. But, no matter what they are, learning is the meaningful organization of elements of experience. Imagery and verbal organization have strong effects on remembering, and the discussion of them will be saved for Part II of the book, on the topic of memory.

Another tenet of cognitive psychology is belief in the active mind. Associationism has a passive subject as an unwritten premise. If specified events with a specified temporal relationship occur in experience, learning will occur, otherwise not, according to associationism. There is nothing the subject need do about the events, or, indeed, can do about them. If the events are properly experienced the learning automatically will happen. Cognitive psychology, on the other hand, has a mentally active subject. No matter whether human or lower animal, there is the active relating of information in the environment, thinking about it, hypothesizing about it, judging it, and deciding about it. Associationism is much more of a psychology of the "out there," in which events in the environment are the prime determiners of behavior. Cognitive psychology would hardly deny the importance of events "out there," but it imputes significance to them only insofar as they are used by the subject's active mind. Events in the environment are objective, and their touchable, seeable, hearable quality has given the advocates of associationism strong feelings of being objective. Everyone accepts the objectivism of associationism, but the inner events of cognitive psychology can be studied with objectivity too. Inner events are untouchable, unseeable, and unhearable, but they can be objectified by empirical operations and studied, just as physicists study the unobservable electron and atom.

OPERANT VERBAL LEARNING

Tolman's cognitive theory of learning was discussed in Chapter 4. Tolman said that learning was the perception of pertinent relations among events of the learning situation. Hypotheses about events are tested on the learning trials, and confirmation of a relevant hypothesis, such as reinforcement always following a particular response class, produces the behavior that we called learned. Tolman's theory raised two questions which continue to divide learning psychologists: To what extent is conscious hypothesis behavior part of the learning process? To what extent is conscious knowledge of the situation, the response, and the reinforcement required for learning? These questions seem innocent enough, but they gain in substance when we look at the position of E. L. Thorndike in the psychology of learning and contrast it to Tolman's.

There was systematic laboratory work being done on animal learning by the end of the 19th century, and a major figure to step forward was E. L. Thorndike. He was the strong beginning of research on reinforced learning in the United States, and his approaches and ideas are still with us, both in the laboratory and out. If Thorndike had been a highly specialized psychologist who worked on a narrow class of problems the significance of his ideas might have been lost or at least delayed for a time, but he was a man of wide interests. He started out as an animal psychologist (as a Harvard student he was ordered out of his rooming house because he was raising chickens in his room for research), and he came to work extensively on human learning. In his lifetime he saw his ideas taught in every department of psychology and every college of education in the country.

Thorndike's doctoral dissertation (Thorndike, 1898) was mostly about reward learning. We have come to have a good understanding of reward learning; so Thorndike's work might seem trite from our mature stance, but in historical context it was not trite but emerged as a stand against the prevailing psychology of the day. The human psychology of the time was structuralism that introspectively analyzed one's own consciousness to determine its elements and structure. The animal psychology of that period was under the influence of Darwinism, and its literature had accounts of animal behavior in terms of intelligence and reasoning as adaptive mechanisms, speculations about consciousness in animals and where it emerged on the phylogenetic scale, and the kinds of animal behavior that did or did not require consciousness. Thorndike's interpretation of reward learning was a strong stand against these prevailing mentalistic conceptions of animal behavior, as well as running counter to structuralism.

Thorndike said that an animal did not use conscious reasoning and active thought processes in learning. Instead, learning is a trial and error process. The animal makes many random movements in the situation, and one of them leads to reward. The reward causes the successful movement to receive an increment in strength, and it is boosted in relation to all of the other movements that can occur in the situation. These other movements, by not being reinforced, are extinguished. Rewarding of the correct movement on subsequent trials steadily increases its likelihood of occurrence, and when its dominance is complete the learning is complete. Later, Thorndike used his conception of animal learning to explain human learning. A child learning to solve an arithmetic problem will make various wrong answers, but when the correct response does occur the teacher will reward it by saying "Right." As in animal learning, rewards for the correct responses eventually cause them to occur with good regularity. Thorndike had no more use for conscious, active mental processes in human learning than in animal learning. For Thorndike, the reward acts to strengthen the response in a wholly automatic fashion, whether the person (or animal) is consciously aware of it or not. Thorndike (1935, p. 62) said that "a person may increase the probability that certain situations will evoke certain responses without knowing at the time that he is doing so or afterward that he has done so." Similarly, Thorndike (1935, p. 63) said that reward will strengthen the connection "regardless of the learner's knowledge about the tendency or ability to identify, describe, or control it." This position is known as the *behaviorist* viewpoint, and is to be contrasted to the cognitive viewpoint. Behaviorism was a movement in psychology that began in 1913 (Watson, 1913), and its rejection of consciousness and its emphasis on laws that relate observable stimuli and responses complemented Thorndike's position. Behaviorism has had a full life and is still a robust movement in the United States.

Tolman's cognitive psychology has an organism who is mentally active during the learning process and who is not a passive recipient of reinforcement. Hypotheses are entertained during learning about what leads to what and about the implications of the reward for behavioral options. Tolman (1958, pp. 109–112) believed that conscious awareness can accompany human hypothesis behavior, although he saw no necessity for it.

The cognitive descendants of Tolman in the 1960s and 70s took a stronger position than Tolman's and held that hypothesis behavior is a conscious aware process, and that learning does not occur until the subject has become aware of the stimulus-response-reinforcement relationship. Reinforcement does not automatically inflict an increment of habit. Instead it is but a signal which informs the subject of the expected response, and the subject proceeds to test various hypotheses until discovering what reinforcement means for his behavior. Learning is a problem-solving situation, and when the problem is solved the subject produces the response with high reliability and regularly earns the reward. Behaviorists, of course, deny all of this in debate and experiment, and a main arena for the confrontation is *operant verbal learning*. Theoretical and experimental papers on this topic number in the hundreds, and it is instructive to examine some of them and see how the two theoretical forces operate in defense of their positions. It is not surprising that human verbal learning is the arena because conscious awareness can be given a definition at the human level as we shall see. What awareness might mean for animals is not clear. Expectedly, cognitive psychologists are interested mostly in human behavior with far fewer of them having an interest in animal behavior. Behaviorists operate freely in both provinces.

In the context of operant verbal learning "awareness" means a grasp of the principle of reinforcement in which the subject knows the kind of responses that will produce reinforcement. Thorndike and Rock (1934) were the first to do an experiment on operant verbal learning. A subject was presented with a list of words and for each one was required to give the first association that came to mind as quickly as possible. If the response was sequentially related to the stimulus word as in speaking or writing, the experimenter rewarded the subject by saying "Right." Otherwise the experimenter said nothing or "Wrong." For example, YOURS–TRULY was rewarded but YOURS–MINE was not. Learning definitely occurred, with the average number of responses correct going from about 3 to 6 from the first to the 30th block of 10 responses. But what about awareness? And how do we know an aware subject? There are two methods that have been used to define an aware subject. One is to ask the subject to verbalize the principle of reinforcement. The other is to examine individual learning curves for "insightful" jumps to near 100 percent correct. This latter method assumes that after becoming aware of the principle of reinforcement, a subject should be able to respond almost perfectly all of the time. Thorndike and Rock used this second method. They examined their data for insightful leaps in performance and found none, and they concluded that learning can occur without awareness. This study is the pioneering one for the field, and investigators have been reacting to it ever since.

An experiment of the kind that is commonly done today is by Cohen et al. (1954, Experiment 1), and it also supports the behavioristic position by finding evidence for learning without awareness. They used the Sentence Construction Task, developed by Taffel (1955). The stimulus for eliciting a response was a card with a verb and six pronouns printed on it: *I, we, he, they, she,* and *you.* The subject's task was to make up a sentence using the verb and one of the pronouns. There were 80 such cards, each with a different verb and with the order of the pronouns randomized on each one. The rewarded response class was sentences that used *I* and *we,* and subjects of the experimental group had them rewarded with "Good" from the experimenter. Nothing was said to a control group. The results appear in Figure 8–3. The rewarded subjects learned and, for our theoretical concerns here, none were found aware of the principle of reinforcement in a postexperimental interview.

A tilt toward the behaviorist's position in this experiment by Cohen et al. should not be taken as decisive because there are other experiments which support the cognitive view and shift the balance back again. Consider an experiment by Levin (1961). Cohen et al. used four questions in the postexperimental interview, and it was Levin's thesis that the four questions insufficiently probed for awareness. Perhaps the learning without awareness which Cohen et al. found was because of aware subjects who were misclassified as unaware. Levin repeated the

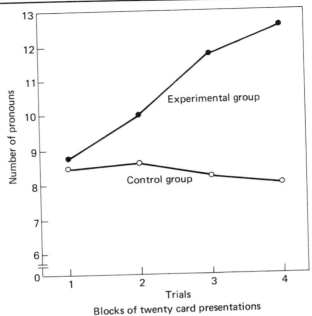

Source: B. D. Cohen, H. I. Kalish, J. R. Thurston, and E. Cohen, Experimental manipulation of verbal behavior. *Journal of Experimental Psychology*, 1954, 47, 106–110. Reprinted by permission of the American Psychological Association.

FIGURE 8–3
The effect of rewarding subjects with "Good" every time they composed a sentence that began with *I* or *we*.

Cohen et al. experiment but used instead an extended interview of 16 questions, the first 4 being the same as Cohen et al. Learning without awareness was found when the subjects were classified with the first four questions, which is the same as Cohen et al. found. But when the probing for awareness was deeper with the extended interview, some of the subjects classified as unaware by the first four questions were now classified as aware. Looking at the data again with this new classification of subjects, only aware subjects now learned. Levin's experiment highlights the continuing problem of how awareness should be determined.

A well-known experiment by DeNike (1964) also supports the cognitive view of operant verbal learning. DeNike had his subjects say any words whatsoever that came to mind, and from this verbal outpouring he selected human nouns for reinforcement. The reinforcement might look like this:

| Subject: | "Is | girl | happily | do | architect," | etc. |
| Experimenter: | "Mmm-hmm" | | | | "Mmm-hmm," | etc. |

Each subject was required to say 300 words. After every 25 words there was a pause and the subject was required to write thoughts about the experiment, which was the source of information about awareness. De-Nike's study had two groups of subjects, an experimental group and a control group. The experimental group first had 50 words without reinforcement to determine the baseline for human nouns without reinforcement, followed by 250 words in which human nouns were reinforced. Learning would be shown by an increase in the number of human nouns from the baseline. The control group also had the first 50 words without reinforcement and random reinforcement of the remaining words 10 percent of the time. The procedure for the control group is considered a good one because it received "Mmm-hmm" events from the experimenter just as the other group, but since they were not response contingent, they could not contribute to learning.

DeNike's results are shown in Figure 8–4. Using the verbal reports, DeNike classified the subjects of his experimental group as aware or

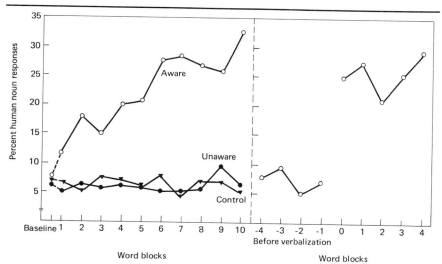

Source: C. D. Spielberger, and L. D. DeNike, Descriptive behaviorism versus cognitive theory in verbal operant conditioning. *Psychological Review*, 1966, 73, 306–326. Reprinted by permission of the American Psychological Association.

FIGURE 8–4

Effects of reinforcing human nouns as the subjects spoke any words that came to mind. The curves on the left show that the only subjects who learn are those aware that human nouns are being reinforced. The data on the right show the sharp increment in performance that results at the point of awareness.

unaware, depending on whether a subject was able to verbalize the principle of reinforcement when writing thoughts about the experiment after every 25 trials. These data are on the left-hand side of Figure 8–4; notice that they handily fit the cognitive conception of learning. Only a subject aware of the principle of reinforcement learns. The right-hand side of Figure 8–4 is another plot of DeNike's data, and it is also in keeping with the assumptions of cognitive psychology. Here the data of the aware subjects of the experimental group are plotted with respect to the block of trials in which the principle of reinforcement was first reported. Cognitive theorists contend that there should be a dramatic leap in performance level at the point of discovering the principle of reinforcement, and indeed so. Probably the reason that Thorndike and Rock (1934) did not find an insightful jump in performance was that their subjects were required to respond as fast as possible, and so they did not have time to use the principle of reinforcement even though they might have known it. Weiss (1955) presents evidence in support of this possibility.

Investigators of operant verbal learning who have concerned themselves with these theoretical issues have almost always studied acquisition and have not appreciated the implications of extinction. The typical behaviorist today accepts the empirical facts of extinction without a theory to explain them. Cognitive psychologists have not particularly bothered to theorize about extinction either, but nevertheless their position has implications for extinction. One implication is that the decline in performance that is extinction occurs because the subjects entertains new hypotheses about the changed conditions of reinforcement, and these cause them to try other responses in an attempt to acquire reinforcement again. The outcome is a decline in occurrence of the criterion response that had been receiving reinforcement. But notice that the criterion response is not weakened—subjects only elect not to give it as they try other response possibilities. If asked, the subject should be able to give the response fully again. Another implication is that extinction need not occur if subjects perceive the continued occurrence of the criterion response as a requirement of them. An example of failure to extinguish is found in Cohen et al. (1954, Experiment II). Patty and Page (1973, p. 312) report a subject who failed to extinguish because he thought that the experimenter was testing persistence. When the trade is in voluntary thought processes, a subject's perception of the situational demands becomes important.

Patty and Page (1973) tested the implication that the extinguished response could be reinstated in full strength if the subject were asked. They used the Sentence Construction Task, with "Good" being the reinforcement for sentences beginning with *They*. Reinforced training continued until a performance criterion of 13 correct out of 15 was met. Withdrawal of reinforcement followed for 45 trials, and then the exper-

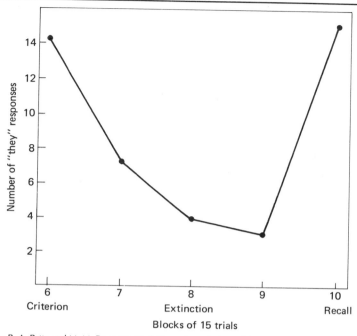

source: R. A. Patty and M. M. Page, Manipulations of a verbal conditioning situation based upon demand characteristics theory. *Journal of Experimental Research in Personality*, 1973, 6, 307–313. Reprinted by permission of Academic Press, Inc.

FIGURE 8–5
The extinction of a verbal operant response in Trial Blocks 7–9 after reaching the criterion of acquisition in Block 6. Block 10 shows response reinstatement on request.

imenter stopped and gave these instructions before giving 15 trials more:

> OK. Let's pause for a moment. I'm going to give some further instructions; it's important that you don't answer me or talk back in any way, just listen. You remember that for a long time I said "Good" after some of your sentences. Now for a long time I haven't said anything. This next part is a test to see if you knew, and can still remember, what it was that you did that made me say "Good" before. I'm going to show several more cards and won't be saying anything, but I want you to make your sentences in such a way that I would have said "Good" before. This way you will demonstrate by your actions that you knew why I said "Good." Let's start again.[1]

The results are shown in Figure 8–5. The decline in performance that is extinction readily occurred, but notice that it does not represent a per-

[1] *Journal of Experimental Research in Personality*, 1973, 6, pp. 308–309. Reprinted by permission of Academic Press, Inc.

manent weakening of response tendency. The subjects fully reinstated the criterion response when asked, as cognitive psychology implies.

DeNike's experiment (DeNike, 1964) is representative of a number which show a strong correlation between learning and reports of awareness, and one would think that the behaviorists would collapse under the onslaught of such convincing evidence. Never. That awareness is a mediating event on which learning depends is the cognitive position, and the behaviorists acknowledge it as one possibility. There are two other main possibilities, however, and the behaviorists are attracted to both of them (Greenspoon and Brownstein, 1967; Kanfer, 1968). One is that the cognitive psychologists have it backwards. Awareness does not mediate learning. Rather, it is learning that mediates awareness, and so awareness is incidental and after the fact. Reinforcement produces a change in response probability, the subject notices the change, and becomes aware of the principle of reinforcement as a byproduct. The other possibility is that awareness is a verbal report in its own right, and it is wrong to conceptualize it as consciousness. Given that the verbal report is a function of the same variables as the criterion response, they will be correlated, but correlation is not causality, as generations of students in statistics courses have heard their instructors say (a correlation between barrooms and churches in cities does not mean that drinking causes religion or vice versa). In truth, all three of these possibilities are plausible and, in sad truth, there is no incisive experimental data that allows us to choose among them. However, a new threat to the behaviorist's position is the extinction data of Patty and Page (1973) in Figure 8–5. From a behavioristic stance it is hard to see how extinction can be reversed on request. Perhaps extinction will be the skirmish ground of the future.

FREE RECALL

Each response in serial anticipation learning and in paired-associate learning has its own identifiable stimulus, but there is no necessity in the study of verbal learning for an identifiable stimulus. A list of words or nonsense syllables can be presented and the subject then can be asked to recall as many as possible in any order. This is the method of *free recall*.

An effect in free recall which has attracted the theoretical interests of cognitive psychologists is *clustering* because it says something about how the mind organizes and structures the elements of the world that impinge on it. The gist of clustering is that words which are presented in an unsystematic way will show some degree of organization in recall. The basic clustering effect was demonstrated in a study by Bousfield (1953), in which it was discovered. Bousfield presented his subjects a list of 60 nouns, with 15 in each of 4 different categories: animals, proper names, vegetables, and professions. The 60 words were presented in a random order, and in free recall Bousefield found a significant tendency for words of a category to be recalled together, or to cluster. This should not imply that a subject would necessarily recall, say, all the animals from the list that he could remember, followed by all the vegetables that he could remember, and so on. Rather, he might recall three animal words, one vegetable word, four professions words, two vegetable words, etc. As the name of the phenomenon says, there is clustering. Bousfield set the direction of research on clustering by using lists with words of several conceptual categories, but clustering is not limited to words of conceptual categories. Apparently any dimension of a list which the subject can perceive can be used as a basis for clustering. Hintzman, Block, and Inskeep (1972) and Nilsson (1973, 1974) found that clustering occurred on the basis of sensory modality when some of the words of the list were visually presented and some were auditorily presented. In other experiments of Hintzman et al., they found that the type of lettering for visually presented words was a basis of clustering, as was the voice of the speaker in auditory presentation.

What are some of the other variables that determine clustering? An obvious one is amount of practice. Using Bousfield's list of 60 nouns with four conceptual categories, Bousfield and Cohen (1953) gave five groups of subjects one to five presentations of the list. The number of words correctly recalled increased with practice, and the number of clusters essentially doubled from one presentation to five. Another fundamental variable is whether the words of a category are blocked together or not when they are presented. As might be expected, it is easier to relate items and promote their clustering at recall when the category words are presented together. Cofer, Bruce, and Reicher (1966) found that blocking increased the clustering of conceptually related words by about 50 percent. To the extent that the presentation becomes less and less blocked and more and more disorganized and random, the clustering will decline. Kintsch (1970, pp. 368–369) observed that items presented together tend to cluster, and as the number of items between any two words of a category increases, their tendency to be recalled together decreases.

Psychologists have had a theoretical interest in clustering because it pits the old rivals, cognitive and associationist psychology, against one another again. Cognitive psychology sees clustering as an example of the organizing powers of the mind that perceives the regularities among the randomly presented words and uses these regularities in guiding the recall (Tulving, 1968). A strong cognitive position would contend that learning in free recall is a matter of giving organization to the list's items, and that increasing amount recalled over practice trials is a function of increasing organization of the items. This cognitive stance is very similar to Köhler's position, mentioned earlier in this chapter, that organizing is the fundamental nature of associative learning (Köhler, 1947).

Associationist psychologists can contend that there is no need to invoke the organizing powers of the mind to explain clustering in free recall. Words that tend to cluster at recall can be words that have been associated in past experience, and the strength of the clustering is a function of the strength of association. These associative relationships between words can be known in free association tests. Suppose, in a free association test, you were given the stimulus word HORSE and you gave RIDER as the first response that came to mind. Then, if HORSE and RIDER were items in a list presented to you it would not be surprising if they occurred together in free recall, and all in the absence of conceptual relatedness.

Jenkins and Russell (1952) and Jenkins, Mink, and Russell (1958) were the first to show that free association norms can predict clustering in free recall. Pairs of words from a free association test were randomly presented in a list for free recall, and there was a significant tendency for them to occur together.

Marshall (reported by Cofer, 1965) presented data which showed how clustering in free recall is a function of association, and that associative relatedness is not the whole story. He calculated an index based on all the associations that any two words had in common, and with the index he was able to define lists for free recall in which words were associatively related in varying degrees. Figure 8–6 shows a clustering score plotted as a function of four practice trials and six values of the index. The greater the number of associations between words the greater the clustering. But is this all there is to clustering? It could be, because words which are conceptually related also tend to be associatively related; so maybe the explanation in terms of association is the more fundamental one. DOG and CAT are conceptually related as animals, but they are also associates of one another in a free association test. Marshall went on to evaluate the contributions of cognitive and associative relations by using lists of words that had the index of association held constant but that were conceptually related or unrelated. The results in Figure 8–7, presented in terms of a clustering score, show that conceptual categories contribute something in their own right, over and beyond the associative relations among words. The associative position and the cognitive position both seem correct. That associations contribute to clustering is true, but that they cannot account for all of the clustering is also true.

How can clustering occur for items that have neither conceptual nor associative relatedness from past language experience? Tulving (1962) demonstrated increasing clustering with practice for unrelated nouns,

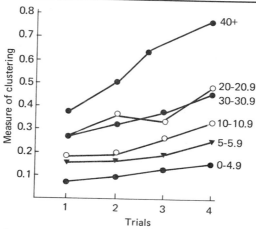

Source: C. N. Cofer, On some factors in the organizational characteristics of free recall. *American Psychologist,* 1965, 20, 261–272. Reprinted by permission of the American Psychological Association.

FIGURE 8–6

The tendency to cluster items in free recall as a function of an index of the associative related-ness among items. The value for the index is specified beside each curve.

and Allen (1968) found increasing clustering over practice trials with unrelated nonsense syllables. How can a subject come to give XIB, JEK, and LAV together? The answer is rote practice. Rundus (1971) had his subjects vocalize their rehearsal patterns of unrelated nouns that were presented for free recall, and he found there was much more going on

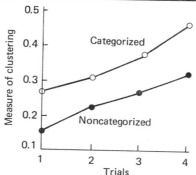

Source: C. N. Cofer, On some factors in the organizational characteristics of free recall. *American Psychologist,* 1965, 20, 261–272. Reprinted by permission of the American Psychological Association.

FIGURE 8–7

The tendency to cluster items in free recall when associative relatedness is held constant and items differ in being categorically (conceptually) related or not.

than studying the item that was being displayed. Rundus found that at any particular moment a subject was rehearsing a set of items. He was rehearsing the item that was showing, he was usually rehearsing the immediately preceding item also, and he had some chance of rehearsing items more distant in the list. The probability of any two items being recalled together in a cluster depended upon the number of times that the two were rehearsed together. Rehearsal was the sole explanation of clustering of unrelated words in Rundus' experiment, but when the words were conceptually related and categorized, apparently the categories were perceived because the rehearsal rate and the performance level were higher. The cognitive organization of the material determined the amount of rehearsal and the level of performance that is a function of it.

Summary

That animals can learn important dimensions of the English language has changed our thinking about the intellectual capabilities of animals, the nature of similarities and differences between the humans and animals, and the meaning of language communication. One of the reasons that previous attempts to teach the English language to chimpanzees have failed is that the vocal apparatus of the chimpanzee is inadequate for the job. A successful attempt by Gardner and Gardner (1971) capitalized on the excellent motor capabilities of the chimpanzee. They taught their chimpanzee, named Washoe, the American Sign Language, the manual language of the deaf of North America. In four years Washoe learned 132 words, some of them conceptual words, and she made many sentences of 3 words or more. Research has shown that Washoe's language compares favorably to a preschool human child. Despite these successes, there are critics who doubt that Washoe is a creative language user like the human.

The interest in animal language learning is relatively new, but the interest in human verbal learning is old. The experimental study of human verbal learning goes back to the 19th century, with an interest in verbal associations as its ancestor. As far back as ancient Greek philosophers, but most notably the British empirical philosophers of the 17th–19th centuries, there has been concern with the association of ideas and how these associations are related to a theory of thought. Hermann Ebbinghaus, in the 19th century, began the experimental study of verbal learning and how verbal items are associated.

There are three main verbal learning procedures: serial learning, paired-associate learning, and free recall. Serial learning requires that a list of verbal items be recalled in the order presented. Paired-associate learning presents the verbal items in pairs, in which one item is the stimulus term and the other the response term. The subject must learn to associate the two items and give the response term when the stimulus term is presented. Free recall allows a subject to recall a list of verbal items in any order.

References

Allen, M.   Rehearsal strategies and response cueing as determinants of organization in free recall. *Journal of Verbal Learning and Verbal Behavior,* 1968, *7,* 58–63.

Angell, J. R.   Memory. *Psychological Review,* 1894, *1,* 435–438.

Asch, S. E.   The doctrinal tyranny of associationism: Or what is wrong with rote learning? In T. R. Dixon and D. L. Horton (Eds.), *Verbal behavior and general behavior theory.* Englewood Cliffs: Prentice-Hall, 1968, pp. 214–228.

Battig, W. F.   Procedural problems in paired-associate learning research. *Psychonomic Monograph Supplements,* 1965, *1,* No. 1, pp. 1–12.

Bousfield, W. A.   The occurrence of clustering in the recall of randomly arranged associates. *Journal of General Psychology,* 1953, *49,* 229–240.

Bousfield, W. A., & Cohen, B. H.   The effects of reinforcement on the occurrence of clustering in the recall of randomly arranged associates. *Journal of Psychology,* 1953, *36,* 67–81.

Bronowski, J., & Bellugi, U.   Language, name, and concept. *Science,* 1970, *168,* 669–673.

Brown, R.   The development of Wh questions in child speech. *Journal of Verbal Learning and Verbal Behavior,* 1968, *7,* 277–290.

Calkins, M. W.   Association. In Münsterberg, H. (Ed.), *Studies from the Harvard Psychological Laboratory* (II.). *Psychological Review,* 1894, *1,* 441–495.

Cieutat, V. J., Stockwell, F. E., & Noble, C. E.   The interaction of ability and amount of practice with stimulus and response meaningfulness (m, m') in paired-associate learning. *Journal of Experimental Psychology,* 1958, *56,* 193–202.

Cofer, C. N.   On some factors in the organizational characteristics of free recall. *American Psychologist,* 1965, *20,* 261–267.

Cofer, C. N., Bruce, D. R., & Reicher, G. M.   Clustering in free recall as a function of certain methodological variations. *Journal of Experimental Psychology,* 1966, *71,* 858–866.

Cohen, B. D., Kalish, H. I., Thurston, J. R., & Cohen, E.   Experimental manipulation of verbal behavior. *Journal of Experimental Psychology,* 1954, *47,* 106–110.

DeNike, L. D.   The temporal relationship between awareness and performance in verbal conditioning. *Journal of Experimental Psychology,* 1964, *68,* 521–529.

Ebbinghaus, H.   *Memory: A contribution to experimental psychology.* (H. A. Ruger & C. E. Bussenius, trans.) New York: Dover, 1964.

Gardner, B. T., & Gardner, R. A. Two-way communication with an infant chimpanzee. In A. M. Schrier & F. Stollnitz (Eds.), *Behavior of nonhuman primates* (Vol. 4). New York: Academic Press, 1971, pp. 117–184.

Gardner, B. T., & Gardner, R. A. Evidence for sentence constituents in the early utterances of child and chimpanzee. *Journal of Experimental Psychology: General,* 1975, *104,* 244–267. (a)

Gardner, R. A., & Gardner, B. T. Early signs of language in child and chimpanzee. *Science,* 1975, *187,* 752–753. (b)

Greenspoon, J., & Brownstein, J. A. Awareness in verbal conditioning. *Journal of Experimental Research in Personality,* 1967, *2,* 295–308.

Hayes, K. H., & Nissen, C. H. Higher mental functions of a home-raised chimpanzee. In A. M. Schrier & F. Stollnitz (Eds.), *Behavior of nonhuman primates* (Vol. 4). New York: Academic Press, 1971, pp. 59–115.

Hintzman, D. L., Block, R. A., & Inskeep, N. R. Memory for mode of input. *Journal of Verbal Learning and Verbal Behavior,* 1972, *11,* 741–749.

Jenkins, J. J., Mink, W. D., & Russell, W. A. Associative clustering as a function of verbal association strength. *Psychological Reports,* 1958, *4,* 127–136.

Jenkins, J. J., & Russell, W. A. Associative clustering during recall. *Journal of Abnormal and Social Psychology,* 1952, *47,* 818–821.

Kanfer, F. H. Verbal conditioning: A review of its current status. In T. R. Dixon & D. L. Horton (Eds.), *Verbal behavior and general behavior theory.* Englewood Cliffs: Prentice-Hall, 1968, pp. 245–290.

Kellogg, W. N. Communication and language in the home-raised chimpanzee. *Science,* 1968, *162,* 423–438.

Kintsch, W. Models for free recall and recognition. In D. A. Norman (Ed.), *Models of human memory.* New York: Academic Press, 1970, pp. 331–373.

Köhler, W. *Gestalt psychology.* New York: Liveright, 1947.

Lenneberg, E. H. Of language, knowledge, apes, and brains. *Journal of Psycholinguistic Research,* 1971, *1,* 1–29.

Levin, S. M. The effects of awareness on verbal conditioning. *Journal of Experimental Psychology,* 1961, *61,* 67–75.

Lieberman, P. Primate vocalizations and human linguistic ability. *Journal of the Acoustical Society of America,* 1968, *44,* 1574–1584.

Lieberman, P. D., Klatt, H., & Wilson, W. Vocal tract limitations of the vocal repertoires of rhesus monkeys and other nonhuman primates. *Science,* 1969, *164,* 1185–1187.

Limber, J. Language in child and chimp? *American Psychologist,* 1977, *32,* 280–295.

Linden, E. *Apes, men, and language.* Baltimore: Penguin, 1976.

Nilsson, L. Organization by modality in short-term memory. *Journal of Experimental Psychology,* 1973, *100,* 246–253.

Nilsson, L. Further evidence for organization by modality in immediate free recall. *Journal of Experimental Psychology,* 1974, *103,* 948–957.

Noble, C. E.   An analysis of meaning. *Psychological Review*, 1952, *59*, 421–430.

Patty, R. A., & Page, M. M.   Manipulations of a verbal conditioning situation based upon demand characteristics theory. *Journal of Experimental Research in Personality*, 1973, *6*, 307–313.

Premack, D.   On the assessment of language competence in the chimpanzee. In A. M. Schrier & F. Stollnitz (Eds.), *Behavior of nonhuman primates* (Vol. 4). New York: Academic Press, 1971, pp. 185–228.

Premack, D.   *Intelligence in ape and man.* Hillsdale: Erlbaum, 1976.

Rumbaugh, D. M. (Ed.)   *Language learning by a chimpanzee: The LANA project.* New York: Academic Press, 1977.

Rundus, D.   Analysis of rehearsal processes in free recall. *Journal of Experimental Psychology*, 1971, *89*, 63–77.

Spielberger, C. D. & DeNike, L. D.   Descriptive behaviorism versus cognitive theory in verbal operant conditioning. *Psychological Review*, 1966, *73*, 306–326.

Taffel, C.   Anxiety and conditioning of verbal behavior. *Journal of Abnormal and Social Psychology*, 1955, *51*, 496–502.

Thorndike, E. L.   Animal intelligence: An experimental study of the associative processes in animals. *Psychological Review Monograph Supplement*, 1898, *2*, No. 4 (Whole No. 8).

Thorndike, E. L.   *The psychology of wants, interests, and attitudes.* New York: Appleton-Century, 1935.

Thorndike, E. L., & Rock, R. T., Jr.   Learning without awareness of what is being learned or intent to learn it. *Journal of Experimental Psychology*, 1934, *17*, 1–19.

Tolman, E. C.   *Behavior and psychological man.* Berkeley: University of California Press, 1958.

Tulving, E.   Subjective organization in free recall of "unrelated" words. *Psychological Review*, 1962, *69*, 344–354.

Tulving, E.   Theoretical issues in free recall. In T. R. Dixon and D. L. Horton (Eds.), *Verbal behavior and general behavior theory.* Englewood Cliffs: Prentice-Hall, 1968, pp. 2–36.

Watson, J. B.   Psychology as the behaviorist views it. *Psychological Review*, 1913, *20*, 158–177.

Weiss, R. L.   The influence of 'set for speed' on 'learning without awareness.' *American Journal of Psychology*, 1955, *68*, 425–431.

Young, R. K.   Serial learning. In T. R. Dixon & D. L. Horton (Eds.), *Verbal behavior and general behavior theory.* Englewood Cliffs: Prentice-Hall, 1968, pp. 122–148.

9

Applications of research on learning

THE MORE mature a science becomes the more useful it is. When we have good scientific laws and use them in practical situations, we can change events in behalf of human goals. In recent years extensive applications have been made of our knowledge of learning, and it is a sign of our growing understanding of variables that influence the learning process. Most of the understanding has come from research on animals. The reader with an interest in human behavior might have been impatient with the coverage of animal learning that has been given, but it is justifiable because it is a source of so much of our knowledge that is applied to human behavior.

One of the visible phenomena of our time is *behavior modification*, which is an effort in applied psychology that uses the principles of learning to change behavior for useful ends. Thus the principles of learning can be used in hospitals or clinics in which clientele cannot function well or are suffering because of their psychological problems. The branch of behavior modification that uses principles of learning to ease human suffering is called *behavior therapy*. The assumption of behavior therapy is that maladaptive behavior is learned, and that the extinction of inappropriate behavior, and maybe the teaching of more appropriate, new responses, will cure the patient. Behavior therapy has abandoned the "medical model," which is based on the belief that neuroses are disease entities, such as smallpox, for which a cure, such as a smallpox vaccine, can be found. A psychologist who is looking for a drug to eliminate a neurosis is using a medical model. As deeply intrenched in psychology as the medical model is, and as valid as it is for some human ailments, the behavior therapists have done well for themselves by abandoning it and relying on a learning model instead.

This chapter will examine aspects of behavior modification. Various uses of positive reinforcement will be examined, including biofeedback, as well as the cure of abnormal human fears.

Some applications of positive reinforcement

Using the principles of positive reinforcement is an easy way to get rid of certain kinds of undesirable behavior. The procedure is to define the undesirable response, identify the reinforcer that is sustaining it, and then withdraw the reinforcer to extinguish the unwanted behavior. In some cases the elimination of undesirable behavior is not enough; it may be necessary to reinforce a new, more suitable response to replace the old one that has been eliminated. Most often behavior modification methods are used to change the behavior of individuals, although it is also used to redirect the behavior of entire groups, such as a classroom of students or a ward of patients in a mental hospital.

THE MODIFICATION OF INDIVIDUAL BEHAVIOR

An example of behavior modification (Hart et al., 1964) is a four-year-old boy who cried excessively in preschool, although he was otherwise normal and healthy, and the investigators hypothesized that the crying was being sustained by adult attention. An episode of crying behavior was defined as a cry loud enough to be heard 50 feet away which persisted for five seconds or more, and it was this response class that was manipulated, using teacher attention as the reinforcer. The sequence of events and the results are shown in Figure 9–1. To determine a baseline of the crying behavior so that change in it could be known, a teacher kept track of the number of crying episodes with a pocket counter for the first ten days. During this time the boy was treated in the normal manner, receiving the usual attention from the teachers whenever he cried spontaneously. For the next ten days the teachers completely withdrew their attention when he cried (this did not apply if the crying was caused by injury, such as from a playground fall). Notice in Figure 9–1 how the offensive behavior extinguishes. Then, for the next ten days, to show how crying was under the control of reinforcement, the teachers reinstated their old attentive behavior and the crying was readily reestablished. A second extinction series followed for the next ten days, and once again the crying stopped.

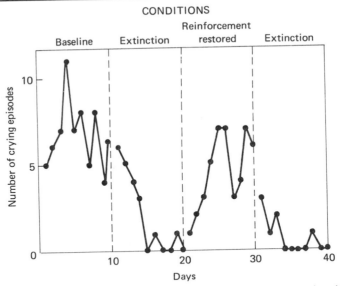

CONDITIONS

Source: B. M. Hart, E. Allen, J. S. Buell, F. R. Harris, and M. M. Wolf, Effects of social reinforcement on operant crying. *Journal of Experimental Child Psychology*, 1964, *1*, 145–153. Reprinted by permission of Academic Press, Inc.

FIGURE 9–1
Number of a child's crying episodes extinguished on two occasions by the withdrawal of adult attention, which was serving as a reinforcer.

Visual attending is particularly critical for the deaf because circumstance has denied them a primary sense channel, and Craig and Holland (1970) report an interesting experiment on increasing the frequency of visual attentive behavior among young deaf children in a classroom situation. As in the case of the boy's crying behavior that was discussed above, attentive behavior had to be defined, and primarily it was a matter of looking at the picture or object that the teacher was using in the instructional task of the moment. In front of each child on the desk was a small box with a light; and if the child was visually attentive for ten seconds the light flashed. At the end of the session the child received a piece of candy for each light flash received. Figure 9–2 shows the sequence of procedures and the results that were obtained. A baseline first was established in the initial classroom sessions and reinforcement was then introduced. The result of reinforcement was an impressive increase in visual attention. The reinforcement was then withdrawn in the final sessions and the attentive behavior extinguished.

Self-imposed starvation is a disorder called *anorexia nervosa*, and it is not to be confused with weight reduction through a rational dieting

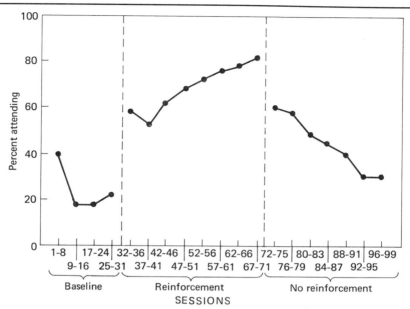

Source: H. B. Craig, and A. L. Holland, Reinforcement of visual attending in classrooms for deaf children. *Journal of Applied Behavior Analysis,* 1970, 3, 97–109. Reprinted by permission of Editor, *Journal of Applied Behavior Analysis.*

FIGURE 9–2
The acquisition and extinction of visual attentiveness in deaf children.

plan. Patients with this disorder can die, and tube feeding has been among the treatments that have been used to forestall such a grim consequence. Garfinkel, Kline, and Stancer (1973) assumed that the disorder was primarily behavioral, not physiological, and they used positive reinforcement to bring weight gains in five young women patients who had been hospitalized for the ailment. The five patients had lost 24–40 percent of their original weight at the time of hospitalization. The plan was to reward the patients with privileges such as weekend passes and off-ward socializing with friends if they gained 0.15 kg (.34 lb) per day or 1 kg (2.2 lb) per week. The results for the five are shown in Figure 9–3. By the end of the treatment they had regained 87–95 percent of their original weight.

THE MODIFICATION OF GROUP BEHAVIOR

One of the important ways that the behavior of a group can be changed with the principles of positive reinforcement is by the use of a

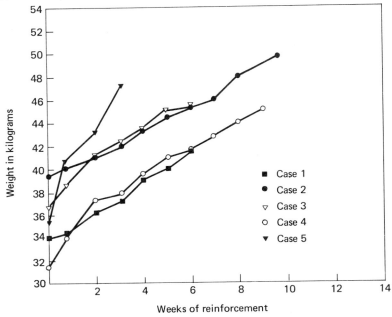

Source: P. E. Garfinkel, S. A. Kline, and H. C. Stancer, Treatment of anorexia nervosa using operant conditioning techniques. *Journal of Nervous and Mental Disease*, 1973, *157*, 428–433. Reprinted by permission of The Williams & Wilkins Co., Baltimore.

FIGURE 9–3
Gains in weight for five patients suffering from anorexia nervosa, a drastic loss of weight imposed by self-starvation. The cure was reward for gains in weight.

token economy. Tokens are symbolic rewards, such as poker chips or points, which are dispensed whenever the desired behavior occurs. Having received a token, the subject can exchange it for "backup reinforcers" of value to the subject. The type of backup reinforcer that will work depends on the subject population. Tokens will have value for children in a primary school classroom if they can be exchanged for toys, but in a mental hospital with adult patients, cigarettes, toilet articles, or extra food serve better as backup reinforcers.

The term "economy" in "token economy" derives from tokens being used as payment when the members of a group behave in a defined way, just as members of our society receive money when they perform acts that are valued, and so tokens become a medium of exchange in an "economy." There is no reason why tokens cannot be used for modifying the behavior of a single individual, but it seems that they are most often used as a reward that can be efficiently administered when members of a group perform acceptably. Later, and leisurely, the tokens can be exchanged for backup reinforcers.

Consider this study by Mann and Moss (1973), who were concerned with the socially maladaptive behavior of a group of young veterans in an acute treatment facility of a Veterans Administration hospital. The men were under the age of 30, with police and drug records common among them. Half of the patients had a record of violent assault, both before hospitalization and during it. As a group, their behavior was socially maladaptive, and they lacked vocational and social skills to find a job and to get along with people. Mostly they preferred to sit around the hospital—eating, sleeping, and watching television. With aluminum discs as tokens, the patients were placed on a very extensive token regime in an effort to socialize them. Tokens were earned for socially desirable behavior such as cleaning the ward, bed-making, attendance at a daily business meeting, and attendance at group therapy sessions. In particular, token rewards for job-seeking or employment were generous. Payment with tokens was required for many of the amenities of everyday life. Snacks, coffee, game room privileges, and weekend passes required tokens. A bed was provided, but tokens were required for the purchase of a mattress; and tokens were required to buy a pass for entry into the main dining hall.

Figure 9–4 has an example of the Mann and Moss data, and it shows how the token reward affected attendance at daily business meetings.

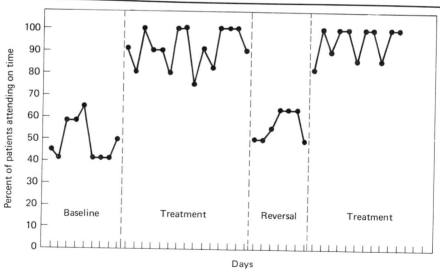

Source: R. A. Mann, and G. R. Moss, The therapeutic use of a token economy to manage a young and assaultive inpatient population. *Journal of Nervous and Mental Disease*, 1973, *157*, 1–9. Reprinted by permission of The Williams & Wilkins Co., Baltimore.

FIGURE 9–4

Token rewards were administered during the treatment periods, and the effect on attendance at daily business meetings by patients of a hospital ward is shown.

The baseline period, before the token economy program began, shows that about half of the patients bothered to attend the meeting on time, but after token reward was introduced the attendance jumped to 85–100 percent. The reversal condition is a dissociation of response and reward, in which the tokens were given regardless of whether the meeting was attended or not. We would not expect the behavior to be affected by reward when the reward is not contingent on the response, and this expectation was fulfilled in the reversal period because the attendance returned to baseline level. When reward was reinstated in the second treatment period, the attendance jumped to a high level again.

GENERALIZATION

The most fundamental question of all is whether the new behavior will generalize to other situations. Will the patients of the Mann and Moss study continue to be concerned with neatness, punctuality, and productive employment after their release from the hospital and when they are in a totally different environment? Mann and Moss did not conduct a follow-up and test for *generalization*, as it is called. In the context of behavior modification, generalization means the transfer of the new, desired behavior to other situations and its continued use there. This is superficially the same as the kind of generalization that was discussed in Chapter 5. The generalization of Chapter 5 was stimulus generalization, in which similar values of a stimulus elicit the response, but behavior modification uses generalization in a wide sense because it is quite willing to use any reasonable technique to maintain behavior in new situations.

How behavior that has been trained with positive reinforcement can be maintained in new situations is a difficult problem. A reliance on stimulus similarity to maintain the response, as in stimulus generalization, may be a useful principle, but with or without stimulus similarity there is the major problem that a new situation is often one in which reinforcement for the behavior no longer occurs. The withdrawal of reinforcement is extinction, and so the expectation would be for performance to decline. Extinction cannot be eliminated, but it can be slowed by using intermittent reinforcement in training, as we saw in Chapters 2 and 3. Occasional reapplication of reinforcement may be required to reinstate the extinguished response. Sometimes it might be possible to avoid extinction entirely by relying on naturally occurring reinforcers in the new situations. For example, suppose a therapist has been reinforcing a shy child for more active social behavior. When the child gets away from the therapist and in a social situation with other children, there is a good chance that the children themselves will reward appropriate social behavior.

Still another possibility is to give varied training. There are lines of evidence that converge on the principle that variety in training situations produces good transfer to new situations. Learning set, that was discussed in Chapter 5, is an example. In Chapter 14 we will meet another version of it under the heading of schema. For behavior modification it means that variations of the desired behavior should be reinforced in a variety of situations.

Whatever is done, there must be planning for generalization. If one trains new responses without a plan, the achievement of generalization will be accidental. Stokes and Baer (1977) called this "the train and hope method." Train and hope characterizes half of the studies of generalization in the field of behavior modification, they say.

PROGRAMMED LEARNING

If we can shape behavior of the pigeon in the laboratory and the untidy patient in the hospital with positive reinforcement, why can we not use it to mold academic skills in our schools? Skinner (1961, 1968) contends that any academic subject matter is an elaborate set of responses, usually verbal, and can be shaped with positive reinforcement like any other elaborate set of responses of any organism. Skinner, who has orchestrated so much of the modern research on positive reinforcement, sees five difficulties with our present classroom practices:

1. They are based on punishment so that the pupil must give the correct response to avoid punishment. That learning can occur this way is established in the history of education and elsewhere (see Chapter 6), but Skinner regards it as a poor way. The student might indeed learn under threatening circumstances, but the punishment also might create a chronic absentee who avoids the fearful classroom.

2. Reinforcement is usually delayed. A student will hand in a set of arithmetic problems and have them returned three days later.

3. Positive reinforcement is unstructured and infrequent when it is used at all. Some teachers are conscientous in commenting with something like "Right" and "Wrong" about the student's efforts, but some hardly bother.

4. The members of a class are expected to learn at the same pace, which is an unrealistic expectation because it fails to consider individual differences in learning rates. Some students learn rapidly and spend a good portion of their time in boredom, and other students learn slowly and struggle to keep abreast of the class pace.

5. The structure of a course of study is often inefficient, considering the complex kinds of behavior to be learned. Of course the organization of a course depends on the skill of the instructor, and many courses are

well organized. A realist must admit, however, that some courses lie on that colorless plain between chaos and distinction.

Skinner contends the result of our present-day instructional methods is inefficient learning and a system that excites neither teacher nor pupil. However, he maintains, it need not be. Why cannot a course be laid out in progressive steps with positive reinforcement contingent on the accomplishment of each step? The organization of these steps could be structured by experts, and then this ideal program of study could be put on a machine for use by students everywhere. And why could not a student study independently with a pace adjusted to personal learning capabilities? Exactly this kind of thing has been done, and the devices to conduct programmed learning are called *teaching machines*. The unit of the program is a question or a problem, and the student who responds correctly to it is immediately informed of the correctness and is moved on to the next step. Skinner recommends that the steps be small so the chance of error is small and the chance of success and reward correspondingly high. And all of this proceeds at the student's own pace.

The first teaching machine was invented by E. L. Pressey of Ohio State University (Pressey, 1926). Pressey's original interest was the automatic administration of a test, such as an intelligence test, and he invented a device with four keys for response and a window for presenting multiple choice test items. The pressing of a key turned up a new question, and the correct responses were tallied on a counter at the back of the machine. Pressey made the perceptive observation that the machine could teach as well as test if the subject was allowed to continue responding to an item until the correct answer was found, and he designed his machine for this mode also. Pressey's original teaching machine is shown in Figure 9–5.

After about 50 years the modern teaching machine has come to use a digital computer for the storage and control of the information, and the largest developmental effort underway is the PLATO system at the Uni-

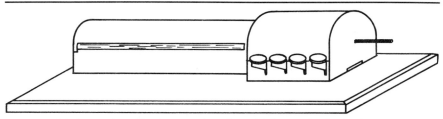

Source: S. L. Pressey, A machine for automatic teaching of drill material. *School and Society*, 1927, 25, 549–552. Reprinted by permission of the Society for the Advancement of Education, Inc.

FIGURE 9–5
The first teaching machine, invented by S. L. Pressey.

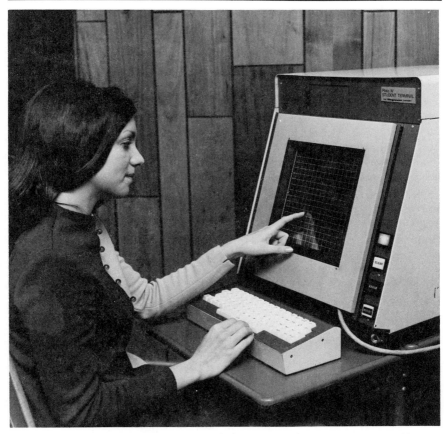

Reproduced by permission of the Computer-Based Education Research Laboratory, University of Illinois at Urbana-Champaign.

FIGURE 9–6
A student using PLATO, a computer-based teaching machine developed by the University of Illinois.

versity of Illinois (Bitzer and Skaperdas, 1970). PLATO is an acronym for Programmed Logic for Automated Teaching Operations. Figure 9–6 shows a student at a PLATO station. In 1979 there were 1,000 terminals in operation, and more to come. At present, PLATO is teaching courses that range from psychology and chemistry to exotic languages. Audio units produce sound that is synchronized with the visual presentation for foreign language instruction. Pictorial presentations are a part of the system also. Computer graphic techniques can draw anything on the display from a map to a cartoon-like rat pressing a bar for a vivid point about reinforcement, and slides are used to present photographs.

Biofeedback

The operations of biofeedback can reasonably be subsumed under positive reinforcement, and so should be a continuation of the previous section, but there are sufficient differences in the responses classes that are manipulated, the motives of the investigators, and the applications that are sought to justify a separate section. The term "biofeedback" refers to procedures which provide the subject with information about the state of a covert physiological response. Biofeedback research is in the tradition of instrumental learning (Chapter 3). The physiological response occurs, information about it is given, and the increase in response probability that occurs is interpreted as learning.

Traditionally, the psychology of learning has had overt behavior as its province, but the field of biofeedback has changed that by turning attention to the learning of processes under the skin. There are ramifications of this development for both basic and applied science. On the side of basic science, the interest is in laws of learning for the new physiological response classes and in how these laws integrate with those derived from overt behavior. On the side of applied science, the interest is in feedback as part of the treatment for certain clinical disorders. Both basic and applied science have had their efforts clouded somewhat by extravagant claims for biofeedback, but nevertheless there has been a core of serious research that has entered the main body of psychology and medicine and seems destined to remain there.

Basic science is committed to distilling laws from regularities in observation and to organizing the laws into theory. Applied science, on the other hand, has human betterment as its goal. Basic and applied science are not independent enterprises because applied science often turns the findings of basic science to human ends, and applied science can uncover data which basic science can use. Regardless of this meshing, basic and applied science are sufficiently different in motive to warrant a separate discussion of the two.

THE BASIC SCIENCE POINT OF VIEW IN BIOFEEDBACK

One cannot understand what the topic of biofeedback means for basic law and theory without understanding the similarities and differences between Pavlovian conditioning and instrumental learning, and why experimental psychologists consider the similarities and differences to be interesting. If we were confident in one set of laws, there would be no need to present instrumental learning and classical conditioning as separate chapters in this book. That separate chapters are still maintained represents psychology's uncertainty about one set of laws, and in this section the reasons for that uncertainty are examined. The topic is a long-persisting one in the psychology of learning, bred in years of pondering the similarities and differences between classical conditioning and instrumental learning.

SIMILARITIES BETWEEN CLASSICAL CONDITIONING AND INSTRUMENTAL LEARNING

There is reason to believe that classical conditioning and instrumental learning are the same if we believe that things equal to the same thing are equal to each other. Many of the standard phenomena of instrumental learning, such as changes in performance measures as a function of acquisition trials, extinction, effects of partial reinforcement on extinction, spontaneous recovery, stimulus generalization, etc., are present in both classical conditioning and instrumental learning (Kimble, 1961, pp. 81–98), and they certainly encourage us to believe that the two kinds of learning are probably the same. And, by comparing the procedures for the two kinds of learning, one can see distinct similarities. Consider a salivation response being acquired by classical conditioning, with a tone as the CS, food as the UCS, and salivation as the UCR. Consider a bar press being acquired by instrumental learning, with a tone as the CS, food as the positive reinforcement, and salivation and eating the food as the UCR. Obviously there is a parallel between the two, and when so many behavioral phenomena are common to both kinds, it is easy to see why so many psychologists feel that the two kinds of learning differ only in surface ways and are really the same underneath. The feeling is held in check, however, because there are differences between the two kinds of learning, and for some the differences are more compelling than the similarities.

DIFFERENCES BETWEEN CLASSICAL CONDITIONING AND INSTRUMENTAL LEARNING

Skinner (1938, pp. 19–21) pointed out that there is a considerable body of behavior that is emitted rather than elicited by a stimulus; the response simply occurs without an identifiable stimulus. Emitted behavior, whenever it occurs, can be learned instrumentally, and Skinner called this kind of behavior *operant behavior*. Classical conditioning, on the other hand, is a kind of behavior that always has an eliciting stimulus, and Skinner called it *respondent behavior*. Some are tempted to assume that somewhere there is an eliciting stimulus for operant behavior if we were only clever enough to find it, but, when evidence for it is missing, the assumption is rash. Someday we may be able to find eliciting stimuli for all the kinds of operant responses, but until we do we have a class of behavior that is different from classically conditioned responses in a fundamental way.

A second difference is that the CR is similar to the UCR in classical conditioning, but in instrumental learning the learned response can be totally different from the UCR to the reinforcement, and usually is. Pavlov (1927) believed that the CS came to substitute for the UCS, and the CR that was learned in response to it had survival value for the organism. Conditioned salivation, for example, lubricates the mouth in anticipation for the food to follow, and so it is the same as the salivation that accompanies eating. This has been called *stimulus substitution theory*. Instrumental learning, however, ordinarily will have a response learned that is topographically much different than the UCR associated with the reinforcement. Bar pressing is completely different than the eating of the food reward or the drinking of the water reward. As valid as this difference between the two kinds of learning might seem, it is weakened somewhat because the stimulus substitution theory is false in its strong form—a CR may be similar to the UCR, but it is not the same. In the case of salivation, the amount and rate of conditioned salivation is less than unconditioned salivation, and even the viscosity has been reported as less for conditioned salivation (Terrace, 1973, p. 82). The conditioned eyeblink response, in which an airpuff is used to elicit the blink that is the UCR, comes to occur in anticipation of the airpuff and is not the same as the UCR. Notwithstanding, and without pressing the point too hard, the CR and the UCR certainly are similar in classical conditioning more often than in instrumental learning.

The third difference that has persisted over the years is that classical conditioning and instrumental learning apply to different response classes. The responses that have been classically conditioned usually have been products of the autonomic nervous system, which controls glandular and visceral responses, such as salivation or the heart-rate response. Exceptions mainly have been the eyeblink and the knee-jerk response. On the other hand, instrumental learning has been found only for nonautonomic responses involving skeletal, or striped, muscle; there has been no evidence of the reward learning of autonomic responses.

THE INSTRUMENTAL LEARNING OF GLANDULAR AND VISCERAL RESPONSES

The distinction between responses based on skeletal muscles and responses based on glandular and visceral activity is an old one (Miller, 1969). Ancient Greek philosophers distinguished between the superior rational mind in the head and the inferior body below. Ideas and thoughts were considered to be of a higher form than emotions, for example. Later, neuroanatomists gave this distinction physiological credence when they distinguished between the cerebrospinal nervous system of the brain and the spinal cord that controlled skeletal responses, and the autonomic nervous system that controlled glandular and visceral responses. The autonomic nervous system was considered essentially independent of the cerebrospinal system (its name "autonomic" reflects the belief in autonomy from the cerebrospinal system). That we can control the movement of a hand but apparently not our heart rate was the kind of evidence taken in support of this distinction. With this distinction in our scientific history, and with many instances of the classical conditioning of glandular and visceral responses, and the many instances of the reward learning of skeletal responses, it is not surprising that learning psychologists have maintained the separation of classical conditioning and instrumental learning for so long.

It has been only recently that learning psychologists have given serious consideration to the instrumental learning of autonomic responses. In retrospect, the tardy concern with this topic is not surprising. A motor act like pressing a bar is observable and available for reward when it occurs, but responses of the autonomic nervous system are remote and hidden, and only when we deliberately seek them out and externalize them with sophisticated instrumentation do they become available for reward. Because reward is an event that is fed back to the subject and informs about the adequacy of the response, and because the responses are physiological events, this research area is known as *biofeedback.* Primarily, it was the work of N. E. Miller and his colleagues at Rockefeller University that caused us to turn toward biofeedback.

Salivation has been a commonly used response for classical conditioning since Pavlov, but Miller and Carmona (1967) viewed it anew and asked if its occurrence could be altered by reward. Dogs were their subjects, and they brought tubing from the parotid duct through a hole in the cheek to a system for measuring the spontaneous flow of saliva. Depending upon the experimental condition, either the spontaneous increase or decrease in the flow of saliva was rewarded with a 20 ml. shot of water in the mouth. Sessions in which either increase or decrease in salivation was rewarded lasted for up to 40 days. The results are shown in Figure 9–7. Contrary to long-held beliefs, there can be a controlling of salivation by reward.

A knotty problem for understanding the instrumental learning of glandular and visceral responses is that it may be mediated by skeletal, or somatic, response learning and not directly learned at all. For example, in the Miller & Carmona study, the water may have rewarded rate of breathing or struggling in the apparatus, which in turn affected rate of salivation. Rate of salivation, then, would be a byproduct of reward, not an explicit product. Miller and Carmona recorded additional mea-

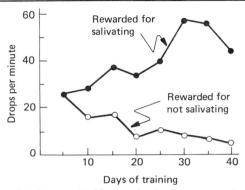

Source: N. E. Miller and A. Carmona, Modification of a visceral response, salivation in thirsty dogs, by instrumental training with water reward. *Journal of Comparative and Physiological Psychology,* 1967, 63, 1–6. Reprinted by permission of the American Psychological Association.

FIGURE 9–7

The instrumental learning of salivation. Thirsty dogs were rewarded with water for either an increase or a decrease in salivation.

sures in their study, such as frequency of respiration, and they made additional tests to check some of these possibilities. They concluded that somatic mediation was not operating and that true instrumental learning of salivation had occurred. The Miller and Carmona study is a good one, but it would have been more convincing if somehow the mediation of somatic responses was eliminated altogether, and this was the approach taken in other experiments from Miller's laboratory.

How related but irrelevant processes can exert an influence on the autonomic response under investigation is best exemplified by the instrumental learning of heart rate. Lynch and Paskewitz (1971) capture the flavor of the problem:

> No one would be surprised if an individual claimed he could control his heart rate by jumping up or down, or by running, or holding his breath; in such cases the mediation of heart rate activity via other physiological mechanisms would be clear to us all. In such a case it is also clear that the individual has not "learned" to control his heart rate directly, rather he has altered other mechanisms which in turn reflexively affect heart rate.[1]

Miller and DiCara (1967) used the drug curare as a way of eliminating these influences on heart rate during reward learning. Curare has the interesting property of being able to block neural impulses to the muscles, and so its effect is paralysis, but without blocking the reception and

---

[1] *Journal of Nervous and Mental Disease,* 1971, 153, pp. 207–208. Reprinted by permission of The Williams & Wilkins Co., Baltimore.

processing of stimuli. The paralysis can be so complete that a respirator must be used for breathing because the muscles of the lungs are inoperative. For some years it has been established that electrical stimulation of the medial forebrain bundle of the brain with implanted electrodes is rewarding for responses such as bar pressing and maze running, and Miller and DiCara used this as reward for change in the heart rate of the curarized rat when a signal occurred. Heart rate had been instrumentally conditioned before, but none of the earlier work was theoretically decisive because the mediation of skeletal muscles had not been controlled. Animals were rewarded for either low or high heart rates, and the results are shown in Figure 9–8. The heart rate appears amenable to instrumental learning when the potential influence of skeletal muscles is ruled out.

Miller and his colleagues also demonstrated the instrumental learning of urine flow (Miller and DiCara, 1968), changes in peripheral blood flow (DiCara and Miller, 1968b), and blood pressure (DiCara and Miller 1968a). All of this was exciting to psychologists who saw a wider scope for the laws of instrumental learning than ever before, but their enthusiasm was dampened when the findings on the instrumental learning of heart rate in a curarized animal could not be reliably replicated (Miller and Dworkin, 1974). The reasons for the failure are not com-

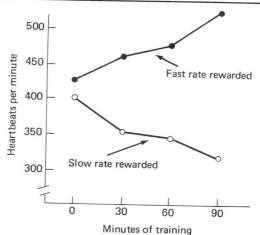

Source: N. E. Miller, and L. DiCara, Instrumental learning of heart rate changes in curarized rats: Shaping, and specificity to discriminative stimulus. *Journal of Comparative and Physiological Psychology*, 1967, 63, 12–19. Reprinted by permission of the American Psychological Association.

FIGURE 9–8

The rewarding of rats for either fast or slow heart rates. The rats were curarized to eliminate the effect of muscular activity on heart rate.

pletely clear, but it is now evident that the curarized rat preparations used in the early studies did not do a good job of maintaining the animal's vital functions. Much work has been done on refining the laboratory techniques used with curarized animals (Dworkin and Miller, 1977), but the instrumental learning of heart rate in the curarized rat still cannot be reliably obtained.

To date, there is no evidence that heart rate can be instrumentally learned without somatic mediation. If somatic mediation is the underlying basis for learning by functions of the autonomic nervous system, then basic science will have a diminished interest in it because it has been training motor activities for a long time. The theoretical issue is not whether responses of the autonomic nervous system can be learned, but whether they can be learned without somatic mediation.

The applied science point of view in biofeedback

It is unfair to say that applied science is disinterested in the question of pure visceral learning, but it is fair to say that they are willing to get on with the problem of helping people with the knowledge at hand without waiting for resolution of theoretical issues. Applied science has a pragmatic way of using whatever knowledge it can whenever it can, and often long before the knowledge fits a conceptual framework that is satisfying to basic science. Good bridges were being built before mechanics became a formalized part of physics.

Biofeedback, operating as it does at the interface of psychology and medicine, is being seen as part of a new discipline called behavioral medicine. Behavioral medicine is concerned with physiological responses which patients learn and can have under voluntary control. The hope is that a patient can have a physiological response under voluntary control and ease his discomfort or even remove a threat to his life. The power to self-regulate heart rate is an example; it would be therapeutic for certain heart ailments and an advance for behavioral medicine if it could be achieved.

SKIN TEMPERATURE

Skin temperature is principally influenced by two factors: the air temperature and the dilation of peripheral blood vessels. The dilation and contraction of blood vessels is under control of the autonomic nervous system. Raynaud's disease is a good reason for the study of biofeedback control of skin temperature because the patient experiences episodes of constriction of blood vessels in the hands, and sometimes the feet, which leaves them feeling cold. The hope is that those afflicted with Raynaud's disease can acquire self-control of skin temperature through biofeedback training.

An experiment by Taub (1977) is a good example of the biofeedback training of skin temperature. Temperature was measured by a sensor on the back of the hand. After establishing baseline temperature (which is about 90°F under conditions of normal room temperature), some of the subjects were instructed to increase their skin temperature and some to decrease it. A feedback light increased in intensity whenever temperature went up and decreased whenever temperature went down. The findings for subjects who were instructed either to increase their skin temperature or decrease it are shown in Figure 9–9. A daily training session was 15 minutes, and the control of skin temperature developed rapidly. The average change is small.

After original training, some of the best subjects were given additional training in reversing the direction of their temperature control. The data of one of these subjects for a single session are shown in Figure 9–10. Direction could be changed at will, and the range of temperature control was as much as 15 degrees. Taub observed that a well-trained subject like this is very good at localizing his control of skin temperature. Training for one hand can be diffuse in the beginning, with temperature changes occurring in both hands, but as training progresses the control localizes in the desired hand. Localization can be as specific as a finger.

Is temperature a matter of somatic mediation? Taub did not think so, although his evidence is preliminary. Electromyographic records (electrical activity of the muscles) was not particularly related to temperature control. Nor was the amount of muscular activity which subjects were seen to exert in their effort to gain temperature control.

Taub tried his technique on patients with Raynaud's disease, and he found their ability to control skin temperature to be as good as normal subjects. Outbreaks of the disease usually occur when the patient is emotionally upset or when exposed to cold, and it could not be claimed that the training overcame the attacks. Nevertheless, Taub's research, and other work like it (see Blanchard and Young, 1974) is provocative and has promise for the control of Raynaud's disease.

HEART RATE

The conditioning of heart rate without somatic mediation is in doubt, but some control of heart rate with somatic mediation involved is not. Patients with certain kinds of heart ailment have been taught to control their heart rate with some success.

Premature ventricular contraction is a heart ailment, commonly described as the heart skipping a beat, and one form of it is called

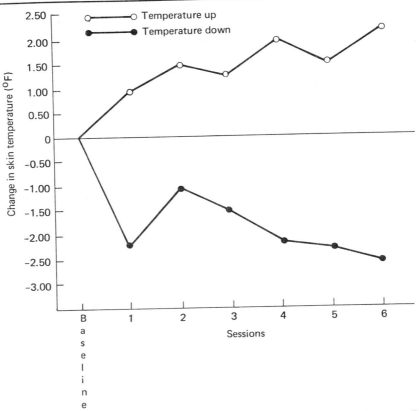

Source: E. Taub, Self-regulation of human tissue temperature. In G. E. Schwartz and J. Beatty (Eds.), *Biofeedback: Theory and research.* New York: Academic Press, 1977, pp. 265–300. Reprinted by permission of Academic Press, Inc.

FIGURE 9–9
The biofeedback control of skin temperature. A feedback light increased in intensity when temperature increased and decreased when temperature decreased. One group of subjects was instructed to increase temperature, another group to decrease it.

"bigeminy" in which a normal beat alternates with an abnormal one. Patients can control bigeminy through exercise, but exercise is not always possible because a patient may be weak or the social situation will not allow it. Learning how to speed up the heart voluntarily through biofeedback training would be a useful technique for a patient. Miller and Dworkin (1977) report a case from their laboratory in which a patient was taught to increase his heart rate without the use of exercise. The biofeedback training involved a signal light that came on whenever heart rate increased, or a needle on a meter that indicated heart rate. He

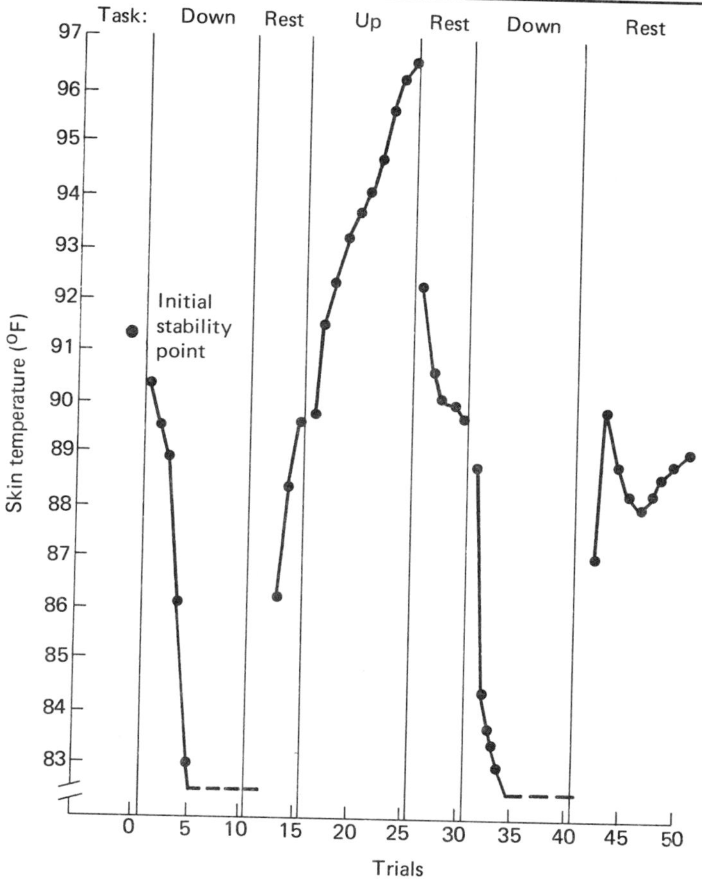

Source: E. Taub, Self-regulation of human tissue temperature. In G. E. Schwartz and J. Beatty (Eds.), *Biofeedback: Theory and research.* New York: Academic Press, 1977, pp. 265–300. Reprinted by permission of Academic Press, Inc.

FIGURE 9–10
Performance of a subject who was given biofeedback training in the reversal of skin temperature.

was able to increase his heart rate by as much as 40 beats a minute. Results like these have been reported in other studies (Blanchard and Young, 1974; Engel, 1977).

BLOOD PRESSURE

Hypertension (high blood pressure) is a public health problem that occurs in 5–10 percent of the population, and the elevated blood pressure that it induces is the suspected villain in a number of dangerous disorders. Drugs are used to lower blood pressure, but the complex and widespread character of high blood pressure produces an interest in other therapeutic techniques that look promising. Biofeedback control is one of them.

Systolic pressure and diastolic pressure are two dimensions of blood pressure, and the biofeedback control of both of them has been studied. Systolic pressure is the peak pressure following contraction of the heart, and diastolic pressure is the pressure following contraction when systolic pressure has declined and before the next heart beat. The standard procedure in a biofeedback experiment is to use a blood pressure cuff wrapped around the upper arm. Average blood pressure as the baseline for the subject is first established, and then the subject is rewarded with a light or a tone whenever blood pressure goes above (or below) the baseline.

The gist of the evidence so far is that biofeedback control is probably possible for both systolic and diastolic pressure (Blanchard and Young, 1974; Shapiro et al., 1977). One of the good questions that investigators ask is whether the reward signal is not actually affecting heart rate, of which blood pressure is a function. This is a definite possibility, and findings on it are mixed (Shapiro et al., 1977). Schwartz (1977), in a sophisticated account of the interdependence of physiological processes such as these, has preliminary evidence that blood pressure and heart rate can be independently manipulated.

The use of biofeedback for the control of high blood pressure is a long way off because the effects are small, and they vary substantially from study to study (Blanchard and Young, 1974; Shapiro et al., 1977). As a technique, routine use of it as a proven therapeutic agent is not yet justified. However, it is an easy, harmless technique that would deserve a try if other treatment techniques were not having much success.

BRAIN WAVES (THE EEG)

Heretofore we have been talking about biofeedback control of functions of the autonomic nervous system, and now we shift to brain waves and the central nervous system. First, a definition and some background.

The electroencephalogram (EEG) is a record of the minute electrical waves of the brain and it is also a remote physiological response that appears to be subject to instrumental learning effects, although the learning is not without its problems of interpretation. The EEG can have different wave forms, and they are often characterized in terms of levels of wakefulness, ranging from focussed attention and high alertness to deep sleep. For our purposes here we will be concerned only with *alpha*

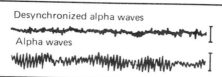

FIGURE 9–11
EEG alpha waves and their desynchronization.

waves and *alpha desynchronization*, both of which are shown in Figure 9–11. Alpha waves have a frequency of 8–13 Hz, with moderate amplitude, and they often accompany a relaxed, calm state of wakefulness. Alpha desynchronization has a faster wave, greater than 13 Hz, with low amplitude. Alpha waves can be desynchronized by a variety of events, and among them are paying attention, anxiety and frustration, active thoughts, muscle activity, and, most of all, visual stimulation.

As with responses of the autonomic nervous system, it was long thought that EEG was subject only to classical conditioning. The classical conditioning of EEG received preliminary interest in the 1930s, but by the 1940s there was systematic interest in the topic (e.g., Jasper and Shagass, 1941; Shagass, 1942; Shagass and Johnson, 1943). A typical experimental setup would be a light as the UCS to desynchronize alpha, and a tone as the CS. At the outset the tone would leave the alpha waves unchanged, but with repeated pairings of the light and the tone, the tone alone would come to desynchronize alpha, which is the CR. Not much interest developed in the classical conditioning of EEG because the phenomenon was variable and unstable, although it appears to be real enough (Albino and Burnand, 1964). The classical conditioning of EEG was a concern with the learning of alpha desynchronization, which is a lessening of alpha, but the modern work on instrumental learning is concerned with *increasing* alpha wave production.

Why should anyone be interested in increasing the production of alpha waves? One can see how basic scientists could become interested in increasing the production of alpha waves because it would extend their understanding of nature and how it operates, but less apparent is the popular interest that has developed. In the 1960s there began a social restlessness among young adults, and a product of the restlessness was fascination with new dimensions of emotions that led to a pursuit of new experiences, often with drugs. The serenity of Zen Buddhists and Yogi masters in their meditation was thought to be a new emotional state for the West, and the attainment of it was seen as exciting and desirable.

Alpha waves are often associated with a contemplative, relaxed state of mind. Because some think that a calm state of mind is desirable, biofeedback training of EEG is seen as the road to serenity. This line of thought has not been hurt by the findings that contemplative Indian Yogis and Zen Buddhists are good at producing alpha waves in an awakened, meditative state. Anand, Chhina, and Singh (1961) obtained EEG recordings on four Indian Yogis before and after meditation. All four showed an increase in alpha activity during meditation. Two of these Yogis were subjected to explicit external stimuli before and during meditation: strong light, loud sound, touching with a hot glass tube, and a vibrating tuning fork. All of these stimuli desynchronized alpha before but not during meditation. Kasamatsu and Hirai (1966) conducted a related study of 48 Japanese Zen Buddhist priests and disciples. Experience in meditation ranged from 1 to over 20 years. Comparison was with control subjects with no training in meditation. The control subjects had no change in their EEG records, but the Zen Buddhists increased their alpha production during meditation, and the amount of alpha activity increased with experience in meditation.

Biofeedback entered the picture with the work of Kamiya and his associates who reported that alpha waves could be instrumentally learned. Nowlis and Kamiya (1970) tested their subjects in a moderately darkened room. A tone was sounded whenever alpha waves were produced, and at the end of training a majority of the subjects were generating more alpha waves than before the biofeedback training began. If alpha waves can be produced by biofeedback, and if alpha waves are correlated with serenity among Indian Yogis and Zen Buddhists, then it logically followed for some that biofeedback was the route to serenity. Western science had penetrated the mysticism of the East.

A good scientist is a doubter, never being wholly convinced that things are as they seem, and some psychologists believed that it was uncritical to assume that biofeedback will produce the meditative states of the East. There are more mundane explanations of alpha increase, they said. A first point of questioning is to ask whether alpha learning truly occurs. The Nowlis and Kamiya experiment is suggestive but not decisive for learning. Control conditions are needed. How do we know that a control group without feedback would not show an increase in alpha over the same period? Subjects ordinarily are apprehensive when they enter an experiment, which would tend to desynchronize alpha and, as they become relaxed during the course of the experiment, desynchronization would decrease, alpha would increase, and "learning" would be observed. Another kind of control group could be given noncontingent feedback, in which feedback and alpha are unrelated. This is a better control group than one with no feedback because they receive the same events as an experimental group except that response and reward are uncorrelated. How do we know that a noncontingent control group would not show an increase in alpha?

Lynch, Paskewitz, and Orne (1974, Experiment I) compared a contingent feedback group with a noncontingent feedback group in the instrumental learning of alpha waves. Feedback was a green light for alpha waves and a red light for their absence. The baseline condition at the start was three minutes in a totally darkened room, and then ten trials were given, with a trial being two minutes of feedback and one minute of resting between trials with the feedback lights turned off. The results are given in Figure 9–12, in which the alpha on the feedback and resting segments of a trial are plotted separately. Feedback, whether contingent or noncontingent, produced "learning"; *both* feedback curves steadily climb over trials. A demonstration of learning must also take the alpha increase beyond the alpha resting level, which is the control baseline. The feedback alpha curve in Figure 9–12 is indeed increasing, but the question is whether it will advance beyond the alpha resting curve. The low level of the feedback alpha curve makes an overtake of the alpha resting curve somewhat unlikely. Plotkin (1978) gave every opportunity for alpha learning to overtake the level of the alpha baseline by extending the training to ten one-hour sessions. He found no evidence of alpha learning either. There is now agreement among leading workers in this field that feedback training does not increase

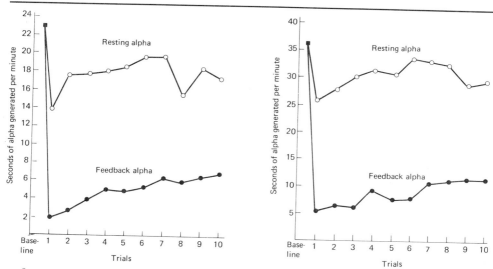

Source: J. J. Lynch, D. A. Paskewitz and M. T. Orne, Some factors in the feedback control of human alpha rhythm. *Psychosomatic Medicine*, 1974, 36, 399–409. Reprinted by permission of the American Psychosomatic Society, Inc.

FIGURE 9–12

The curves on the left show effects of reinforcing the occurrence of EEG alpha waves by making the feedback contingent upon alpha production. The curves on the right show that the same effects are obtained when feedback is noncontingent and unrelated to the occurrence of alpha.

alpha beyond the resting level (Lynch, Paskewitz, and Orne, 1974; Paskewitz and Orne, 1973, 1974; Johnson, 1977, p. 74; Plotkin, 1978; Orne and Wilson, 1977, p. 108), and so learning as we know it for other response classes does not occur for alpha.

Granting that alpha increase with feedback is not learning as we ordinarily define it, there is a learning-like effect in Figure 9–12 nevertheless. Furthermore, we have seen that alpha increases with experience for Zen Buddhist priests. What is the explanation? Lynch and Paskewitz (1971) have the hypothesis, which was applied to the data shown in Figure 9–12, that learning-like effects for alpha occur as a subject ceases to attend to stimuli that desynchronize alpha. As the power to block incoming stimuli increases, the proportion of alpha increases and "learning" is observed. Peper (1971), Mulholland and Peper (1971), and Plotkin (1976) believe that alpha is influenced by motor activity in this way. Motor movements and tensions will desynchronize alpha, and so alpha will increase as a subject becomes increasingly quiescent and relaxed. The production of alpha comes from control of stimuli that desynchronize it, not from alpha learning per se.

Whether true alpha learning occurs or not, it may nevertheless be true that sustained alpha produces a calm, serene state of mind. Walsh (1974) tested the hypothesis that the relaxed mental states are not produced by alpha but by the demands of the experimental situation as the subject perceives them, or by deliberate instructions from the experimenter. Before receiving feedback training, Walsh's subjects received either alpha instructions or neutral instructions. The alpha instructions explained biofeedback training and the "alpha state" as calm, contemplative, and dreamlike. The neutral instructions gave a matter-of-fact account of EEG and biofeedback training. The dependent measure was a description of subjective experiences associated with the feedback signal which judges rated for its correspondence to the "alpha state." The results were that a contemplative "alpha state" accompanied alpha only when the subjects were instructed in it and led to expect it. On the basis of the Walsh experiment it is not surprising that Yogis and Zen Buddhists have serene subjective states that accompany their alpha waves during meditation. Walsh has shown us that these subjective states can be controlled by situational factors, and the situational factors for Yogis and Zen Buddhists are compelling religious ones.

Conclusion on brain waves There has been a considerable amount of work on biofeedback and EEG, but it would seem to be the least useful of the biofeedback efforts. There is no evidence that alpha increases with biofeedback operations and is learned. What appears as learning is the operation of behavioral strategies to ignore or control stimuli that depress alpha, which is not alpha learning but the learning of activity correlated with alpha. Nor is there evidence that sustained alpha produces a serene state of mind. The serene state comes from suggestion, nothing more.

MUSCLE POTENTIALS

When a neural impulse traveling down an axon reaches the motor endplate on a muscle fiber, the fiber contracts, then relaxes, and there follows a minute electrical discharge into surrounding tissue. The field which specializes in the recording of this electrical activity is *electromyography*, or EMG. The recording is done either by electrodes placed on the surface of the skin, or by fine wire electrodes inserted directly into the muscle like a hypodermic needle (Basmajian, 1974).

Budzynski et al. (1970) showed how EMG can be used therapeutically by revealing muscular activity to a patient with biofeedback techniques. Tension headaches are associated with sustained, excessive contractions of the head and neck muscles, and EMG is used to provide feedback about the tension. Budzynski et al. used a tone to inform the subject about the level of tension, with a higher pitch tone being associated with a higher level of EMG activity. EMG surface electrodes were placed on the forehead. The patient was urged to relax in the biofeedback training sessions and keep the tone as low pitched as possible. In addition to the biofeedback training, the patient was encouraged to practice relaxation at home at least once a day. The patient also was required to keep a record of headaches and to judge each one on a rating scale. The average results for five patients are shown in Figure 9–13. Both the headache intensity and the EMG level decreased steadily over the four weeks of feedback after the baseline period.

EMG biofeedback is now becoming a useful tool for the retraining of muscles that have become impaired by accident or illness. Neural impulses are often capable of reaching inoperative muscles and activating them, but the patient has inadequate internal feedback about his muscular intentions and actions. Biofeedback procedures present these low key, often tiny, muscle activities to the patient and show him muscular capabilities that he did not think he had. Booker et al. (1969) used EMG feedback on a patient who had been in an accident and could not control the muscles of the left side of the face or blink the left eye or close it. By giving biofeedback about EMG activity on both sides of the face, the patient could compare movements of the damaged side with the normal side, and strive to equalize them. At first she obtained some movement of facial muscles by shoulder movement, but eventually she activated the facial muscles alone. This program took several months to complete, and it was successful.

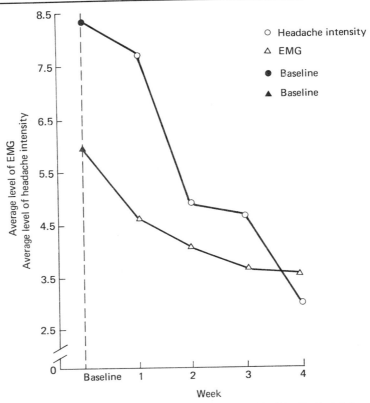

Source: Adapted with permission from T. Budzynski, J. Stoyva, and C. Adler, Feedback-induced muscle relaxation: Application to tension headache. *Journal of Behavior Therapy and Experimental Psychiatry*, 1970, *1*, 205–211. Copyright 1970, Pergamon Press, Ltd.

FIGURE 9–13
Effects of biofeedback training to reduce muscular tension and thus tension headaches. As the muscular tension, measured by EMG, decreased, the rated severity of the headache decreased.

CONCLUSION ON BIOFEEDBACK

Biofeedback has had a brief but active research history, and the best that can be said of it is that it looks promising enough to justify the research that is continuing. The basic science side of learning is bedeviled with the somatic mediation problem; it has not proved that pure visceral learning can occur. Applied science, on the other hand, hovers between doubt and optimism. In two major summaries of the clinical usefulness of biofeedback, Legewie (1977, p. 473) said "I have not been able to do away with my scepticism about the clinical use of biofeedback" and Blanchard and Young (1974, pp. 587–588) said ". . . it would seem premature to hail biofeedback training as a panacea for psychosomatic and other disorders." The biofeedback area that seems on the soundest turf of all is EMG feedback (Blanchard and Young, 1974, p. 579; Tarler-Benlolo, 1978), but even here caution is deserved because few follow-up studies of long-term benefits have been run (Tarler-Benlolo, 1978). The other areas may realize their promise as research succeeds in uncovering more of their facts and in untangling their problems.

The elimination of phobias

Behavior therapy is the clinical arm of behavior modification that uses the laws of learning to adjust the maladaptive behavior of mentally distressed individuals. In the first part of this chapter, some therapeutic uses of positive reinforcement by behavior therapists were discussed. In this section, we will discuss the elimination of unrealistic fears that can cripple the effectiveness of an individual. These unrealistic fears are called *phobias*.

Many fears are beneficial, such as the fear of fire which keeps you from putting your hand in a flame. Other fears can be beneficial under some circumstances and absurd under others. Consider a fear of height. It is a healthy attitude to be respectfully fearful when on the edge of a 1,000-foot cliff, but it is abnormal for your heart to pound wildly when standing on a chair in your kitchen. It is a wise person who does not put a hand in a nest of cobras, but it is abnormal to break into a sweat when handed a plastic snake. The psychotherapist does a lively business in the extinction of unrealistic fears such as these.

At the beginning of Chapter 6 a pioneering experiment by Watson and Rayner (1920) on the conditioning of human fears was discussed. They used a classical conditioning procedure and taught a baby to be afraid of a white rat and similar white objects. Using the Watson and Rayner study as point of departure, Jones investigated the extinction of fears in children. After trying several possibilities (Jones, 1924a), Jones settled on "the method of direct conditioning" as the most useful and she reported on its use with the case of little Peter, a child of three years (Jones, 1924b). Tests had established that Peter was afraid of rabbits, and Jones' method of fear extinction was to associate a rabbit with the pleasurable act of eating. At first the rabbit was kept at a distance from Peter while he ate, but as the fear lessened Jones was able to bring the rabbit closer and closer until eventually Peter's fear disappeared. Today this method of extinction is called *counterconditioning*.

Not much came of Jones' findings for a while, probably because the treatment of phobia in the 1920s was dominated by Freudian psychoanalysis (psychoanalysis is still with us but it has competitors). Psychoanalysis is an *insight therapy,* in which the analyst conducts a long probing inquiry into the patients' unconscious mind in an effort to turn up the origin of the phobia that is repressed there. Once the origin is revealed the cure is accomplished, according to psychoanalytic theory. This state of affairs prevailed until three things happened: Eysenck amassed statistics that showed the ineffectiveness of psychoanalysis and insight therapies like it (Eysenck, 1952); Eysenck (e.g., 1959) argued how psychotherapy can be rooted in learning theory; and Wolpe (1954, 1958, 1962) published a theory of phobia elimination based on countercondi-tioning. These events did not stand alone in their influence on behavior therapy and its growth, but they came at an intellectually restless mo-ment and were a catalyst for it.

Eysenck's 1952 message was hard-hitting. After examining the recov-ery rate of neurotics in mental hospitals, neurotics given routine com-fort and medication but not psychotherapy, and neurotics given psychoanalysis and other insight therapies, Eysenck found that about two thirds of them recovered within two years of the onset of illness regardless of what was done to them. While these data are not strict disproof of any therapeutic method, they nevertheless gave cause for reflective pause.

Subsequently, Eysenck (1959) argued that if learning is a very influen-tial factor for our behavior, which no one denies, then it is difficult to deny that neurotic reactions have a large learning component and are importantly determined by the laws of learning. Maladaptive behavior is not a symptom of repressed forces in the unconscious mind. "Get rid of the symptom and you have eliminated the neurosis," Eysenck said, and doing it is a straightforward matter of extinction.

How are human phobias extinguished? Wolpe (1954, 1958, 1962) said that the core of neurotic behavior lies not in maladaptive behavior but in the fear that underlies it, and it is fear that must be extinguished if the undesirable behavior is to be eliminated. Wolpe followed the research of Jones (1924a, 1924b) with studies of his own on counterconditioning, and he concluded that an antagonistic response could eliminate fear, as Jones said. Wolpe (1962, p. 562) stated his principle of fear extinction this way: "If a response inhibitory to anxiety (fear) can be made to occur in the presence of anxiety-evoking stimuli, it will weaken the connec-tion between these stimuli and the anxiety responses." Wolpe, how-ever, felt that eating had limited usefulness as fear's antagonist. Eating worked well enough with animals and children, but not with adults, he said. It is muscular relaxation which he recommended for adults as the response antagonistic to fear. The psychotherapeutic procedure, which he called "systematic desensitization" (hereafter called desensitization), involves teaching the phobic patient how to relax in the presence of fearful stimuli, and the outcome is extinction of the fear. We will now turn to the details of desensitization, as well as other learning-based methods of psychotherapy.

Learning-based methods of psychotherapy

DESENSITIZATION

Wolpe's desensitization procedure, outlined in the previous section, needs only a few more details to be useful in the clinic. After interviews to establish the details of the phobia, the patient is instructed in relaxation of various muscle groups, which is the response that is considered antagonistic to the fear and which will extinguish it. In addition, a hierarchy of feared objects and events, from the least to the most fearful, is constructed from the interview data. A patient who has a fear of heights when there is no danger of falling might have a hierarchy that begins with standing on a box, standing on a chair, looking out of a first-floor window, looking out of a second-story window, and so on. In the desensitization session the therapist begins by asking the patient to image the least feared item of the hierarchy, and to relax at the same time. If the anxiety persists, the patient is told to stop imagining the scene and to practice relaxation. Wolpe believes it important to keep anxiety at a minimum level at all times because of evidence that an antagonistic response can only extinguish a relatively weak fear (Wolpe, 1962, p. 654). The therapist continues to work through the hierarchy in this way until the fears are absent for the items of the hierarchy and, eventually, the real objects and events themselves.

Some clinical skill may be required on the part of the therapist to identify the troublesome fear because the patient's maladaptive behavior may not always reveal it directly. A student may stay in his room all of the time and profess a fear of diseases that he might catch outdoors. Actually, the fear may be fear of failure at school, and the outdoors is no more than the medium through which he must walk to reach the school.

IMPLOSIVE THERAPY

Desensitization uses counterconditioning as the method of fear extinction, but implosive therapy, and flooding therapy described in the next section, use the more common method of extinction in which reinforcement is withdrawn and the response is repeatedly evoked in the presence of its eliciting stimulus; relaxation is not part of it. We saw in Chapter 6 that avoidance behavior is dependent on fear reduction, according to Mowrer's two-factor theory. The principle of anxiety conservation, also discussed in Chapter 6, holds that the extinction of fear is difficult because the avoidance response removes the subject from the fearful situation at the first tiny feelings of fear, with the result that the fear response hardly occurs at all and so hardly extinguishes. To extinguish fear, the situation must be structured so that the fear response is repeatedly aroused in the presence of its eliciting stimuli. This is the rationale of implosive therapy.

In contrast to desensitization which minimizes the elicitation of fear, implosive therapy tries to maximize the fear of the patient. The therapist gets information about the patient's fears in preliminary interviews, and then uses this information to generate fearful scenes for the patient's imagination. "Generate as much fear as possible and face it" is the guiding principle. With the fear repeatedly generated and faced, and with the patient given no opportunity to avoid it, the result is extinction. Notice that it is sufficient to confront the memory of fearful stimuli, not the actual fearful stimuli themselves. It will not be lost on the reader that the recollection of painful memories is at the heart of Freudian psychoanalysis.

Implosive therapy was devised by T. G. Stampfl. The best single paper for the student who wishes to examine implosive therapy in more detail is by Stampfl and Levis (1967). Levis and Hare (1977) provide a more recent account.

FLOODING

Flooding was discussed in Chapter 6 as a way of extinguishing animal fears, and it has a direct counterpart in the clinical elimination of phobias. Repeatedly expose an animal to a fearful stimulus, with avoidance disallowed, and eventually his fear will subside and his avoidance of the stimulus will cease. Repeatedly expose a phobic patient to the actual stimuli of which he is afraid, not memories of them, with avoidance disallowed, and eventually his fear will subside and his symptoms will cease. Whatever the merit of flooding, there is the inconvenience of exposing the patient to the actual stimuli that frighten him. If he is afraid of heights, he may be taken to the top of a building, for example. It is much easier to deal in imagined stimuli as desensitization and implosive therapy do.

A COMMENT

Notice that all three of these modern techniques for treating phobias involve the arousal of fear. They differ in the fearfulness of the stimulus scene that is presented on each occasion, and they differ in whether the feared stimuli are real or imagined, but nevertheless they all involve engagement with fearful stimuli in one way or another. There are some who believe that this is the main element in the extinction of phobias, and that other elements such as relaxation, or real versus imagined, do not matter much. Research on psychotherapeutic techniques engages questions of this kind.

Do learning-based psychotherapies work?

What does it take to prove that a method of psychotherapy works? The three methods that we have discussed have their roots in laboratory research on fear, which provides empirical and theoretical support for them, but therapists want to see the methods tested in the actual context of neurotic patients and the clinic.

One would think that an experimental group given a particular method of therapy and a control group not given it would suffice as evidence of the method's effectiveness. There are many experiments of this sort in the literature, and they are of interest, but they do not suffice as good evidence. The reason is that a factor called the *placebo effect* is involved, and the experimental versus control group design makes no provision for it.

THE PLACEBO EFFECT

"Placebo" is from the Latin and it means "I shall please." Medically, a placebo is a pharmacologically neutral substance that may be administered by a physician for two reasons: (1) The physician knowingly administers the placebo because there are reasons for not using an active medical agent. This does not mean there is no expectation of cure, as we shall see. (2) The physician knowingly administers the placebo for research purposes so that a control baseline is established for comparison with an experimental drug of interest. In psychology the term placebo is used in an analogous way—it is any kind of activity or treatment that the psychologist believes to be neutral and will have no effect on the subject. What is fascinating about placebos is that they often are not neutral and *do* affect behavior, just as neutral drugs can have a therapeutic medical effect.

The best examples of placebos come from the field of medicine in which physicians have administered neutral substances to patients in the sincere belief that they had curative powers. The history of medicine is littered with these therapeutic efforts, and the history is not finished because even in our advanced day physicians are sincerely administering medication that the future will prove worthless. Shapiro (1960), a keen analyst of placebos from the medical point of view, says that scientific medicine began a scant 100 years ago; so it is fair to say that most drugs up until relatively recent times were useless. This statement is easy to believe because the sophistication to do a good research evaluation of drugs is recent (e.g., Grenfell et al., 1963). What is more difficult to believe is that cures have been obtained with these worthless prescriptions over the centuries. Hippocrates, that Greek physician of about 460 B.C. who is the father of medicine, had no drugs of apparent value and yet he was a respected, useful member of his society (Shapiro, 1960, p. 111). Unquestionably he obtained cures with the "flesh of vipers, the spermatic fluid of frogs, horns of deer, animal secretions, and holy oil," although documentary evidence is lacking. Evidence, however, is available on crushed worm as a cure for toothache. In 1794, Dr. Ranieri Gerbi, a professor at Pisa, said that a toothache could be cured by crushing a worm species, called curculio antiodontaligious, between the thumb and forefinger of the right hand and rubbing it on the aching tooth. An investigatory commission established that it stopped 431 of 629 toothaches immediately. Later, Dr. Carradori, court physician at Weimar, found that the crushed ladybug beetle worked as well. During the same period an English paper reported about the same level of cure for toothache from filling the mouth with milk and shaking it until it turned to butter. The list of bizarre prescriptions, many of which undoubtedly had their successes, is endless (Shapiro, 1960, 1971; Frank, 1973). One does not have to go back to ancient times for cures with bizarre treatments, however. In our time, brightly colored, inert dye has been found to be as good as any other treatment of warts including surgery, and 70 percent of patients who had their peptic ulcers treated with distilled water showed excellent results lasting over a period of a year (Frank, 1973, p. 140).

How the expectancy of cure can actually cure is one of the mysteries of medicine (and psychology). Several variables have been cited as important for the placebo effect (Frank, 1973; Shapiro, 1960, 1971; Jones, 1977). The patient must have a strong belief in the curative powers of the treatment. A placebo must be convincing as a treatment (a bitter placebo pill that tastes like "medicine" will produce more cures than one that tastes like sugar candy). The administering agent must be part of a respected, established institution of society. The medical doctor has these qualifications in modern society (Shapiro et al., 1954), but in less modern societies witch doctors fulfill them equally well. When all of these factors come together, unwittingly or otherwise, the chances of cures via the placebo effect are good. In fact, the recommendation has been made that physicians capitalize on the placebo effect whether it is understood or not. Only half jokingly, physicians have been urged to treat as many patients as possible with the new drugs while they still have the power to heal (Shapiro, 1960, p. 114).

What does all of this have to do with psychotherapy? A great deal. Medicine has had a parade of worthless drugs over the centuries that have worked because of the placebo effect, and similarly, psychology has had a parade of psychotherapies that have gotten cures for the same reason. Witch doctors, medicine men, faith healers, and hypnotists, as well as professionally trained psychologists and psychiatrists, have used a large array of strange therapies in which they ardently believed and which produced enough cures of neurotic ailments to sustain their beliefs. Even charlatans with contrived but convincing treatment programs achieve enough cures to keep them in profitable business. And then there is the clergyman or friend who sometimes help the disturbed by simply being his warm, understanding self. The power to be a useful psychotherapist is widespread. When the question is raised about the best method of psychotherapy, we may be tempted to agree with Lewis Carroll's *Alice's Adventures in Wonderland:*

> They all crowded round, panting, and asking, "But who has won?" This question the Dodo could not answer without a great deal of thought. . . . At last the Dodo said, "*Everybody* has won, and *all* must have prizes."

Maybe the Dodo is willing to give everybody prizes, but scientists are not. The variables that affect behavior can be known, and the psychotherapy wins that specifies the correct working of these variables for a particular kind of neurotic behavior. But in the search for these variables, the investigator of psychotherapeutic methods cannot ignore all the diverse ways that cures can be obtained, just as the investigator of drugs cannot ignore the unbelievable catalog of drugs that has cured virtually every human ailment. The placebo effect is just as potent for psychology as for medicine, and the investigator of variables in the psychotherapeutic process must weigh it.

There are two approaches to the placebo effect in the search for variables in the psychotherapeutic process. One is a long-run quest for understanding of the placebo effect. Assuming no accidental, genuine pharmacological effects, why should a mixture of crocodile's blood and camel dung cure gallstones? Why should the beating of drums and pleas to the god Buwala cure a fear of being enclosed in a small space? We will be scientifically stronger when we understand the determinants of human expectancy for cure and how they affect medical and psychological processes. The second approach is a short-term one because every experiment on psychotherapy contains the placebo effect as a contaminant that clouds the understanding of variables under scrutiny. An experiment that does not include an assessment of the placebo effect probably will not produce results that can be clearly interpreted.

How is the placebo effect evaluated? In a drug evaluation study the experimental substance and an identical appearing neutral substance (the placebo) are used in a "double-blind" experiment (e.g., Grenfell et al., 1963) in which neither the subjects nor the investigator know which substance is which; neither substance can benefit from expectations of the participants. A study on psychotherapy has considerations of its own. There are five central features of a well-designed experiment on the effectiveness of a psychotherapy method:

1. An experimental group that receives the psychotherapy method of particular interest.
2. A placebo control group that receives "pseudotherapy" which has all the trappings of psychotherapy for the subjects, and is convincing to them, but lacks scientific rationale insofar as anyone knows.
3. There must be equal expectation of cure for the subjects of the experimental group and the placebo control group. As with the double blind drug experiment, the expectation of cure must be the same for the experimental and the neutral treatment.
4. A control group that receives no treatment and has no expectation of cure.
5. Several therapists should be balanced over the subjects of the groups. The warmth and status of the therapist, as well as his confidence in a method of psychotherapy, undoubtedly are variables in the rate of cure. Without control of this factor, the outcome of the experiment is influenced by the characteristics of a therapist as well as the psychotherapeutic method.

These requirements increase the complexity of an experiment on psychotherapeutic methods. In fact, most experiments on the topic fail to meet them (Morganstern, 1973; Kazdin and Wilcoxon, 1976). An experiment on desensitization by Paul (1966), to which we turn next, is an exception.

EXPERIMENTAL EVALUATIONS

The Paul experiment The Paul study compared desensitization with insight therapy, and it is a strong study because it had all the controls necessary for drawing sound inferences about a cure for anxiety. The fear of public speaking was targeted for study. The undergraduate students in a large class in public speaking at the University of Illinois were given a battery of anxiety and personality tests at the beginning and end of the course, including two that measured fear of public speaking. One of these two was called "Personal Report of Confidence as a Speaker," and those who were most anxious about public speaking as measured by it were chosen for the experiment.

There were five groups in the experiment, two experimental groups and three control groups:

1. *Desensitization group.* An experimental group. Desensitization as was described earlier in this chapter, was administered.
2. *Insight group.* An experimental group. An interview procedure, standard to several kinds of insight therapy, was used where the therapist attempted to reduce the anxiety of the subject by giving him insight into the origins and dynamics of his problem.
3. *Placebo control group.* This group had a pseudotherapy administered to it. The pseudotherapy was convincing to the subjects, but Paul had no reason to believe that it had power to cure anxiety. The subjects were told that anxiety about speech making was the result of low tolerance for stress, and this could be overcome by training to work and think effectively under stress. The training was working with a stressful task while under the influence of a "tranquilizer" (actually a capsule of sodium bicarbonate). The task was presented as a stressful one that was used in the training of astronauts, but it was only a tape of auditory signals from which aperiodic signals had to be detected. The subjects were told that a tolerance for stress would develop with this teaching regime, including the stress of public speaking, even without the "tranquilizer."
4. *No-treatment control group.* This group followed the same procedures as the Desensitization, Insight, and Placebo Control groups except that no psychotherapy treatment was given. Does simply paying attention to subjects, with their awareness that they are in an experiment, make a difference?
5. *No-contact control group.* These subjects took the test battery at the beginning and end of the course but were unaware of being part of an experiment.

In addition to the test battery at the beginning and end of the course, four other measures were used, and they were the main measures of the experiment. All subjects except those of the no-contact control group were required to give a test speech at the beginning and at the end of the experiment, and the four measures were taken at those times as indices of anxiety stress. The desensitization, insight, and placebo control groups received their respective therapies in the time between the two speeches. The four measures were:

1. A behavioral checklist for performance anxiety. Rather than inferring about the state of anxiety, the observer rated the behavioral manifestations of it, like a quavering voice. Four trained observers rated each subject.

2. A test, called the Anxiety Differential, revealed the subject's perception of his own fear.
3. Pulse rate.
4. Plamar Sweat Index. This measure was recorded with a laboratory instrument. We are all familiar with the sweating palm as an index of anxiety.

The main results of Paul's experiment are presented in Figure 9–14. The four basic measures are shown, as well as a "physiological composite" score which combined pulse rate and the palmar sweat index into one measure. Shown in Figure 9–14 is the reduction from the first to the second test speech for a measure. The greater the reduction, the less the anxiety about public speaking. Notice that desensitization therapy has the greatest anxiety reduction of all measures. Moreover, the five therapists rated desensitization therapy as inducing the greatest improvement. Clearly, desensitization is better than insight therapy, which has enjoyed status in psychotherapy for so long. However, insight therapy is not worthless because it is distinctly better than the no-treatment control group. Insight therapy helps ease anxiety, but the

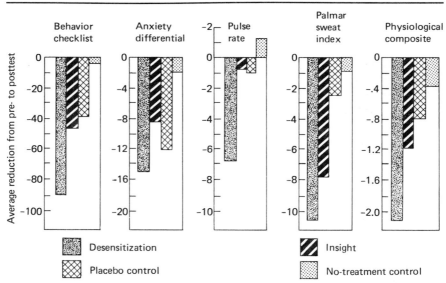

Source: Adapted from G. L. Paul, *Insight versus desensitization in psychotherapy.* Stanford: Stanford University Press, 1966. Reprinted with the permission of the publishers, Stanford University Press. © 1966 by the Board of Trustees of the Leland Stanford Junior University.

FIGURE 9–14
The reduction in anxiety about public speaking. The four main groups of the Paul study are shown. The greatest reduction was for the group that had desensitization therapy.

contrived psychotherapy administered to the placebo control group does just as well. This is a good example of the curative powers of a placebo. In fact, the no-treatment control group had less anxiety than the no-contact control group as measured by the measures of fear of public speaking in the test battery, and all that happened was that someone paid attention to them. "Even a losing horse wins," Paul observed.

OTHER RESEARCH

What can be said about the experiments on implosion and flooding therapies? None of them have the controls of the Paul study on desensitization; so a conclusion about them is difficult. A review of the literature on this topic (Morganstern, 1973) concluded that the failure to conduct proper controls, primarily placebo controls, made the cause-effect relationship between treatment, either implosion or flooding, and outcome, difficult to assess. Both treatments are consistent with laboratory research and theory of fear extinction, however, which is in their favor.

CONCLUSION ON THE EXTINCTION OF PHOBIAS

The extinction of fear by behavior therapy has an impressive body of research on animals and humans to support it, which is more than any other school of psychotherapy can say. Yet, for all the strength, questions are still being asked and answers still being sought through research. Behavior therapists carry on lively debates and research on variables in the acquisition and extinction of fear. As a sobering note, phobias are only 3 percent of mental disturbances (Frank, 1973); so there remains a long way to go for a full understanding of mental illnesses and their cures.

Summary

The applied psychology effort which uses the principles of learning to change behavior for useful ends is called *behavior modification*. The branch of behavior modification that uses the principles of learning to change maladaptive behavior in the clinic and the hospital is called *behavior therapy*. The assumption of behavior therapy is that maladaptive behavior is learned, and that extinction of the inappropriate behavior, and maybe the teaching of more appropriate, new responses, is the route for cure.

Positive reinforcement techniques are used to modify human behavior in practical situations. Both normal and abnormal behavior have been changed in this way. Reinforcers are sometimes dispensed to groups of subjects, such as patients in a hospital ward, in an effort to change their behavior. These programs with groups are called token economies.

Another use of positive reinforcement techniques is to change remote physiological responses that can be known only with instrumentation which makes their characteristics accessible. This is the area of *biofeedback*. Of interest are responses like heart rate and blood pressure. The hope is that through learning these responses can be manipulated in ways to help individuals who have difficulty with them. For example, an individual with high blood pressure may be able to keep it under control with biofeedback techniques. Biofeedback has had its laboratory successes, and some clinical success.

A common clinical problem is the elimination of phobias, which are abnormal fears. Psychologists, working mostly with animals, have given a great deal of research attention to research on fear for 60 years. Procedures and theory from this research is now having its impact in the clinic. Desensitization, implosion, and flooding are three related kinds of psychotherapy that are used to extinguish fears. Desensitization requires the subject to imagine a graded series of fearful stimuli, while relaxing at the same time. Relaxation is believed to contribute to the extinction of fear by the process of counterconditioning which assumes that relaxation is antagonistic to fear. Implosion theory requires the imagination of the graded series of fearful stimuli, but without the relaxation procedures. The repeated arousal of fear in the absence of reinforcement is the condition of extinction, and so the phobia gradually disappears as the treatment continues. Flooding is the same as implosion therapy except that real rather than imagined stimuli are used. The most convincing research has been done on desensitization therapy, and the evidence is that it works.

References

Albino, R., & Burnand, G. Conditioning of the alpha rhythm in man. *Journal of Experimental Psychology*, 1964, 67, 539–544.

Anand, B. K., Chhina, G. S., & Singh, B. Some aspects of electroencephalographic studies in Yogi. *Electroencephalography and Clinical Neurophysiology*, 1961, 13, 452–456.

Basmajian, J. V. *Muscles alive.* 3rd Ed. Baltimore: Williams & Wilkins, 1974.

Bitzer, D., & Skaperdas, D. The economics of a large-scale computer-based education system; PLATO IV. In W. H. Holtzman (Ed.), *Computer-assisted instruction, testing and guidance.* New York: Harper & Row, 1970, pp. 17–29.

Blanchard, E. B., & Young, L. D. Clinical applications of biofeedback training. *Archives of General Psychiatry*, 1974, 30, 573–589.

Booker, H. E., Rubow, R. T., & Coleman, P. J. Simplified feedback in neuromuscular retraining: An automated approach using electromyographic signals. *Archives of Physical Medicine and Rehabilitation*, 1969, *50*, 621–625.

Budzynski, T., Stoyva, J., & Adler, C.   Feedback-induced muscle relaxation: Application to tension headache. *Journal of Behavior Therapy & Experimental Psychiatry*, 1970, *1*, 205–211.

Craig, H. B., & Holland, A. L.   Reinforcement of visual attending in classrooms for deaf children. *Journal of Applied Behavior Analysis*, 1970, *3*, 97–109.

DiCara, L. V., & Miller, N. E.   Instrumental learning of systolic blood pressure responses by curarized rats: Dissociation of cardiac and vascular changes. *Psychosomatic Medicine*, 1968, *30*, 489–494. (a)

DiCara, L. V., & Miller, N. E.   Instrumental learning of vasomotor responses by rats: Learning to respond differentially in the two ears. *Science*, 1968, *159*, 1485–1486. (b)

Dworkin, B. R., & Miller, N. E.   Visceral learning in the curarized rat. In G. E. Schwartz & J. Beatty (Eds.), *Biofeedback: Theory and research*. New York: Academic Press, 1977, pp. 221–242.

Engel, B. T.   Biofeedback as treatment for cardiovascular disorders: A critical review. In J. Beatty & H. Legewie (Eds.), *Biofeedback and behavior*. New York: Plenum, 1977, pp. 395–401.

Eysenck, H. J.   The effects of psychotherapy: An evaluation. *Journal of Consulting Psychology*, 1952, *16*, 319–324.

Eysenck, H. J.   Learning theory and behaviour therapy. *Journal of Mental Science*, 1959, *105*, 61–75.

Frank, J. D.   *Persuasion and healing*. Rev. Ed. Baltimore: Johns Hopkins Press, 1973.

Garfinkel, P. E., Kline, S. A., & Stancer, H. C.   Treatment of anorexia nervosa using operant conditioning techniques. *Journal of Nervous and Mental Disease*, 1973, *157*, 428–433.

Grenfell, R. F., Briggs, A. H., & Holland, W. C.   Antihypertensive drugs evaluated in a controlled double-blind study. *Southern Medical Journal*, 1963, *56*, 1410–1416.

Hart, B. M., Allen, E., Buell, J. S., Harris, F. R., & Wolf, M. M.   Effects of social reinforcement on operant crying. *Journal of Experimental Child Psychology*, 1964, *1*, 145–153.

Jasper, H., & Shagass, C.   Conditioning the occipital alpha rhythm in man. *Journal of Experimental Psychology*, 1941, *28*, 373–388.

Johnson, L. C.   Learned control of brain wave activity. In J. Beatty & H. Legewie (Eds.), *Biofeedback and behavior*. New York: Plenum, 1977, pp. 73–93.

Jones, M. C.   The elimination of children's fears. *Journal of Experimental Psychology*, 1924, *7*, 382–390. (a)

Jones, M. C.   A laboratory study of fear: The case of Peter. *Pedagogical Seminary*, 1924, *31*, 308–315. (b)

226

Jones, R. A. *Self-fulfilling prophecies.* Hillsdale: Erlbaum, 1977.

Kasamatsu, A., & Hirai, T. An electroencephalographic study on the Zen meditation (Zazen). *Folia Psychiatrica Neurologica Japonica,* 1966, *20,* 315–336.

Kazdin, A. E., & Wilcoxon, L. A. Systematic desensitization and nonspecific treatment effects: A methodological evaluation. *Psychological Bulletin,* 1976, *83,* 729–758.

Kimble, G. A. *Conditioning and learning.* (2nd Ed.), New York: Appleton-Century-Crofts, 1961.

Legewie, H. Clinical implications of biofeedback. In J. Beatty & H. Legewie (Eds.), *Biofeedback and behavior.* New York: Plenum, 1977, pp. 473–485.

Levis, D. J., & Hare, N. A review of the theoretical rationale and empirical support for the extinction approach of implosive (flooding) therapy. In M. Hersen, R. M. Eisler, and P. M. Miller (Eds.), *Progress in behavior modification* (Vol. 4). New York: Academic Press, 1977. pp. 299–376.

Lynch, J. J., & Paskewitz, D. A. On the mechanisms of the feedback control of human brain wave activity. *Journal of Nervous and Mental Disease,* 1971, *153,* 205–217.

Lynch, J. J., Paskewitz, D. A., & Orne, M. T. Some factors in the feedback control of human alpha rhythm. *Psychosomatic Medicine,* 1974, *36,* 399–409.

Mann, R. A., & Moss, G. R. The therapeutic use of a token economy to manage a young and assaultive inpatient population. *Journal of Nervous and Mental Disease,* 1973, *157,* 1–9.

Miller, N. E. Learning of visceral and glandular responses. *Science,* 1969, *163,* 434–445.

Miller, N. E., & Carmona, A. Modification of a visceral response, salivation in thirsty dogs, by instrumental training with water reward. *Journal of Comparative and Physiological Psychology,* 1967, *63,* 1–6.

Miller, N. E., & DiCara, L. Instrumental learning of heart rate changes in curarized rats: Shaping and specificity to discriminative stimulus. *Journal of Comparative and Physiological Psychology,* 1967, *63,* 12–19.

Miller, N. E., & DiCara, L. V. Instrumental learning of urine formation by rats: Changes in renal blood flow. *American Journal of Physiology,* 1968, *215,* 677–683.

Miller, N. E., & Dworkin, B. R. Visceral learning: Recent difficulties with curarized rats and significant problems for human research. In P. A. Obrist, A. H. Black, J. Brener, & L. V. DiCara (Eds.), *Cardiovascular psychophysiology.* Chicago: Aldine, 1974, pp. 312–331.

Miller, N. E., & Dworkin, B. R. Critical issues in therapeutic applications of biofeedback. In G. E. Schwartz and J. Beatty (Eds.), *Biofeedback: Theory and research.* New York: Academic Press, 1977, pp. 129–161.

Morganstern, K. P. Implosive therapy and flooding procedures: A critical review. *Psychological Bulletin,* 1973, *79,* 318–334.

Mulholland, T. B., & Peper, E. Occipital alpha and accommodative vergence, pursuit tracking, and fast eye movements. *Psychophysiology*, 1971, *8*, 556–575.

Nowlis, D. P., & Kamiya, J.   The control of electroencephalographic alpha rhythms through auditory feedback and the associated mental activity. *Psychophysiology*, 1970, *6*, 476–484.

Orne, M., & Wilson, S.   Alpha, biofeedback and arousal/activation. In J. Beatty and H. Legewie (Eds.), *Biofeedback and behavior*. New York: Plenum, 1977, pp. 107–120.

Paskewitz, D. A., & Orne, M. T.   Visual effects on alpha feedback training. *Science*, 1973, *181*, 361–363.

Paul, G. L.   *Insight vs. desensitization in psychotherapy*. Stanford: Stanford University Press, 1966.

Pavlov, I. P.   *Conditioned reflexes*. (G. V. Anrep trans.). Oxford: Oxford University Press, 1927.

Peper, E.   Reduction of efferent motor commands during alpha feedback as a facilitator of EEG alpha and a precondition for changes in consciousness. *Kybernetik*, 1971, *9*, 226–231.

Plotkin, W. B.   On the self-regulation of the occipital alpha rhythm: Control strategies, states of consciousness, and the role of physiological feedback. *Journal of Experimental Psychology: General*, 1976, *105*, 66–99.

Plotkin, W. B.   Long-term eyes-closed alpha-enhancement training: Effects on alpha amplitudes and on experiential state. *Psychophysiology*, 1978, *15*, 40–52.

Pressey, S. L.   A simple device which gives tests and scores—and teaches. *School and Society*, 1926, *23*, 373–376.

Pressey, S. L.   A machine for automatic teaching of drill material. *School and Society*, 1927, *25*, 549–552.

Schwartz, G. E.   Biofeedback and patterning of autonomic and central processes: CNS-cardiovascular interactions. In G. E. Schwartz and J. Beatty (Eds.), *Biofeedback: Theory and research*. New York: Academic Press, 1977, pp. 183–219.

Shagass, C.   Conditioning the human occipital alpha rhythm to a voluntary stimulus. *Journal of Experimental Psychology*, 1942, *31*, 367–379.

Shagass, C., & Johnson, E. P.   The course of acquisition of a conditioned response of the occipital alpha rhythm. *Journal of Experimental Psychology*, 1943, *33*, 201–209.

Shapiro, A. K.   A contribution to a history of the placebo effect. *Behavioral Science*, 1960, *5*, 109–135.

Shapiro, A. K.   Placebo effects in medicine, psychotherapy, and psychoanalysis. In A. E. Bergin and S. L. Garfield (Eds.), *Handbook of psychotherapy and behavior change*. New York: Wiley, 1971, pp. 439–473.

Shapiro, D., Mainardi, J. A., & Surwit, R. S.   Biofeedback and self-regulation in essential hypertension. In G. E. Schwartz & J. Beatty (Eds.), *Biofeedback: Theory and research*. New York: Academic Press, 1977, pp. 313–347.

Skinner, B. F. *The behavior of organisms.* New York: Appleton-Century, 1938.

Skinner, B. F. *Cumulative record.* New York: Appleton-Century-Crofts, 1961.

Skinner, B. F. *The technology of teaching.* New York: Appleton-Century-Crofts, 1968.

Stampfl, T. G., & Levis, D. J. Essentials of implosive therapy: A learning-theory based psychodynamic behavioral therapy. *Journal of Abnormal Psychology,* 1967, *72,* 496–503.

Stokes, T. F., & Baer, D. M. Am implicit technology of generalization. *Journal of Applied Behavior Analysis,* 1977, *10,* 349–367.

Tarler-Benlolo, L. The role of relaxation in biofeedback training: A critical review of the literature. *Psychological Bulletin,* 1978, *85,* 727–755.

Taub, E. Self-regulation of human tissue temperature. In G. E. Schwartz and J. Beatty (Eds.), *Biofeedback: Theory and research.* New York: Academic Press, 1977, pp. 265–300.

Terrace, H. S. Classical conditioning. In J. A. Nevin (Ed.), *The study of behavior.* Glenview: Scott, Foresman, 1973, pp. 71–112.

Walsh, D. H. Interactive effects of alpha feedback and instructional set on subjective state. *Psychophysiology,* 1974, *11,* 428–435.

Watson, J. B., & Rayner, R. Conditioned emotional reactions. *Journal of Experimental Psychology,* 1920, *3,* 1–14.

Wolpe, J. Reciprocal inhibition as the main basis of psychotherapeutic effects. *A.M.A. Archives of Neurology and Psychiatry,* 1954, *72,* 205–226.

Wolpe, J. *Psychotherapy by reciprocal inhibition.* Stanford: Stanford University Press, 1958.

Wolpe, J. The experimental foundation of some new psychotherapeutic methods. In A. J. Bachrach (Ed.), *Experimental foundations of clinical psychology.* New York: Basic Books, 1962, pp. 554–575.

two

MEMORY

10

An overview of memory

THE AVERAGE person has a good deal of practical wisdom about learning, undoubtedly because learning is the source of so many skills that are necessary for livelihood and, indeed, survival. The parent will have plenty of advice about learning for a child whose school grades are deficient, and the advice can be sound and lead to improvement in grades. But what advice does the lay person have when poor performance is caused by a deficiency in memory methods? The remembering of knowledge and skills is just as important for livelihood and survival as learning, and yet the experiences of lay people with remembering do not produce much practical wisdom.

Actually people know more about memory than they think they do because learning and memory are not independent processes, and so the person's knowledge about learning also represents some knowledge about memory. Chapter 1 said that learning and memory are different sides of the same behavioral coin, and so to know something about one is to know something about the other. Learning is concerned with the operations that place a relatively stable behavior potential in memory in the first place, and memory is the storage of that potential over time and its activation when recollection takes place. The time between learning and the attempt to activate the memory is called the *retention interval*, and any loss that occurs between learning and test is called a *retention loss* or *forgetting*.

231

The first part of this book was devoted to learning, and the last part will be devoted to storage and retrieval, which is the topic of memory. In the study of *storage* we ask such questions as: How does rehearsal affect the retention of material? What are the effects of encoding with imagery? How is material lost from storage? *Retrieval* is getting the response out of storage, and it has status as a topic of memory because an item can be in storage in full strength and would occur if only it could be found and stimulated. Subjectively, we all have faced retrieval problems when we have a response on the tip of our tongue, have a feeling of knowing the response, and have searched our memory for it.

Some history and background of memory

The interest in memory goes back to the very beginnings of recorded civilization (Gomulicki, 1953). The ancient Greeks, who are among the earliest of our intellectual forebears, had memory in their mythology as the goddess Mnemosyne. Zeus was the supreme god of the ancient Greeks, and through Mnemosyne he fathered nine daughters who were called the Muses and who were the patron saints of the various arts. Plato (427–347 B.C.) was a philosopher among those ancient Greeks, and he asked what form memory might take in people and what some of its properties are. Plato (translated edition, 1892) wrote:

> I would have you imagine, then, that there exists in the mind of man a block of wax, which is of different sizes in different men; harder, moister, and having more or less purity in one than another, and in some of an intermediate quality. . . . Let us say that this tablet is a gift of Memory, the mother of the Muses, and that when we wish to remember anything which we have seen, or heard, or thought in our own minds, we hold the wax to the perceptions and thoughts, and in that material receive the impression of them as from the seal of a ring; and that we remember and know what is imprinted as long as the image lasts; but when the image is effaced, or cannot be taken, then we forget and do not know. (Pp. 254–255.)

Plato was saying that memory must be soft (change with experience) and erode with time (show forgetting).

Aristotle (384–322 B.C.) was another famous philosopher among the ancient Greeks, and was a student of Plato's. He began a long line of physiological speculation about the location of memory in the body. The significance of the brain was unappreciated by Aristotle because he assigned most of the brain's functions to the heart, and memory was among them. From Aristotle we still have the expression "learned by heart," and even today young children know that learning something by heart is to have it completely in memory and available on call. Aristotle's ideas about the heart as the locus of memory were short-lived, however. Erasistratus (310–250 B.C.), who was Aristotle's own grandson, doubted Aristotle's ideas about the heart. He did the first dissections of the brain and concluded that the nervous system was the seat of mental functions, and from that time on the brain was properly cited as the location of mental functions. Not all concerns with memory were physiological. In addition to his physiological interests, Aristotle undertook a description of mental activity at the level of ideas or behavior, and he outlined principles about how one thought would lead to another. The concern with the association of ideas reached its peak in 17th–19th century England among the British Associationists (Chapter 8).

Perhaps a more direct, visible ancestor for the behavioral study of memory is Hermann Ebbinghaus (1850–1909). He was interested in the association of ideas also, and he took his interests and moved them from armchair speculation, which was the style of the British Associationists, to objective research in the laboratory (Ebbinghaus, translated edition, 1964). Chapter 8 discussed Ebbinghaus as the founder of the objective study of verbal learning, which indeed he was, but left unsaid that he developed an objective method of verbal learning as the route to an objective study of human memory. Ebbinghaus varied the amount of practice of the lists that he learned, and he was the first to show that the more rehearsal the less forgetting. Ebbinghaus also varied the length of the retention interval and became famous for the "curve of forgetting," showing recall as a function of the time between learning and recall. His procedure was to learn eight lists of 13 nonsense syllables each to a criterion of two errorless repetitions, put them aside for the duration of the retention interval, and then relearn them to the same criterion as before. His measure of forgetting was the savings score, or the amount of time to relearn relative to the time to learn originally. If it took 1,000 seconds to learn a list originally and only 300 seconds to relearn it after the retention interval, the savings would be 700 seconds or 70 percent. Savings should be less as the retention interval increased because less would be remembered as time went on, and more time would be required for relearning. The curve of forgetting, plotted in terms of the saving score as a function of time, is shown in Figure 10–1. The curve of forgetting was entrenched in psychology for a long time, but modern textbooks shy from it because psychologists no longer think in terms of *the* curve of forgetting. Forgetting is a function of many factors and there are many curves of forgetting.

Ebbinghaus set the objective tone for research on memory, and later investigators often used verbal lists in their investigation of it, although occasionally they branched out and studied the retention of other forms of behavior, such as prose passages and motor skills. It is fair to say that

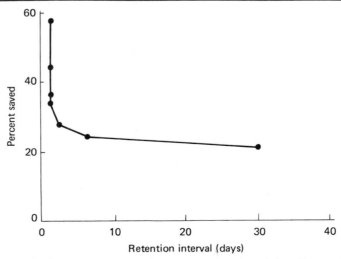

Source: H. Ebbinghaus, *Memory: A contribution to experimental psychology*. (Ruger and Bussenius, trans.) New York: Dover, 1964. Adapted from tabled values by permission of Dover Publications, Inc.

FIGURE 10–1
Classic curve of forgetting by Ebbinghaus.

memory was a low-key interest of psychologists for about 75 years after Ebbinghaus. Learning, as discussed in the first half of this book, became one of the dominant research interests of experimental psychologists, and memory remained in the background. The period of the 1930s to the 1950s was one of intensive theorizing about learning, much of it animal learning, and the theories contained little or no mention of memory (e.g., Hull, 1943). Psychology might have continued on this course if it had not been for two papers on short-term verbal retention in the late 1950s, one by Brown (1958) in England and the other by Peterson and Peterson (1959) in the United States.

SHORT-TERM VERBAL RETENTION

The Ebbinghaus tradition was a verbal list as the unit of study and retention intervals that were long—hours and days. There is nothing wrong with the Ebbinghaus method, but Brown (1958) and Peterson and Peterson (1959) set it aside and studied the retention of a single nonsense syllable over intervals of seconds. To the astonishment of psychologists they found that human subjects had dramatic forgetting in but a few seconds, and this caused psychologists to think that memory might have unsuspected complexities.

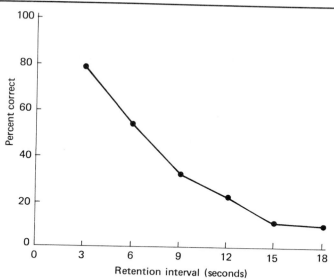

Source: L. R. Peterson, and M. J. Peterson, Short-term retention of individual verbal items. *Journal of Experimental Psychology,* 1959, *58,* 193–198. Adapted by permission of the American Psychological Association.

FIGURE 10–2
Short-term retention function for a single verbal item.

The Peterson and Peterson data, which have been replicated many times, are shown in Figure 10–2, and the method for getting them was simple. The experimenter spelled a three-unit consonant syllable (e.g., BDX) as the item for the subject to learn and remember, and then spoke a three-digit number as a cue for the subject to immediately begin counting backwards by threes (or fours). Retention intervals were 3 to 18 seconds before recall was attempted. The purpose of counting backwards was to prevent the subject from covertly rehearsing the item in the retention interval and offsetting any forgetting that might occur. The data in Figure 10–2 are no surprise when one stops and thinks about everyday experiences in forgetting. Who among us has not forgotten a telephone number in the few seconds between finding it in the telephone book and dialing it?

VISUAL MEMORY

There was another line of research, occurring at about the same time as the work on short-term verbal retention, which was influential in directing research and theory about memory. This research was on *vi-*

sual memory or *iconic memory*, and it opened the general topic of sensory memories. Sperling (1960) and Averbach and Coriell (1961) were the first to document the temporal characteristics of the visual trace for verbal materials. They found that the trace persisted in the visual system for about 200 milliseconds, which is a very short-term retention system, and different from the short-term retention that was found by Peterson and Peterson, which was measured in seconds (Figure 10–2). An implication of research on visual memory is that all senses have memories, and time has borne out the implication. The next chapter will give a more detailed account of research on sensory memories.

The Atkinson and Shiffrin model

If Ebbinghaus and those that followed in his tradition of learning lists of words can be said to have had a theory of memory, it was a strength theory, in which the habit strength of verbal items increased with rehearsal repetitions and decreased with length of the retention interval. Strength theory outlived its usefulness for verbal recall because there was no easy way that the findings of Peterson and Peterson on short-term verbal retention and the findings on visual memory could be incorporated in it. These different properties of memory, as well as the long-term retention of well-learned material, would have to be related by any model of memory worthy of the name. The model that did the job and captured the interests of psychologists in the 1960s and into the 1970s was by Atkinson and Shiffrin (1968).

An important characteristic of the Atkinson and Shiffrin model is that it expresses an information-processing point of view, where the flow and transformation of information is emphasized, and it is often expressed as a digital computer analogy. The human memory and a digital computer have a number of similarities. A computer has the input and the output of information, a working memory of limited capacity and a central memory of large capacity. Information is transferred from one memory to the other, and information is processed, transformed, compared, decided upon, searched, scanned and retrieved. By introspection of our own memory we can come up with operations that are similar to these, and it is easy to assume that the digital computer and human memory have the same, or closely analogous, processes.

The Atkinson and Shiffrin model is shown in Figure 10–3. The model has three stores: sensory memory (actually it is visual memory because insufficient evidence existed at the time to justify memories for the other sense modalities), short-term memory, and long-term memory. The dotted line in Figure 10–3 is for the contact that verbal inputs must make

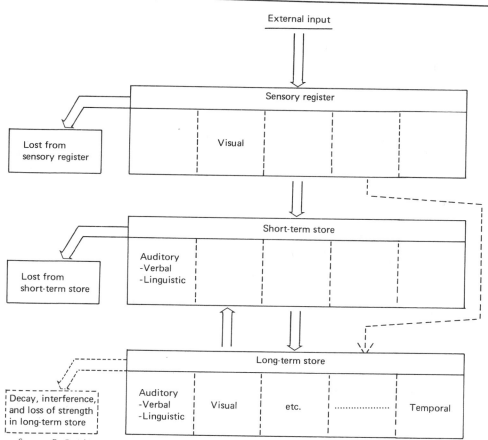

Source: R. C. Atkinson, and R. M. Shiffrin, Human memory: A proposed system and its control processes. In K. W. Spence & J. T. Spence (Eds.), *The psychology of learning and motivation* (Vol. 2). New York: Academic Press, 1968, pp. 89–195. Reprinted by permission of Academic Press, Inc.

FIGURE 10–3

Information-processing model of verbal memory by Atkinson and Shiffrin.

with their learned representations in long-term memory so that they can be recognized and named, and it is this information that is entered into short-term memory. Sensory storage is very brief, as we noted before. Loss from sensory memory is from rapid decay and from interference with newly arrived information.

The short-term memory is a temporary store of limited capacity, but not as temporary as sensory memory. The limited capacity of short-term memory is commonly called memory span, which is the number of items that can be immediately recalled without error, and Atkinson and Shiffrin derived it from the decay of items in short-term memory and from rehearsal that restores the decaying item. Considering the decay rate and the rehearsal rate, there is a limited number of items which can be processed, and this limited number is the capacity, or memory span. Memory span is five to eight items, and the transfer of these items from short-term memory to long-term memory is determined by amount of time in short-term store. Decay and rehearsal are determiners of time in short-term memory, but so is interference from incoming items which knocks out old items and replaces them with new ones.

One final property that short-term memory came to have was the acoustic coding of items stored there; the items were encoded in terms of their sounds. Being in short-term memory, a verbal item was in the stage prior to long-term memory where its associations and meaning reside. Atkinson and Shiffron did not make much of acoustic encoding in their original formulation, but it came to figure prominently in the thinking of investigators who sought to verify the model. As we shall see below, acoustic coding became one of the defining properties of short-term memory and one of its justifications.

Long-term verbal memory is the repository of established knowledge and language (and might better be called semantic memory—see Chapter 15). Information is retrieved from long-term memory by searching for it, although it might not always be there to be found because it could be lost through decay or interference. Sometimes the searching is easy, as when we immediately recall an item; but other times it can be difficult, as when an item is on the tip of the tongue and it takes a long search to find it. The subject's memory and its utilization are under conscious control—the subject can decide what information to take in, what and when to rehearse, whether to form an image, or when to search memory and retrieve information or not. Atkinson and Shiffrin call these voluntary actions in behalf of memorization and recall "control processes," and in giving a central place to them makes the model undeniably cognitive.

The Atkinson and Shiffrin model depended importantly on the conception of short-term memory. Sensory memory was on sound research turf. Moreover, the defense of long-term memory is easy. Who can deny the storage of information from a lifetime of experience? What is the empirical justification for short-term memory having the properties assigned to it? The definition of short-term memory in the model sets it apart from sensory memory and long-term memory. Do the facts support the definition? Data on rapid forgetting, memory span, acoustic coding, and brain trauma were assembled in defense of short-term memory.

ARGUMENTS FOR A SHORT-TERM MEMORY SYSTEM

Rapid forgetting One of the standing arguments for a short-term memory system is rapid forgetting, in which the complete loss of information is believed to occur in about 30 seconds. Thirty seconds is a convention, based on data like those in Figure 10–2. Fast forgetting is taken to define a short-term memory system because long-term memory, the major compartment of memory, retains information for so much longer than 30 seconds that a short-term memory system with special properties is implied.

Memory span An old finding in experimental psychology is *memory span* (Jacobs, 1887). Memory span is defined as the ability to reproduce immediately, after one presentation, a series of discrete stimuli in their original order (Blankenship, 1938). Any normal person can recall one item immediately after it is presented, but what about five items? Ten? The number that can be reliably recalled without error is the memory span and it is commonly believed to be about seven (Miller, 1956). The literature of memory span is large, and representative findings are found in a study by Jahnke (1963). Either five, six, seven, eight or nine randomly ordered consonants were read to college student subjects at a rate of one per second for immediate recall. The recall for 5, 6, 7, 8 or 9 items was, respectively, 100, 96, 83, 62, and 57 percent. The ability for immediate recall of briskly presented verbal material is very definitely limited.

Prior to our modern concern with memory, the interpretation of memory span was in terms of individual differences, not memory theory. Jacobs (1887), in the first report of memory span, described how it was related to age, sex, and academic achievement. The memory span correlated with intelligence, and it has received considerable attention in the field of mental testing. In more recent times the memory span has been seen as the capacity of short-term memory. The reasoning went like this: We have a vast capability to recollect the material in long-term memory, such as yesterday's argument, last year's funeral, and the arithmetic that was learned in primary school. The store of material in long-term memory is enormous. Why, then, is immediate recall so poor? Part of the answer came to be that short-term memory, which is used for immediate recall, has a limited capacity.

Acoustic coding Suffice to say at this point that there are circumstances in which the learning of one response will interfere with the recall of another. There is a large literature on verbal interference, and one of the variables established for it is semantic similarity—words that are similar in meaning tend to interfere (Adams, 1967, Chapter 4). It was Conrad (1964) who did the basic study which showed that verbal items that sound alike can also interfere with one another, and it was this finding that had implications for short-term memory.

Conrad's approach to acoustic interference required two experiments. His first experiment was an auditory discrimination experiment. Letters were recorded on tape against a background of white noise at a rate of one per five seconds, and the task of the subject was to write down the letter that she or he thought was spoken. The results were not unexpected. Letters that sounded alike, such as B, T, and V, or S, F, and X, were often confused. Conrad's second experiment was short-term retention, in which six-letter sequences were presented *visually* at a 0.75-second rate for immediate recall. The finding which became of interest for memory theory is that subjects confused letters that sounded alike, just as they had in the auditory discrimination experiment.

The puzzle in Conrad's data had two dimensions. One was the finding of acoustic interference when the history of interference research had targeted only semantic interference, in which only words of similar meaning would interfere. The other was that visually presented material produced errors along an acoustic dimension. Memory theorists decided that short-term memory is fundamentally an acoustic store, and it differs from long-term memory, which is semantic in character. The theoretical assumption came to be that verbal material presented in any sense modality is transformed into acoustical form and stored in short-term memory. It was never quite clear how the transformation was accomplished. Presumably auditory inputs could enter the acoustically based short-term memory directly, and visual inputs would undergo transformation to acoustic form, perhaps by the act of covert verbalization (Sperling, 1967).

Brain trauma   In these enlightened times epileptic seizures are usually held in check with drugs, but success is not 100 percent. There are an unfortunate few among epileptics who cannot benefit from drugs. They can have several grand mal seizures a day during which they are smitten unconscious and fall down, twitching and contorting. These severe cases can be helped with brain surgery (e.g., Penfield and Jasper, 1954; Penfield and Perot, 1963). For our purposes here, surgical relief from epileptic seizures can be at the price of new learning, and this has implications for memory theory. Milner (1959, 1966), who has been the most systematic analyst of these cases, cites a postoperative patient who could not learn the address of his new house, or know that he had read a magazine the day before (he would read the same magazine over and over with no sense of familiarity with the contents). He could not find the lawnmower that he had put away after using it yesterday, and he would do a jigsaw puzzle over and over with no knowledge of having seen it before. Yet the patient was not stupid because his IQ from before the operation was unchanged. Nor did he lack memory. His long-term memory was sound because all of his preoperative skills and knowledge were intact, and he had short-term retention if he rehearsed the item over and over to himself. When he stopped refreshing the item with rehearsal, however, it quickly became unavailable for recall. Thus, he had all the mechanisms of a normal mind, but he lacked the capability of change through experience. Barbizet (1963) calls this misfortune *amnesie de memoration* (defect of memorizing). What was interesting for memory theory is that a short-term and a long-term memory system were separately identifiable by an absence of the mechanism which transferred material from one to the other.

THE DECLINE OF THE ATKINSON AND SHIFFRIN MODEL

A scientific theory never collapses from a blow by one decisive experiment that strikes down a central assumption and leaves the theory crippled forevermore. Rather there are criticisms and experiments that nibble at the foundations of a theory and raise doubts in the minds of scientists, making the theory vulnerable to competing theories. An example of the kind of experiment that raised doubts was on the topic of rehearsal and its effects on retention.

Since Ebbinghaus we have had many demonstrations that the greater the number of practice repetitions the greater the retention, and Atkinson and Shiffrin handled this finding by having rehearsal transfer information from short-term memory to long-term memory. The longer an item is in short-term memory the more the transfer to long-term memory, and rehearsal is an operation that prolongs time in short-term memory. However, evidence has come forward that not all rehearsal leads to improvement in retention. Today we have cause to distinguish between *maintenance rehearsal,* in which a verbal item is held by rehearsal until the immediate need for it is satisfied and from which no long-term benefits derive; and *elaborative rehearsal,* in which an item is thought to be linked to long-term memory with its associations, meanings, and images. Only elaborative rehearsal will benefit retention. That all rehearsal does not benefit retention is discussed in detail in Chapter 12 on coding strategies; so let it suffice to say that the Atkinson and Shiffrin assumption that all rehearsal leads to improved retention is probably wrong.

As a result of difficulties of this sort, two new models have come forward in an effort to replace the Atkinson and Shiffrin model. Shiffrin (1975, 1976) is responsible for one of the new models to replace the earlier one for which he was partly responsible, and it is an interesting departure from the model which he and Atkinson devised. The other model of verbal memory is called "levels of processing." Craik and Lockhart (1972) are responsible for the levels of processing theory.

The Shiffrin model

Figure 10–4 is Shiffrin's portrayal of his model of verbal memory. He abandoned the route of sensory memory to short-term memory to long-term memory. Complex sensory information, with all its features, from all modalities, now goes automatically to long-term memory. Short-term memory is less a separate structural store than it is the activation of elements of long-term memory. The activation of sensory information is very brief, and the information quickly drops back to long-term memory unless it is given selective attention and held in short-term memory by control processes that mark it for rehearsal, imagery elaboration, or verbal encoding. The selection of some information from long-term memory for action is what selective attention means in this formulation.

Rehearsal of an item in short-term memory is mostly a maintaining function, with elaboration in long-term memory a lesser outcome. Maintenance rehearsal, the decay of the item trace, and interference all interact to influence forgetting in short-term memory. Rapid decay occurs unless forestalled by maintenance rehearsal. The input of interfering items prevents rehearsal, thus allowing decay. The capacity of short-term memory is not as important for Shiffrin's revised model as it

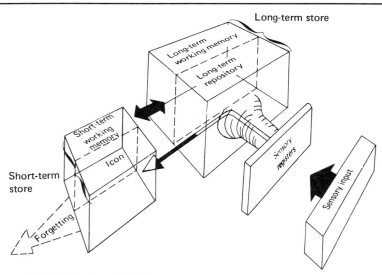

Source: R. M. Shiffrin, Capacity limitations in information processing, attention, and memory. In W. K. Estes (Ed.), *Handbook of learning and cognitive processes.* (Vol. 4.) Hillsdale: Erlbaum, 1976, pp. 177–236. Reprinted by permission of Lawrence Erlbaum Associates, Publishers.

FIGURE 10–4
The model of memory proposed by Shiffrin.

was for Atkinson and Shiffrin's model. Short-term memory can have a great deal of information, as when it is momentarily filled with a rich sensory input, or it can have little information, as when a few items are being maintained by rehearsal.

Elaboration is the main mechanism to move information from short-term memory to long-term memory. The material held in short-term memory gains stability by making contact with associations, concepts, and images that are already in long-term memory.

The levels of processing model

The Shiffrin model has less of the computer analogy and "boxes" that characterized the Atkinson and Shiffrin model, and the levels of processing model of Craik and Lockhart (1972) has even less of the computer analogy.

The basic idea of the Craik and Lockhart model is that there are levels of processing, and the greater the depth of processing the less the forgetting. The first level is a preliminary stage, where the processing is concerned with the sensory and physical features of the stimulus input. At a somewhat deeper level of processing the stimulus might be recognized, and at the deepest level the stimulus can engage the mature, sophisticated knowledge of the perceiver. An example of levels of processing is reading. We can handle the material at a simple sensory level, where we are aware of the printed page but do not recognize or understand the words. We can process at a somewhat deeper stage and recognize that we have experienced the material before. Or, we can process it at the deepest level where associations are aroused and where meaning is explored.

An incidental learning procedure is commonly used in experiments on levels of processing theory. Incidental learning is contrasted to intentional learning. The difference between the two is degree of orientation to the learning task. In an intentional learning situation the learning task and its requirements are honestly described to the subject at the outset. In an incidental learning situation the subject is told that the task has one purpose and then is tested on another. Consider a list of words, in which each word is written on a different background color. An intentional learning group would be honestly told that the task is to learn the words, and after practice they would be tested on the words. An incidental learning group would be told that the task would be to learn the colors, and after practice they would be unexpectedly tested on the words to which only incidental attention was seemingly required. In an experiment on levels of processing a subject might be shown words and for each word either asked questions about their typography (shallow processing) or their meaning (deep processing). At the end there is an unexpected test of recall. The problem with an experiment of this kind, which is like many of the experiments on levels of processing, is that there is no independent measure of depth; depth is a variable defined by the intuitive judgment of the investigator. To avoid the hazards of intuition, some investigators have turned toward processing time as an objective index of depth. If a subject takes longer to respond to a question about a word's meaning than its typography, then meaning has greater depth than typographical features. According to the theory, the word whose meaning was explored will be remembered better than the word whose typography was emphasized.

Craik and Tulving (1975) report experiments that exemplify the problems of levels of processing theory. A subject was asked a question about a word just before it was briefly exposed. Following the word, the subject answered Yes or No in response to the question with two response keys. The time between presentation of the word and the key response was the processing time that the question had created for the word. An unexpected recall test of the words followed their presentation. Three kinds of questions were asked in one of their experiments, and each kind of question was designed for a different level of processing. A typescript question on whether the word was in uppercase or lowercase type was asked, and it was intended to induce a low level of processing. "Does the word rhyme with TRAIN?" is an example of a rhyme question intended to produce a somewhat deeper level of processing than the typescript question. Semantic questions were asked about a word's meaning, e.g., "Would the word fit the following sentence: The girl placed the _____ on the table." Semantic questions were intended to induce the deepest level of processing. Processing time was used to verify the depth of processing, and it was found, as hoped, that typescript questions had the least processing time, rhyme questions had an intermediate amount of processing time, and semantic questions had the longest times. According to theory, processing time and recall should be directly related, which they were. The amount recalled was the least for typescript questions, intermediate for rhyme questions, and the most for semantic questions.

The Craik and Tulving experiment is a good one, but it needs a follow-on experiment that asks more about the validity of processing times as a measure of levels. Suppose, a shallow, nonsemantic task was made difficult to perform. The level of processing would presumably be a shallow one, but it would be contradicted by a long processing time. Moreover, it should be possible to find a semantic task, easy to perform, that would have a brief processing time. How would recall be affected? This is the experiment that Craik and Tulving ran next. The nonsemantic task involved deciding about the vowels and consonants that made up a word, and the semantic task was a sentence completion task of the kind that was used in their experiment described above. An unexpected test of recognition followed, in which the 40 test words that were presented had to be picked from among 80 distractor words. Results were that processing time was longer for the nonsemantic task but recognition was best for the semantic task, which is opposite to expectation if processing time is a good index of level. Processing time is weakened as an independent measure of level by this experiment and, being weakened, leaves the definition of level at the intuitive mercies of the investigator, which is a flaw for any science that seeks objectivity. Levels of processing theory is now under criticism (Nelson, 1977; Baddeley, 1978), and it is difficult to know whether it will be repaired or replaced by new theory.

Summary

This chapter has traced the concern with memory from ancient times to the present. Plato, the great philosopher of ancient Greece, viewed memory metaphorically as a wax tablet that was soft and could change with experience, and which would erode with time as a means of accounting for forgetting. In the 19th century, Hermann Ebbinghaus introduced the experimental study of verbal learning and forgetting, and the curve of forgetting over hours and days which he obtained was commonly cited into the 1950s as the nature of the forgetting function. In the late 1950s, however, rapid short-term forgetting in a matter of seconds was established, causing psychologists to think that memory was more complex than had been suspected. At about the same time, research established that human sensory systems had short-term forgetting characteristics also. Starting in the early 1960s, the output of research on memory vastly increased, and new theorizing about memory accompanied it.

The Atkinson and Shiffrin model of memory, emphasizing an information processing point of view and the flow of information and its control as a computer might do, was prominent in the 1960s and into the 1970s. The model had very brief sensory memory, a short-term memory for intermediate storage, and long-term memory as storage compartments. The subject used voluntary processes such as rehearsal and imagery formation for the transformation and control of the material.

Two new models of memory place less reliance on compartments of memory than the Atkinson and Shiffrin model, and so are less computer-like in their storage and control of information. A model by Shiffrin is too new for it to have undergone the test of very many critical experiments about it. The levels of processing model, which says that the deeper verbal information is processed, from the sensory level to the semantic level, the less the forgetting.

The main criticism that is being made of the levels of processing model is that the concept of levels is not independently and objectively defined, as an independent variable in science must be.

References

Adams, J. A. *Human memory.* New York: McGraw-Hill, 1967.

Atkinson, R. C., & Shiffrin, R. M. Human memory: A proposed system and its control processes. In K. W. Spence & J. T. Spence (Eds.), *The psychology of learning and motivation* (Vol. 2). New York: Academic Press, 1968, pp. 89–195.

Averbach, E., & Coriell, A. S. Short-term memory in vision. *Bell System Technical Journal,* 1961, *40,* 309–328.

Baddeley, A. D. The trouble with levels: A reexamination of Craik and Lockhart's framework for memory research. *Psychological Review,* 1978, *85,* 129–152.

Barbizet, J. Defect of memorizing of hippocampal-mammillary origin: A review. *Journal of Neurology, Neurosurgery and Psychiatry,* 1963, *26,* 127–135.

Blankenship, A. B. Memory span: A review of the literature. *Psychological Bulletin,* 1938, *35,* 1–25.

Brown, J. Some tests of the decay theory of immediate memory. *Quarterly Journal of Experimental Psychology,* 1958, *10,* 12–21.

Conrad, R. Acoustic confusions in immediate memory. *British Journal of Psychology,* 1964, *55,* 75–84.

Craik, F. I. M., & Lockhart, R. S. Levels of processing: A framework for memory research. *Journal of Verbal Learning and Verbal Behavior,* 1972, *11,* 671–684.

Craik, F. I. M., & Tulving, E. Depth of processing and the retention of words in episodic memory. *Journal of Experimental Psychology: General,* 1975, *104,* 268–294.

Ebbinghaus, H. *Memory: A contribution to experimental psychology.* (H. A. Ruger and C. E. Bussenius, trans.). New York: Dover, 1964.

Gomulicki, B. R. The development and present status of the trace theory of memory. *British Journal of Psychology Monograph Supplements,* 1953, No. 29.

Hull, C. L. *Principles of behavior.* New York: Appleton-Century, 1943.

Jacobs, J. Experiments on "prehension." *Mind,* 1887, *12,* 75–79.

Jahnke, J. C. Serial position effects in immediate serial recall. *Journal of Verbal Learning and Verbal Behavior,* 1963, *2,* 284–287.

Miller, G. A. The magical number seven, plus or minus two: Some limits on our capacity for processing information. *Psychological Review,* 1956, *63,* 81–97.

Milner, B. The memory defect in bilateral hippocampal lesions. *Psychiatric Research Reports,* 1959, *11,* 43–52.

Milner, B. Amnesia following operation on the temporal lobes. In C. W. M. Whitty & O. L. Zangwill (Eds.), *Amnesia*. London: Butterworths, 1966. Pp. 109–133.

Nelson, T. O. Repetition and depth of processing. *Journal of Verbal Learning and Verbal Behavior*, 1977, *16*, 151–171.

Penfield, W., & Jasper, H. *Epilepsy and the functional anatomy of the human brain*. Boston: Little, Brown, 1954.

Penfield, W., & Perot, P. The brains record of auditory and visual experience: A final summary and discussion. *Brain*, 1963, *86*, 595–696.

Peterson, L. R., & Peterson, M. J. Short-term retention of individual verbal items. *Journal of Experimental Psychology*, 1959, *58*, 193–198.

Plato. *The dialogues of Plato* (Vol. 4) (3rd ed.). (B. Jowett, trans.). Oxford: Clarendon Press, 1892.

Shiffrin, R. M. Short-term store: The basis for a memory system. In F. Restle, R. M. Shiffrin, N. J. Castellan, H. R. Lindman, and D. B. Pisoni (Eds.), *Cognitive theory* (Vol. 1). Hillsdale: Erlbaum, 1975, pp. 193–218.

Shiffrin, R. M. Capacity limitations in information processing, attention, and memory. In W. K. Estes (Ed.), *Handbook of learning and cognitive processes* (Vol. 4). Hillsdale: Erlbaum, 1976, pp. 177–236.

Sperling, G. The information available in brief visual presentations. *Psychological Monographs*, 1960, *74* *(Whole No. 498)*.

Sperling, G. Successive approximations to a model for short-term memory. *Acta Psychologica*, 1967, *27*, 285–292.

11

Sensory memories

In one way or another, modern models of memory have a place for brief retention of information in sensory form. The senses are the first stop for incoming information, and they have some capability for storing the information. At the time of the Atkinson and Shiffrin model, which was reviewed in the last chapter, visual memory was the only sensory memory to be reckoned with. Since that time there has been a lively acceleration of research on sensory storage, and it has been broadened to include nonvisual sensory memories. This chapter documents the modern work on sensory memories. The remarks that were made about visual memory in the last chapter are expanded, and research on other sensory memories is presented.

Visual memory

BASIC DATA ON VISUAL MEMORY

The last chapter said that the visual trace lasts but a fraction of a second, and such phenomena require special apparatus for their study. Typically, a laboratory device called a tachistoscope is used. A tachistoscope is a device for controlling the time of visual presentation, often measured in milliseconds. A tachistoscope might be used to present a word for 50 milliseconds, or it might be used for more elaborate sequences such as a word for 50 milliseconds, a blank time interval of 100 milliseconds, and a second word for 75 milliseconds. Very brief presentation of visual events can preclude the occurrence of eye movements, which take about 200 milliseconds to get underway. There are times when it is desirable to eliminate the effects of eye movements, and the study of visual memory is one of them. A movement of the eye to a new position creates a second visual input which complicates the study of a single input.

Sperling (1960) and Averbach and Coriell (1961) were the first to define the properties of visual memory, and their research methods are in common use today. Averbach and Coriell used a tachistoscope to present a 2 × 8 array of randomly chosen letters for 50 milliseconds (Figure 11–1). The display went blank after the letters appeared, which signified a delay interval the length of which varied from trial to trial and was the retention interval for the visual input. At the end of the delay a signal appeared at one of the positions, and the subject attempted recall of the letter that had appeared at that position. Before a trial the subject never knew which 16 letters would be shown. Depending on the experiment, a bar marker above the top row or beneath the bottom row, or a circle around the letter, was used to designate the letter for recall. Figure 11–2 shows the order of events that was used. Figure 11–3 has the results of the three subjects of the experiment, and the measure of performance is percent of letters correctly named adjusted for guessing. Notice that the longer the items are in visual memory the greater the forgetting, with the trace dissipated and leveled off at about 200 milliseconds (that the curves level off at a nonzero value suggests the operation of unknown long-term memory factors as a minor contaminant of the sensory memory data). Two hundred milliseconds is not a fixed constant for the visual trace. The brightness of the display makes a

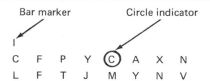

FIGURE 11–1

The visual array which Averbach and Coriell used in their research on the visual trace. Either the circle indicator or the bar marker occurred at the end of the retention interval to indicate the letter for recall.

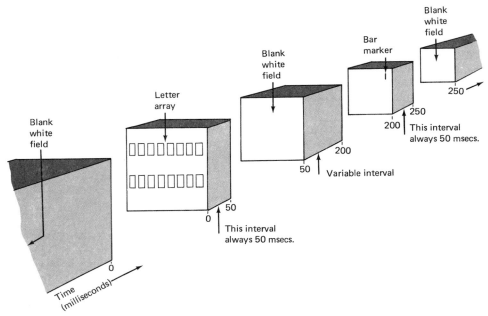

Source: E. Averbach, and A. S. Coriell, Short-term memory in vision. *Bell System Technical Journal*, 1961, *40*, 309–328. Reprinted with permission from the *Bell System Technical Journal*, The American Telephone and Telegraph Company.

FIGURE 11–2
Sequence of events on a trial which Averbach and Coriell used in their research on the visual trace.

difference, with better performance associated with the brighter display (Keele and Chase, 1967). Averbach and Sperling (1961) also found that brightness of the screen before and after item presentation is a variable for duration of the visual trace. When the preexposure and postexposure fields are bright, the trace fades rapidly, as in the Averbach and Coriell study, but when they are dark the duration of the trace is increased several times.

FORGETTING IN VISUAL MEMORY

Why are items lost (forgotten) from the visual trace? *Trace decay* and *interference* are two theories of forgetting that have concerned psychologists for a long time (see Chapter 13), and both of them can apply to the visual trace. Trace decay is spontaneous degeneration of the trace. Time alone, in the absence of any other variables, is sufficient to produce

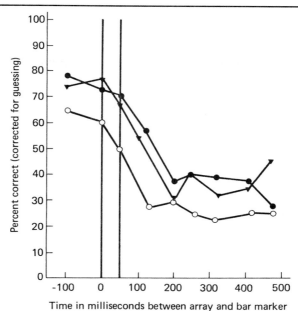

Source: E. Averbach, and A. S. Coriell, Short-term memory in vision. *Bell System Technical Journal,* 1961, *40,* 309–328. Reprinted by permission from *The Bell System Technical Journal,* The American Telephone and Telegraph Company.

FIGURE 11–3

Primary findings of the experiment by Averbach and Coriell on the visual trace. The three curves represent three different subjects. The decay of the trace is complete in about 200 milliseconds.

forgetting. Forgetting is inevitable. Interference, on the other hand, ascribes forgetting to events that occur in time, not time itself. Forgetting may or may not occur, depending on the intruding events.

Trace decay The experimental proof of trace decay requires empty time, assurance that intervening events have not occurred as a potential source of interference, and guarantees that rehearsal to offset the forgetting has not occurred. We are confident that trace decay is operating for the visual trace because the retention intervals that were studied were brief, and it is impossible to believe that rehearsal could occur, and difficult to believe that interfering events could intrude unless deliberately put there.

The experimental data by Eriksen and Collins (1968) speak explicitly for a decaying visual trace. Their approach was based on Figure 11–4. When the two nonsense patterns in Figure 11–4 are presented simultaneously with a tachistoscope, the letters HOV are seen. But if the two nonsense patterns are presented with a delay between them, then inte-

Source: C. W. Eriksen, and J. F. Collins, Sensory traces versus the psychological moment in the temporal organization of form. *Journal of Experimental Psychology*, 1968, 77, 376–382. Reprinted by permission of the American Psychological Association.

FIGURE 11–4

The successive presentation of the two nonsense patterns at the top will result in the pattern HOV at the bottom. Experimental study of the time between presentations permitted the decay function for the visual trace to be inferred.

gration of the two should depend on the amount of decay that has taken place for the one presented first (if trace decay is true). When the delay is short the first nonsense pattern should still be strong, fuse readily with the second nonsense pattern, and be read easily as HOV. As the delay increases, however, the trace of the first nonsense pattern should become weaker and weaker, decreasing the chances that enough of the first nonsense pattern will be available when the second one occurs to be readable as HOV. Another variable should be the intensity of the nonsense pattern. The brighter the first nonsense pattern the stronger its visual trace and the greater the chances that it will be available when the second one occurs. Eriksen and Collins found support for both of these implications. Decay of the visual trace was definitely established, with persistence being in the same 100–200 millisecond range that has been inferred by other techniques (Averbach and Coriell, 1961). The brightness level of the first nonsense pattern also met expectations. Higher brightness levels gave the best accuracy in reading the meaningful letters.

Interference It would be theoretically tidy if trace decay were the entire explanation of forgetting in visual memory, but the world is not so simple. Interference applies also. Averbach and Coriell found that if they designated the letter to be recalled with the circle instead of the bar marker (Figure 11–1), there was a marked decrement in recall beyond that normally found for the bar marker. Figure 11–5 shows a comparison of the circle and the bar marker. The individual recall functions for the three subjects show substantially poorer performance with the circle indicator. Somehow, the circle interferes and makes the letter less available. The two principal theories of interference in visual memory are *interruption* and *integration* (Kahneman, 1968). Interruption theory says that the second, or masking, stimulus, stops the visual action of the criterion stimulus (it has been called "erasure"). Averbach and Coriell believe that erasure is adaptive in a normal, constantly changing environment because it always insures that old information is out of the visual system when new information occurs. Without erasure, they argue, old and new visual information would be merged and the world would be blurred. Eriksen and his associates (e.g., Eriksen and Hoffman, 1963), favor a version of integration theory in which, instead of interruption, the second stimulus combines with the first and makes it less discriminable. Two stimuli, each with sufficient brightness and contrast for clear discriminability, combine and can have insufficient discriminability for clear perception.

Integration theory has the advantage of conceptual richness over interruption theory because it implies that the clarity of the pattern can increase or decrease, depending upon the second stimulus; the second

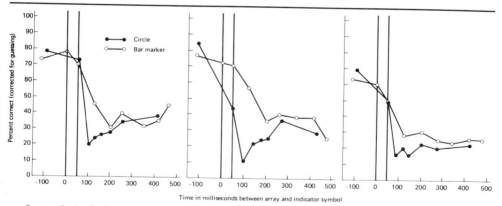

Source: E. Averbach, and A. S. Coriell, Short-term memory in vision. *Bell System Technical Journal,* 1961, 40, 309–328. Reprinted with permission from the *Bell System Technical Journal,* The American Telephone and Telegraph Company.

FIGURE 11–5

Figure 11–1 had the circle indicator and the bar marker as two different ways to cue the letter to be recalled. Here we see the curves for three subjects, and the effects of the two indicators are not the same. The circle indicator exerts an interference effect.

stimulus may complement or degrade the clarity of the first stimulus. Interruption theory would predict only degradation as the second stimulus disrupts the visual trace of the first stimulus and reduces its clarity. Schultz and Eriksen (1977) designed various second stimuli that would either enhance or degrade the first stimulus if integration theory is true. Their results supported integration theory. Both enhancement and disruption were obtained, depending whether the second stimulus complemented the first or not.

READOUT

How do we get verbal information out of the visual code so that we might operate upon it? The process is called *readout*, or scanning. The visual trace need not necessarily be translated into a verbal code. The translation could be from the visual trace to a nonverbal visual image.

Readout is a process that is poorly understood, but nevertheless there are four points to be made about it:

1. It is similar to attention; without it we have no perception of the input.

2. Readout is a matter of making contact with stable, well-learned elements in long-term memory. A digit 9 is unavailable for recall while in visual memory, and only after it has made contact with well-learned representations of the digit does a potential for recall exist. And the better the internal representation has been learned the faster and more accurate the readout. Mewhort, Merikle, and Bryden (1969), using a tachistoscope and procedures like those of Averbach and Coriell, presented arrays of letters that were either random or an approximation to English words. The best performance was with the letters that approximated words based on well-established language habits.

3. Readout is very rapid. Sperling (1963) collected data on readout and demonstrated its speed. A tachistoscope was used and the experimental variable was amount of exposure time for an array of letters before an undifferentiated visual pattern was switched on to "erase" the letters just entered into visual memory. Sperling related number of letters correctly read to exposure time, and he found that the letters could be read out at the rate of 10–15 milliseconds per letter, which is 65–100 letters per second.

4. Although readout is rapid, and the visual trace persists long enough to be extensively "read," the amount that can be reported from any visual input is small. Use a tachistoscope to present an array of 16 letters, as in Figure 11–1, and the subject will be able to report only five of them or so. This has been called the *span of apprehension*, and it is a close relative of memory span that was discussed in the last chapter. Figure 11–3 shows that most any of the 16 letters can be reported when

the request is immediate and for one letter; any of the letters are available and accessible in the visual trace when the request is for a small number of them. But when the request is for a full report of the 16 letters the subject can give only five or so. In other words, we can see more than we can say. There is a limit on the number of items that the readout mechanism can process, the number that can be stored after readout, or the number that the output (response) mechanism can handle.

Auditory memory

There is an auditory memory system, just as there is a visual memory system, and it has been called by several names. Neisser (1967) called it *echoic memory*. Crowder and Morton (1969), and Crowder (1970, 1972), call it *precategorical acoustic storage*, where by "precategorical" they mean that the items are being held in unprocessed sensory form before being read out. Here, this auditory system will be called *auditory memory* to imply in a direct way that it is one of the sensory memories.

A main difference between visual memory and auditory memory is that items in auditory memory have a longer persistence. The decay time in visual memory is a fraction of a second, but the time in auditory memory is longer. The support for auditory memory comes from evidence which shows effects on recall that are particularly auditory in origin. Saying items aloud leads to better recall than silent reading, auditory presentation produces better retention than visual presentation, and a rather wide, nonspecific range of auditory information can interfere with auditory material that has just been presented for recall. Each of these lines of evidence will be surveyed in turn.

BASIC DATA ON AUDITORY MEMORY

Effects of vocalization There is a body of experimental literature which shows that saying material aloud during learning will improve its retention, presumably because it is the condition of a strong auditory trace. Consider an experiment by Pollack (1963) on the short-term retention of digits. A subject was presented a six-digit sequence visually, followed by reading other digits in a 12-second retention interval to prevent rehearsal before recall of the six was signaled. Pollack had his subjects say the six digits silently without moving the lips, silently with lips moving, or speaking aloud. The percent correct for these three conditions, respectively, was 72, 80, and 87. A clear advantage occurs when an item is vocalized during learning. Tell (1971) reported similar findings from an experiment which used the Peterson and Peterson method (Chapter 10) for studying short-term verbal retention. Subjects were presented a nonsense syllable visually and were required to say it to themselves, whisper it, or say it aloud. The best recall was for the vocalized item, whispering next best, and silent study the worst of all.

Present a series of items for recall, and then plot recall in terms of the order that the items were presented. The result is the *serial position curve*, shown in Figure 11–6. Sometimes investigators plot items correct, and sometimes errors, but it does not matter which they do because the two plots are reciprocals of one another. The characteristics of a serial position curve are that performance is poorest in the middle and best on the ends. The good performance for the first positions is called the *primacy effect*, and the good performance for the final positions is called the *recency effect*. The recency part of the curve takes on particular interest for sensory memory because the effects of auditory memory primarily are reflected there.

Conrad and Hull (1968) are among those who have shown that vocali-

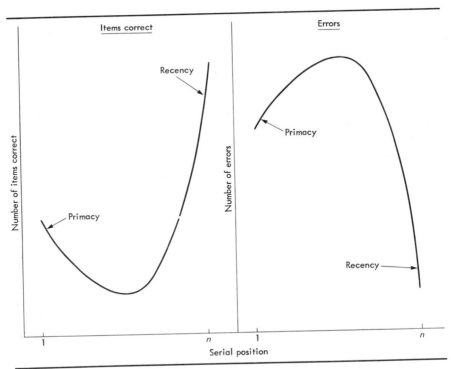

FIGURE 11–6

A plot of recall as a function of the position of the item in a list is called the serial position curve. The left-hand curve is plotted in terms of number of items correct at each position. The right-hand curve is in terms of number of errors.

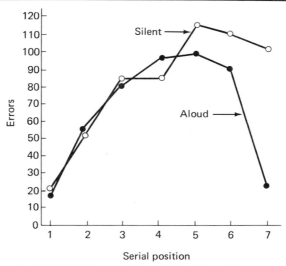

Source: R. Conrad, and A. J. Hull, Input modality and the serial position curve in short-term memory. *Psychonomic Science*, 1968, *10*, 135–136. Reprinted by permission of The Psychonomic Society, Inc.

FIGURE 11–7
Vocalization of verbal items aids their recall. The benefit for a series is in the recency part of the serial position curve.

zation produces its advantage by reducing errors in the recency part of the serial position curve. Sequences of seven digits were presented visually for immediate recall in order with either silent reading or vocalization during presentation. The results are shown in Figure 11–7. Saying the item aloud benefits recency, not primacy.

Effects of sense modality The second line of evidence that urges an auditory memory upon us is research on sense modality and retention, in which the visual and auditory modes of presenting verbal items are compared. The evidence is that the auditory mode of presentation produces retention that is superior to the visual mode. And the retention advantage appears in the recency part of the serial position curve, just as with vocalization.

Watkins and Watkins (1977) presented lists of eight common words at a one-second rate by either the auditory or the visual mode. Recall was immediate, with instructions to recall in serial order. The results are shown in Figure 11–8. The most recently presented items have a large advantage when the presentation mode is auditory. Modern thinking contends that an auditory memory can hold the final items for several seconds, and the auditory persistence gives these items an advantage at recall.

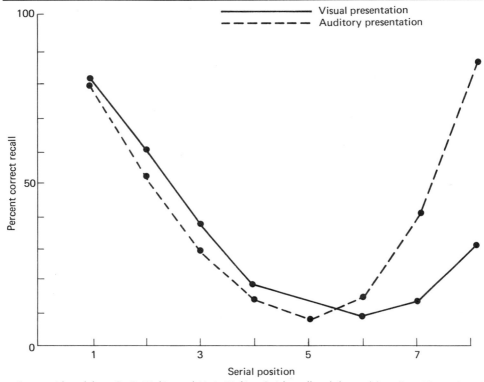

Serial position

Source: Adapted from O. C. Watkins and M. J. Watkins, Serial recall and the modality effect: Effects of word frequency. *Journal of Experimental Psychology: Human Learning and Memory,* 1977, *3,* 712–718. Copyright 1977 by the American Psychological Association. Reprinted by permission.

FIGURE 11–8
Serial position curves for auditory and visual modes of presenting verbal material. The auditory mode gives extra recall benefits to the most recently presented items at the end of the list.

FORGETTING IN AUDITORY MEMORY

We saw that both trace decay and interference were plausible mechanisms of forgetting for visual memory, and the same applies to auditory memory.

Trace decay   Relative to visual memory, decay of the auditory trace is considered to be long, and this makes for possibilities of rehearsal and interfering events in the retention interval. How to control for rehearsal and interference is not yet defined; so what is said here about the time course of auditory trace decay must be accepted with caution.

Estimates of decay time for the visual trace are accurate when compared to estimates of the auditory trace. Crowder (1970, p. 159) has the estimate at two seconds, and Glucksberg and Cowen (1970) have it at about five seconds. About ten seconds is another estimate and, while it is long by some theorists' thinking, there are three experiments that agree on it. Consider an experiment by Estes (1973). The item for short-term retention was four consonants. The subject either vocalized each of the letters aloud or categorized it as "high" if a letter fell in the first half of the alphabet or "low" if the letter fell in the second half of the alphabet. The purpose of vocalization was to create a strong acoustic trace, and the purpose of categorization was to create suppression of the acoustic trace. The retention interval ranged from .4 to 14.4 seconds and during the interval the subjects read digits aloud as a rehearsal-preventing measure. The retention curves for the two conditions are shown in Figure 11–9, and they again show that vocalization produces superior recall. Of importance for our purposes here is the time course of the decay—the advantage for vocalization ceases at 9.6 seconds. Estes also examined confusion errors, or the substitution of a letter that sounds like the correct one. These acoustic confusions lasted for about 9.6 seconds also. It will be remembered that our first hint of acoustic factors in memory came from the work of Conrad (1964), and he based his analysis on confusion errors of this type. In an experiment which has its similarities to Estes' study, Tell and Ferguson (1974) found the positive effects of vocalization on retention to persist for 8 seconds, which is comfortably close to Estes' finding.

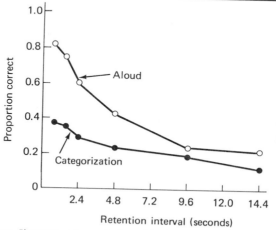

Source: W. K. Estes, Phonemic coding and rehearsal in short-term memory for letter strings. *Journal of Verbal Learning and Verbal Behavior*, 1973, *12*, 360–372. Reprinted by permission of Academic Press, Inc.

FIGURE 11–9

Vocalization improves short-term verbal recall, and the time course of the advantage lasts about ten seconds.

Using an entirely different approach, Eriksen and Johnson (1964) also found decay time in the ten-second range. Their subjects were comfortably seated in an experimental room with the main task of reading an interesting novel. Occasionally a brief low-intensity tone would sound, and after a delay the reading lamp would go off and the subject would indicate whether he heard the tone or not by pressing a key. The time interval between the tone and the reading lamp going off varied from zero to ten seconds. They found that detection of the tone decreased steadily from zero to ten seconds. Even at ten seconds the detection of the tone was slightly higher than chance guessing, suggesting that the duration of the acoustic trace may be even slightly longer than ten seconds.

Interference   Interference in auditory memory is best documented by the *suffix effect*. Crowder and Morton (1969) have been visible in their efforts for defining the properties of auditory memory, and they have relied heavily on the suffix effect. The experimental procedure for demonstrating the suffix effect is simple. A typical experiment has a short string of digits presented aurally for immediate recall. In a control condition the subject hears 296714385 (for example) and she tries to recall 296714385. In the experimental, or suffix condition, she hears 2967143850 and, like the control condition, must try and respond with 296714385. The only difference is that the experimental condition has a single digit added by the experimenter, and the result of it is a large recall decre-

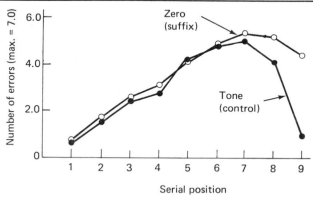

Source: R. G. Crowder, Visual and auditory memory. In J. F. Kavanagh and I. G. Mattingly (Eds.), *Language by ear and eye: The relationships between speech and reading.* Cambridge, Massachusetts: M. I. T. Press, 1972, pp. 251–275. Reprinted by permission of the M. I. T. Press.

FIGURE 11–10

The suffix effect, in which the occurrence of a single stimulus after the item series to be remembered will interfere and produce an increase in errors. The increase occurs primarily in the recency part of the serial position curve.

ment in the recency part of the curve. Typical serial position data by Crowder (1972) are shown in Figure 11–10, in which the word "zero" was the suffix and a simple tone was a control event administered in the same place in the sequence as "zero." In later work, Morton, Crowder and Prussin (1971) manipulated the characteristics of the suffix in a number of ways and obtained the suffix effect consistently. The experimenter could say "Naught," "Recall," or any of a number of random words, as the suffix, and they all produced a decrement in the recall of digits. Instead of digits, lists of common words were the items for recall in another of their studies, and the suffix was a word either similar or dissimilar in meaning to the words of the list. In both cases decrement was obtained, and it was uninfluenced by meaning. Whether the voice that spoke the suffix was the same or different from that which spoke the items to be remembered made a difference in decrement, however. Decrement occurred for any voice, but it was greatest for the same voice. There is no doubt that the acoustic trace is subject to interference from many kinds of sounds, and the absence of effects from word meaning implies operation of a precategorical sensory trace before it has been read out.

Motor memory

Just as with vision and audition, the sensory trace of motor movement has both trace decay and interference as forgetting processes.

Trace decay The first research statement in behalf of decay of the motor trace was a study by Adams and Dijkstra (1966). The movement was a displacement of the arm, the distance of which was defined by having the blindfolded subject move a slide along a linear track until it hit a stop. Amount of practice was a variable in their experiment, and the number of times that the subject made the movement to the stop before the retention interval began defined amount of practice. One, 6, and 15 practice repetitions were made, and retention intervals of 5, 10, 15, 20, 50, 80, and 120 seconds were used. Recall after the retention interval was with the stop removed and was an attempt to reproduce the length of the movement that was made originally. The results are shown in Figure 11–11 in terms of absolute error in movement (regardless of whether it was too short or too long) at recall. There are two distinctive features to the curves. One is that error decreases as a function of amount of practice, which is a routine rehearsal effect and nothing new. The other is the rate at which error increases as a function of the retention interval. Error increases steadily over 80 seconds, at which time it levels off. Adams and Dijkstra interpret the forgetting as decay of the motor trace. Adams, Marshall, and Goetz (1972) and Burwitz (1974) have

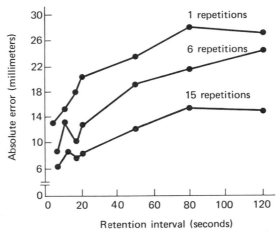

Source: J. A. Adams and S. Dijkstra, Short-term memory for motor responses. *Journal of Experimental Psychology*, 1966, *71*, 314–318. Reprinted by permission of the American Psychological Association.

FIGURE 11–11

Motor recall error as a function of length of the retention interval and amount of rehearsal. The decay appears to continue for about 80 seconds.

since added support to the decay interpretation with their motor retention studies.

The estimate of an 80-second motor trace has explanatory power that goes beyond motor movements. Both overt vocalization and subvocalization have motor elements accompanying them in the act of speaking (Hardyck and Petrinovich, 1970; McGuigan and Winstead, 1974), and so their motor traces would combine with the auditory trace to influence the course of short-term verbal retention and undoubtedly prolong it. Behavior can often have multiple sensory consequences, and so we must be alert to the effects of the compound. Hintzman (1967) pointed out that the auditory consequences of speech are confounded with motor elements, and so it is hard to untangle their influences on short-term verbal retention. Untangling the auditory and motor influences is a scientific assignment that we must accept, but understanding the effects of them together in a sensory compound is an equally important assignment.

Interference The motor trace does not appear to be different from the visual and auditory traces; it is susceptible to interference from motor events that occur in the retention interval. Kantowitz (1972) gives us an example of interference with the motor trace. Using a task such as that which Adams and Dijkstra used, in which position of the displaced arm had to be remembered, the subjects were required to freely move the control slide during a 20-second retention interval. The outcome was decrement in the movement that was being remembered and unmistakable evidence for motor interference.

Tactile memory

The sensory memory for touch is subject to forgetting from both interference and trace decay.

FORGETTING IN TACTILE MEMORY

Interference In our discussions of visual, auditory, and motor memories, we saw that events in the same modality as the criterion material to be remembered will cause a decrement in recall, and the same phenomenon holds for tactile memory. Abramsky, Carmon and Benton (1971) used an electromechanical stimulator for the study of interference (or masking, as it is often called in sensory psychology) among tactile stimuli. The instrument stimulates the skin by dropping and holding weights on it, which permits accurate control of the force duration, rate of application, and area of stimulation. The stimulator in this experiment controlled two tactile stimuli and the time interval between them. The masking stimulus and the criterion stimulus could occur together, the masking stimulus could follow the criterion stimulus by 30, 60, or 100 milliseconds, or the masking stimulus could precede the criterion stimulus by these same intervals. Thus, both forward and backward masking were studied. The locations of the two stimuli on the forearm were different, and the subject's task was to respond with a footswitch upon feeling the touch of the criterion stimulus. The results are shown in Figure 11–12, plotted in terms of an index of masking. A value of 1.0 is no masking, and values greater than 1.0 signify masking. The greatest interference is when the two stimuli occur together, and the greater their temporal separation the less the masking. In another experiment reported in this same paper, Abramsky et al. found that masking is directly related to the force of the masking stimulus and inversely related to the force of the criterion stimulus.

Trace decay A study by Schurman, Bernstein, and Proctor (1973) is the main one which demonstrates trace decay for tactile stimuli and reports the time function for retention. They stimulated the skin with a "von Frey hair," which is a pressure control device. The experimenter strikes the skin vertically with the hair (it is often made of nylon today), and the touch to the skin has a controlled intensity because the hair bends at a known pressure. Schurman and his colleagues touched a subject on the skin with the hair, and then one to ten seconds later

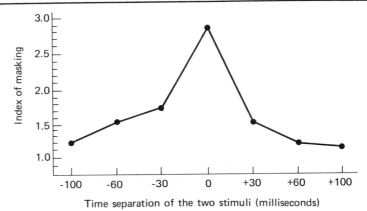

Source: O. Abramsky, A. Carmon, and A. L. Benton, Masking of and by tactile pressure stimuli. *Perception & Psychophysics*, 1971, *10*, 353–355. Reprinted by permission of The Psychonomic Society, Inc.

FIGURE 11–12
The masking (interference) function generated by the successive presentation of two tactile stimuli. The vertical axis is an index of masking, with a value of 1.0 being no masking. The horizontal axis has the order and the time separation of the two stimuli. + means that the masking stimulus precedes the criterion stimulus; − means that the masking stimulus follows the criterion stimulus.

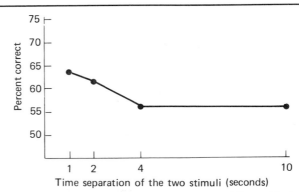

Source: D. L. Schurman, I. H. Bernstein, and R. W. Proctor, Modality-specific short-term storage for pressure. *Bulletin of the Psychonomic Society*, 1973, *1*, 71–74. Reprinted by permission of The Psychonomic Society, Inc.

FIGURE 11–13
The decay function for touch lasts about four seconds.

touched the skin again and the subject judged whether or not the same point on the skin had been touched. One group of subjects was a counting group, in which the subjects counted backward by threes from a number spoken by the experimenter at the start of each retention interval (except the one-second interval, which was too brief). And, of course, there was a no-counting group. If the subjects were remembering the location of the touch with the aid of verbal factors, then counting should reduce their rehearsal and lower the accuracy of tactile judgments relative to the no-counting group.

The results are shown in Figure 11–13. The curve represents the counting and no-counting group combined because there was no difference between them, demonstrating an absence of verbal factors in the judgments. The decay was largely completed in four seconds, and this value is reasonably close to that which other investigators have found. Murray, Ward, and Hockley (1975) found that the decay ran for four to eight seconds, varying with the part of the body stimulated. Like audition, tactile decay time is relatively long.

Summary

The first stage of processing information for retention is one or more sensory memories. For example, visual memory alone would be involved if a verbal item is presented visually for immediate recall but, if the subject vocalizes the visually presented item before recall, then the act of speaking will add the effects of auditory, motor and tactual memories to visual memory.

Both trace decay and interference are the processes of sensory forgetting. Trace decay is the spontaneous degeneration of the material in store, and interference is the action of new inputs in the same modality that degrade those in storage. Trace decay in visual memory may be complete in 200 milliseconds. Other sensory memories appear to have longer storage times, although their duration is the subject of investigation and sometimes controversy. Auditory memory may range from 2–10 seconds, tactual memory about 4–8 seconds, and motor memory as long as 80 seconds.

References

Abramsky, O., Carmon, A., & Benton, A. L. Masking of and by tactile pressure stimuli. *Perception & Psychophysics,* 1971, *10,* 353–355.

Adams, J. A., & Dijkstra, S. Short-term memory for motor responses. *Journal of Experimental Psychology,* 1966, *71,* 314–318.

Adams, J. A., Marshall, P. H., & Goetz, E. T. Response feedback and short-term motor retention. *Journal of Experimental Psychology*, 1972, *92*, 92–95.

Averbach, E., & Coriell, A. S. Short-term memory in vision. *Bell System Technical Journal*, 1961, *40*, 309–328.

Averbach, E., & Sperling, G. Short-term storage of information in vision. In C. Cherry (Ed.), *Information theory*. London: Butterworths, 1961, pp. 196–211.

Burwitz, L. Short-term motor memory as a function of feedback and interpolated activity. *Journal of Experimental Psychology*, 1974, *102*, 338–340.

Conrad, R. Acoustic confusions in immediate memory. *British Journal of Psychology*, 1964, *55*, 75–84.

Conrad, R., & Hull, A. J. Input modality and the serial position curve in short-term memory. *Psychonomic Science*, 1968, *10*, 135–136.

Crowder, R. G. The role of one's own voice in immediate memory. *Cognitive Psychology*, 1970, *1*, 157–178.

Crowder, R. G. Visual and auditory memory. In J. F. Kavanagh and I. G. Mattingly (Eds.), *Language by ear and eye: The relationships between speech and reading*. Cambridge: M.I.T. Press, 1972, pp. 251–275.

Crowder, R. G., & Morton, J. Precategorical acoustic storage (PAS). *Perception & Psychophysics*, 1969, *5*, 365–373.

Eriksen, C. W., & Collins, J. F. Sensory traces versus the psychological moment in the temporal organization of form. *Journal of Experimental Psychology*, 1968, *77*, 376–382.

Eriksen, C. W., & Hoffman, M. Form recognition at brief durations as a function of adapting field and interval between stimulations. *Journal of Experimental Psychology*, 1963, *66*, 485–499.

Eriksen, C. W., & Johnson, H. J. Storage and decay characteristics of nonattended auditory material. *Journal of Experimental Psychology*, 1964, *68*, 28–36.

Estes, W. K. Phonemic coding and rehearsal in short-term memory for letter strings. *Journal of Verbal Learning and Verbal Behavior*, 1973, *12*, 360–372.

Glucksberg, S., & Cowen, G. N., Jr. Memory for nonattended auditory material. *Cognitive Psychology*, 1970, *1*, 149–156.

Hardyck, C. E., & Petrinovich, L. F. Subvocal speech and comprehension level as a function of the difficulty level of reading material. *Journal of Verbal Learning and Verbal Behavior*, 1970, *9*, 647–652.

Hintzman, D. L. Articulatory coding in short-term memory. *Journal of Verbal Learning and Verbal Behavior*, 1967, *6*, 312–316.

Kahneman, D. Method, findings, and theory in studies of visual masking. *Psychological Bulletin*, 1968, *70*, 404–425.

Kantowitz, B. H. Interference in short-term motor memory: Interpolated task difficulty, similarity, or activity? *Journal of Experimental Psychology*, 1972, *95*, 264–274.

Keele, S. W., & Chase, W. G. Short-term visual storage. *Perception & Psychophysics,* 1967, *2,* 383–386.

McGuigan, F. J., & Winstead, C. L., Jr. Discriminative relationship between covert oral behavior and the phonemic system in internal information processing. *Journal of Experimental Psychology,* 1974, *103,* 885–890.

Mewhort, D. J. K., Merikle, P. M., & Bryden, M. P. On the transfer from iconic to short-term memory. *Journal of Experimental Psychology,* 1969, *81,* 89–94.

Morton, J., Crowder, R. G., & Prussin, H. A. Experiments with the stimulus suffix effect. *Journal of Experimental Psychology Monograph,* 1971, *91,* 169–190.

Murray, D. J., Ward, R., & Hockley, W. E. Tactile short-term memory in relation to the two-point threshold. *Quarterly Journal of Experimental Psychology,* 1975, *27,* 303–312.

Neisser, U. *Cognitive Psychology.* New York: Appleton-Century-Crofts, 1967.

Pollack, I. Interference, rehearsal, and short-term retention of digits. *Canadian Journal of Psychology,* 1963, *17,* 380–392.

Schultz, D. W., & Eriksen, C. W. Do noise masks terminate target processing? *Memory & Cognition,* 1977, *5,* 90–96.

Schurman, D. L., Bernstein, I. H., & Proctor, R. W. Modality-specific short-term storage for pressure. *Bulletin of the Psychonomic Society,* 1973, *1,* 71–74.

Sperling, G. The information available in brief visual presentations. *Psychological Monographs,* 1960, *74,* Whole No. 498.

Sperling, G. A model for visual memory tasks. *Human Factors,* 1963, *5,* 19–31.

Tell, P. M. The influence of vocalization on short-term memory. *Journal of Verbal Learning and Verbal Behavior,* 1971, *10,* 149–156.

Tell, P. M., & Ferguson, A. M. Influence of active and passive vocalization on short-term recall. *Journal of Experimental Psychology,* 1974, *102,* 347–349.

Watkins, O. C., & Watkins, M. J. Serial recall and the modality effect: Effects of word frequency. *Journal of Experimental Psychology: Human Learning and Memory,* 1977, *3,* 712–718.

12

Strategies of verbal memorization

"STRATEGIES OF memorization" imply that the subject has a choice in the way that he memorizes. Atkinson and Shiffrin (1968) in their model of memory which was discussed in Chapter 10 called these different ways of memorizing "control processes." That the learner has choice is not always true because the learning situation can be constrained to restrict the way that memorization is done. Nevertheless, learning situations are often open-ended, allowing the subject to choose his method of memorization. Giving the subject an active role in the learning process makes this view of verbal memorization a cognitive one (Chapter 8).

This chapter is about three main ways to memorize verbal responses: rehearsal, verbal mediation, and imagery.

Rehearsal

Rehearsal is rote learning, in which the item to be remembered is repeated over and over. The repetition often results in improved recall. Ebbinghaus (translated edition, 1964), in his pioneering studies of memory published in 1885, showed that the more practice repetitions a list of words is given the better the recall. This principle has been known by laymen for a long time. It is common for a layman to repeat items that he wants to secure in memory.

We will begin this account of rehearsal with data which show that practice repetitions benefit recall. Then recent studies will be discussed which compromise the generalization by showing that it is not always true. There would appear to be conditions of rehearsal that do not improve recall. The distinction is between *elaborative rehearsal* which improves recall, and *maintenance rehearsal* which does not.

ELABORATIVE REHEARSAL

A good example of rehearsal benefitting retention is a study by Hellyer (1962) who used a short-term retention procedure. A memory drum was used to present a consonant syllable, e.g., KBJ, 1, 2, 4, or 8 times, which the subject read aloud. The retention intervals were either 3, 9, 18, or 27 seconds, and they were filled with reading digits aloud to prevent rehearsal. The results are shown in Figure 12–1. Forgetting steadily increased over the retention interval, but the greater the amount of rehearsal the better the recall.

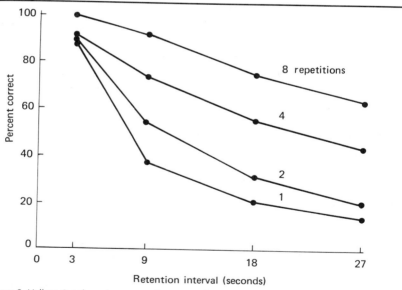

Source: S. Hellyer, Supplementary report: Frequency of stimulus presentation and short-term decrement in recall. *Journal of Experimental Psychology*, 1962, 64, 650. Reprinted by permission of the American Psychological Association.

FIGURE 12–1

Short-term retention of single verbal items as a function of number of rehearsal repetitions.

MAINTENANCE REHEARSAL

The idea that rehearsal might leave recall unaffected was influenced by levels of processing theory (Chapter 10), and the methods being used to investigate it are similar. Levels of processing theory would say that an item could be given such shallow processing during rehearsal that its recall would be unlikely. The item would be maintained at the shallow level for immediate use, but it would leave no effects that would give it long-term availability. Shallow processing is induced by incidental learning procedures, in which the subject thinks that he is learning one aspect of the task but is tested on another which was made to seem incidental to him. A good example of the incidental learning procedure and how it gives evidence for maintenance rehearsal is an experiment by Glenberg, Smith, and Green (1977).

Glenberg et al. presented a four-digit number for two seconds, one or three words for two seconds, and then a blank slide for 2, 6, or 18 seconds, which was the retention interval. A tone sounded every two seconds in the retention interval as a signal for the subject to repeat the word(s). Recall of the digits was then requested. Using different digits and words, this sequence was repeated 63 times. From the subject's point of view it was a typical short-term retention procedure in which digits were presented for learning and later recall and the words were distractor activity to prevent rehearsal. Psychologists have been running experiments like this for years, but Glenberg et al. introduced a switch by having the subjects recall as many words as possible after Trial 63; they made an incidental learning paradigm out of a short-term retention paradigm. The issue: Will repetitions of the word(s) in the retention interval make a difference in the level of their recall? The answer was No. In the one-word condition the subjects' recall averaged 11, 7, and 12 percent for the 2-, 6-, and 18-second rehearsal intervals. These percentages, respectively, were 3, 4, and 5 percent for the three-word condition. The overall level of recall was very low, and amount of rehearsal had no effect. Nine times more rehearsal was given in the 18-second interval than in the 2-second interval, and yet there was little difference between them. Rundus (1977) obtained similar findings with a similar procedures. He had rehearsal intervals of 4, 5, 6, 8, 9, 10, 12, and 15 seconds and had recall of 15, 17, 19, 15, 17, 10, 19, and 18 percent, respectively. Amount of recall is not always related to amount of rehearsal, and so an idea like maintenance rehearsal, in balance with elaborative rehearsal, deserves to be held.

Why does some rehearsal benefit recall and some not? What are the conditions under which elaborative rehearsal occurs? We are only beginning to scratch the surface of the topic. Complications are beginning to appear, and when we untangle them we will be much further along toward a theory of rehearsal. In the experiment above by Glenberg et al. we saw no effect of rehearsal when the item was presented once and the subject repeated it over and over in the retention interval after the item was removed. However, when the repetition is visual rather than vocal, then rehearsal benefits recall (Nelson, 1977; Rundus, 1977). Advances in science come from solving puzzles like this.

Natural language mediation

Rote rehearsal is a strategy of memorization that we all know and often use. We have known about it since we were young. Rehearsal is probably the only effective strategy in the mental arsenal of the child. But as we grow older and language develops, other options open up to us. A more complex verbal strategy is *natural language mediation*, in which the subject organizes an item with any verbal association that meaningfully relates them.

Suppose the pair to be learned is DOG–HOG. When confronted with this pair a subject might organize these two words by thinking to herself that DOG and HOG are both animals, that a DOG is a smaller animal than a HOG, that DOG is the name of another animal that rhymes with HOG, or that both are three-letter words for the names of domesticated animals. There are no restraints in the formation of a natural language mediator; it is up to the subject and will vary from subject to subject and item to item. And natural language mediators are not dependent on meaningful words being in the item. Many nonsense syllables induce easy natural language mediators. The pair BUS–BUT might be translated into "The bush is beautiful." Ebbinghaus was wrong when he thought that nonsense syllables were free of associations.

Having acquired a natural language mediator in learning, the subject is faced with the problem of making use of it at recall. When the stimulus word appears, the subject must remember the natural language mediator and must remember how to decode it and obtain the response word which is required. If the natural language mediator is that the response term is the name of an animal that rhymes with the stimulus term DOG, the subject must not only recall the aid but also remember how to use it and obtain the response term HOG. The natural language mediator could be a poor one and yield the response POLLYWOG. With all these problems of getting a good natural language mediator in the first place, remembering it, and properly decoding it, one would think that natural language mediators might be a hindrance. Not so, as will be documented shortly.

EFFECT ON LEARNING RATE

The effect of natural language mediators on the learning process is to make it faster than when learning is by rote. Adams, McIntyre, and Thorsheim (1969) gave their subjects a list of ten paired associates to learn over eight trials by the anticipation method. The procedure was to have the subject report the response term, if possible, when the stimulus term alone was showing, as is standard for the anticipation method. The next presentation for the item was the stimulus and response terms together, which is also standard for the anticipation method as an informing and study event, except here the subject also was asked to report his natural language mediator to the experimenter if he had one. If he did not have a mediator, then he was to report "Rote," and it was presumed that the item was being learned by rote practice repetitions. A four-second rate was used so there was ample time for these reports. The reason for obtaining the verbal report at each presentation of each item was to place the recording of the natural language mediator very near the point of its use. When a subject is asked about his mediators

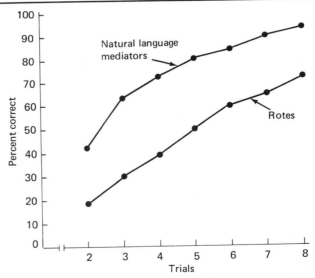

Source: J. A. Adams, J. S. McIntyre, and H. I. Thorsheim, Natural language mediation and interitem interference in paired-associate learning. *Psychonomic Science*, 1969, *16*, 63–64. Reprinted by permission of The Psychonomic Society, Inc.

FIGURE 12–2
A comparison of mediated and rote verbal learning. Paired associates were learned by the anticipation method.

only at the end of the experiment, there is the possibility that faulty memory of some mediators may cause errors to creep in.

The results of the study were that subjects were mediating 46 percent of their items at the end of practice. The percent of responses correctly anticipated on each trial is shown in Figure 12–2, and they are shown for both rote and mediated items. A substantial advantage was found for mediated items. Over all eight trials, the average superiority of mediated over rote items was 28 percent.

EFFECTS ON SHORT-TERM RETENTION

Kiess (1968) compared mediated and rote learning for the short-term retention of single nonsense syllables. The experimental procedure was to present a syllable visually for three seconds, at which time the subject would report a natural language mediator if one came to her. She then read from arrays of random digits as the rehearsal-preventing activity during the retention interval, which could range from 0 (immediate recall) to 30 seconds. The recall attempt for the item and the natural language mediator, if one had been reported, followed. Association value of the syllables was a main variable of the study because Kiess hypothesized that the number and the quality of natural language mediators would depend on it. A low association-value item might be ZOJ, which is unlike a word and for which an association is difficult. A high association-value syllable is a word (SUN), or nearly a word (TEL), and associations should be easy for them. Kiess found association value to be related positively to the formation of natural language mediators, as expected, with natural language mediators occurring for 32 percent of low association-value items and 87 percent of high association-value items. The recall of natural language mediators was virtually perfect; so the forgetting of syllables could not be assigned to the forgetting of mediators. The syllable retention data appear in Figure 12–3. For items of both low and high association value, the mediated ones were recalled best, with the largest benefits going to unfamiliar items of low association value. The low association-value items are rare in everyday experience and the natural language mediation is a way of making them memorable by converting them to the familiar and commonplace. The high association-value items are common in everyday experience, and benefit far less from natural language mediation.

Bower and Clark (1969) showed how natural language mediation can dramatically affect the recall of entire lists of words. A subject was given 12 successive lists of ten nouns each, with instructions to learn the words of each list in order. The subjects of the control group could learn the words in any way that they wished, but subjects of the experimental group were told to weave a meaningful story about the ten words of a

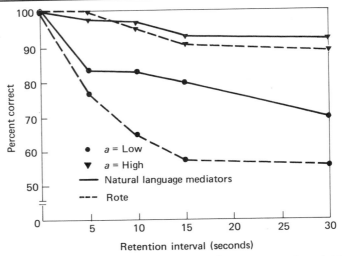

Source: H. O. Kiess, Effects of natural language mediators on short-term memory. *Journal of Experimental Psychology*, 1968, *77*, 7–13. Reprinted by permission of the American Psychological Association.

FIGURE 12–3
Effect of low and high association value (a) of nonsense syllables on short-term verbal retention. Learning was either by rote or natural language mediation.

list. For example, consider the list LUMBERJACK, DART, SKATE, HEDGE, COLONY, DUCK, FURNITURE, STOCKING, PILLOW, MIS-TRESS. One subject made up this narrative: "A LUMBERJACK DARTed out of a forest, SKATEd around a HEDGE past a COLONY of DUCKs. He tripped on some FURNITURE, tearing his STOCKING while hastening toward the PILLOW where his MISTRESS lay." After the 12 lists had been learned, the subjects were asked to recall as many of the words of the 12 lists as possible, with only the first word of a list as cue. They were scored for recalling the words in correct order. The experimental group averaged 93 percent correct, the control group 13 percent.

EFFECTS ON LONG-TERM RETENTION

Montague, Adams, and Kiess (1966) conducted an experiment similar to the Kiess study but with a retention interval of 24 hours. The outcome of the two studies is similar, but Montague et al. had substantial forgetting of natural language mediators whereas Kiess (1968) did not, and the consequences of it are interesting and important. A long list of 96 nonsense syllable pairs was used, and each pair was presented once. The study time for a pair in acquisition was an experimental variable, and was either 15 or 30 seconds. Mediation takes time, and the number of natural language mediators should be determined by the amount of study time for an item. The other variable was low, e.g., TAC–ZIG, and high, e.g., VET–BAT, association value of the nonsense syllables that made up the pairs, much the same as in the Kiess study. During the study of a pair, the subject wrote down a natural language mediator if one occurred to him, and at recall with the stimulus term displayed he wrote the response term of a pair if he could remember it as well as the natural language mediator if the item had been mediated originally. Recording the mediator at both learning and recall was to assess effects of forgetting the mediator at recall.

The results of the study by Montague et al. are shown in Tables 12–1 and 12–2. Table 12–1 has percent of items that had a natural language mediator in acquisition. As anticipated, the longer the study time the more frequently a mediator is formed. Number of mediators was also related positively to association value, which is the same finding as the Kiess experiment. Table 12–2 has the recall data. There are three categories of items in Table 12–2: (1) rote learning, in which there was no natural language mediator reported; (2) mediated learning, in which a natural language mediator was formed in acquisition and remembered at recall; and (3) mediated learning, in which the natural language mediator was formed in acquisition and forgotten at recall. Recall after rote learning was poor, which is not unexpected because not much study time was allowed for an item. The forgetting of a natural language mediator had a devastating effect on recall, with recall level near zero. By contrast, the remembering of the natural language mediator gave an

TABLE 12–1

Percent of items mediated for each of four experimental conditions.

Study time (seconds)	Association value	
	Low	High
15	33	62
30	53	78

Source: W. E. Montague, J. A. Adams, and H. O. Kiess. Forgetting and natural language mediation. *Journal of Experimental Psychology*, 1966, *72*, 829–833. Reprinted by permission of the American Psychological Association.

TABLE 12–2
Percent of items correctly recalled after 24 hours.

Experimental condition		Item category		
Association value	Study time (seconds)	Mediator remembered	Mediator forgotten	Rote learning
Low	15	46	1	3
Low	30	46	0	5
High	15	80	2	8
High	30	86	3	11

Source: W. E. Montague, J. A. Adams, and H. O. Kiess. Forgetting and natural language mediation. *Journal of Experimental Psychology,* 1966, *72,* 829–833. Reprinted by permission of the American Psychological Association.

excellent level of recall, particularly for items of high association value. Natural language mediation is a very successful memorization strategy providing that the mediator is correctly recalled.

Smith (1969) extended the study by Montague, Adams, and Kiess (1966). He demonstrated that the trends in Table 12–2 for a 24-hour retention interval also hold for longer intervals. Each of Smith's three groups learned a list of nonsense syllable pairs of intermediate association value by the correction method (Chapter 8). After the criterion of learning had been met, the subject wrote the natural language mediator for each item if one was used; otherwise the subject indicated rote learning. A group then had a retention interval of either one, three, or nine days, and was tested at recall for both the response term of the pair and the natural language mediator. His results are shown in Table 12–3. Notice that the very high retention which Montague et al. found

TABLE 12–3
Percent of items correctly recalled after 1, 3, and 9 days.

Retention interval (days)	Item category		
	Mediator remembered	Mediator forgotten	Rote learning
1	98	70	72
3	97	62	75
9	96	17	35

Source: W. R. Smith. Retention as a function of natural language mediation and of time. *Psychonomic Science,* 1969, *14,* 288–289. Reprinted by permission of The Psychonomic Society, Inc.

when the natural language mediator was remembered holds up for at least nine days, and is not limited to the modest one-day interval which Montague et al. used. Notice, too, that the most forgetting occurred when learning was mediated and the natural language mediator went unremembered. Rote learning occupies an intermediate level of retention, also confirming Montague et al. The absolute level of the percentages in Tables 12–3 and 12–2 cannot be compared, only the relative trends, because different acquisition methods and materials were used in the two studies.

ENCODING AND DECODING OF THE NATURAL LANGUAGE MEDIATOR

What is the nature of learning and recall processes for mediated items? During acquisition there is mental exploration for a suitable association to encode the item, and the success of the exploration increases with longer study time and higher association value (Table 12–1). Over the retention interval the subject must not only remember the natural language mediator, which now embodies the item to be remembered, but also how to decode the mediator at recall and obtain the item from it. WESTERN as the natural language mediator for the pair WES–TER would be easy to decode, but THE PIZZA HAS MOZZARELLA CHEESE for the item PIZ–MOL should be difficult because the element PIZ and MOL are both imbedded in words of a sentence and somehow must be extracted and verified at recall. The column *mediator remembered* in Table 12–2 shows that this process is relatively easy for pairs of high association value, which often yield simple natural language mediators that preserve the item in a rather direct form, e.g., WESTERN for the item WES–TER, and are easily decoded into the correct response at recall. Low association value items are another matter. The level of correct recall for them is only 46 percent, indicating unsuccessful decoding of mediators even though they were successfully recalled. Undoubtedly their mediators were complex with more decoding steps (e.g., THE PIZZA HAS MOZZARELLA CHEESE for the item PIZ–MOL), and the decoding procedure could not always be remembered at the time of recall. Natural language mediation is very helpful for remembering a verbal item *if* the mediator can be remembered *and* decoded.

The best research on the decoding of natural language mediators is by Prytulak (1971). Consonant-vowel-consonant nonsense syllables were used. They were presented one at a time, and the subject wrote a natural language mediator for each one. At the completion of the series, the subject was given the natural language mediators and asked to reconstruct the nonsense syllable from each one. Table 12–4 lists various nonsense syllables, examples of natural language mediators that were

278

TABLE 12–4

Examples of nonsense syllables, natural language mediators, and the probability of correctly decoding the natural language mediators.

Nonsense syllables and their natural language mediators	Probability of correct decoding
PIN–PIN	.88
LOV–LOVE	.89
WOD–WOOD	.88
FEX–FLEXIBLE	.78
PYM–PAYMENT	.71
JEK–JERK	.68
ZEL–ZEAL	.59
FOH–FOREHEAD	.57
KUT–CUT	.52
VAQ–VANQUISH	.44
KOZ–COZY	.40
YIT–YET	.36
BYF–BYE	.36
WIQ–WICK	.29
BUH–BUNCH	.24
ZYT–ZEST	.20
JYZ–JAZZ	.20

Source: L. S. Prytulak, Natural language mediation. *Cognitive Psychology*, 1971, *2*, 1–56. Reprinted by permission of Academic Press, Inc.

formed for them, and the probability of correctly decoding the natural language mediators. The decoding probability was high when the natural language mediator had the same letters as the nonsense syllable preserved in the same order. But when the natural language mediator did not preserve all of the letters of the syllable, then the probability of correct decoding was low. Decoding the nonsense syllable LOV from the natural language mediator LOVE is easy, but decoding JYZ from JAZZ is not.

Prytulak took the natural language mediators which his subjects gave him and developed a classification system for the kind and number of transformations relating the nonsense syllable and the natural language mediator. Consider the nonsense syllable WOD. One type of transformation was the internal addition of a constant, giving the natural language mediator WORD. This is a one-step transformation. The internal addition of a constant, and the addition of a suffix, gives the natural language mediator WONDER, which is a two-step transformation. And so on. Prytulak correctly surmised that the probability of correctly decoding a natural language mediator is inversely related to the number of transformation steps, and the plot of his data for this relationship are given in Figure 12–4. Prytulak theorized that the transformations are

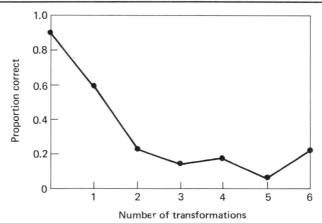

Source: L. S. Prytulak, Natural language mediation. *Cognitive Psychology*, 1971, 2, 1–56. Reprinted by permission of Academic Press, Inc.

FIGURE 12–4
Verbal recall as a function of the number of steps in decoding natural language mediators.

"stacked" in the subject's mind according to complexity, and in encoding an item the subject works down the stack until finding one that applies. The decoding of the natural language mediator to retrieve the item requires an application of the transformation in reverse.

CONCLUSION ON NATURAL LANGUAGE MEDIATION

Natural language mediation is a powerful mechanism for remembering. Good advice that can be given for increasing retention is this: Form an association, any association, for the material at the time of learning. Then, try and remember the association at recall and from it try to recover the material to be remembered. If you are successful at all of this, your reward will be an impressive level of recall.

Imagery

It has been said that if you doubt a role for mental imagery in memory, then ask yourself how you know the answer to this question: How many windows do you have in your house? Almost certainly you have never made a deliberate count of your windows; so a verbal response from previous experience is not available to you in memory. What is available to you are the products of sensory experience with your house, which are memory images with spatial representation. In a manner that is hardly understood at all, you stroll through the mental image of your house, as a Victorian lady through her garden, and count the windows. Natural language mediation is a verbal strategy, and imagery is a non-verbal strategy. Anyone who has had a dream knows what an image is. In recent years there have been active concerns with developing objective indices of them and inquiring about their role in retention.

The image has travelled an uneven road in psychology. The image was an unquestioned concept at the turn of this century when structuralism was the dominant school of American psychology. The method of structuralism was introspective analysis of one's own consciousness, and when the mind's eye was turned inward the analyst saw images. Images were a consequence of experience and an essential element of thought, according to the structuralists. Then, in the early part of this century, behaviorism emerged as a school of psychology. Its fundamental tenet was that consciousness and the images that populated it were unnecessary for a science of behavior (Chapter 8). The behaviorists did not deny images, but they did deny that images had a place in the laws and theories of psychology. Objective stimuli and responses were the elements of psychology's laws, not images, they said. The philosophy of behaviorism, which is alive and thriving today, dominated psychology's thinking about images for 50 years. It was not until the mid-1960s, under the leadership of the Canadian psychologist Allan Paivio (see Paivio, 1971), that the image was returned to psychology's arena. Today, as the remainder of this chapter will testify, psychology is convinced of the importance of the image for psychological law and theory, and there are plenty of experiments to prove it.

MODERN APPROACHES TO IMAGERY

The image as analog representation The subjective experience of an image is one thing, but objectifying the image in a manner that satisfies scientists is another. Several approaches have been used, and the most fascinating of them has been the work of Shepard and his associates. Their basic work (Shepard and Metzler, 1971; Metzler and Shepard, 1974) appears to require an image for its explanation, and it has the objectivity that science requires. Their procedure was to time the mental rotation of forms, and they used pairs of line drawings as the item of study. The two forms could be the same with one rotated in the picture plane (A in Figure 12–5), could be the same with one rotated in depth (B in Figure 12–5), or different (C in Figure 12–5). The amount of rotation ranged from zero to 180 degrees. The subject had a lever for each hand, and he was instructed to pull the right-hand lever as soon as he determined that the two forms were the same, and the left-hand as soon as he

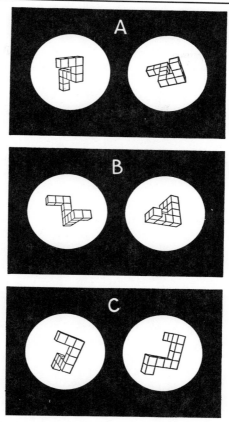

Source: R. N. Shepard and J. Metzler, Mental rotation of three-dimensional objects. *Science*, 1971, *171*, 701–703. Copyright 1971 by the American Association for the Advancement of Science.

FIGURE 12–5

Forms that were used to demonstrate that images are a mental analog of the objects in the world that they represent. See text for explanation of the three parts of the figure.

determined that the two forms were different. To do this the subject had to carry out a mental rotation of the form, and the lever timed the act of mental rotation. The results are shown in Figure 12–6. The time to decide that identical pairs were the same was a direct, linear function of the amount that one form was rotated with respect to its twin. The more the form out there in the world was rotated the longer it took to rotate its image, and Shepard and his colleagues concluded that the image is an *analog representation* of the world. The image behaves in a fashion that corresponds to the behavior of objects in the world.

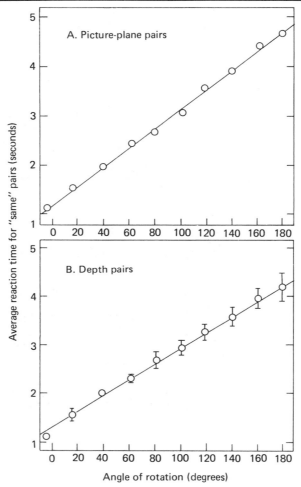

A. Picture-plane pairs

B. Depth pairs

Average reaction time for "same" pairs (seconds)

Angle of rotation (degrees)

Source: R. N. Shepard and J. Metzler, Mental rotation of three-dimensional objects. *Science,* 1971, *171,* 701–703. Copyright 1971 by the American Association for the Advancement of Science.

FIGURE 12–6

The mental rotation of the forms shown in Figure 12–5 was timed, and the amount of time taken to rotate them was found proportional to the amount of rotation that actual objects in the real world would require. The proportionality is shown for mental rotation in the picture plane and in depth.

The symbolic-distance effect   If one can mentally rotate an image then one ought to be able to compare images. An experiment by Moyer (1973), which has stimulated a number of experiments on mental comparison, suggests the possibility that images can be compared, although the interpretation is not accepted by everyone. Consider the question, "Which is larger, an elephant or a fly?" A comparison of the mental images of these two animals should be easy and fast. However, the question, "Which is larger, a fly or a bumblebee?" should be difficult and slower. Moyer displayed pairs of animal names to his subjects who were required to throw a switch on the side of the name of the larger animal. Reaction time was recorded. The results are shown in Figure 12–7. The smaller the difference in animal sizes the longer the reaction time. Just as it would take longer in the world to discriminate a fly and a bumblebee, so it is with mental images. Here again there is an indication that images stand in an analog relationship with corresponding objects of the world. Findings like Moyer's have come to be known as the *symbolic distance effect*.

The image is seen as an explanation of the symbolic distance effect by some (e.g., Paivio, 1975), but there are those who are cautious about the interpretation. Moyer himself questions it (Moyer and Dumais, 1978). One criticism is that at least some of the comparisons can be made with size labels and do not seem to need images at all. An elephant carries the label "large" and a fly has the label "small", and our verbal processing of these labels is sufficient for a speedy comparison. Another criticism is that the symbolic distance effect is found for digits. Parkman (1971) presented subjects with pairs of digits 0–9 with the requirement to press a switch on the side of the larger digit. The greater the separation between digits the faster the reaction time. It is hard to see how images are involved in the comparison of digits. Some may find theoretical indecisiveness like this uncomfortable, but it does not bother scientists very much because the world is clouded with uncertainty in their eyes and they are tolerant of it. At any moment, given the facts that are available, a scientist will pass tentative judgments on the mechanisms that are required to explain the facts, and then will get on with the job of research to refine the judgments and reduce the uncertainty. A judgment that is made by some psychologists is that findings on mental comparison are explained by the image.

The instructional approach   Another approach to imagery is to instruct subjects to form images and use them in learning. Bower and Winzenz (1970) required the paired-associate learning of noun pairs. One group of subjects was instructed to learn by rote. One group had each noun pair imbedded in a sentence, which is an experimenter-provided natural language mediator. Each subject of another group was instructed to form an image that related each noun pair. A recall test

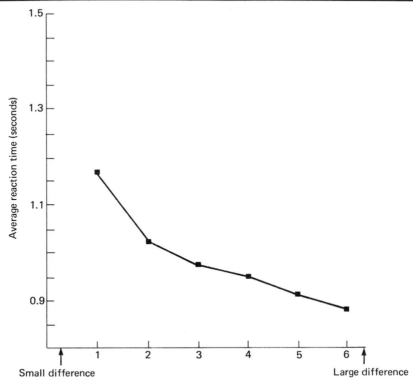

Source: R. S. Moyer, Comparing objects in memory: Evidence suggesting an internal psychophysics. *Perception & Psychophysics,* 1973, *13,* 180–184. Reprinted by permission of The Psychonomic Society, Inc.

FIGURE 12–7
An approach to showing that mental objects are an analog representation of the world is to record the time that it takes to discriminate whether two of them differ in size or not. The discrimination takes longer when the two objects are about the same size. The discrimination between mental objects that have a large difference in size is done more rapidly.

found that imagery gave the best performance, natural language mediation next best, and rote repetition the poorest of all. In addition to demonstrating the instructional approach to imagery, the experiment demonstrates that imagery is superior to natural language mediation as a strategy of memorization, and both are better than rote rehearsal.

Mnemonic systems

Mnemonic systems are structured memory aids, and imagery systems are the oldest of them. Imagery mnemonics originated with the ancient

Greeks, and it is only with the modern interest in imagery that we have taken a scientific interest in them and have experimentally verified their effectiveness in the laboratory. The Method of Loci (locations) is the oldest memory aid of them all.

THE METHOD OF LOCI

Remembering a speech without notes has always been an art, and it was a valued art among the ancients. Before printing, all was oral communication, and effective oral communication placed a premium on the memory for events and their organization. The art of rhetoric undoubtedly was a more refined skill then than now, and the Roman Cicero (106–43 B.C.) in his treatise *De Oratore* (translated edition, 1959), discussed the importance of memory for rhetoric. He tells a story about the discovery of the first mnemonic device:

> There is a story that Simonides was dining at the house of a wealthy nobleman named Scopas at Crannon in Thessaly, and chanted a lyric poem which he had composed in honour of his host, in which he followed the custom of the poets by including for decorative purposes a long passage referring to Castor and Pollux; whereupon Scopas with excessive meanness told him he would pay him half the fee agreed on for the poem, and if he liked he might apply for the balance to his sons of Tyndareus, as they had gone halves in the panegyric. The story runs that a little later a message was brought to Simonides to go outside, as two young men were standing at the door who earnestly requested him to come out; so he rose from his seat and went out, and could not see anybody; but in the interval of his absence the roof of the hall where Scopas was giving the banquet fell in, crushing Scopas himself and his relations underneath the ruins and killing them; and when their friends wanted to bury them but were altogether unable to know them apart as they had been completely crushed, the story goes that Simonides was enabled by his recollection of the place in which each of them had been reclining at table to identify them for separate interment; and that this circumstance suggested to him the discovery of the truth that the best aid to clearness of memory consists in orderly arrangement. He inferred that persons desiring to train this faculty must select localities and form mental images of the facts they wish to remember and store those images in the localities, with the result that the arrangement of the localities will preserve the order of the facts, and the images of the facts will designate the facts themselves, and we shall employ the localities and images respectively as a wax writing tablet and the letters written on it.[1]

---

[1] Cicero. *De Oratore* (Books I and II.) (Rev. ed.) (E. W. Sutton and H. Rackham, trans.). Cambridge: Harvard University Press, 1959, pp. 352–355. Reprinted by permission of Harvard University Press.

The technique has come to be known as the *Method of Loci*, based as it is on the placing of distinctive visual images of the items to be remembered in the locations of a spatial image. Retrieval at the time of recall is a matter of mentally moving through the locations of the spatial image, finding the images of the item that are stored, and recalling them. The same locations can be used repeatedly for an indefinite number of memory tasks, it is contended.

Suppose you have ten items to remember. Recollect the image of a familiar place, like your kitchen, and then imagine each of the ten items and place it in a distinctive location in the kitchen image—one in the oven, one under the sink, and so on. At recall you imagine your kitchen again, image the item in the oven, the item under the sink, etc. Cicero recommended that the imagery be vivid and distinctive, and about the only change (from unknown sources) in the Method of Loci in 2,000 years is the suggestion that images be not only vivid but bizarre. Do not simply put the item in the oven. Put it in the mouth of a one-eyed suckling pig wearing sunglasses that you imagine is cooking there.

Does the Method of Loci work? It seems farfetched to some, and yet the Method of Loci has persisted throughout the ages and has been regularly endorsed as a memory aid (Yates, 1966). Memory experts who perform on the stage claim it as one of their techniques. Only in very recent times, however, has the Method of Loci come under experimental scrutiny. Since the mid-1960s, research on imagery has accelerated (Bower, 1970; 1972), and one thrust of research has been the Method of Loci. Some of the research has been demonstration exercises, which is a beginning, but Groninger (1971) has a suitably designed experiment on the topic.

After instructing them in the Method of Loci, Groninger sent each subject of an imagery group into a booth to work out a spatial image with 25 locations that could be easily ordered and was very familiar. A typical subject took about ten minutes to do this, then was given a pack of 25 cards, each with a word on it, and told to learn them in order, using the Method of Loci. A control group of subjects was simply given the cards and told to learn them in order, using any method they wished. That all subjects knew the words when they came out of the booth was verified, and they were then instructed to return after one week and five weeks. On their return they were administered retention tests. The imagery group recalled 92 percent of the words in correct order after one week and 80 percent after five weeks. Corresponding values for the control group were 64 percent and 36 percent. Interviews with the control group subjects found that most of them learned the list by rote rehearsal; so the data are a comparison of imagery mediation and rote learning as mechanisms of remembering. Imagery clearly wins.

Is it necessary that images be bizarre? Nappe and Wollen (1973) gave their subjects one study-test trial on a list of 48 noun pairs. The nouns were of high imagery value as scaled by Paivio, Yuille, and Madigan (1968); so mostly they were concrete objects, such as TREE or DOG, and would easily arouse an image. The study time for each pair was self-paced because a subject was required to form an image for each pair and the time for it varied from item to item and subject to subject. A memory drum was used for presentation. Written beside each pair was "common" or 'bizarre," indicating the kind of image that should be conceived for the item. Half of the items were designated "common" and half "bizarre." The act of image creation was timed, with the subject pressing a switch after forming an image. The subject then gave a verbal description of the image, which was tape-recorded, before going on to the next pair. No evidence was found that bizarre images benefited retention. Sixty-eight percent of the pairs with common images were recalled correctly, and 65 percent of the pairs with bizarre images were correct—an inconsequential difference. Common images had the advantage of faster formation time. On the average, common images were formed in four seconds and bizarre images in six seconds. As a check on the commonness and bizarreness of the images, judges rated the descriptions of the images that had been recorded. The judges concluded that "common" images were indeed commonplace, and "bizarre" images were typically unusual.

In another experiment on bizarreness, Wollen and his associates (Wollen, Weber, and Lowry, 1972) tested the hypothesis that image bizarreness might be concealing a more fundamental variable for imagery and retention. Their example of the problem is the pair SOFA–ELEPHANT to be learned with imagery. For a bizarre image, undoubtedly you would come up with something like an elephant sitting on a sofa, but in creating this bizarre image you also have an image where the two elements are interacting. Is it bizarreness or interaction that is important? Most cases of bizarre imagery would involve interacting elements; so the two variables are confounded. Wollen et al. performed an experiment that untangled these two variables. They had their subjects learn noun pairs like PIANO–CIGAR by the study-test method, and with each pair there was one of four possible line drawings depicting the objects as bizarre or not or interacting or not. This approach deliberately gave the subject the image, rather than letting a subject freely create an image of his own. An example of the four kinds of drawings is given in Figure 12–8. The four line drawings constitute four experimental conditions of the study in which each of four experimental groups learned a list with one type of drawing. A control condition learned the pairs without a drawing. Recall was immediate, and the results indi-

Noninteracting, nonbizarre

Noninteracting, bizarre

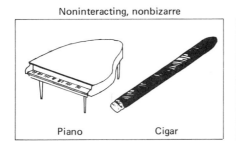

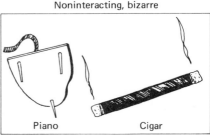

Piano	Cigar

Piano	Cigar

Interacting, nonbizarre

Interacting, bizarre

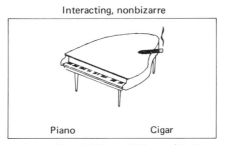

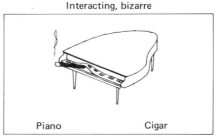

Piano	Cigar

Piano	Cigar

Source: K. A. Wollen, A. Weber, and D. H. Lowry, Bizarreness versus interaction of mental images as determinants of learning. *Cognitive Psychology*, 1972, *3*, 518–523. Reprinted by permission of Academic Press, Inc.

FIGURE 12–8
Example of the four kinds of drawings that accompanied word pairs when they were presented for study in the Wollen et al. experiment. The intent was to encourage bizarre imagery or not, and interaction among image elements or not.

cated benefits for retention when elements of the image interacted, not when they were bizarre. In fact, bizarreness affected retention adversely, giving a level of recall below that of the control group.

At this stage of our knowledge the rule seems to be that elements of the image should be integrated in a way that is meaningful and consistent with everyday experience. For the Method of Loci it is better to place the item to be remembered in the oven amidst the baking potatoes rather than in the mouth of a one-eyed suckling pig wearing sunglasses.

THE PEGWORD METHOD

The Method of Loci can be used to recall items in order or otherwise. You can choose to wander through your mental locations sequentially if you wish for the retrieval of items in order, or you can wander through the locations aimlessly and retrieve items in any order. When the interest is solely order information, however, there is an imagery mnemonic system called the *Pegword Method* designed solely for that purpose. You can use the

Pegword Method to recall ten items in their correct order, or you can give the ninth item on request, or any other item for that matter. A nightclub memory expert, using the Pegword Method, can stand by the door, meet the guests as they enter, and then flawlessly recall all their names in a flashy display of recollection. Or, if asked, he can recall the name of the 63d person that entered the club.

The Pegword Method requires the memorization of a jingle which has the pegs on which the items to be remembered are hung with imagery. The most common jingle in use today goes on in this vein: One is a bun, two is a shoe, three is a tree," etc. After learning this mnemonic device you can take on the learning of any series of items, with imagery as the mechanism. Suppose the first word of a list is LADY. Conjure an image of a LADY sitting in a bun, as if she were a hot dog. If the second word is SCISSORS, image a scissors cutting a shoe in half. And so on. At recall you go through the jingle, and the rhyme arouses the image that you constructed for it and allows you to retrieve the item.

Does the Pegword Method work? In a laboratory evaluation, Bugelski (1968) instructed the subjects of an experimental group in the uses of imagery, thoroughly schooled them in the one-bun mnemonic device, and then had them learn six lists of ten nouns each. There was a control group, and they were given the lists and instructed to learn them in serial order, with nothing said about imagery or mnemonic devices. The outcome was that the experimental group recalled 63 percent of the words in their correct positions, and the control group only 22 percent.

Bower and Reitman (1972) compared two ways of using the Pegword Method with the Method of Loci. The jingle they used for lists of 20 noun pairs to be learned by the Pegword Method is given in Table 12–5. A separate-images group learned five lists by the Pegword Method,

TABLE 12–5

Rhymes for numbers 1–20 used by Bower and Reitman (1972) in their experiment on mnemonic devices and imagery.

One is a gun	Eleven is penny-one, hotdog bun
Two is a shoe	Twelve is penny-two, airplane glue
Three is a tree	Thirteen is penny-three, bumble bee
Four is a door	Fourteen is penny-four, grocery store
Five is knives	Fifteen is penny-five, big bee hive
Six is sticks	Sixteen is penny-six, magic tricks
Seven is oven	Seventeen is penny-seven, go to heaven
Eight is plate	Eighteen is penny-eight, golden gate
Nine is wine	Nineteen is penny-nine, ball of twine
Ten is hen	Twenty is penny-ten, ball point pen

Source: G. H. Bower, and J. S. Reitman, Mnemonic elaboration in multilist learning. *Journal of Verbal Learning and Verbal Behavior*, 1972, 11, 478–485. Reprinted by permission of Academic Press, Inc.

with a separate set of images for each list. A progressive elaboration group learned the five lists by the Pegword Method also, but by progressively enlarging the imagery scene around each pegword. Suppose the first words of Lists 1, 2, and 3 were HUNTER, HOUND, and FOX. The peg is "One is a gun." For List 1 the subject might get the image of a hunter with a gun, and for List 2 he might elaborate this to be a hunter with a gun who has his hound beside him, and for List 3 the image might be a hunter with a gun and his hound who are pursuing a fox. The idea was that separate images might cause some confusion among items of the lists and cause errors at recall, whereas progressive elaboration has all of the items of a given serial position in a single integrated image, which should lessen the chances of confusion. The third group was the loci group, which used the Method of Loci, with locations of the subject's own choosing. The loci group also used progressive elaboration. Needless to say, all groups were thoroughly pretrained in imagery and the mnemonic device assigned to them. At the end of the learning session of one trial per list, all subjects attempted immediate recall of the 100 items of the five lists, and then attempted recall once again a week later. The results for items in their correct list positions are shown in Figure 12–9. The strongest variable for recall is the progressive elaboration technique, whether the Pegword Method or the Method of Loci was used, and it remains effective over the one-week retention interval. Separate images serve the most recently learned lists reasonably well for an immediate recall test, but after a week their effectiveness is negligible.

THE KEYWORD METHOD

The learning of foreign vocabulary is never easy. The chore is typically done by rote rehearsal in which a foreign word is related to its English equivalent. Atkinson and Raugh (1975) have demonstrated that imagery can be a substantial benefit for the learning and remembering of foreign language vocabulary, and they call their approach the *Keyword Method.*

A keyword is an English word that sounds like part of the foreign word. Other than sound there is no relationship between the keyword and the foreign word. After getting the keyword, the next step is to associate a mental image of the keyword interacting with the English translation of the foreign word. For example, the Russian word ZVONÓK means BELL. The pronunciation is "zvahn-oak," with the emphasis on the last syllable, and it has a sound that resembles the English word OAK. With the English word OAK as the keyword, one could conjure the image of an oak tree with little bells as acorns, or an oak tree growing under a large bell jar.

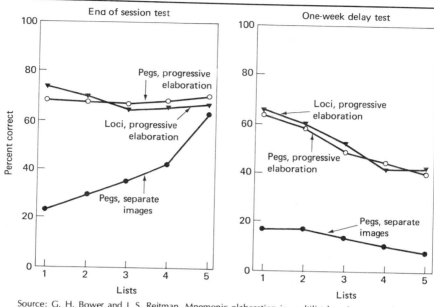

Source: G. H. Bower and J. S. Reitman, Mnemonic elaboration in multilist learning. *Journal of Verbal Learning and Verbal Behavior*, 1972, *11*, 478–485. Reprinted by permission of Academic Press, Inc.

FIGURE 12–9

A comparison of the Pegword Method and the Method of Loci as mnemonic devices that use imagery. Whether the image was separately conceived for each item of each list or progessively elaborated across items of the several lists that were learned, was also studied.

Atkinson and Raugh experimentally evaluated the effectiveness of the keyword method. Subjects learned a vocabulary of 120 Russian words. The control subjects during learning were shown the Russian word paired with its English translation, and they learned by rote, as we all have done when we have learned foreign vocabularies. The keyword group, instructed in the Keyword Method, had a keyword presented with each Russian word and its English translation. After three days of learning, all were given a test of the 120 words on Day 4. About six weeks later, they were given the test again. On the Day 4 test, the keyword group had 72 percent correct and the control group had 46 percent correct. On the test after six weeks, the keyword group remembered the meaning of 43 percent of the Russian words, while the control group recalled only 28 percent. There was forgetting over six weeks, which is expected, but the keyword group retained its superiority nevertheless. The Keyword Method gave an advantage, and the advantage persisted.

Imagery theory

What is the source of an image? Or course we are not sure, but there is the long-standing assumption that the source is sensory experience. The self-arousal of an image in the absence of events that defined it in the first place is a kind of re-creation of those events. David Hartley, the 18th century British associationist, wrote of the image as a conditioned sensation, but his definition probably would not be acceptable today because it could imply that the image is a copy of the scene that was experienced. Perhaps faithful copying sometimes occurs, but psychologists today would prefer not to see images as unanalyzed sensations. Rather, images are seen as remembered perceptions that derive from the stimuli that we organize, attend to, and process.

There are several things to notice about this conception of an image. First, it is objective in principle because it derives from experience, and experience can be manipulated. Second, it does not necessarily imply that consciousness and images are the same; there is no reason why one cannot have unconscious images. Third, images can be in any sense modality even though the term "image" has an implication of visual experience. And fourth, images should not necessarily be considered high fidelity representation of sensory experience; a visual image is not necessarily a clear color photograph in the head. Being a remembered perception, the image is probably as much a product of the perceiver as the sensory input from the world.

For whatever analysts of imagery say about theory, it is hard to escape the feeling they are talking about a mental picture which the subject perceives subjectively and uses to guide his responding. Analysts call this the *picture metaphor*. Scientists will sometimes deny use of the picture metaphor because it is based on subjective experience. Whether scientists endorse the picture metaphor or not, they come close to it in their thinking without necessarily embracing it. The kinds of experiments that are done and the inferences that are drawn suggest that a picture metaphor is often guiding the thinking of the investigator. Whether the picture metaphor is guiding the behavior of the subject is another matter. Indeed, it is the issue.

Paivio (1971), the pioneer of the modern interest in imagery, considers a picture-like image as an influential mediator of behavior, but insufficient in itself. Images are a nonverbal code, and he combines them with the verbal code to form the *dual-coding hypothesis*. The image code and the verbal code are used in different degrees for pictures, concrete words, and abstract words. A picture that defies verbal description is processed entirely by imagery. A picture that lends itself to verbal description is processed mostly by imagery but has some verbal code combined with it. Concrete words that describe explicit sensory events such as houses and cars shift more toward the verbal code, although some imagery is used. Abstract words use only the verbal code. By including the verbal code, Paivio shows how imagery interacts with other memory processes.

Pylyshyn (1973) tries for even a more fundamental conception by asserting that both verbal and imagery systems are based on abstract propositions. A sentence or an image has particular features, but the proposition that determines them is general. The more economical a theory the better, and Pylyshyn strives for economy by trying to replace Paivio's dual theory with a unitary one. Propositional theory has been criticized on the grounds that evidence does not distinguish it from the picture metaphor very well (Anderson, 1978), probably because neither position is stated explicitly enough. If two theories imply the same thing then either they are identical or they are so loosely specified that it is never clear that one theory predicts something that the other does not.

The modern research interest in imagery dates only from the mid-1960s, so it is not surprising that there is theoretical uncertainty. Data give direction and precision to theory, and it may be a while before we have enough of it to do a good theoretical job.

Summary

The method by which verbal material is memorized influences the amount recalled. These methods are called strategies of memorization, and there are three basic ones: rote rehearsal, natural language mediation, and imagery.

Rote rehearsal is the best known strategy to insure the retention of verbal information in memory. Repetition of an item to be remembered can improve recall—the more repetitions the better the recall. The modern picture of rehearsal is complicated by the finding that not all rehearsal leads to improved retention. We now distinguish between maintenance rehearsal, which does not improve retention, and elaborative rehearsal which does. Research is trying to untangle the determinants of these two kinds of rehearsal so that they will be clearly distinguished.

Natural language mediation is the verbal encoding of an item to be remembered, and it is positively related to retention also. A natural language mediator is an effective mnemonic aid only if the subject remembers it and can remember how to decode it and retrieve the to-be-remembered item. When these requirements are met a natural language mediator is several times more effective than rote rehearsal.

Imagery and retention are positively related. Embodying a to-be-remembered verbal item in an image has the same requirements as the natural language mediator if it is to be effective: The image must be remembered, as must be the method of decoding it.

Imagery is the oldest strategy of memorization. A technique called the

Method of Loci goes back to the ancient Greeks, and it uses a spatial image in which the items to be remembered are stored. At recall the spatial image is remembered and the items are retrieved from it. The Pegword Method is another imagery device to aid retention, and it is tailored for the remembering of items in a sequence. The Keyword Method uses imagery to facilitate the learning of foreign language vocabulary.

The main theories of imagery are the picture metaphor, the dual-coding hypothesis, and propositional theory. The picture metaphor says that the subject using imagery is responding to a picture-like entity with real world properties that he subjectively sees. The dual-coding hypothesis says that verbal behavior and imagery, as nonverbal behavior, anchor the two ends of a continuum. Behavior can be guided by either or an interaction of the two. Propositional theory says that both language and images are derived from a more fundamental abstraction, called the proposition.

References

Adams, J. A., McIntyre, J. S., & Thorsheim, H. I. Natural language mediation and interitem interference in paired-associate learning. *Psychonomic Science,* 1969, *16,* 63–64.

Anderson, J. R. Arguments concerning representations for mental imagery. *Psychological Review,* 1978, *85,* 249–277.

Atkinson, R. C., & Raugh, M. R. An application of the mnemonic keyword method to the acquisition of Russian vocabulary. *Journal of Experimental Psychology: Human Learning and Memory,* 1975, *104,* 126–133.

Atkinson, R. C., & Shiffrin, R. M. Human memory: A proposed system and its control processes. In K. W. Spence & J. T. Spence (Eds.), *The psychology of learning and motivation* (Vol. 2). New York: Academic Press, 1968, pp. 89–195.

Bower, G. H. Analysis of a mnemonic device. *American Scientist,* 1970, *58,* 496–510.

Bower, G. H. Mental imagery and associative learning. In L. Gregg (Ed.), *Cognition in learning and memory.* New York: Wiley, 1972, pp. 51–88.

Bower, G. H., & Clark, M. C. Narrative stories as mediators for serial learning. *Psychonomic Science,* 1969, *14,* 181–182.

Bower, G. H., & Reitman, J. S. Mnemonic elaboration in multilist learning. *Journal of Verbal Learning and Verbal Behavior,* 1972, *11,* 478–485.

Bower, G. H., & Winzenz, D. Comparison of associative learning strategies. *Psychonomic Science,* 1970, *20,* 119–120.

Bugelski, B. R. Images as mediators in one-trial paired-associate learning. II: Self-timing in successive lists. *Journal of Experimental Psychology,* 1968, *77,* 328–334.

Cicero. *De Oratore* (Books I and II). (Rev. ed.) (E. W. Sutton and H. Rackham, trans.). Cambridge: Harvard University Press, 1959.

Ebbinghaus, H. *Memory: A contribution to experimental psychology.* (H. A. Ruger and C. E. Bussenius, trans.). New York: Dover, 1964.

Glenberg, A., Smith, S. M., & Green, C. Type I rehearsal: Maintenance and more. *Journal of Verbal Learning and Verbal Behavior,* 1977, *16,* 339–352.

Groninger, L. D. Mnemonic imagery and forgetting. *Psychonomic Science,* 1971, *23,* 161–163.

Hellyer, S. Supplementary report: Frequency of stimulus presentation and short-term decrement in recall. *Journal of Experimental Psychology,* 1962, *64,* 650.

Kiess, H. O. Effects of natural language mediators on short-term memory. *Journal of Experimental Psychology,* 1968, *77,* 7–13.

Metzler, J., & Shepard, R. N. Transformational studies of the internal representation of three-dimensional objects. In R. L. Solso (Ed.), *Theories in cognitive psychology: The Loyola Symposium.* New York: Wiley, 1974, pp. 147–201.

Montague, W. E., Adams, J. A., & Kiess, H. O. Forgetting and natural language mediation. *Journal of Experimental Psychology,* 1966, *72,* 829–833.

Moyer, R. S. Comparing objects in memory: Evidence suggesting an internal psychophysics. *Perception & Psychophysics,* 1973, *13,* 180–184.

Moyer, R. S., & Dumais, S. T. Mental comparison. In G. H. Bower (ed.), *The psychology of learning and motivation.* (Vol. 12). New York: Academic Press, 1978, pp. 117–155.

Nappe, G. W., & Wollen, K. A. Effects of instructions to form common and bizarre mental images on retention. *Journal of Experimental Psychology,* 1973, *100,* 6–8.

Nelson, T. O. Repetition and depth of processing. *Journal of Verbal Learning and Verbal Behavior,* 1977, *16,* 151–171.

Paivio, A. *Imagery and verbal processes.* New York: Holt, Rinehart and Winston, 1971.

Paivio, A. Perceptual comparisons through the mind's eye. *Memory & Cognition,* 1975, *3,* 635–647.

Paivio, A., Yuille, J. C., & Madigan, S. A. Concreteness, imagery, and meaningfulness values for 925 nouns. *Journal of Experimental Psychology Monograph Supplement,* 1968, *76,* No. 1, Part 2.

Parkman, J. M. Temporal aspects of digit and letter inequality judgments. *Journal of Experimental Psychology,* 1971, *91,* 191–205.

Prytulak, L. S. Natural language mediation. *Cognitive Psychology,* 1971, *2,* 1–56.

Pylyshyn, Z. W. What the mind's eye tells the mind's brain: A critique of mental imagery. *Psychological Bulletin,* 1973, *80,* 1–24.

Rundus, D. Maintenance rehearsal and single-level processing. *Journal of Verbal Learning and Verbal Behavior,* 1977, *16,* 665–681.

Shepard, R. N., & Metzler, J. Mental rotation of three-dimensional objects. *Science,* 1971, *171,* 701–703.

Smith, W. R. Retention as a function of natural language mediation and of time. *Psychonomic Science,* 1969, *14,* 288–289.

Wollen, K. A., Weber, A., & Lowry, D. H. Bizarreness versus interaction of mental images as determinants of learning. *Cognitive Psychology,* 1972, *3,* 518–523.

Yates, F. A. *The art of memory.* Chicago: University of Chicago Press, 1966.

13

Verbal forgetting processes

TRACE DECAY and interference were discussed as two theories of forgetting in sensory memory in Chapter 11. Sensory memory is precategorical memory, in which the material exists as the internal persistence of a sensory event until it is processed or read out. Once having been processed, what theory or theories of forgetting apply? To follow Plato's metaphor (Chapter 10), what has happened to the impression that experience has placed on the wax tablet of the mind? Has time eroded it? Do new items get written on the tablet and obscure older ones? Does the presence of other tablets make a particular tablet hard to find and identify? In more modern and less picturesque terms, we ask if the response potential has decayed with time, if the learning of other responses has interfered with the to-be-remembered response, or if the response potential is in high strength but our retrieval operations have failed to recover it. These statements represent three main theories in modern psychology about the causes of forgetting: trace decay, interference, and failure to retrieve.

We say that forgetting has occurred when a performance loss is observed after a retention interval. Keep in mind that a retention loss and a memory loss are not necessarily the same. Retention could be poor because motivation has dropped or fatigue is present. Or an item might not have been learned; so we cannot be expected to remember something that has not entered memory in the first place. But even with such variables as motivation and fatigue held constant on the learning and the retention test, and even insuring that the item has been learned in the first place, there is no guarantee that the loss of an item on the retention test means a loss from memory storage. An item may exist in full strength in memory and yet not occur at the retention test. Assume that you once learned the name of an early American patriot who invented bifocals, but now you cannot recall it when asked. The item may have disappeared totally from memory, requiring you to learn it anew, but it also could be fully in memory but inaccessible to your recovery efforts. Suppose a friend said teasingly to you, "Of course you can remember his name! Let me give you some hints. He signed the Declaration of Independence. He was a delegate to the Constitutional Convention. He was the first secretary of the American Philosophical Society." Then you say, "I've got it! Thomas Jefferson!" Your friend replies, "No! I'll give you one more hint. He invented the lightning rod." And you say, *"Now* I've got it! Benjamin Franklin!" The item was in your memory store all of the time, but it took some jogging to arouse it. Subjectively, you had a strong feeling of knowing the answer. William James, founder of the first psychological laboratory in the United States, captured the feeling of retrieval very nicely:

> Suppose we try to recall a forgotten name. The state of our consciousness is peculiar. There is a gap therein; but no mere gap. It is a gap that is intensively active. A sort of wraith of the name is in it, beckoning us in a given direction, making us at moments tingle with the sense of our closeness, and then letting us sink back without the longed-for term. (James, 1890, p. 251)

Memory recovery mechanisms come under the heading of *retrieval from memory.* Having an item in memory and being able to use it are two different things. Tulving and Pearlstone (1966) distinguished between an item that is *available* in memory but not necessarily *accessible.* A book may be available in the library, but if the card is missing from the catalog it may not be accessible to you.

The means by which we can access items that are full-strength in memory is a rather new research interest in psychology, and today we are less inclined to equate retention loss with memory loss. There are those who believe that once information is processed in memory it is permanently available and that remembering is entirely a matter of retrieval; everything is remembered indefinitely and in principle can be retrieved. Evidence for this strong assertion would be techniques that would allow us to remember anything we had ever learned. The abolition of forgetting would be an enormous achievement (and a mixed blessing), but there is no indication that it is attainable. The evidence at present supports an intermediate position. Feats of retrieval are certainly possible because daily we experience instances like the Benjamin Franklin example, and retrieval has been amply demonstrated in the laboratory, but there is no evidence that all forgetting is nothing more than a failure to retrieve. Interference, and probably trace decay, operate also.

Interference, trace decay, and retrieval will be developed in detail in the sections that follow.

Interference

The *interference theory of forgetting* is an active theory because it contends that events within time, not time itself, cause forgetting. Forgetting may or may not occur over the retention interval, depending upon the nature and frequency of interfering events. So many things are forgotten so often that some feel a need for an inevitable forgetting process independent of experience like trace decay, but interference theorists say that widespread forgetting occurs because active organisms have a high likelihood of encountering events that will interfere.

Experimental psychologists have been vigorous in their conduct of laboratory experiments on interference. Much of the research on interference has the implicit assumption that the laws that are found will explain forgetting because the interference theory of forgetting says that the laws of interference and the laws of forgetting are the same. First let us examine representative laboratory research on the laws of interference, and then examine their value as an explanation of forgetting.

DESIGN OF EXPERIMENTS FOR INTERFERENCE

Interference is produced by two basic kinds of experimental designs, which produce retroactive interference and proactive interference.

Retroactive interference is defined as decrement in recall produced by events between learning and recall. The experimental design for retroactive interference is:

	Learning	Retention interval	Recall
Experimental group	Learn A	Learn B	Test A
Control group	Learn A	—	Test A

If activity B causes a decrement in the test of activity A for the experimental group relative to the test of activity A for the control group, then retroactive interference has occurred. Activity B may not always interfere; it can be neutral or even transfer positively to A on the test.

Proactive interference is defined as a decrement in recall of a criterion activity produced by events that occurred before learning of the criterion activity. The experimental design for proactive interference is:

	Prior learning	Learning	Retention interval	Recall
Experimental group	Learn B	Learn A	—	Test A
Control group	—	Learn A	—	Test A

If the prior learning of activity B causes a decrement in Test A for the experimental group when compared to Test A for the control group, then proactive interference has occurred.

Most research on interference has been with lists of verbal paired associates. A standard laboratory arrangement for interference with paired associates is to have companion pairs in the two lists A and B whose stimuli are the same and whose responses are different. For example, for retroactive interference, a pair of criterion List A could be HOUSE–TRACTOR, and its learning could be followed by the learning of an interfering List B which has the pair HOUSE–TREE. Recall of criterion List A would then follow. In the case of proactive interference, the interfering List B with HOUSE–TREE would be learned before learning and recall of criterion List A with the companion pair HOUSE–TRACTOR.

REPRESENTATIVE DATA ON RETROACTIVE INTERFERENCE

An experiment by Briggs (1957) nicely presents fundamental facts about retroactive interference. Briggs investigated amount of practice on each of the two lists, which were comprised of paired adjectives whose stimulus terms were the same and whose response terms were different. The criterion list was given 2, 5, 10, or 20 trials, and the interfering list was given either 0 (control), 2, 5, 10, or 20 trials. Recall on the criterion list followed. The amount of retroactive interference for the various conditions was measured by a formula which Briggs called Relative Retroactive Interference:

$$100 \times \frac{\text{Control group score} - \text{Experimental group score}}{\text{Control group score}}$$

The formula tells us how much an interfering list reduced recall of the criterion list below that of the control group which had only learn and recall of the criterion list. Consider an example from Briggs' own data. A control group with 20 trials on the criterion list (and no trials on the interfering list) had 9.44 responses correct on the recall test. An

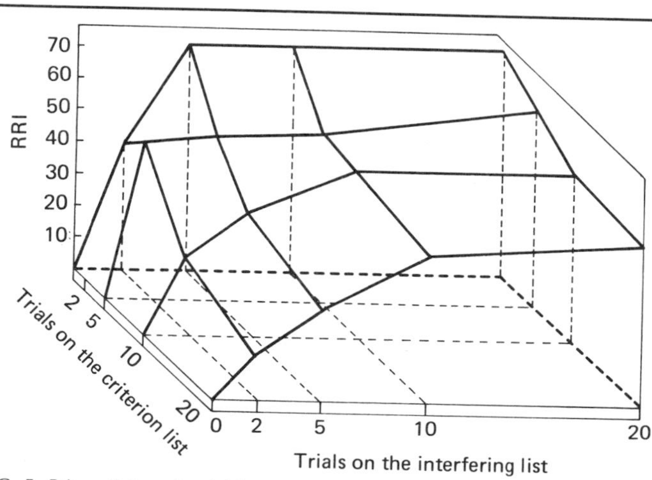

Source: G. E. Briggs, Retroactive inhibition as a function of the degree of original and interpolated learning. *Journal of Experimental Psychology,* 1957, 53, 60–67. Reprinted by permission of the American Psychological Association.

FIGURE 13–1

Retroactive interference in paired associates as a function of amount of practice on the criterion list to be recalled and the interfering list.

experimental group with 20 trials on the criterion list (and 20 trials on the interfering list) had 4.38 responses correct on the recall test. Thus,

$$100 \times \frac{9.44 - 4.38}{9.44} = 54\% \text{ Relative Retroactive Interference}$$

Brigg's results, in terms of Relative Retroactive Interference, are shown in Figure 13–1. Interference is related positively to amount of practice on the interfering list, and inversely to amount of practice on the criterion list.

REPRESENTATIVE DATA ON PROACTIVE INTERFERENCE

Amount of prior interfering activity and length of the retention interval are two main variables for proactive interference. Data on effects of amount of prior activity are given in a study by Archer (reported in Underwood, 1957), and they are shown in Figure 13–2. Using serial learning, Archer's subjects learned lists of 12 adjectives. Each list was learned to a criterion of one perfect trial and recalled 24 hours later. Immediately after recall the next list was learned to criterion, then recalled 24 hours later, and so on, for nine lists. Percent recall declined steadily from 71 percent for the first list to 27 percent for the ninth list.

302

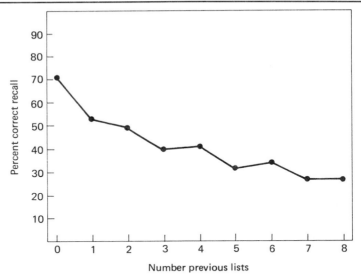

Source: B. J. Underwood, Interference and forgetting. *Psychological Review,* 1957, 64, 49–60. Reprinted by permission of the American Psychological Association.

FIGURE 13–2
Proactive interference steadily increases as a function of the number of prior lists learned and recalled.

An experiment by Greenberg and Underwood (1950) demonstrates the effects of both number of lists and length of the retention interval on proactive interference. There were three groups of subjects and each group successively learned and recalled four lists of ten paired adjectives. The retention interval between learning and recall was the same throughout for a group, but was different for each group—10 minutes, 5 hours, and 48 hours. One group learned List 1, rested ten minutes, recalled List 1, learned List 2, rested ten minutes, recalled List 2, and so on for four lists. Other groups did the same but each with a different retention interval. The results are shown in Figure 13–3. Retention is unaffected by number of prior lists when the retention interval is brief, but sizable effects are obtained as the retention interval increases. Archer, whose data are shown in Figure 13–2, used a 24-hour interval, and we can see from the Greenberg and Underwood data that the interval was properly chosen to give a substantial proactive interference effect.

Single verbal items in the paradigm for short-term retention (e.g., Peterson & Peterson, 1959) exert proactive interference effects just as verbal lists do. Figure 13–4 shows data from Wickens (1970), and they show increasing decrement in recall as successive items are learned and recalled. The three curves are for different classes of verbal materials: three consonants, three numbers, or three words. The retention interval was 20 seconds throughout for the words, and 10 seconds for the other two kinds of material. Regardless of kind of material, there is a buildup of interference, shown by the progressive decline in recall over trials. The buildup is rather rapid, leveling off after the initial items.

Wickens' data in Figure 13–4 show high retention for the first item and less thereafter, suggesting that there would be little short-term forgetting without prior items and the interference they produce. This possibility was explored and supported in experiments by Keppel and Underwood (1962). They used trigram consonant syllables, e.g., QXF, as their verbal materials, and in one of their experiments they manipulated both the number of items learned and recalled as well as the retention interval. Their results are shown in Figure 13–5. Retention was perfect for one item learned and recalled where there were no prior items to exert proactive interference. But, when two or three items were learned and recalled, there is proactive interference and the rapid forgetting that

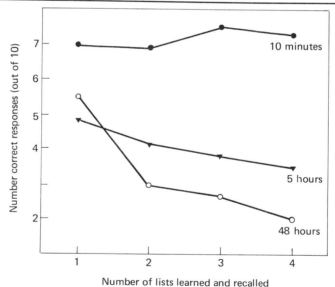

Source: R. Greenberg, and B. J. Underwood, Retention as a function of stage of practice. *Journal of Experimental Psychology,* 1950, 40, 452–457. Reprinted by permission of the American Psychological Association.

FIGURE 13–3

Proactive interference as a function of number of prior lists learned and recalled, and length of time interval between learning and recall of a list (shown as curve parameter).

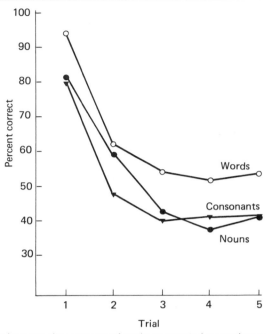

Source: D. D. Wickens, Encoding categories of words: An empirical approach to meaning. *Psychological Review*, 1970, *77*, 1–15. Reprinted by permission of the American Psychological Association.

FIGURE 13–4
Proactive interference in short-term retention as a function of the number of single items learned and recalled. Curves for three types of verbal material are shown.

we identify with short-term retention. The Keppel and Underwood study gave encouragement to the view that the short-term forgetting which Peterson and Peterson (1959), and Brown (1958), obtained was a consequence of interference.

HOW GOOD IS THE INTERFERENCE THEORY OF FORGETTING?

Interference is easily obtained in the laboratory, but this does not prove that forgetting is caused by interference. How do we test the interference theory of forgetting? Because the interference theory of forgetting is an active theory that depends upon the occurrence of events to interfere with the ones stored in memory and being remembered, a straightforward test would be to eliminate the interfering events. If the theory is true, elimination of interfering events should eliminate forgetting. There have been two approaches to this issue. One

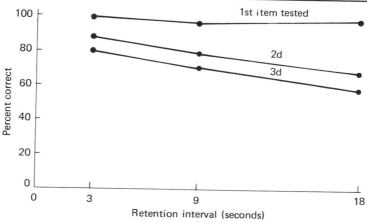

Source: G. Keppel and B. J. Underwood, Proactive inhibition in short-term retention of single items. *Journal of Verbal Learning and Verbal Behavior,* 1962, *1,* 153–161. Reprinted by permission of Academic Press, Inc.

FIGURE 13–5
Proactive interference as a function of retention interval and number of prior items learned and recalled. Short-term forgetting is absent for one item where the conditions of proactive interference are absent.

approach has been to have subjects sleep during the retention interval on the assumption that sleep insulates the subject from incoming stimuli, some of which can interfere. Comparisons are with subjects who have been awake during the retention interval. The other approach has been to compare implications of the interference and trace decay theories of forgetting in the same experiment to see whether time or events in time is the variable for forgetting. Pitting rival hypotheses against one another in an experiment is a standard approach in science.

The sleep studies The implications of sleep during the retention interval for the interference theory of forgetting was seen over 50 years ago by Jenkins and Dallenbach (1924) in a classic experiment. Two subjects were used, and they had serial learning of many lists of nonsense syllables over many sessions as they participated in all experimental conditions. The variables of the experiment were retention intervals of one, two, four, and eight hours, and whether the interval was spent asleep or awake. The results are presented in Figure 13–6. Over twice as many items were recalled after sleeping than after being awake. Sleep did not totally eliminate forgetting, but it was effective enough to be in comfortable agreement with the interference theory of forgetting. The investigators conclude that ". . . forgetting is not so much a matter of the decay of old impressions and associations as it is a matter of the

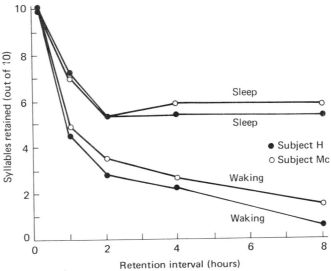

Source: J. G. Jenkins and K. M. Dallenbach, Obliviscence during sleep and waking. *American Journal of Psychology,* 1924, 35, 605–612. Reprinted by permission of the University of Illinois Press.

FIGURE 13–6
Verbal retention over intervals of sleeping and waking for two subjects.

interference, inhibition, or obliteration of the old by the new" (Jenkins and Dallenbach, 1924, p.. 612). Subsequent experiments (Ekstrand, 1967, 1972; Barrett and Ekstrand, 1972; Spight, 1928; Van Ormer, 1932) also found the superiority of sleeping over waking for retention, and so the original Jenkins and Dallenbach finding is a secure one in psychology.

An example of the more modern work that is consistent with Jenkins and Dallenbach is a study by Ekstrand (1967). His subjects learned a list of verbal paired associates and recalled them after eight hours. One group of subjects slept during the retention interval and the other was awake. The awake subjects had 73.3 percent correctly recalled, while the sleep subjects had 84.6 percent correct. This is not a large difference, but it is significant and in the same direction as the one that Jenkins and Dallenbach found. The same finding of a small but significant difference in favor of subjects who slept was also found in another study by Ekstrand (1972).

If the interference theory of forgetting is empirically true and if sleep is a mechanism that denies registry of incoming stimuli, then there should be no forgetting whatsoever for subjects who sleep in the retention interval. This was not so, however, because all of the studies found some forgetting for sleeping subjects, although not much forgetting in some cases. These findings could mean several things:

1.   Interference theory is not the sole explanation of forgetting. Some forgetting occurs even with sleep controlling all of the interference; so some other factor must contribute to the forgetting.

2.   The sleep experiments conform to a retroactive interference paradigm in which the interfering material, presumably controlled by sleep, occurs between the original learning and recall of the criterion material. The sleep experiments, however, do not control for proactive interference from prior learned material and it could be the cause of decrement for the sleeping subjects. The Jenkins and Dallenbach study is particularly vulnerable to this criticism because the two subjects learned and recalled many lists, and so most lists had the learn and recall of other lists preceding them. The Ekstrand experiments were better in this respect. Ekstrand had his subjects learn and recall only one list, and the forgetting was considerably less as a result. Nevertheless, some forgetting was found.

3.   Sleep is an imperfect mechanism for controlling potentially interfering events; it is not the control that investigators think it is. The brain is a mass of electrical activity, and one way to monitor it is with the electroencephalogram (EEG) which is a record of the brain's electrical activity obtained from electrodes pasted on the skull (the EEG was discussed in Chapter 9 under biofeedback). For our purposes here the EEG is informative about levels of sleep and wakefulness. Figure 13–7 shows the different kinds of EEG records that are obtained for the awake-sleep continuum, and during a night's sleep we fluctuate in and out of these levels. Simon and Emmons (1956), in an experiment on learning while asleep, presented their sleeping subjects with questions and answers at five-minute intervals while simultaneously recording the EEG to determine the level of sleep at the time the item was presented. An example question was: "In what kind of store did Ulysses S. Grant work before the war?" and its answer was: "Before the war, Ulysses S. Grant worked in a hardware store." Upon waking the questions were presented again and the recall of answers was attempted. Recall was about 80 percent correct for state A (Figure 13–7), about 50 percent correct for state B, about 5 percent correct for state C, and essentially zero-level recall thereafter. For their purposes, Simon and Emmons saw the data as denying the popular thesis that learning can occur while asleep because they found no learning in states D, E, and F where sleep was genuinely present. For the purpose of analyzing sleep and memory experiments, their data emphasize that sleep is imperfect for insulating subjects from potentially interfering stimuli because subjects sometimes fluctuate into semiawake states that allow stimuli to be received and responses to be learned.

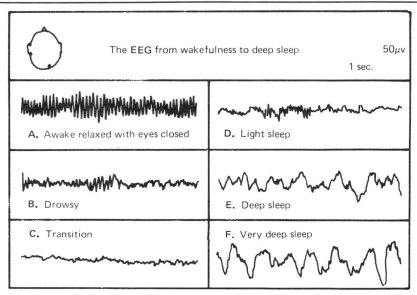

The EEG from wakefulness to deep sleep   50μv

1 sec.

A. Awake relaxed with eyes closed

D. Light sleep

B. Drowsy

E. Deep sleep

C. Transition

F. Very deep sleep

Source: C. W. Simon and W. H. Emmons, Responses to material presented during various levels of sleep. *Journal of Experimental Psychology*, 1956, 51, 89–97. Reprinted by permission of the American Psychological Association.

FIGURE 13–7
The EEG function is related to depth of sleep. The function was used in an experiment that related verbal learning and recall to depth of sleep.

Trace decay theory

Interference has received the bulk of the research effort, but the trace decay theory of forgetting has had intuitive appeal for psychologists and it is common to find it assumed in their theorizing. Empirical tests of the trace decay theory of forgetting have been few in the history of experimental psychology, however, and for good reason. One reason is that a strict test of the theory requires empty time in which the memory trace can spontaneously decay, and this is very difficult to achieve. An organism has experiences in time, and the experiences could be the cause of forgetting rather than time itself, which is support for the interference theory of forgetting. Another reason is that humans deliberately offset verbal forgetting processes with self-generated rehearsal in the supposedly empty retention interval. Only a very few experimental studies have faced trace decay head-on.

Waugh and Norman (1965) did an experiment that compared trace decay and interference as explanations of short-term retention, and trace decay fared poorly in the comparison. An item for the subject was auditory presentation of a list of 16 digits, with the last digit called the probe digit, accompanied by a tone. The probe digit had occurred only once before in the list, and the subject's task was to give the digit that immediately followed it in the series. The experimental variables were presentation rate and amount of retroactive interference. Presentation rates were one digit per second and four digits per second. Interference was defined by the number of digits between first occurrence of the probe digit in the list and its second occurrence as the signal for recall. The critical comparison between trace decay and interference theories was this: If trace decay accounts for forgetting in the time between a digit's presentation and its recall, then time, as defined by presentation rate, should be the controlling variable; but if interference is the primary determiner of forgetting, then the number of intervening digits should be the determining factor. The results are shown in Figure 13–8. There are no differences between the rates of presentation; only number of intervening digits controls performance at recall. Events in time, not time itself, control the amount forgotten.

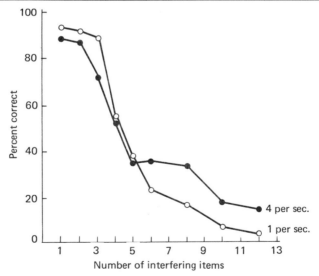

Source: N. C. Waugh and D. A. Norman, Primary memory. *Psychological Review*, 1965, 72, 89–104. Reprinted by permission of the American Psychological Association.

FIGURE 13–8
Short-term retention as a function of number of interfering items between learning and recall and item presentation rate. Only number of interfering items affected recall, which supports the interference theory of forgetting.

One potential problem for the Waugh and Norman experiment is that rehearsal is uncontrolled and could be a variable to conceal evidence of trace decay. If trace decay is true, then the rate of one digit per second should produce more forgetting than the four-per-second rate. But, the rate of one digit per second also allowed more time between digits for rehearsal, which would offset the greater amount of forgetting that was expected. There was no evidence for or against rehearsal, however. Only four experienced, sophisticated subjects were used over and over again in the various experimental conditions, and this weighs against the rehearsal argument because the subjects undoubtedly were informed about rehearsal and its upsetting effects for the issues at hand. An experimental design that used many naive subjects would have run a greater risk of contamination from rehearsal.

Reitman (1971) undertook the difficult assignment of defining procedures for empty time to test for trace decay theory. In addition, in other conditions of the same experiment, she had filled time for an evaluation of the interference theory of forgetting. A short-term retention paradigm was used. The task was three words presented visually, and their recall was solicited after a 15-second retention interval. The procedure for creating empty time over the retention interval was based on a study by Johnston et al. (1970) who found that the storage, rehearsal, and recalling of words during the concurrent performance of a motor task caused a worsening of motor performance. Reitman reasoned that if a difficult discrimination task filled the retention interval, there should be a drop in its performance relative to a control condition if verbal rehearsal occurred, and so she filled the interval with a tonal detection task in which a brief 1,000 Hz tone occurred in a background of white noise. The subject had to press a key every time the tone was heard. A control condition had the same task requirement except that the words did not have to be recalled and so there was no incentive to rehearse. A comparison of the experimental and control conditions on the tonal detection task failed to turn up evidence of rehearsal. Postexperimental interviews with the subjects also failed to find evidences of rehearsal. Reitman had some of the retention intervals without any tones for detection whatsoever; so if there was no rehearsal and no tones in the interval, then a state of empty time existed and trace decay theory could be legitimately tested. She found retention to be 93 percent over the empty retention interval, which is very high. Thirteen of her 18 subjects had 100 percent correct. Reitman properly accepted her findings as evidence against trace decay theory because there was almost no forgetting over empty time. In other conditions Reitman had verbal interference in the retention interval, during which the discrimination task was detection of the syllable "toh" in a tape recording among a background series of "doh." Sometimes the subjects had to report the detection by pressing a key, as in the tonal detection task, and sometimes the reporting was saying "toh" aloud. The percent correct recall for silent and vocal syllabic detection tasks was respectively 77 percent and 70 percent. Reitman concluded in behalf of the interference theory of forgetting and against trace decay theory. Interpolated verbal events degraded verbal recall; so events that fill time, not time alone, cause forgetting.

An appreciation of the conceptual frame of reference for the Reitman study is necessary for an understanding of her findings and an acceptance of them. Her kind of experiment is called divided attention, and a common assumption of such experiments is that the human has limited processing capacity. A subject given a primary task to perform will use a certain amount of that capacity. Give him a secondary task to perform at the same time and it is assumed that the remainder of the capacity will be used or exceeded. If capacity is exceeded, the subject no longer has the resources to perform efficiently, and decrement in the primary and/or the secondary task will result. Reitman is assuming that the detection task in the retention interval occupies the processing capacity fully, and an insufficient capacity to sustain concurrent rehearsal results in decrement for the detection task. It is in this way, she reasons, that a decrement in the detection task is an index of covert rehearsal. But is it so? It is possible that the detection task and rehearsal could be done together with no decrement in either. We do many things together with high efficiency, such as walking and talking; so it is possible that detection and rehearsal can be done together without impairment. The conclusions about interference and trace decay are acceptable only if it can be shown that decrement in detection occurs whenever rehearsal occurs.

Another problem with the Reitman study is the ease of the memory task. The three words were shown for two seconds and had to be remembered for only 15 seconds. Maybe this task is so easy that little forgetting would occur no matter what the mechanism. The absence of forgetting that led her to conclude against trace decay may have been due to a ceiling effect.

Constructive criticism by peers is common in science, but constructive self-criticism is the best of all. In a second series of experiments (Reitman, 1974), Reitman answered the objections of the ceiling effect and undetected rehearsal. She increased the memory load from three to five words, which should increase task difficulty and the chances of forgetting. And she introduced a new experimental condition in which the subjects were instructed to rehearse deliberately while performing the tonal detection task. This new condition was a check to see if rehearsal actually does induce detection decrement, which it did. With this evidence, and following the logic of the 1971 experiment, she was able to interpret retention over the 15-second interval with greater confidence. This time, when rehearsal was absent by her definition, forgetting was definitely found. This is evidence for trace decay. That events in the retention interval can be interfered with is nothing new, but evidence that events also decay is new, and Reitman concludes for both trace decay and interference as mechanisms of forgetting. The popular appeal of trace decay for psychologists is now backed with objective evidence. Whether Reitman's generalization will stand depends on whether the logic of her experiments, based on divided attention, survives critical analysis, some of which is beginning to appear (Roediger, Knight, and Kantowitz, 1977). Survive or not, her experiments are an inventive attempt to create empty time and ask if the material being remembered decays in it.

Retrieval from memory

Retrieval from memory can occur in the absence of any apparent stimulus, as when we sit alone in a room and try to recall the name of Socrates' wife. Virtually all of psychological research on retrieval, however, has used a stimulus at recall as means of arousing forgotten responses. This approach is called *prompting*, and the reminder stimulus is called the *prompter*. We all know that a prompter can be stimulating for forgotten responses. Recalling the name of the invincible character of movies and television who sheds his ordinary identity and clothing in a phone booth is helped if we know that his name begins with S. Recalling is helped even more if we know that awestruck people look into the sky and say. "It's a plane, it's a bird, it's S_____!" Recall is cue-dependent in the prompting situation, and undoubtedly psychologists are attracted to prompting for the study of retrieval because prompters can be systematically manipulated and related to the efficacy of recall.

THE RETRIEVAL OF WORDS

The study that stimulated the interest in retrieval mechanisms in recent years was by Tulving and Pearlstone (1966). They presented their subjects with lists of nouns that were blocked according to conceptual categories and accompanied by the category name in each case. For example, during presentation the category word WEAPONS would be followed by the words BOMB and CANNON, and the category word PROFESSIONS would be followed by ENGINEER and LAWYER. Only instance words such as BOMB, CANNON, ENGINEER, and LAWYER needed to be learned and remembered; the subjects were instructed not to learn the category words. Free recall was used, and it was either cued with the category names as prompters, or noncued. Prompting produced superior recall.

A study on prompting by Bahrick (1969) is a good example of the systematic manipulation of the characteristics of prompters. Bahrick had his subjects learn a list of 20 paired associates (Table 13–1), most of them simple nouns, to a criterion of six correct anticipations. One experimental variable was retention intervals of zero (immediate test), two hours, two days, or two weeks. The retention test had unprompted recall followed by prompted recall. Unprompted recall was a version of standard recall for paired-associate learning—the subjects were given a written list of the stimulus terms and were asked to recall as many of the response terms as they could. Prompted recall followed, to see how many of the items that were forgotten on the unprompted test could be stimulated by prompters. The stimulus term for each missed item was presented again, and while the subject looked at it and tried to recall the response again, the experimenter spoke a prompter word. The main experimental variable was the associative relationship between the response terms and the prompters. Table 13–1 illustrates. The prompter probability levels in the table represent the probability that the response term will be elicited by the prompter in a free association test. In a free association test the prompter is presented as a stimulus and a subject gives the first response that comes to mind. For example, in Table 13–1, the word VELVET elicits the response BLUE 3 percent of the time in a free association test. The word SKY, on the other hand, elicits BLUE 66 percent of the time. Bahrick presumed, and correctly, that the probability relationship between the prompters and the response terms of the list would be an effective variable for retrieval. His results are shown in Table 13–2. Notice how the percentage of correct recall for the responses that had been forgotten in the unprompted test increases steadily as a function of prompter level. Prompter Level 5 has a high associative relationship between prompters and responses, and the subjects recover an impressive 70–86 percent of their forgotten responses.

One word can prompt another word, but even fragments of a word can be effective prompters. Horowitz, White, and Atwood (1968) used fragments of a word as prompters for the retrieval of the whole word. After seeing a list of words once, a subject would be shown one third of each word as a prompter, and he had to make an effort to recall the word. Initial segments of words were the best prompters, final segments next best, and middle segments the poorest. Retrieval time was the fastest with initial segments.

TABLE 13–1

The paired-associate list and the five levels of prompters in the Bahrick study.

Paired-associate list		Prompter probability levels				
Stimulus	Response	1 (0.01–0.08)	2 (0.09–0.21)	3 (0.23–0.36)	4 (0.38–0.59)	5 (0.61–0.86)
Time	Blue	Velvet 0.03	Grey 0.10	Green 0.28	Azure 0.58	Sky 0.66
Shoe	Book	Print 0.02	Comic 0.15	Read 0.35	Chapter 0.59	Author 0.65
Top	Chair	Leg 0.02	Cushion 0.09	Upholstery 0.36	Furniture 0.48	Table 0.74
Went	Telephone	Pole 0.04	Extension 0.17	Communication 0.33	Dial 0.59	Operator 0.75
Tile	Girl	Child 0.03	Cute 0.18	Feminine 0.26	Coed 0.54	Boy 0.86
Party	Water	Desert 0.05	Drink 0.12	Swim 0.23	Fountain 0.44	Faucet 0.68
Abrupt	Flower	Tree 0.03	Fragrant 0.15	Pollen 0.35	Rose 0.54	Blossom 0.82
Effect	Car	Journey 0.01	Travel 0.15	Gas 0.23	Truck 0.56	Trolley 0.80
Sign	Cold	Weather 0.05	Winter 0.09	Cough 0.25	Ice 0.56	Hot 0.83
Sorry	Fast	Scurry 0.03	Haste 0.10	Accelerate 0.24	Rapid 0.40	Slow 0.80
Wing	Sleep	Trance 0.05	Retire 0.14	Pillow 0.30	Dream 0.47	Doze 0.81
Fail	Horse	Pasture 0.03	Chariot 0.20	Ranch 0.30	Gallop 0.58	Saddle 0.79
Bitter	Light	Sun 0.04	Electric 0.16	Switch 0.34	Dark 0.54	Illuminate 0.71
Marble	Flag	Parade 0.04	Patriotism 0.18	Salute 0.23	Allegiance 0.38	Banner 0.65
Business	Short	Small 0.02	Stocky 0.10	Stubby 0.34	Tall 0.52	Long 0.77
Sack	Fire	Forest 0.04	Smoke 0.14	Burn 0.27	Extinguish 0.50	Blaze 0.64
Rope	School	Teacher 0.08	Institute 0.15	Academy 0.32	Elementary 0.55	Prep 0.75
Door	Talk	Pep 0.06	Whisper 0.13	Speech 0.26	Chatter 0.51	Converse 0.83
Stop	Apple	Banana 0.07	Pie 0.12	Fruit 0.30	Orchard 0.56	Cider 0.61
Window	Doctor	Hospital 0.08	Prescription 0.21	Medicine 0.36	Nurse 0.53	Physician 0.71
	Average	0.041	0.141	0.295	0.521	0.743

Source: H. P. Bahrick. Measurement of memory by prompted recall. *Journal of Experimental Psychology*, 1969, 79, 213–219. Reprinted by permission of the American Psychological Association.

TABLE 13-2

Percent of correct recall on the prompted recall test as a function of the associative relationship between the response and the prompter (the prompter level—see Table 13-1), and the time interval between training and testing.

Prompter level	Retention interval				Overall average
	0	2 hours	2 days	2 weeks	
1	18	16	13	14	15
2	48	43	42	27	40
3	49	55	58	50	53
4	79	72	62	63	69
5	86	80	70	80	79
Overall average	56	53	49	47	

Source: H. P. Bahrick. Measurement of memory by prompted recall. *Journal of Experimental Psychology*, 1969, *79*, 213–219. Reprinted by permission of the American Psychological Association.

THE RETRIEVAL OF FORM

There is more to the topic of retrieval than words. From common experience there is every reason to believe that such events as odors or emotional reactions can be very effective in the arousal of memories. In form perception a fragment of a picture could prompt our recollection of the entire picture. This latter possibility stimulated an experiment by Bower and Glass (1976). Subjects were shown a series of patterns and then were shown prompters of the patterns. A prompter was elements of a pattern, and the subject had to recall the pattern by drawing it after seeing the prompter (this experiment has similarities to the one by Horowitz and his associates on word fragments, described in the previous section). The prompters were rated good, mediocre, and poor, depending upon their similarity to the pattern. Three example patterns and their prompters are shown in Figure 13-9. Two judges rated the drawings. Good, mediocre, and poor prompters stimulated, respectively, good, mediocre, and poor recall of the whole patterns.

IS RETRIEVAL THE EXPLANATION OF INTERFERENCE?

Is the decrement in performance that is created by interference a matter of retrieval difficulty? This is a fundamental kind of question to ask because it is an attempt to reduce one theory to another. If true, we would have only trace decay and retrieval as theories of forgetting, rather than trace decay, retrieval, and interference. A gain in explanatory power is made every time a science reduces the number of its theories.

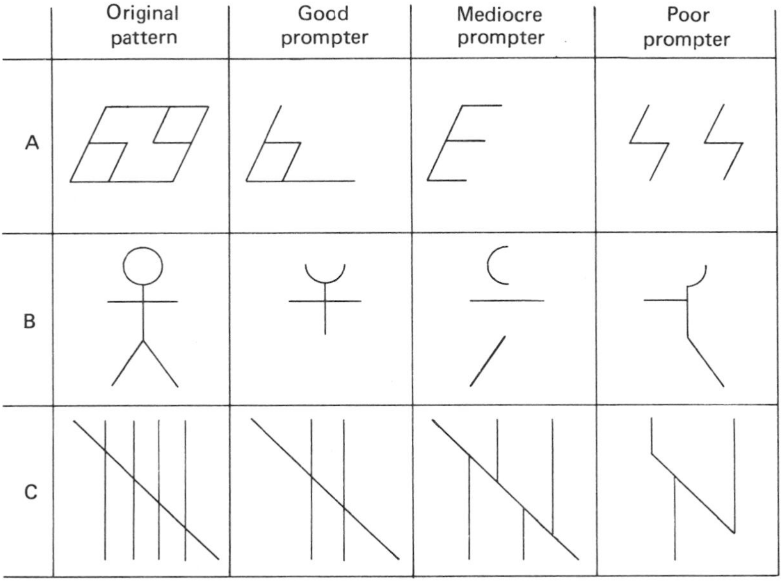

Source: Adapted from G. H. Bower and A. L. Glass, Structural units and the redintegrative power of picture fragments. *Journal of Experimental Psychology: Human Learning and Memory*, 1976, 2, 456–466. Copyright 1976 by the American Psychological Association. Reprinted by permission.

FIGURE 13–9
Examples of good, mediocre, and poor prompters that were used to retrieve the original patterns that had been presented earlier. The retrieval of the patterns was by drawing them.

The history of research on verbal interference, which had its strong beginnings in the 1930s, shows several theories of interference. In the 1930s a viable theory of interference was the *independence hypothesis*. The independence hypothesis held that interfering responses compete at recall, and the strongest one in the competition is the one that occurs. In a retroactive interference design, in which the learning of A and B are followed by the recall of A, the decrement in recall of A is explained by the dominance of B. The successor to the independence hypothesis was the *unlearning hypothesis*, which held that the decrement in A at recall was because the learning of B had brought about the extinction of A in part. Subsequently there was the *differentiation hypothesis*, which asserted that interference reduced the discriminability, or differentiation, of the material. The learning of B reduces the discriminability of A and decreases its availability at recall.

In their own way these older theories distinguished between retrieval and storage. An interfered-with response under the independence hypothesis and the differentiation hypothesis would seem to have full strength in storage but would be difficult to retrieve. The storage-retrieval distinction is vague for the unlearning hypothesis because it was never quite clear what "unlearning" meant. There has been an attempt to bring unlearning in on the side of retrieval (Petrich, 1975), however.

Modern-day retrieval theorists have a wealth of interference data from the past for theorizing, but there has been rather little new data collected from the stance of contemporary thinking on retrieval and memory processes. Pertinent data, with an explicit retrieval orientation, are now making their appearances in the psychological literature, however. Reynolds (1977) used two lists of paired associates as a way of generating retroactive interference and studying the effects of retrieval on it. For both lists, the stimulus terms were nonsense syllables. The response terms of List 1, in which the interference decrement would be induced by List 2, were words in several conceptual categories, like colors or animals. The response terms of List 2 were unrelated to those of List 1. As the retroactive interference design requires, recall of List 1 followed the learning of Lists 1 and 2. The subjects in a retrieval condition had names of the conceptual categories for the response terms of List 1 available as prompters at recall, while control subjects did not. The results were that the prompters lessened the interference decrement. Enthusiasm for the retrieval interpretation of interference may have to be contained because the prompters failed to overcome all of the interference decrement, as might be expected if retrieval failure is the sole explanation of interference. There is always the possibility that better retrieval cues can be found, however. One of the problems with retrieval theory today is that we do not know enough to specify the characteristics of prompters. If a test of retrieval theory fails it may only be because an inadequate prompter was used, not that the theory is fundamentally wrong. In time we will come to know enough about retrieval cues so that retrieval theory can be defined more exactly.

Concluding remarks on theories of forgetting

Theories of forgetting have been under scrutiny since ancient times, and we still have a long way to go. Thousands of experiments on memory have been conducted, and they document many determinants of retention, but rather few studies bear incisively on why forgetting occurs. This chapter has documented difficult problems involved in testing theories of forgetting, and so it is not surprising that the topic is unresolved.

What is the status of the three basic theories of forgetting? There is no doubt that interference is a factor in forgetting. Interference is an empirical fact, and when it occurs in the retention interval it can be a force for decrement. Similarly, there is no doubt that failure to retrieve is a factor in forgetting. Material can lie in memory in full strength but be impotent until the proper conditions of retrieval occur. Trace decay has the flimsiest support of all, but the recent studies of Reitman have given it more credibility than before.

Summary

What are the theories to account for the forgetting of material that has passed through sensory memory and into more stable memory beyond? Three theories of forgetting prevail today: interference, trace decay, and failure to retrieve.

The interference theory of forgetting says that events which occur between the learning of material and its recall, or before the learning of material and its recall, can interfere with the material and induce decrement in its recall. Interference is an active theory of forgetting—without interfering events there is no forgetting.

Trace decay theory says that the trace of the material stored in memory spontaneously decays with time, like the spontaneous disintegration of radioactive materials. Trace decay is a passive theory—forgetting occurs regardless of the subject's experience. Experimental comparisons of trace decay and interference theories weigh toward interference, although there is evidence that trace decay and interference are both valid.

Failure to retrieve as a theory of forgetting says that the material exists at high strength in memory but that we cannot find it and so cannot recall it. The common method of studying retrieval is prompting, in which a cue is presented at recall in an effort to stimulate otherwise unavailable material. Experiments generously support the concept of retrieval.

It would be scientifically elegant if one of the three theories accounted for all of the circumstances of forgetting that we know, with the other two failing to qualify. Unfortunately, elegance does not prevail—there is evidence for all three theories. Interference theory and failure to retrieve are both sound explanations of forgetting. Trace decay has the weakest support of all, but some support for it does exist.

References

Bahrick, H. P.   Measurement of memory by prompted recall. *Journal of Experimental Psychology*, 1969, 79, 213–219.

Barrett, T. R., & Ekstrand, B. R.   Effect of sleep on memory: III. Controlling for time-of-day effects. *Journal of Experimental Psychology*, 1972, 96, 321–327.

Bower, G. H., & Glass, A. L.   Structural units and the redintegrative power of picture fragments. *Journal of Experimental Psychology: Human Learning and Memory,* 1976, *2,* 456–466.

Briggs, G. E.   Retroactive inhibition as a function of the degree of original and interpolated learning. *Journal of Experimental Psychology,* 1957, *53,* 60–67.

Brown, J.   Some tests of the decay theory of immediate memory. *Quarterly Journal of Experimental Psychology,* 1958, *10,* 12–21.

Ekstrand, B. R.   Effect of sleep on memory. *Journal of Experimental Psychology,* 1967, *75,* 64–72.

Ekstrand, B. R.   To sleep, perchance to dream (about why we forget). In C. P. Duncan, L. Sechrest, and A. W. Melton (Eds.), *Human memory: Festschrift in honor of Benton J. Underwood.* New York: Appleton-Century-Crofts, 1972, pp. 59–82.

Emmons, W. H., & Simon, C. W.   The nonrecall of material presented during sleep. *American Journal of Psychology,* 1956, *69,* 76–81.

Greenberg, R., & Underwood, B. J.   Retention as a function of stage of practice. *Journal of Experimental Psychology,* 1950, *40,* 452–457.

Horowitz, L. M., White, M. A., & Atwood, D. W.   Word fragments as aids to recall: The organization of a word. *Journal of Experimental Psychology,* 1968, *76,* 219–226.

James, W.   *Principles of psychology* (Vol. 1). New York: Holt, 1890.

Jenkins, J. G., & Dallenbach, K. M.   Obliviscence during sleep and waking. *American Journal of Psychology,* 1924, *35,* 605–612.

Johnston, W. A., Greenberg, S. N., Fisher, R. P., & Martin, D. W.   Divided attention: A vehicle for monitoring memory processes. *Journal of Experimental Psychology,* 1970, *83,* 164–171.

Keppel, G., & Underwood, B. J.   Proactive inhibition in short-term retention of single items. *Journal of Verbal Learning and Verbal Behavior,* 1962, *1,* 153–161.

Peterson, L. R., & Peterson, M. J.   Short-term retention of individual verbal items. *Journal of Experimental Psychology,* 1959, *58,* 193–198.

Petrich, J. A.   Storage and retrieval processes in unlearning. *Memory & Cognition,* 1975, *3,* 63–74.

Reitman, J. S.   Mechanisms of forgetting in short-term memory. *Cognitive Psychology,* 1971, *2,* 185–195.

Reitman, J. S.   Without surreptitious rehearsal, information in short-term memory decays. *Journal of Verbal Learning and Verbal Behavior,* 1974, *13,* 365–377.

Reynolds, J. H.   Unavailable and inaccessible information in retroactive inhibition of paired associates. *Journal of Experimental Psychology: Human Learning and Memory,* 1977, *3,* 68–77.

Roediger, H. L., III, Knight, J. L., Jr., & Kantowitz, B. H.   Inferring decay in short-term memory: The issue of capacity. *Memory & Cognition,* 1977, *5,* 167–176.

Simon, C. W., & Emmons, W. H. Responses to material presented during various levels of sleep. *Journal of Experimental Psychology*, 1956, *51*, 89–97.

Spight, J. B. Day and night intervals and the distribution of practice. *Journal of Experimental Psychology*, 1928, *11*, 397–398.

Tulving, E., & Pearlstone, Z. Availability versus accessibility of information in memory for words. *Journal of Verbal Learning and Verbal Behavior*, 1966, *5*, 381–391.

Underwood, B. J. Interference and forgetting. *Psychological Review*, 1957, *64*, 49–60.

Van Ormer, E. B. Retention after intervals of sleep and waking. *Archives of Psychology*, 1932, No. 137.

Waugh, N. C., & Norman, D. A. Primary memory. *Psychological Review*, 1965, *72*, 89–104.

Wickens, D. D. Encoding categories of words: An empirical approach to meaning. *Psychological Review*, 1970, *77*, 1–15.

14

Recognition

RECOGNIZING a face that you saw yesterday or a tune that you heard last week is not a matter of recalling and repeating a response that has been reinforced or rehearsed before. Recall is the production of a response, but *recognition* is deciding that a stimulus has been experienced before.

Methods for studying recognition

Two basic methods are used for studying recognition behavior in the laboratory, and both have their parallels in everyday life. One is called the method of single stimuli and the other is called the forced-choice method. Both methods first expose the subject to stimuli, and then in a later recognition test they require the subject to identify the old stimuli from among new ones that have not been presented before. The two methods differ in the conduct of the recognition test.

METHOD OF SINGLE STIMULI

The *method of single stimuli* has the old and new stimuli mixed and presented one at a time at the test, with the subject judging each one "old" or "new." The difficulty with this procedure is response bias in which, in the extreme case, a subject can identify all of the old stimuli correctly or fail to identify any of them. With an indifferent attitude the subject can designate all of the stimuli as "old." All old stimuli will be correctly classified, and 100 percent recognition will be scored. All new stimuli will be falsely classified, however. Or the subject can be very conservative and designate all stimuli as "new" because he or she is not absolutely sure that the old stimuli have been experienced before. All new stimuli will be correctly classified, but all old stimuli will be falsely classified and the percent recognition score will be zero. For these reasons percent correctly recognized is an inadequate measure for the method of single stimuli. The percent correct measure assumes that an item is either recognized or not, or that we guess at it. By using a statistical correction for guessing, we get a "true" measure of recognition; but in failing to consider response bias, the percent correct measure fails to account for a subject's motivation to respond with laxness or strictness. Commonly, the motivation level which the subject adopts is called the *criterion*. An approach which abandons the percent correct measure and its assumptions, and which takes criterion into account, is the *Theory of Signal Detection.*

Psychologists first applied the Theory of Signal Detection to psychophysics, which is the study of sensory behavior. Suppose that a subject is asked to detect a weak tone whenever it occurs. For a long time percent of tones detected was the measure of sensory capability used. However, the measure has the same problem as in a recognition memory experiment: It reflects the sensory capabilities of the auditory system, as the users believed, but it also reflects response bias, which was not considered. The subject may adopt a strict criterion and respond only when absolutely sure that a tone has occurred, or the subject may adopt a lax criterion and respond almost with indifference to the presence of a tone.

The application of the Theory of Signal Detection to recognition memory assumes that items are arranged on a psychological continuum of familiarity, and the subject sets a criterion along the continuum and uses it at the recognition test to make a decision about an item's familiarity. If the feeling of familiarity is greater than the criterion, the item will be judged "old," but if it is less, the judgment is "new."

The essence of the Theory of Signal Detection is that the subject is in a decision situation. A stimulus on the recognition test is either old or new, and the subject must decide "old" or "new" for each stimulus on the basis of criterion. In the Theory of Signal Detection the percentage of "old" responses to old stimuli are called "hits," and the percentage of "old" responses to new stimuli are called "false alarms." With the level of familiarity fixed, these two measures will covary as a subject varies criterion. If a subject has a conservative criterion he or she will be very sure before saying "old"; so there will be a low hit rate and a low false alarm rate. As the criterion relaxes, both the hit rate and the false alarm rate will increase.

The valuable feature of the Theory of Signal Detection is that it separates the sensory-perceptual aspect of the situation from the criterion and provides a separate measure of each. The index of sensory-perceptual discrimination is called d' (d prime), and the index of the criterion is called β (beta). These are easily calculated (Hochhaus, 1972; Theodor, 1972).

FORCED-CHOICE METHOD

The *forced-choice method* is a method of multiple stimuli, in which a test item is an old stimulus presented simultaneously with one or more alternative new stimuli and the subject must discriminate the old one from the new ones. Here the response bias problem does not apply because the subject is forced to discriminate the features of the several stimuli of the test and declare one as "old." Percent correct is a valid measure of recognition when the forced-choice method is used. One would think that the forced-choice method gives a "true" measure of recognition, but this is not so because different ways of defining the test will give different recognition levels. Both the similarity and the number of alternative stimuli affect recognition accuracy.

It is an intuitive expectation that the more similar the alternatives the lower the level of recognition because the similarity makes it more difficult to discriminate an old item from the alternatives. This intuitive expectation has been borne out in several experiments (Bahrick and Bahrick, 1964; Bruce and Cofer, 1965; Klein and Arbuckle, 1970). Moreover, the greater the number of alternatives in the forced-choice test the lower the recognition level (Bruce and Cofer, 1967; Underwood, 1972). From his data on the recognition of words, Underwood (1972) estimated that each alternative in the forced-choice test adds 6 percent to recognition error. Measurement problems such as these would seem an uncomfortable handicap for research on recognition, but they are not. Even though a measure is not a "true" one it can be used for relative comparisons. Thus, we can study the recognition of stimuli over different retention intervals just so long as all subjects use, say, the forced-choice method where each test item has four stimuli.

Recognition of complex stimuli

VISUAL STIMULI

A truly remarkable feature of human memory is the excellence of recognition. You see a Rembrandt painting and know that you have seen it before (your teacher in second grade had it above her desk). As a child you ride on a train pulled by a steam locomotive, and 20 years later you recognize the chug and wheeze of the engine when you hear it on a radio program. All of us are convinced of our great powers of recognition when we reflect on incidents such as these, but more convincing than informal recollection is psychological research which shows that everything we ever suspected about our powers of recognition can be true.

Research on the recognition of complex visual stimuli such as pictures has been going on for a long time in psychology (e.g., Strong, 1912, 1913), but none of the early investigators seemed particularly aware of the high capacity which the human has for visual recognition. Recent investigators, however, have become sensitive to the human power of recognition and have pursued it in their experiments. Shepard (1967) allowed his subjects one chance to study at their own pace 612 pictures of common scenes (they averaged six seconds per picture), and then gave them an immediate recognition test. They averaged 97 percent correct. Nine out of 35 subjects had 100 percent correct. An even more remarkable demonstration is by Standing, Conezio, and Haber (1970). They had their subjects study 2,560 slides of common scenes for ten seconds each over two to four days. In an immediate retention test the group averaged 90 percent correct, with one subject having a score of 95 percent correct. The poorest subject, if he can be called that, correctly recognized 85 percent of the pictures.

All of this is very impressive and conforms to a great deal of our everyday experience, but Goldstein and Chance (1970) remind us that these studies used dissimilar pictures culled from popular periodicals, and that this is only one kind of everyday recognition experience. Often we must recognize a complex visual stimulus from highly similar ones, such as recognizing our child from among many classmates or recognizing our car among 500 others in a parking lot. To balance our understanding, they used similar faces, ink blots, and photographs of snow crystals as stimuli in their experiments. Each stimulus was presented for two to three seconds. Faces were best recognized, with 71 percent correct. Ink blots had 46 percent correct, and snow crystals had 33 percent correct. These values are not as high as Shepard (1967) and Standing, Conezio, and Haber (1970) found for dissimilar stimuli.

AUDITORY STIMULI

The history of recognition memory is almost entirely one of visual recognition. Recently, however, as part of the modern interest in memory, there has been research on the recognition of complex auditory stimuli that has run parallel to the research on complex visual stimuli, and with similar results. Heterogeneous, dissimilar auditory stimuli have been found to have the same high level of recognition as dissimilar visual stimuli.

Lawrence and Banks (1973) had their subjects listen to a tape with such diverse sounds as machinery, laughing, sneezing, horses neighing, tap-dance routines, and thunder. The tape had 194 different sounds, and each one was presented for 30 seconds. The test tape followed after a five-minute break, and the subjects had to discriminate the old sounds from new ones. The level of recognition was very high, ranging from 85–89 percent for the different types of stimuli. As with visual stimuli, the recognition level for highly similar sounds should be lower.

Variables for recognition

We saw in previous chapters that recall is a function of many variables, and no less can be said for recognition. Familiarity and verbal mediation are two prominent variables that have been given thorough study.

FAMILIARITY

Exposure time   The basic operation for recognition is sensory experience, and it is common to refer to it as the familiarity variable. Potter and Levy (1969), in their study of recognition and exposure time, show how recognition is positively related to the amount of sensory experience.

Potter and Levy devised eight short films, where in each film there was a sequence of 16 color photographs. Each film was projected at a different rate, and it was followed by a recognition test in which the projected pictures were mounted on cardboard and had to be selected from among new pictures. Seven different exposure rates were used, ranging from ⅛ second (125 milliseconds) to 2 seconds (2,000 milliseconds) per picture. One group of subjects was given the shorter intervals and another group the longer intervals. Figure 14–1 has the data of the experiment. One hundred twenty-five milliseconds per picture gives a trivial level of recognition, but the trend is a steadily increasing one, and by the time the rate has increased to two seconds the subjects are recognizing almost all of the pictures correctly. Findings like these help us understand the very high level of recognition obtained by Shepard (1967) and Standing, Conezio, and Haber (1970). Shepard used self-paced presentation which averaged six seconds per picture, and Standing et al. allowed ten seconds per picture. While six to ten

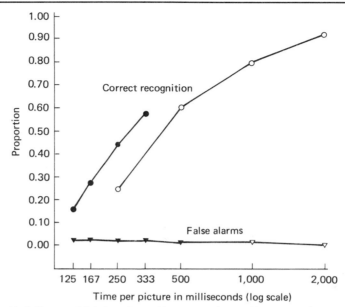

Source: M. C. Potter, and E. I. Levy, Recognition memory for a rapid sequence of pictures. *Journal of Experimental Psychology*, 1969, *81*, 10–15. Reprinted by permission of the American Psychological Association.

FIGURE 14–1
Recognition accuracy for pictures as a function of exposure duration. The break in the curves represents two groups of subjects, one which had short exposures and one which had the longer exposures. The upper function is for the correct recognition of old stimuli, and the lower function is for incorrectly identifying new stimuli as old (false alarms).

seconds is not long to gaze at a picture, the Potter and Levy data tell us that it is more than enough to guarantee a high level of recognition.

The perception and registration of visual detail From reading the familiarity literature there is no reason to doubt that the form which is experienced by one (or sometimes more) of the senses is not registered in memory, completely, in all of its detail. Rock, Halper, and Clayton (1972) challenged this thesis that memory for form is like a photographic record.

Their approach was to present a form visually for five seconds under incidental learning conditions, during which the subjects thought that they were looking at it for the purposes of forming an after-image, and then to test ten seconds later for recognition. The forms used were meaningless nonsense forms, and the ones presented for study in the various experimental conditions are shown in Figure 14–2. The A form was the basic complex form, in which the contour enclosed an inner configura-

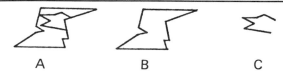

Source: I. Rock, F. Halper, and T. Clayton, The perception and recognition of complex figures. *Cognitive Psychology*, 1972, 3, 655–673. Reprinted by permission of Academic Press, Inc.

FIGURE 14–2
The forms used by Rock, Halper, and Clayton (1972) in their experiments on how much of a complex form is stored and enters into subsequent recognition. Forms B and C are the outer and inner components of Form A.

tion of detail. The B form and the C form represent a separate display of the contour and the inner configuration, respectively. Figure 14–3 has the items of the recognition tests that were used in the various experimental conditions. A ten-alternative test item was used, as shown.

Rock and his associates had several conditions in their main experiment, and the conditions are described along with the results for them in Table 14–1. In Condition 1 the basic complex form (Figure 14–2A) was presented for study and then tested only for the recognition of the inner configuration (Figure 14–3A). With guessing level at 10 percent, the 11 percent that was correctly recognized is equivalent to no recognition at all. Condition 2 asked if the poor level of performance in Condition 1 was because of lack of context in the test; so Condition 1 was repeated except that the recognition test had the ten inner patterns enclosed in a common contour (Figure 14–3B). This time the inner configuration of the study figure was not recognized at all. Condition 3 tested for recognition of only the contour (Figure 14–3C) after study of the whole complex figure (Figure 14–2A), and the recognition level was fairly good

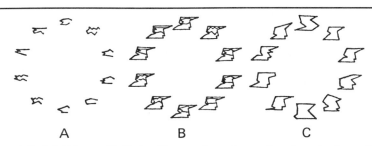

Source: I. Rock, F. Halper, and T. Clayton, The perception and recognition of complex figures. *Cognitive Psychology*, 1972, 3, 655–673. Reprinted by permission of Academic Press, Inc.

FIGURE 14–3
The recognition tests used by Rock, Halper, and Clayton (1972).

TABLE 14–1

Percent of forms correctly recognized for the various presentation and test conditions in the study by Rock, Halper, and Clayton.

Condition	Form exposed	Form tested	Percent correctly recognized
1	Complex (Figure 14–2A)	Inner configuration (Figure 14–3A)	11
2	Complex (Figure 14–2A)	Inner configuration in context (Figure 14–3B)	0
3	Complex (Figure 14–2A)	Outer contour (Figure 14–3C)	56
4	Outer contour (Figure 14–2B)	Outer contour (Figure 14–3C)	69
5	Inner configuration (Figure 14–2C)	Inner configuration (Figure 14–3A)	83

Source: I. Rock, F. Halper, and T. Clayton. The perception and recognition of complex figures. *Cognitive Psychology,* 1972, *3,* 655–673. Reprinted by permission of Academic Press, Inc.

although not as good as in Condition 4 where the outer contour was both studied and tested. Condition 5 was the same as Condition 4 except that the inner configuration was both studied and tested, and here the recognition level was quite good. The purpose of the separate assessment of the contour and the inner configuration in Conditions 4 and 5 was to see if there was something about these elements of the complex form that made them inherently difficult to recognize. The inner configuration is an easy pattern to recognize when studied in isolation (Condition 5), but when it is studied in the context of the complex figure it can be recognized hardly at all (Conditions 1 and 2). Then, to secure the matter, Rock et al. repeated all of the conditions of the experiment using curvilinear figures rather than rectilinear ones. The results were about the same.

In another experiment Rock et al. varied the exposure time for the complex figure from 2–15 seconds, and the recognition of the inner configuraton was affected little or not at all. In still another experiment the question was asked whether the inner configuration had actually been received in memory but had been forgotten very rapidly and was no longer available ten seconds later at the recognition test. Retention intervals of 200 milliseconds and 10 seconds were compared, and no appreciable difference was found. It was concluded that the problem was failure in perception of the inner configuration in the first place, not in memory, and that much of what impinges on the sense receptors in daily life does not necessarily enter memory. Rock et al. remind us of the difficulties we have of discriminating the faces of people of other races;

the details for making these discriminations do not readily enter memory. Although the data of Rock et al. do not show it, we can expect the detail to become recognizable eventually. The details of forms undoubtedly become articulated with enough experience.

Eye fixations and recognition   Rock et al. have shown that the failure to recognize detail is a matter of perception—some elements of the visual scene are not received in the first place. Why is this so? Why do some things enter memory and some not? One possibility is attention as a central mechanism, in which some elements of impinging stimuli are preordained for registration because of their importance for the subject. Without denying the importance of attention, it is likely that the explanation of selective perception in Rock's subjects is in terms of eye fixations. The eye is a highly selective, directional sensor of the visual environment; it is not a passive element like a camera lens. The center of the visual field, called the fovea, is acutely sensitive to color, form, and detail, and through eye movements the subject actively directs the foveal region of the eye to extract key features of the visual scene. One might presume that the simple figures which Rock et al. used in their experiments had compelling outer contours which the subjects saw as informative and which commanded their eye fixations so that the outer contours were the elements that were primarily perceived rather than the inner contours.

But what is the evidence that eye fixations are fundamental in forming the representation in memory that is the basis of visual recognition? The importance of eye fixations for visual recognition has been demonstrated in an excellent experiment by Loftus (1972). He presented pairs of color photographs for various viewing times, and recorded eye fixations throughout the presentation. His results were unequivocal: Recognition is determined by number of eye fixations, not by viewing time itself. Viewing time, as the defining operation of familiarity, was a variable for recognition only insofar as it determined the number of fixations. With viewing time held constant, correct recognition was directly related to the number of fixations (Figure 14–4).

We can now reconcile the familiarity variable with the studies by Rock et al. and by Loftus, and say what it all means for visual recognition. The study by Rock et al. showed that the perception of visual form was imperfect, and that only aspects of it are entered into memory and are available for recognition. The Loftus study demonstrated that only that which is visually fixated can be recognized. By inference, the imperfect perception found in the Rock et al. study could be because eye fixations imperfectly scan the visual scene and enter only parts of the scene into memory.

Eye fixations are fundamental to recognition, and there are additional questions that can be asked about them. How much is seen in a fixation

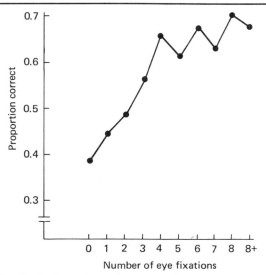

Source: G. R. Loftus, Eye fixations and recognition memory for pictures. *Cognitive Psychology*, 1972, *3*, 525–551. Reprinted by permission of Academic Press, Inc.

FIGURE 14–4
Recognition accuracy for photographs as a function of number of eye fixations.

of the eye? The field of view must be narrow because ordinarily the eye must fixate a picture in a number of places before recognition takes place. Mackworth (1976) defines the *useful field of view* as the largest visual field at which performance is perfect. In his studies of eye movements and visual searching for a target event randomly located among others, Mackworth believes that the useful field of view can be as little as one degree and as great as six or even more, depending upon the demands of the material being scanned. When the material is difficult and dense, such as requiring the subject to find a single letter in a page of closely typed random letters (or a needle in a haystack), the useful field of view is very narrow, as in tunnel vision. When the material is easy, the useful field of view is larger and a bigger part of the scene is taken in each time. A typical picture is a mix of easy and difficult discriminations so that the useful field of view probably changes from fixation to fixation. Mackworth compares the visual system to a zoom lens as it widens or narrows its useful field of view in adaptation to the varying demands of the material.

All of this points to the importance of the narrow but powerful foveal region in the center of the visual field. But what about peripheral vision? Does it play no part in recognition? We do see things in the periphery, as we all know. Simple detection of stimulus change occurs as far out as 58 degrees from center, and more complex discriminations become possible as the stimulus is moved toward the center (Edwards and Goolkasian, 1974). In one of his experiments Loftus (1972) instructed his subjects to attend to only one of the pictures of the pair so that one picture received eye fixations and the other was viewed in peripheral vision. Recognition was found only for the picture that had been fixated, and Loftus concluded against a role for peripheral vision in recognition.

A recent experiment by Parker (1978), however, is at odds with the Loftus finding on peripheral vision. Measuring eye movements, Parker presented a picture (not a picture pair, as in the Loftus experiment) for viewing and then had recognition test trials in which the pictures were either the same, or different with objects changed or omitted. Parker found that the subjects fixated a changed object in the test picture earlier than the same object when it had not been changed. He concluded that both foveal and peripheral information in a test picture are encoded, and that they are compared with the representation of the picture stored in memory at the time of original viewing. Coarse information is derived from peripheral vision and is used to direct eye fixations for more detailed information on which to base a confident decision about whether the picture had been experienced before.

It is safe to say that we have not heard the last of this matter of peripheral vision and recognition. Peripheral vision has been an area of traditional interest in psychology because of its importance for the understanding of visual mechanisms, but the Loftus and the Parker studies indicate its importance for the understanding of memory as well.

VERBAL FACTORS

The standard literature on familiarity and recognition says that the representation of sensory experience that is laid down in memory is related positively to exposure time, and the generalization has validity. What is left unsaid is that processes can occur in the exposure time. We have seen that eye fixation is one of the processes, and for humans another likely process is verbal labeling and description. Rather than simply sensing a stimulus and judging whether it has been experienced before, a subject may also recall verbal labels and descriptions that were generated when the stimulus was presented before. The issue is whether this verbal recalling is a variable for recognition.

We are all aware of verbal codes that can occur for form stimuli. Some are obvious, such as the association *A* when the form *a* is presented. Other associations are not so obvious, such as a billowy cloud reminding us of Santa Claus. We have complex, diverse associations to the random shapes that are inkblots, and some psychologists and psychiatrists think that these responses to inkblots in the Rorschach test have diagnostic value for mental disorders. For our purposes here, verbal responses will sometimes play a positive role in form recognition.

Scientists always strive for control and quantification of their subject matter, and the topic of verbal factors and recognition is no exception. One cannot study verbal factors and recognition with stimuli representing common objects such as houses, trees, and dogs because they all elicit elaborate verbal descriptions from human subjects; all subjects have the full value of the verbal variable all of the time. To get around this problem, investigators generated random, or nonsense, shapes of different complexities according to specified rules (Attneave, 1957; Attneave and Arnoult, 1956), and then scaled them for their power to arouse verbal associations. Adapting methods that have been used for the scaling of verbal material (see Underwood and Schulz, 1960, chap. 2), Vanderplas and Garvin (1959) scaled random shapes of several complexity levels that have come to be used in research on form recognition. They presented random forms one at a time and asked the subjects if the form reminded them of anything or not. The associative value for a form was the proportion of subjects who had an association for it. The tendency was for simple forms with 4–6 sides to have more associations than complex forms with 16–24 sides. Nonsense shapes of intermediate complexity with 12 sides are shown in Figure 14–5, to illustrate the general kind of form that was used.

Ellis (1968) used the Vanderplas and Garvin forms to study the relevance and meaningfulness of verbal labels. Ellis' labels were either meaningful and relevant for the forms, meaningful and irrelevant, or indifferent. Meaningful and relevant labels were the most typical ones given by subjects in another experiment (Ellis and Muller, 1964), and so they had a good chance of being the labels that any one might associate with the forms. For example, a form might have an oval center and two long projections from the top, and a meaningful, relevant label might be "steer." A meaningful but irrelevant label that might be assigned to this form would be "book." The indifferent labels were nonsense syllables. Paired associate training of the labels and forms preceded the recognition test, and Ellis found a positive effect for verbal factors in recognition, with relevant labels producing the primary benefit. The meaningful and relevant labels gave better recognition performance than either irrelevant or indifferent labels, which had about the same level of recognition performance. Verbal factors are beneficial for form recognition as long as the form and the verbal label stand in a meaningful, relevant relationship to one another.

How do verbal associations work to benefit recognition? Ellis (1973) believes that a verbal label operates at the time of input when the subject is studying the form. Through the verbal labeling process the sub-

Source: J. M. Vanderplas and E. A. Garvin, The association value of random shapes. *Journal of Experimental Psychology*, 1959, *57*, 147–154. Reprinted by permission of the American Psychological Association.

FIGURE 14–5
Examples of random shapes which were scaled for association value by Vanderplas and Garvin (1959).

ject directs attention to prominent parts of the visual form, and these prominent parts become more noticeable at the recognition test and the subject has a greater chance of correctly recognizing the form. In effect, Ellis is saying that the verbal label shapes the visual representation of the form that is stored in memory. An alternate hypothesis is by Adams and Bray (1970). They contend that the verbal factors operate at the time of the recognition test, not at the time of input. Adams and Bray found that correct recall of responses that had been associated with stimuli increased the probability of stimulus recognition and the subject's confidence in the recognition. They reasoned that the availability of the correct response at the test gives the subject a feeling of confidence about the stimulus and increases the chances that he will recognize it. Santa and Ranken (1972) also provided evidence that verbal factors operate after the input stage, as Adams and Bray contend. They used counting backwards during the retention interval as a verbal interfering activity, and it lowered the level of recognition. Presumably the interference degraded the verbal label of the stimulus being remembered and decreased its effectiveness at the recognition test. A more direct comparison of these two hypotheses someday might come from the study of eye movements and the recognition process. If verbal labeling directs where the subject looks during input then there should be a relationship between the content of the verbal label and eye movements. If this correlation is low then the Adams and Bray output hypothesis is likely to be true.

With evidence on the positive role of verbal factors for visual recognition, we might think that recognition and recall of verbal responses are one and the same and that recognition is no more than retrieval of the verbal associate. This is not so. Keep in mind that visual recognition is fundamentally based on a sensory code and that the verbal code is only a supplement to it. It is the code from sensory experience that is basic, not the verbal code, and there are several lines of evidence to support the preeminence of the sensory code:

1.   Recognition occurs even though the verbal label has been forgotten (Ellis and Daniel, 1971). Something else besides the verbal label must be operating.

2.   The capacity for storing visual stimuli for later recognition is enormous, as we saw earlier in this chapter. Hundreds, indeed thousands, of stimuli can be stored after only a brief exposure. Verbal recall has no such capacity.

3.   We recognize far more detail than is in a verbal code. The verbal code is gross. We can identify one hat from among many others that differ by very slight details. The verbal label would be "hat" in all instances and could not be the basis of the discriminations.

4.   Pictures are recognized better than the names of the same objects (Jenkins, Neale, and Deno, 1967; Kaplan, Kaplan and Sampson, 1968; Paivio and Csapo, 1969). If the presentation time is long enough, the picture can have a verbal label *plus* a visual sensory code, which gives it an edge over words that are only verbal.

5.   Abstract forms that defy verbal labeling in most subjects can be easily recognized. This effect is present in any experiment that uses abstract visual forms of low association value (e.g., Clark, 1965).

EFFECTS OF THE RETENTION INTERVAL

Visual recognition is not immune to the forces of forgetting. Using meaningless forms, Clark (1965) found no forgetting over intervals of 5–20 minutes, and Arnoult (1956) found no decline in recognition accuracy over five hours, but longer intervals are different. Shepard (1967) had retention intervals up to four months among his experiments, and the recognition accuracy for pictures presented only once was 97 percent in an immediate test and 58 percent after four months. Nickerson (1968), whose subjects viewed ordinary photographs that had been presented once for five seconds, had a retention interval of one year. Eighty percent of the pictures were correctly identified after one day, but the value dropped to about 35 percent after one year.

Despite this evidence of forgetting, there are circumstances in which our remarkable powers of recognition remain so for long periods of time. Certainly you would have little trouble in recognizing your parents after a 20-year absence. Bahrick, Bahrick, and Wittlinger (1975) confirm these expectations from common experience by showing the high recognition of names and faces of members of high school classes over retention intervals of 3 months to 48 years since graduation. The recognition of names remained in the vicinity of 90 percent correct for 14 years, and dropped to only 77 percent after 48 years. Face recognition was even better, remaining in the vicinity of 90 percent for 34 years and dropping to only 73 percent after 48 years.

Is it a contradiction that Bahrick et al. found such high levels of recognition accuracy over many years while Shepard found only 58 percent after 4 months and Nickerson only 35 percent after 1 year? No. Certainly the familiarity variable must account for the difference. Shepard and Nickerson presented their stimuli for only a few seconds each, but subjects in the Bahrick et al. experiment had many hours of exposure to their stimuli over the three years of high school. The longer the exposure the better the recognition is the principle that is operating.

CHANGE IN THE STIMULUS

Patterson and Baddeley (1977) showed their subjects pictures of actors and then gave them a recognition test in which the appearance was either identical or disguised with the addition or removal of beard and/or moustache, the addition or removal of glasses, or a change in hair style. Recognition accuracy was 98 percent when appearance was identical, but only 45 percent when the appearance was disguised. Good advice for a criminal: If you had a beard at the time of the crime, shave it off. If you did not have a beard at the time of the crime, grow one.

Theories of form recognition

How is sensory information stored in memory so that recognition is possible? Psychologists are always challenged by the determinants of behavior that are hidden from them in the dark folds of the brain, and much of psychological theorizing is about the nature of these unseeable events. There are three theories of recognition behavior: template matching, feature matching, and schema matching. As in so much of psychology, recognition has multiple theories. Any science can have competing theories for a subject matter, but the competition often has more entries in psychology, which is a young science. Theories are resolved by empirical data, and a young science often lacks enough of it to decide among the competing theories.

A word of caution: None of the three theories have a place for verbal factors. As important as verbal factors are for recognition, the three theories are concerned only with the subject's internal representation of the environmental stimulus and how it determines recognition. Furthermore, all of the theories focus on visual recognition; none of them face the mechanisms of recognition for other sense modalities.

TEMPLATE MATCHING

Template-matching theory has sensory experience lay down a direct representation of itself (the template) and, at the recognition test, when the stimulus is experienced again, the incoming stimulus is compared with the template. If they correspond and a match occurs, the subject says that the stimulus is familiar and that he recognizes it. If the match fails, however, the stimulus will seem unfamiliar and the subject will have little confidence that it has been experienced before.

Template matching is a theory of recognition that is about as old as recorded history. Plato (translated edition, 1892) wrote about it. Speaking through Socrates, he said:

> . . . when knowing you and Theodorus, and having on the waxen block the impression of both of you given as by a seal, but seeing you imperfectly and at a distance, I try to assign the right impression of memory to the right visual impression, and to fit this into its own print: If I succeed, recognition will take place. . . . (p. 257)

Recall from Chapter 10 that Plato, perhaps metaphorically, saw memory as a wax tablet on which experience imprints its seal. In more modern times the image has filled the role of a template. In Chapter 12 we were concerned with the use of an existing image which the subject has aroused in the situation and uses as mediator in the learning and retention of verbal items.

The strength of the image template in recognition is a function of experience with the stimulus; the more the stimulus is experienced the more familiar it becomes and the more accurate the recognition. As we have seen, a function of visual experience is to increase the opportunities for eye movements to scan the stimulus (Loftus, 1972), presumably enriching the template.

Problems for template matching   The notion of an image template as a direct (although not necessarily high fidelity) representation of sensory experience is an appealing one, and not without scientific merit. Certain classical findings of perception do not fit an image explanation of recognition very well, however. One kind of data that fails is our ability to recognize a form when it undergoes changes in size. How can a sensory input with an altered size on the retina match the image from earlier experience? The image notion carries with it, implicitly, an assumption of one-to-one mapping of the stimulus input and the image, and the easy recognition of a stimulus of altered size violates this assumption.

The same criticism applies when we recognize a form whose orientation has been changed. Tilt a triangle in the recognition test and we all will recognize the triangle, nevertheless. There are limits, of course, to the recognition of forms when their orientation is changed because the change can drastically alter some forms, as the rotation of a square converts to a diamond. Notwithstanding, our capabilities for recognizing forms when their orientation has been changed is a violation of the one-to-one mapping assumption and so can be taken as evidence against template matching.

Perhaps the greatest difficulty for the image template is findings for cross-modal transfer—the discrimination of stimuli in one sense modality and the transfer of the discrimination to another sense modality. Given the visual presentation of a triangle, would you be able to recognize it if it were presented to you in the dark for tactual discrimination? "Yes!" you would reply, but this simple experiment does not prove anything because the verbally clever human would label the triangle during the study period and use the label rather than the brain's sensory systems to mediate recognition. Whether verbal behavior can mediate visual-tactual transfer is not the issue. The issue is whether the transfer can be mediated by sensory mechanisms alone. If the mediation is wholly sensory, then the image can exist in modalities which did not share in the sensory experience that created the image. The image is ordinarily assumed to be a specific product of the sensory channels that participated in the sensory experience with the stimulus.

The challenge of cross-modality transfer to template theory is weakened somewhat by the mix of positive and negative findings for cross-modality transfer (for reviews, see Ettlinger, 1967; von Wright, 1970) that we have today. One might think that the use of nonverbal animal subjects would be the way to avoid language mediators which can contaminate an experiment with human subjects, and yet the animal findings turn out to be less than decisive for cross-modality transfer (Ettlinger 1967; von Wright, 1970). The best positive evidence comes from medical case histories of patients who have had their sight restored with surgery after long-term blindness. The person who has endured long-term blindness necessarily comes to place an enormous reliance on the tactual modality as a source of information. When sight is restored, the issue is: Will tactual experience benefit the newly endowed visual behavior? Recent investigation into the postoperative visual behavior of the newly sighted has answered this question in the affirmative (Gregory and Wallace, 1963; Valvo, 1971).

Gregory and Wallace (1963) studied the single case of a man who had been blind in both eyes from the age of 10 months, and who received corneal graftings and sight at the age of 52 years. (All cases of this sort deal with surgical correction of the eye's front surface, with the retina healthy and intact.) They found that the patient had immediate visual comprehension of uppercase letters, which he had learned by touch, and that he was unable to read lowercase letters, which had not been learned by touch. Valvo (1971) found the same evidence for cross-modal transfer by observing competence in the visual processing of uppercase letters that had been learned earlier by touch and an inability to read lowercase letters.

Each card of the Ishihara Color Vision Test has dots of one color that form a numeral and are on a background of dots of another color. Normally it is used to assess color vision, as the name of the test implies; a subject who is color blind will, depending upon the colors, be unable to discriminate the numeral from the background. Gregory and Wallace found that their subject read every numeral perfectly. The normalcy of color vision after a lifetime of visual inactivity is a worthy finding, but for our purposes here we once again find positive cross-modal transfer because the subject had visual competence in a skill that was acquired by touch. Scientists are polite, persistent critics of one another, and a critic could point out that the subject might really have been making unobtrusive motor movements during the test which were informative of the numeral, and that there might not have been visually reading at all. Granting that the subject could discriminate the colors, a finger might have been used to trace out the pattern in the palm of the hand covertly. Or, maybe eye movements traced the pattern and were informative about the numeral. Gregory and Wallace countered both of these arguments by watching for finger movements during the test (there were none) and by observing eye movements. The eye movements were gross and jerky and could not have informed about much of anything.

FEATURE MATCHING

A feature is a dimension of difference which allows stimuli to be distinguished from one another. The feature-matching theory of recognition holds that distinctive features of the stimulus, not an image representation, is stored in memory. For example, the distinctive features for the uppercase letter D might be a straight line and a curved line that connects with its ends. An uppercase E might be expressed as three equally spaced lines of approximately equal length at right angles to a fourth line. At the time of stimulus input the subject does not process the entire stimulus as is done in the case of template-matching theory. Instead, distinctive features of the input are selectively processed. For visual inputs the stored features could be influenced by the selectivity of eye fixations (Loftus, 1972). Eye fixations are localized points on the scene being scanned, and they could be the basis of the features that are stored. The more exposure to the stimulus (familiarity) the greater the number of key features stored and the more accurate the recognition.

Feature matching has an advantage over template matching because it circumvents the problems that template matching has with size and form orientation. Regardless of size or orientation of the form, as long as the features are present in the stimulus and match those that have been stored, the stimulus will be recognized. Feature matching has been used with some success by scientists trying to engineer machines for pattern recognition, and this is another, and weaker, reason for some to favor feature matching. That a machine uses a particular process in simulating a human function does not mean that the human system uses the same process for the function.

Problems for feature matching   It is not at all clear that the findings on cross-modal matching are embarrassing for feature-matching theory, as they are for template matching theory. Template matching is based on the image which arises out of explicit sensory experiences. Feature matching, being a newer theory, is less clear in its defining principles. Most advocates of feature matching seem to imply that the features are extracted from the impinging stimuli, just as the image derives from impinging stimuli, and so they can be defined only by the modality of the sensory experience. If so, cross-modal matching is the same embarrassment for feature matching as it is for template matching.

SCHEMA MATCHING

A face in the crowd momentarily catches our eye and tomorrow we recognize it when we see it again. Both template-matching and feature-matching theory can explain this act of recognition because both are concerned with the perceptual learning and recognition of a single form. But not all perceptual learning and recognition is of a single form. A goodly amount of our perceptual behavior is with respect to stimulus classes and is closely akin to concept behavior. Concept behavior is a matter of classification and abstraction for the instances of a class of stimuli, and our perceptual processing of a class of stimuli is the same in principle. If we had a high pile of pictures, half of them pictures of various cats and half not, we would most certainly be able to recognize cats and sort cat pictures in one pile and noncat pictures in another. We seem to have a mental representation of cats as a class, and we are able to recognize all instances of the class, whether we have experienced them before or not. Even if the high pile of pictures contained a remote jungle cat that a sorter had never seen before, the chances are high that its picture would be tossed into the cat pile. Thus, the human memory is capable of abstractions and of classifying stimuli with respect to the abstractions. In the realm of perception these abstractions are called prototypes or *schemata*. In recognition by schema matching, it is assumed that a stimulus is compared against the schema for the stimulus class and a decision made about its class membership.

The notion of schema primarily comes to us from Bartlett (1932) who was impatient with the position that memory is a composite of traces, one for every little thing we think and do. In more recent times, in perception, schema was revived as a research topic by Attneave (1957). Today, cognitive psychology, in its concern with higher mental functioning, has a lively interest in the schema. Our research literature is currently debating the conditions under which a schema is formed, and an example of a present-day experiment is by Peterson, Meagher, Chait, and Gillie (1973, their Experiment I).

The general plan of the Peterson et al. experiment was to train subjects on specified kinds of stimulus instances of a form, and then test for recognition on the same and different kinds of stimulus instances of the form. Peterson et al. used four different prototype forms defined by dot patterns: a triangle, the letter F, and two random patterns. Each form class was systematically distorted to provide various instances of it, and the method of distortion was a technique developed by Posner, Goldsmith, and Welton (1967). An example of the triangle prototype and four levels of distortion are shown in Figure 14–6. The Posner et al. technique is a probabilistic one; so a level of distortion in Figure 14–6 represents the kind of figure that is typical of an indefinite number of figures that could be generated with the same degree of distortion.

There were three groups. A group was trained on instances of the four patterns, with either distortion level 1, 5, or 7.7, as illustrated in Figure 14–6 for the triangle (the extreme distortion, level 9.7, was not used). The stimuli were on slides, and the subject responded with four telegraph keys, one for each stimulus class. The subject had to classify each slide as one of the four stimulus classes by pressing a key. After pressing the key, a reinforcement lamp signalled the correct key to the subject. Training continued until 24 consecutive slides were classified correctly. In the recognition test series, with the reinforcement light

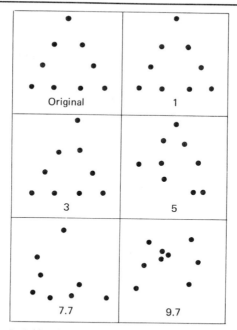

Source: M. I. Posner, R. Goldsmith, and K. E. Welton, Jr., Perceived distance and the classification of distorted patterns. *Journal of Experimental Psychology*, 1967, 73, 28–38. Reprinted by permission of the American Psychological Association.

FIGURE 14–6
Five levels of distortion of a triangle. The distortion is by a probabilistic technique.

removed, each group had to classify slides which were instances of the old training stimuli, the prototype stimuli, and new stimuli for the prototypes with distortion levels 1, 3, 5, and 7.7. Notice that each group had to classify instances of stimuli that had not been experienced before.

The results are shown in Table 14–2. Performance on the old training stimuli is the baseline against which performance on the new instances of the stimuli should be compared. Notice that the formation of abstractions, or the capability for classifying novel instances of stimuli, is facilitated by training on low levels of distortion. Group 1, which trained on Level 1 distortion, had the best performance of all. Not only was the accuracy of identifying the prototypes greater when training was on patterns with low levels of distortion, but more distorted stimuli were correctly classified.

Problems for schema matching   While it is not a problem in a theoretical sense, it pays to keep in mind that schema matching cannot be a general theory of recognition because it does not account for the power

TABLE 14–2
Average errors (out of three instances of a category on transfer test). The meaningful stimuli in training were a triangle and the letter *F*; the random stimuli were meaningless patterns.

Training condition (stimuli)	Old training stimuli	Proto- type pattern	1	3	5	7.7
Group 1						
Meaningful	0.04	0.08	0.09	0.31	0.98	2.40
Random	0.38	0.48	0.34	0.47	0.86	1.58
Average	0.21	0.28	0.22	0.39	0.92	1.99
Group 5						
Meaningful	0.84	0.80	0.96	1.18	1.88	1.76
Random	0.78	1.04	1.44	1.36	1.33	1.89
Average	0.82	0.92	1.20	1.27	1.60	1.83
Group 7.7						
Meaningful	1.04	1.75	1.67	1.76	1.61	1.86
Random	1.08	1.72	1.61	1.73	2.05	2.28
Average	1.06	1.73	1.64	1.75	1.83	2.07

Source: M. J. Peterson, R. B. Meagher, Jr., H. Chait, and S. Gillie. The abstraction and generalization of dot patterns. *Cognitive Psychology*, 1973, 4, 378–398. Reprinted by permission of Academic Press, Inc.

of recognition that develops from a single, brief sensory experience. It is remotely conceivable that a schema could be formed in one experience, but it is generally believed that multiple experiences are required. Whether varied instances of the stimulus class are required for schema learning is another matter. Varied instances are certainly one condition for the acquisition of a schema, as the Peterson et al. experiment testifies, but it may be only one way to do it. Charness and Bregman (1973) report some proficiency with novel instances of a stimulus class when training was only on the prototype stimulus. Intuitively, it would seem that training with the prototype alone would be ideal for deriving the core essentials of the stimulus class. Maybe so, but it is well to keep in mind that intuition is an unreliable companion on scientific campaigns.

All of the theories of form recognition neglect verbal factors, and this neglect seems to be particularly damaging for schema matching because verbal factors could easily give the appearance of schema formation. In the Peterson et al. experiment, some of the subjects certainly must have seen that some of the stimuli were meaningful (triangle, the letter F), verbally labeled them, and then used recall of the label as a basis for the key-pressing classification response. Random shapes were also used but, as we saw in our earlier discussion of the Vanderplas and Garvin (1959) experiment, random shapes do not necessarily eliminate verbal associations. That verbal labeling might have been present in the Peterson et al. experiment does not undermine it. Rather, the implication is that there is another variable to be understood for the concept of schema, and that we should consider broadening the concept to include verbal factors. At present, schema is defined wholly on the perceptual side as a function of sensory experience, and this is a good conception, as far as it goes. It is necessary for us to know if abstractions can be formed solely on the sensory-perceptual side, but we must inquire further and ask if verbal factors contribute to the schema also.

The general sense of the schema concept, as it has evolved by its protagonists (Attneave, 1957), is that it is a genuine abstraction on the sensory-perceptual side, a transcendent entity that embodies all of the essentials of the stimulus instances of the class without embodying the stimulus particulars of any of them. That it is a true abstraction makes schema matching different from template matching and feature matching, which entail the storage of particular aspects of each stimulus. A moment's reflection tells us that a true abstraction is not the only possibility for a schema, however. There is no reason why *each* stimulus could not be stored, either in terms of an image or features, and why the successive stimuli could not build a composite or average that is the schema or "abstraction." If this latter possibility turns out to be so it will reduce schema matching to either template matching or feature matching and also will be an enriching of them. As presently conceived, template matching and feature matching do not gracefully accommodate the human capability for perceptual abstraction.

Search and retrieval factors in recognition

All of the theories of recognition have the assumption that recognition will occur if the second presentation of the stimulus on the test "matches" the traces of the stimulus in memory that were laid down on the first presentation. But is matching all there is to it? In the last chapter we saw search and retrieval as processes of recall. Do search and retrieval processes operate for recognition also? Subjectively it is apparent that we search our memory at recall, but it is not subjectively obvious that search and retrieval operate for recognition. Our thinking about this was changed when Sternberg (1966, 1969) developed data and theoretical reasoning that caused us to consider search and retrieval as factors in recognition. Sternberg's work is in the modern manner of information processing (Chapter 10).

THE STERNBERG THEORY

One of the attractions of Sternberg's work was the classic simplicity of his approach. The use of reaction time to infer about mental processes is one of the oldest approaches in psychology, and Sternberg used it to infer about mental search time. Sternberg (1966) used the ten digits as stimuli. On each trial the subject saw a random series of one to six different digits presented singly for 1.2 seconds each. Then followed a two-second delay, a warning signal, and a test digit. The test digit was a recognition test and the subject had to decide whether it was a member of the set that was just shown. If the subject decided "Yes" one lever was pulled, and if "No" another was pulled. The measure of performance was reaction time, or time between onset of the test stimulus and occurrence of the response. If the test digit was a member of the set it was called a positive set, and if not it was a negative set. Sternberg found that reaction time was a linear increasing function of set size, and it is an effect that is easily obtained. Representative data are shown in Figure 14–7, which is a recent replication by Theios et al. (1973). Notice that the functions for positive and negative sets are the same. Sternberg's interpretation of data such as these is that recognition is a serial scanning process, in which the test digit is compared successively with the digits stored in memory, and the larger the set the longer the search time. That the functions for the positive and negative sets are about the same has the interesting implication that the scanning is exhaustive; even when a match occurs the scanning continues through the entire set. The logic of the argument is that the reaction time to the positive set would be less

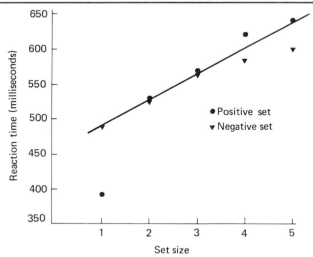

Source: J. Theios, P. G. Smith, S. E. Haviland, J. Traupmann, and M. C. Moy, Memory scanning as a serial self-terminating process. *Journal of Experimental Psychology*, 1973, 97, 323–336. Reprinted by permission of the American Psychological Association.

FIGURE 14–7
Recognition reaction time as a function of stimulus set size.

than to the negative set if the search terminated when a match occurred. Only about half of the items on the average must be searched for a match to occur in a positive set, but all of the items must be examined before the subject can say whether an item is missing and is a member of the negative set. Serial scanning of this sort is contrasted to parallel scanning, as another theoretical possibility, in which all items of the set would be searched simultaneously. One implication of a parallel scanning model is that reaction time would be a horizontal function of set size, in which all set sizes have the same reaction time because all items were tested simultaneously.

The linear relationship between reaction time and set size is a well-established finding in modern experimental psychology, and one would think that Sternberg's interpretation of retrieval processes in recognition would be beyond challenge, but not so. One line of challenge has been to study reaction-time values to the digits within a set. If search is exhaustive, as Sternberg contends, then reaction time should be the

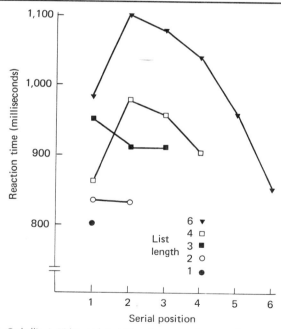

Source: M. C. Corballis, J. Kirby, and A. Miller, Access to elements of a memorized list. *Journal of Experimental Psychology,* 1972, *94,* 185–190. Reprinted by permission of the American Psychological Association.

FIGURE 14–8

Reaction time as a function of number of items in the set and serial position in the set.

same for all digits of a set because all are scanned before the reaction-time response occurs. The study of items as a function of their position in the set is the study of the serial position curve, a phenomenon which we encountered in Chapter 11 within the context of verbal recall; Morin, DeRosa, and Stultz (1967), and Corballis (1967) appear to have been the first to show that reaction time is dependent on serial position. A good demonstration of the serial position effect in the Sternberg's situation is an experiment by Corballis, Kirby, and Miller (1972) which used experimental procedures similar to Sternberg's. Positive sets of one, two, three, four, or six items were used, and a plot of reaction time as a function of serial position for each of the lists is given in Figure 14–8. The serial position effects are sharply defined for the longer lists.

Summary

Recognition is deciding that a stimulus has been experienced before. Recognition accuracy can be very high. Exposure to hundreds, indeed, thousands of pictures, usually can produce a recognition level of 90 percent correct, or more. High similarity of the stimuli can reduce this value, however.

The basic operation for recognition is sensory experience, and the duration of the experience is called the familiarity variable. Recognition accuracy is positively related to exposure time in most experiments. Recent research has shown that eye fixations are a more fundamental determiner of visual recognition than exposure time, and that exposure time is a variable only insofar as it determines number of eye fixations. Verbal factors, as a supplement to a sensory code, are also a variable for recognition. The human subject has a rich propensity for verbal labeling and description, and the labels and descriptions that are hung on a stimulus benefit its recognition.

There are three theories of recognition: template matching, feature matching, and schema matching. Template matching is an image theory, in which the stimulus lays down a rather direct representation of itself. At the recognition test an incoming stimulus is compared with the template, and if a match occurs a sense of familiarity is present and the subject declares that he has experienced the stimulus before. Feature matching is similar to template matching except that only critical features of the stimulus are stored, not an explicit image. Feature matching gives greater versatility in recognition because only critical features of the stimulus need be recognized, not the detailed stimulus. Schema matching is recognition of the members of a stimulus class. Schema matching theory contends that an abstract representation of the members of a stimulus class is stored, and an item is recognized when it is compared against the schema and judged to be a member of the class.

References

Adams, J. A., & Bray, N. W.   A closed-loop theory of paired-associate verbal learning. *Psychological Review,* 1970, *77,* 385–405.

Arnoult, M. D.   Familiarity and recognition of nonsense shapes. *Journal of Experimental Psychology,* 1956, *51,* 269–276.

Attneave, F.   Transfer of experience with a class-schema to identification-learning of patterns and shapes. *Journal of Experimental Psychology,* 1957, *54,* 81–88.

Attneave, F., & Arnoult, M. D.   The quantitative study of shape and pattern perception. *Psychological Bulletin,* 1956, *53,* 452–471.

Bahrick, H. P., & Bahrick, P. O.   A re-examination of the interrelations among measures of retention. *Quarterly Journal of Experimental Psychology,* 1964, *16,* 318–324.

Bahrick, H. P., Bahrick, P. O., & Wittlinger, R. P.   Fifty years of memory for names and faces: A cross-sectional approach. *Journal of Experimental Psychology: General,* 1975, *104,* 54–75.

Bartlett, F. C.   *Remembering: A study in experimental and social psychology.* Cambridge: University of Cambridge Press, 1932.

Bruce, D., & Cofer, C. N.   A comparison of recognition and recall in short-term memory. *Proceedings, 73rd Annual Convention of the American Psychological Association,* 1965, pp. 81–82.

Bruce, D., & Cofer, C. N.   An examination of recognition and free recall as measures of acquisition and long-term retention. *Journal of Experimental Psychology,* 1967, *75,* 283–289.

Charness, N., & Bregman, A. S.   Transformations in the recognition of visual forms. *Canadian Journal of Psychology,* 1973, *27,* 367–380.

Clark, H. J.   Recognition memory for random shapes as a function of complexity, association value, and delay. *Journal of Experimental Psychology,* 1965, *69,* 590–595.

Corballis, M. C.   Serial order in recognition and recall. *Journal of Experimental Psychology,* 1967, *74,* 99–105.

Corballis, M. C., Kirby, J., & Miller, A.   Access to elements of a memorized list. *Journal of Experimental Psychology,* 1972, *94,* 185–190.

Edwards, D. C., & Goolkasian, P. A.   Peripheral vision location and kinds of complex processing. *Journal of Experimental Psychology,* 1974, *102,* 244–249.

Ellis, H. C.   Transfer of stimulus predifferentiation to shape recognition and identification learning: Role of properties of verbal labels. *Journal of Experimental Psychology,* 1968, *78,* 401–409.

Ellis, H. C.   Stimulus encoding processes in human learning and memory. In G. H. Bower (Ed.), *The psychology of learning and motivation* (Vol. 7). New York: Academic Press, 1973, pp. 123–182.

Ellis, H. C., & Daniel, T. C.   Verbal processes in long-term stimulus-recognition memory. *Journal of Experimental Psychology,* 1971, *90,* 18–26.

Ellis, H. C., & Muller, D. G. Transfer in perceptual learning following stimulus predifferentiation. *Journal of Experimental Psychology*, 1964, *68*, 388–395.

Ettlinger, G. Analysis of cross-modal effects and their relationship to language. In F. L. Darley (Ed.), *Brain mechanisms underlying speech and language*. New York: Grune & Stratton, 1967, pp. 53–60.

Goldstein, A. G., & Chance, J. E. Visual recognition memory for complex configurations. *Perception and Psychophysics*, 1970, *9*, 237–241.

Gregory, R. L., & Wallace, J. G. *Recovery from early blindness: A case study*. Cambridge: Heffers, 1963.

Hochhaus, L. A table for the calculation of d' and β. *Psychological Bulletin*, 1972, *77*, 375–376.

Jenkins, J. R., Neale, D. C., & Deno, S. L. Differential memory for picture and word stimuli. *Journal of Educational Psychology*, 1967, *58*, 303–307.

Kaplan, S., Kaplan, R., & Sampson, J. R. Encoding and arousal factors in free recall of verbal and visual material. *Psychonomic Science*, 1968, *12*, 73–74.

Klein, L. S., & Arbuckle, T. Y. Response latency and task difficulty in recognition memory. *Journal of Verbal Learning and Verbal Behavior*, 1970, *9*, 467–472.

Lawrence, D. M., & Banks, W. P. Accuracy of recognition memory for common sounds. *Bulletin of the Psychonomic Society*, 1973, *1*, 298–300.

Loftus, G. R. Eye fixations and recognition memory for pictures. *Cognitive Psychology*, 1972, *3*, 525–551.

Mackworth, N. H. Stimulus density limits the useful field of view. In R. A. Monty and J. W. Senders (Eds.), *Eye movements and psychological processes*. Hillsdale: Erlbaum, 1976, pp. 307–320.

Morin, R. E., DeRosa, D. V., & Stultz, V. Recognition memory and reaction time. *Acta Psychologica*, 1967, *27*, 298–305.

Nickerson, R. S. A note on long-term recognition memory for pictorial material. *Psychonomic Science*, 1968, *11*, 58.

Paivio, A., & Csapo, K. Concrete image and verbal memory codes. *Journal of Experimental Psychology*, 1969, *80*, 279–285.

Parker, R. E. Picture processing during recognition. *Journal of Experimental Psychology: Human Perception and Performance*, 1978, *4*, 284–293.

Patterson, K. E., & Baddeley, A. D. When face recognition fails. *Journal of Experimental Psychology: Human Learning and Memory*, 1977, *3*, 406–417.

Peterson, M. J., Meagher, R. B., Jr., Chait, H., & Gillie, S. The abstraction and generalization of dot patterns. *Cognitive Psychology*, 1973, *4*, 378–398.

Plato. *The dialogues of Plato* (Vol. 4) (3rd ed.). (B. Jowett trans.). Oxford: Clarendon Press, 1892.

Posner, M. I., Goldsmith, R., & Welton, K. E., Jr. Perceived distance and the classification of distorted patterns. *Journal of Experimental Psychology*, 1967, *73*, 28–38.

Potter, M. C., & Levy, E. I. Recognition memory for a rapid sequence of pictures. *Journal of Experimental Psychology*, 1969, *81*, 10–15.

Rock, I., Halper, F., & Clayton, T.   The perception and recognition of complex figures. *Cognitive Psychology*, 1972, *3*, 655–673.

Santa, J. L., & Ranken, H. B.   Effects of verbal coding on recognition memory. *Journal of Experimental Psychology*, 1972, *93*, 268–278.

Shepard, R. N.   Recognition memory for words, sentences, and pictures. *Journal of Verbal Learning and Verbal Behavior*, 1967, *6*, 156–163.

Standing, L., Conezio, J., & Haber, R. N.   Perception and memory for pictures: Single-trial learning of 2,500 visual stimuli. *Psychonomic Science*, 1970, *19*, 73–74.

Sternberg, S.   High-speed scanning in human memory. *Science*, 1966, *153*, 652–654.

Sternberg, S.   Memory Scanning: Mental processes revealed by reaction-time experiments. *American Scientist*, 1969, *57*, 421–457.

Strong, E. K., Jr.   The effect of length of series upon recognition memory. *Psychological Review*, 1912, *19*, 447–462.

Strong, E. K., Jr.   The effect of time-interval upon recognition memory. *Psychological Review*, 1913, *20*, 339–372.

Theios, J., Smith, P. G., Haviland, S. E., Traupmann, J., & Moy, M. C.   Memory scanning as a serial self-terminating process. *Journal of Experimental Psychology*, 1973, *97*, 323–336.

Theodor, L. H.   A neglected parameter: Some comments on "A table for the calculation of d′ and β." *Psychological Bulletin*, 1972, *78*, 260–261.

Underwood, B. J.   Word recognition memory and frequency information. *Journal of Experimental Psychology*, 1972, *94*, 276–283.

Underwood, B. J., & Schulz, R. W.   *Meaningfulness and verbal learning.* New York: Lippincott, 1960.

Valvo, A.   *Sight restoration after long-term blindness: The problems and behavior patterns of visual rehabilitation.* New York: American Foundation for the Blind, 1971.

Vanderplas, J. M., & Garvin, E. A.   The association value of random shapes. *Journal of Experimental Psychology*, 1959, *57*, 147–154.

von Wright, J. M.   Cross-modal transfer and sensory equivalence—a review. *Scandinavian Journal of Psychology*, 1970, *11*, 21–30.

15

Memory for sentences and prose

PSYCHOLOGY has had an upsurge in research on language in recent years, and it is different than the study of verbal learning and memory which has been covered throughout this book so far. The study of verbal learning and memory, which has been with us since psychology's earliest days as an experimental science, did not represent an interest in verbal behavior for its own sake. Rather, verbal behavior was studied as a route to the understanding of general laws, just as any other response class might be studied. In Chapter 7 we saw that for a long time psychology had a philosophy of science which believed in general laws, and with this philosophy the study of one response class is as good as another. With general laws being sought, there was no motivation for studying verbal units that are realistic in the natural language.

Investigators of language today have their interests strongly focused on the natural language with its units of phrases, sentences, and prose, and frequently they reject study of the isolated verbal unit that has been the style of the past. There is no doubt that the tradition of isolated units made a receptive bed for the study of larger, more realistic verbal units, and given the receptive bed, events of the present moved psychologists in new directions. One of the directions was inspired by developments in linguistics by Chomsky (1957, 1965). Studies of sentences and prose can be found along psychology's research routes of the past, but they were never accompanied by ideas that drove scientists to vigorous research action. Chomsky's ideas had this power, and they are embodied in his development of *generative theory*, or transformational grammar as it is often called.

Chomsky's generative theory

Generative theory is a cognitive theory that opposes an associationist view of language. Cognitive theory, with its emphasis on the organizing powers of the mind, has been a long-standing opponent of associationism and of behaviorism with its focus on the learning of responses to stimuli. The modern bout between behaviorists and cognitive psychology in the arena of language began with a paper by Mowrer (1954). Mowrer said that "the sentence is, preeminently, a *conditioning device*, and that its chief effect is to produce new associations, new learning, just as any other paired presentation of stimuli may do." Communication is a transfer of meaning from sign to sign, so that the listener associates one word of the sentence with another and acquires its meaning by virtue of the association. Mowrer's example is John telling Charles that "Tom is a thief," and the assumption is that Charles already has meaning attached to the words "Tom" and "thief." What, then, is the function of the sentence? The sentence is fundamentally a classical conditioning paradigm (Chapter 2), in which "Tom" is a conditioned stimulus and "thief" is an unconditioned stimulus, and by association "Tom" comes to elicit some of the reaction evoked by "thief." For Charles, by the principles of conditioning, "Tom" comes to mean an untrustworthy person who steals, and the next time Charles meets Tom he reacts to him as if he is a thief. Mowrer went on to derive various other characteristics of language behavior from the principles of learning, and they were all well-reasoned, ingenious derivations. In 1957, Skinner published a book *Verbal Behavior,* which also derived language behavior from the behaviorist's point of view (Skinner, 1957). Both Mowrer and Skinner saw language behavior as instances of general laws of learning. The basic determination of the laws has often been with animals or simple human learning situations, and the use of these laws to explain language is the application of them to new situations. General scientific laws have such power.

Chomsky (1959) unleashed a cognitive counterattack in his review of Skinner's 1957 book. Chomsky held that the application of the laws of learning, derived as they were from simple situations, to the complexities of language, was gross and superficial. In other words, the general laws were not as general as Mowrer and Skinner believed them to be. When it comes to the learning of language there is no meaningful identification of stimulus, response, or reinforcement, which are the essential ingredients of the behaviorist's laws, Chomsky argued. And, if learning is so fundamental, how is it that we can speak sentences that we have never spoken before or understand sentences that we have never heard before? Given a knowledge of grammar, the rules of which can generate all the permissible sentences in the language and exclude all those that are not, we seem capable of seemingly infinite variety in language, and it is very difficult to see the conditions of its learning. Miller (1965) estimated that there are 10^{20} sentences 20 words long, and it would take a child 1,000 times the age of the earth just to listen to them. We saw in Chapter 7 that biological endowment establishes the boundary conditions for behavior, determining what can and cannot be learned. Chomsky contends that the rich human capability for language creativity has been sharpened by biological forces and is uniquely human (there is an indication, as we saw in Chapter 8, that the chimpanzee has some of this capability also).

Chomsky's more substantive reply to the associationists was his theory of linguistics (1957, 1965). Much of linguistics is descriptive and of passing interest to the psychologist, but Chomsky's generative theory is different because aspects of it have implications for language as behavior, which is the field of psychology called psycholinguistics.

Of most interest to psychologists was Chomsky's distinction between surface structure, deep structure, and transformational rules. *Surface structure* is a physical form of the sentence as it is observed; *deep structure* contains the abstract, fundamental meaning of the sentence and the grammar functions that relate to meaning; and *transformational rules* relate surface structure to deep structure. The importance of the distinction between deep structure and surface structure can be appreciated when it is noted that different deep structures can have the same surface structure, and different surface structures can have the same deep structure. The ambiguous sentence "They are cooking apples" is an example of how different deep structures can have the same surface structure. It can mean that someone is cooking apples, or that the apples are for cooking. The sentence "The bird ate the seed" and the sentence "The seed was eaten by the bird" is an example of different surface structures but identical deep structure—both sentences have the same meaning. The simple, active, declarative expression of the idea in deep structure is called the *kernel sentence,* and if it is not exactly the same as the idea in deep structure it is the simplest transformation of it that occurs at the surface. Other syntactical forms of the idea are more complex transformations. Consider the kernel sentence "The bird ate the seed." By transformation rules the kernel sentence can be transformed into a passive, a negative, or a question form, or any combination of the three. "The seed was eaten by the bird" (passive), "The bird did not eat the seed" (negative), or "Did the bird eat the seed?" (question). There can be all combinations of these, such as passive + negative, "The seed was not eaten by the bird."

Some psychologists saw implications of Chomsky's theory for memory. One theme lies in surface structure. Different surface structures can express the same meaning and have the same deep structure. Is learning and memory influenced by surface structure or the underlying meaning? Another research theme concerns transformation rules. Miller (1962), working from Chomsky's generative theory, assumed that the number of transformations was important for sentence memory. Do the transformations that lie between deep structure and surface structure make a difference for the retention of sentences?

EFFECTS OF SENTENCE SURFACE STRUCTURE AND MEANING

The study of the surface structure of a sentence is the study of syntax, and it can be separated from semantics for analysis. *Syntax* is a study of the ordering of words or morphemes (the morpheme is the smallest unit of the language that conveys meaning) to form larger language units such as phrases and sentences. *Semantics,* as another fundamental characteristic of sentences, is the study of meaning. The syntactical and semantical structure of sentences can have some independence (Miller and Isard, 1963). A sentence can be syntactically and grammatically correct: "A witness signed the official legal document." A sentence can be syntactically correct but semantically meaningless, or semantically anamolous, as it is often called: "A witness appraised the shocking company dragon." Or a sentence can be syntactically and semantically meaningless: "A diamond shocking the prevented dragon witness." It is in ways like this that syntax can be studied independently of other sentence properties.

Marks and Miller (1964) studied the effects of both syntax and meaning on the recall of sentences. Four kinds of word strings were used. *Normal sentences* were used, with proper syntax and meaning ("Pink bouquets emit fragrant odors"). A second kind of sentence was *semantically anamolous*, in which the syntactic structure was the same as the normal sentences but it was meaningless ("Pink accidents cause sleeping storms"). Two nonsense strings of words were also formed as the other two kinds of word strings, and they were control conditions. One kind, called *anagram strings*, was a random rearrangement of the words of normal sentences ("Bouquets pink odors fragrant emit."). The other kind, called *word lists*, was a random rearrangement of the words of anamolous sentences ("Accidents pink storms sleeping cause."). Five

354

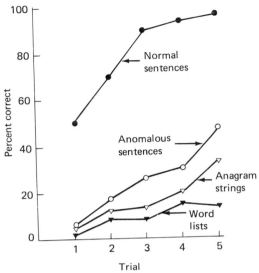

Source: L. E. Marks, and G. A. Miller, The role of semantic and syntactic constraints in the memorization of English sentences. *Journal of Verbal Learning and Verbal Behavior,* 1964, 3, 1–5. Reprinted by permission of Academic Press, Inc.

FIGURE 15–1
Findings of an experiment which separate the influences of syntax and meaning on the recall of sentences.

trials were given, using aural presentation. Recall was immediate and in writing by the method of free recall.

Figure 15–1 has the results in terms of complete word strings correctly recalled. The normal sentences with good syntax and meaning are recalled best of all. Next are anamolous sentences which are meaningless but have good syntax, and the two random strings without syntactical or semantical structure are the poorest of all. Both syntax and meaning are variables for the learning and recall of sentences.

EFFECTS OF NUMBER OF TRANSFORMATIONS

Generative theory holds that the essential idea of the sentence resides in deep structure, and the surface structure of the sentence can reflect the basic meaning of the sentence rather directly or be one or more transformations of it. Miller (1962) took this assumption and turned it into a hypothesis about memory for sentences. He said that the learning of any sentence involves a recoding of it as a kernel sentence, and what is carried in memory is the kernel sentence plus a "footnote" about syntactic structure. If the sentence for remembering is: "The small boy wasn't liked by Joe," the subject would recode it as the kernel "Joe liked the small boy" plus a tag that it is a passive-negative transformation and is two transformations of the kernel. The semantic and the syntactic properties of a sentence are stored separately according to this hypothesis, and presumably can be forgotten independently. The subject might forget the transformations and remember the kernel, and so recall only the simple form of a more complicated sentence.

Mehler (1963) tested Miller's hypothesis, and the logic of his experiment is shown in Figure 15–2. A kernel sentence (K) can be transformed into passive (P), negative (N), interrogative (Q) form, or any combination of the three. The kernel sentence "The boy hit the ball" would have the negative form "The boy hasn't hit the ball." The passive form would be "The ball has been hit by the boy," and the interrogative form is "Has the ball been hit by the boy?" An example of a combination of the three basic transformations is the passive-negative-interrogative form "Hasn't the ball been hit by the boy?" Mehler tested the immediate recall of kernel sentences and their seven transformations. He found that kernel sentences are remembered the best, but this success for Miller's

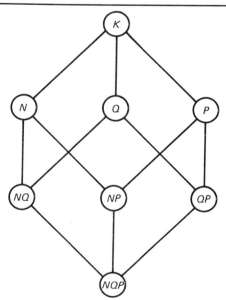

Source: J. Mehler, Some effects of grammatical transformations on the recall of English sentences. *Journal of Verbal Learning and Verbal Behavior*, 1963, 2, 346–351. Reprinted by permission of Academic Press, Inc.

FIGURE 15–2

Representation of the eight types of sentences that were used in the Mehler experiment. Seven transformations of a basic kernel sentence (K) were used. See text for explanation.

hypothesis had a short life because it sank under the weight of failure to replicate (Martin and Roberts, 1966; Roberts, 1968), and arguments about the role of sentence length and its control in these experiments (Martin and Roberts, 1967).

The retention of prose

REPRODUCTION VERSUS CONSTRUCTION

The studies that have been reviewed so far in this chapter have in common their concern with memory for the form and meaning of an individual sentence. Beyond the individual sentence is the processing of multiple sentences, which typically come to us in the form of prose. We can have the literal, exact learning of a prose passage (e.g., Cofer, 1941), but there is little modern-day interest in the rote learning of prose because prose is rarely processed that way. The human would like to have a perfect memory and remember it all, as the memory aids discussed in Chapter 12 help him to do, but the truth is that a great deal of memory is not literal recollection but a mix of such higher mental processes as inference, induction, interpretation, the derivation of concepts, and selective attention to some material and not others. To say this is to have a cognitive emphasis because the thrust is not surface structure but what the subject's active mind does with the surface structure. As we will see, a strict cognitive view must be tempered because we remember more of surface structure than we think we do.

Have a subject read a page of prose and then have her recall it. Very little literal recollection will be obtained, but there will be statements of ideas from the passage, inferences, errors of facts and omissions, etc. Was this behavior a result of processing during learning, with recall a straightforward reporting of what was learned? If so, memory for prose is *reproductive*. Or, was much of the recall content created at the time of recall? The subject could have organized a general abstraction at the time of learning and then created much of the recall report at the time of recall to meet the demands of the recall situation. This point of view of memory for prose is *constructive*. Constructive theory is most prominently associated with Bartlett (1932). Bartlett called the abstraction that is formed in learning, and on which the recall elaboration is based, the *schema*. Bartlett's theory has been influential, with survival longer than most theories in psychology, but in recent times it has been threatened. Experiments by Fredericksen (1975a, 1975b) are in support of the reproductive view, with evidence that inferences from prose occur at the time of learning, not recall.

MEMORY FOR SURFACE STRUCTURE

When the theoretical stance is cognitive, and emphasis is on the meaning of the prose passage, there is a sidestepping of other factors required for the processing of prose. Consider form recognition, which was discussed in Chapter 14. The forms on the page that are the letters, words, and sentences of the prose passage are experienced briefly as we process them in reading. Now a picture can be recognized with good accuracy when seen for only a fraction of a second; so should not the literal recognition of letters, words, and sentences be good also? Undoubtedly many elements on a page are perceived poorly as the eye moves and fixates irregularly across a line of type. Notwithstanding, many elements are perceived very well, and there is no reason why they should not be recognized as well as a briefly presented picture. The same should hold for auditorily presented material.

Keenan, MacWhinney, and Mayhew (1977) recorded the conversation of a faculty luncheon and then made up a recognition test of four-alternative multiple choice items for remarks that were made. The four alternatives were (1) a verbatim statement of the remark, (2) a paraphrase of the remark, (3) a remark that was different in content from the verbatim remark but which was plausible in terms of the discussion, and (4) a paraphrase of (3). There was excellent retention for the verbatim statement of the remark. Recognition of surface structure was excellent. Bates, Masling, and Kintsch (1978) performed a similar experiment and had the same outcome. They had their subjects watch a television soap opera and then gave them a multiple-choice test of statements that the characters in the soap opera made. Once again, recognition accuracy of verbatim statements was good. Even typography, which might seem to have details that would be overlooked in the process of reading, can be recognized 32 days later (Kolers and Ostry, 1974).

EFFECTS OF THE IMPORTANCE OF IDEAS

We have seen that the major processing of the contents of a prose passage appears at the learning stage rather than at recall, and the processing can take various forms, most of which we know little about: inference, abstraction, attending to some material and not others, etc. If so, it is reasonable to assume that some ideas will be processed more thoroughly than others and remembered better. Johnson (1970) had his subjects learn prose passages which independent raters had categorized into linguistic units of seven to eight words between which the reader might pause to catch a breath, give emphasis to the story, or enhance meaning. Other raters then classified the importance of these units for the theme of the passage into six categories. Acquisition was reading the story twice, and recall was in writing after retention intervals of 15 minutes, 7 days, 21 days, or 63 days. The results of one of his experiments are shown in Figure 15–3, with the recall protocol scored in terms of the linguistic units and their importance. Recall declined with length of the retention interval, which is a routine finding, but recall was positively related to the importance of the unit, which is a new finding.

An obvious explanation for this finding of Johnson's is that subjects were spending more study time on the important units. If so, this would reduce the significance of the findings because it would mean that retention is a positive function of study time, a generalization which has been with us since Ebbinghaus. To control for study time, Johnson performed another experiment in which presentation of the linguistic units was with a slide projector and controlled. Recall was immediate or after 21 days, and the results are presented in Figure 15–4. Even with presentation time controlled, importance is a variable. In a manner un-

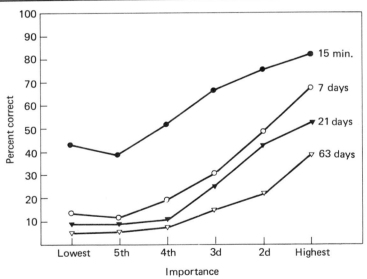

Source: R. E. Johnson, Recall of prose as a function of the structural importance of the linguistic units. *Journal of Verbal Learning and Verbal Behavior,* 1970, 9, 12–20. Reprinted by permission of Academic Press, Inc.

FIGURE 15–3
Recall as à function of importance of the ideas in a prose passage. The curve parameter is retention interval.

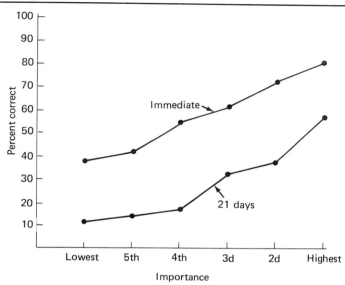

Source: R. E. Johnson, Recall of prose as a function of the structural importance of the linguistic units. *Journal of Verbal Learning and Verbal Behavior*, 1970, 9, 12–20. Reprinted by permission of Academic Press, Inc.

FIGURE 15–4
Immediate and delayed recall (21 days) as a function of importance of the ideas in a prose passage. The study time for the words of the passage that contained each idea was controlled.

known, the human weighs the relative importance of ideas while reading a prose passage, and the processing which he gives them on the basis of his weighting is a variable for retention.

Retrieval from semantic memory

Tulving (1972) made the distinction between *episodic memory* and *semantic memory*. Semantic memory is our stable, long-term knowledge of language and how to use it, and knowledge about the world. Episodic memory is local knowledge associated with time, place, and particular events. For example, the word "five" could be a response required of a subject in a laboratory experiment on verbal learning, and this local memory requirement would be an example of episodic memory. On the other hand, the subject's long-time, stable knowledge of "five" as a word in the language and as part of a number system is outside the local bounds of the laboratory experiment and is part of the subject's semantic memory.

The interest in models of semantic memory comes from the reasonable belief that semantic memory has an organization that is a basis for our use of language and a contributor to our thought processes (there may be more to thought than language, e.g., images). Two models of semantic memory will be presented, the network model and the featural model.

Retrieval time has been a primary way of studying the organization of semantic memory, and its first major use was in test of a network model by Collins and Quillian (1969). Retrieval time is the reaction time used by a subject to ascertain the truth or falsity of a sentence, such as "A canary can fly." If the subject believed the sentence to be true, she would press a button with one hand, and if she thought it to be false she would press a second button with the other hand. The model that was tested is shown in Figure 15–5. The model is a hierarchical or network model which assumes that the descriptive concrete properties of *canary* are stored immediately along with it, and that more abstract properties are stored more remotely. The higher the position in the hierarchy the longer the reaction time to decide about the truth of a sentence. Following Figure 15–5, the sentence "A canary can sing" should have the

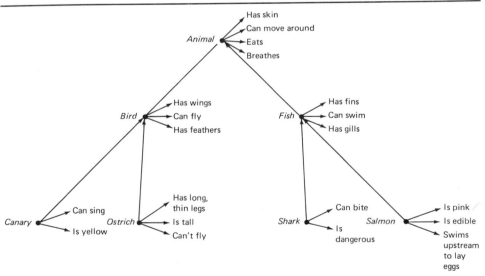

Source: A. M. Collins, and M. R. Quillian, Retrieval time from semantic memory. *Journal of Learning and Verbal Behavior,* 1969, 8, 240–247. Reprinted by permission of Academic Press, Inc.

FIGURE 15–5
A network model of semantic memory. It is assumed that longer processing times are associated with higher positions in the hierarchy.

fastest reaction time of all, "A CANARY CAN FLY" should have a somewhat slower reaction time because flying is a more general property associated with all birds, and "A canary has skin" should have the slowest time because it requires the abstract knowledge that a canary is an animal and that all animals have skin. All of this seems like an orderly dictionary rather than human memory, which can be anything but orderly; but this should not altogether upset testing of the hierarchical arrangement of knowledge, which is the model's main property. That the model has some justification is found in the positive results which Collins and Quillian obtained. The sentence "A canary can sing" had the fastest reaction time, with "A canary can fly" being about 75 milliseconds slower, and "A canary has skin" being about 75 milliseconds slower still. A false sentence such as "A canary has gills" had a relatively slow reaction time, about the same as "A canary has skin." Collins and Quillian surmised that a decision about a false sentence requires the search through several levels in an attempt to verify the assertion, and when verification fails, a false response is reported. Searching through several levels takes more time in the model, and so false sentences have longer reaction times.

FEATURAL MODEL

Rips, Shoben, and Smith (1973) were not content with the network model of Collins and Quillian because of its rationality in which "memory structure mirrors logical structure, and logically valid relations can be read directly from the structure of stored semantic information" (p. 3). They wanted a model that was more psychological, without a dictionary-like quality, and their solution was the concept of *semantic distance*. What they call the "semantic distance effect" is that verification time increases as a function of the relatedness of the two main words in a sentence like "A canary is a bird." The sentence "A canary is a bird" would be expected to have a faster reaction time than "A canary is an animal" because *canary–bird* are more related than *canary–animal*. Determining relatedness or semantic distance, is a matter of having subjects scale various word pairs, which Rips et al. did, and they found that reaction time was related to semantic distance, as they had hypothesized. In a subsequent paper (Smith, Shoben, and Rips, 1974) the position was taken that the semantic distance of word pairs is more fundamentally a function of the *semantic features* which the words have in common. Semantic features are all of the defining characteristics of a word, and some are more salient than others in a hierarchy of features that define the word, according to Smith et al. The reason that *canary–bird* has less semantic distance than *canary–animal* is that *canary* and *bird* have more features in common than *canary* and *animal* and so, for the same reason, the reaction time in verifying "A canary is a bird" is faster than that for "A canary is an animal."

AN ASSOCIATIVE INTERPRETATION

Semantic memory and retrieval from it is in the cognitive tradition, but a worthwhile question is to ask what the older associative view with its emphasis on isolated verbal units, has to offer. We saw in Chapter 8 that association had its origins in antiquity, flowered as a theory of thought under British Associationism in the 17th–19th centuries, and was the goad for so much of the work on verbal associative learning that has been done. It is good science to ask what the associative view has to say about the kinds of data which are in evidence of retrieval from semantic memory. The pitting of rival viewpoints against one another always produces greater scientific advance than asserting one view or the other and doing experiments about it. So far, associative and cognitive views of verbal thought processes have confronted each other little in the laboratory. Clustering in free recall is often given a cognitive interpretation in terms of the organizing powers of the mind, and in Chapter 8 we saw experimental efforts, of some success, to explain clustering in terms of associations.

Rips, Shoben, and Smith (1973) scaled word pairs for "relatedness," using a four-point rating scale, and the rating values were correlated with reaction time measures and became the basis of semantic distance, and more fundamentally semantic features, as theory. But the words of a pair can be associates of one another or have associations in common; so the question is: Are semantic features or associations the fundamental explanation? One way to look at semantic features is that they are the associations which two words have in common. The word pair *canary–bird* have the feature wings in common, but if we asked subjects to give words in free association to *canary* and *bird* it is likely that *wings* would be among them.

Cofer (1957) was the first to show that rated similarity of word pairs and number of associations which the pairs held in common were highly correlated, and he observed that the study "should help to determine to what extent the association-oriented and the meaning-oriented investigators are talking about the same thing" (p. 603). Cofer's study does not stand alone. Garskof and Houston (1963; 1965) also found high relationships between rated similarity and number of associations which the two words had in common. While it is true that Rips, Shoben, and Smith (1973) had their subjects rate pairs for "relatedness" rather than "similarity," it is likely that subjects would rate pairs for relatedness and similarity in about the same way. Underwood and Schulz (1960, Chapter 2) summarize the evidence which shows that the seemingly different ways of scaling verbal materials can be highly correlated. The implication is that the scaled relatedness of word pairs, which is the empirical index of semantic distance and number of semantic features, is highly correlated with the number of associations which word pairs have in common, and so the cognitive and the associative viewpoints are tangled.

Another line of evidence which the advocates of semantic memory should face is associative reaction time, or the time taken to give a word in free association to a verbal stimulus. The research on retrieval from semantic memory is mostly founded on simple sentences like "A canary is a bird." If the mental process of verifying the truth of this sentence is a subject's testing to see if *bird* is an associate of *canary*, then the reaction time data in semantic memory experiments have association as the primary cause. The sentence "A canary is a bird" has a faster reaction time than "A canary is an animal," but Marbe's Law could account for this finding. Marbe's Law is an old relationship in psychology (Woodworth, 1938, p. 360), and it says that the more frequently a response is given by subjects in a free association test the faster its associative reaction time. *Bird* would certainly be a more common associate of the stimulus *canary* than *animal*, and so its reaction time would be faster, according to Marbe's Law.

An associative point of view, for whatever value it might have in explaining the data of semantic memory, is not being given much attention these days. One reason is that most association data are old and too incomplete to be useful, but the main reason is that the associative point of view was strongly linked with behavioristic psychology, which modern cognitive psychology rejects. That the associative point of view was affiliated with a discarded school of psychology does not mean that association data are valueless, however. Kiss (1975) is bringing associative data up to date. He begins with a large set of stimulus words, gets associations to them, then uses the associations as stimulus words for associations again, and so on. He has used 8,400 stimulus words, and he has constructed an associative thesaurus in this fashion. He believes that associations are fundamental to cognition, and that they are a key to retrieval, as when one word suggests another until the item is recovered from memory.

Summary

There is a lively research interest in memory for conventional units of the natural language, with the sentence and the prose passage being the elements of study. Because of the concern with natural language, contemporary research is in touch with developments in linguistics and psycholinguistics.

364

There has been an interest in Chomsky's generative theory from linguistics. Learning psychologists had theorized that the sentence is a learned chaining of verbal response elements, but generative theory rejected this position. Generative theory expresses the versatility and complexity of a sentence in terms of deep structure, surface structure, and transformational rules. Deep structure is the fundamental meaning of a sentence; surface structure is the particular form that the sentence takes when it is expressed; transformational rules express the relationship between deep structure and surface structure. Generative theory stimulated psychological ideas about memory for sentences, but experimental tests of them have not always been confirming.

How we learn and remember prose passages is another main topic of research interest. Memory for prose is usually not literal but it a mix of such higher mental processes as inference, induction, interpretation, the derivation of concepts, and selective attention to some aspects of the passage and not others. Does this processing occur at learning with recall a straightforward report of what was learned? This is the reproductive view. Or was much of the content created at the time of recall from an abstraction of the material formed at the time of learning? This is the constructive view. Research at present favors the reproductive view. These debates on how prose is transformed should not detract from the considerable literal recall of prose material that can occur.

Another research interest of psychology has been semantic memory, or the organization of our stable, long-term knowledge of language and how to use it, and knowledge about the world. Reaction time is used to infer how information is organized in semantic memory and retrieved from it.

References

Bartlett, F. C. *Remembering: A study in experimental and social psychology.* Cambridge: Cambridge University Press, 1932.

Bates, E., Masling, M., & Kintsch, W. Recognition memory for aspects of dialogue. *Journal of Experimental Psychology: Human Learning and Memory,* 1978, 4, 187–197.

Chomsky, N. *Syntactic structures.* The Hague: Mouton, 1957.

Chomsky, N. Verbal behavior (a review). *Language,* 1959, 35, 26–58.

Chomsky, N. *Aspects of the theory of syntax.* Cambridge: M.I.T. Press, 1965.

Cofer, C. N. A comparison of logical and verbatim learning of prose passages of different lengths. *American Journal of Psychology,* 1941, 54, 1–20.

Cofer, C. N. Associative commonality and rated similarity of certain words from Haagen's list. *Psychological Reports,* 1957, 3, 603–606.

Collins, A. M., & Quillian, M. R. Retrieval time from semantic memory. *Journal of Verbal Learning and Verbal Behavior,* 1969, 8, 240–247.

Fredericksen, C. H. Acquisition of semantic information from discourse: Effects of repeated exposures. *Journal of Verbal Learning and Verbal Behavior,* 1975, *14,* 158–169. (a)

Fredericksen, C. H. Effects of context-induced processing operations on semantic information acquired in discourse. *Cognitive Psychology,* 1975, *7,* 139–166. (b)

Garskof, B. E., & Houston, J. P. Measurement of verbal relatedness: An idiographic approach. *Psychological Review,* 1963, *70,* 277–288.

Garskof, B. E., & Houston, J. P. The relationship between judged meaning similarity, associative probability, and associative overlap. *Psychological Reports,* 1965, *16,* 220–222.

Johnson, R. E. Recall of prose as a function of the structural importance of the linguistic units. *Journal of Verbal Learning and Verbal Behavior,* 1970, *9,* 12–20.

Keenan, J. M., MacWhinney, B., & Mayhew, D. Pragmatics in memory: A study of natural conversation. *Journal of Verbal Learning and Verbal Behavior,* 1977, *16,* 549–560.

Kiss, G. R. An associative thesaurus of English: Structural analysis of a large relevance network. In A. Kennedy and A. Wilkes (Eds.), *Studies in long term memory.* New York: Wiley, 1975, pp. 103–121.

Kolers, P. A., & Ostry, D. J. Time course of loss of information regarding pattern analyzing operations. *Journal of Verbal Learning and Verbal Behavior,* 1974, *13,* 599–612.

Marks, L. E., & Miller, G. A. The role of semantic and syntactic constraints in the memorization of English sentences. *Journal of Verbal Learning and Verbal Behavior,* 1964, *3,* 1–5.

Martin, E., & Roberts, K. H. Grammatical factors in sentence retention. *Journal of Verbal Learning and Verbal Behavior,* 1966, *5,* 211–218.

Martin, E., & Roberts, K. H. Sentence length and sentence retention in the free-learning situation. *Psychonomic Science,* 1967, *8,* 535–536.

Mehler, J. Some effects of grammatical transformations on the recall of English sentences. *Journal of Verbal Learning and Verbal Behavior,* 1963, *2,* 346–351.

Miller, G. A. Some psychological studies of grammar. *American Psychologist,* 1962, *17,* 748–762.

Miller, G. A. Some preliminaries to psycholinguistics. *American Psychologist,* 1965, *20,* 15–20.

Miller, G. A., & Isard, S. Some perceptual consequences of linguistic rules. *Journal of Verbal Learning and Verbal Behavior,* 1963, *2,* 217–228.

Mowrer, O. H. The psychologist looks at language. *American Psychologist,* 1954, *9,* 660–694.

Rips, L. J., Shoben, E. J., & Smith, E. E. Semantic distance and the verification of semantic relations. *Journal of Verbal Learning and Verbal Behavior,* 1973, *12,* 1–20.

Roberts, K. H. Grammatical and associative constraints in sentence retention. *Journal of Verbal Learning and Verbal Behavior,* 1968, *7,* 1072–1076.

Skinner, B. F. *Verbal behavior.* New York: Appleton-Century-Crofts, 1957.

Smith, E. E., Shoben, E. J., & Rips, L. J. Structure and process in semantic memory: A featural model for semantic decisions. *Psychological Review,* 1974, *81,* 214–241.

Tulving, E. Episodic and semantic memory. In E. Tulving and W. Donaldson (Eds.), *Organization and memory.* New York: Academic Press, 1972, pp. 381–403.

Underwood, B. J., & Schulz, R. W. *Meaningfulness and verbal learning.* New York: Lippincott, 1960.

Woodworth, R. S. *Experimental psychology.* New York: Holt, 1938.

Author index

Subject index